LIBRARY OF NEW TESTAMENT STUDIES

610

Formerly the Journal for the Study of the New Testament Supplement Series

Editor
Chris Keith

Editorial Board
Dale C. Allison, John M.G. Barclay, Lynn H. Cohick, R. Alan Culpepper, Craig A. Evans, Robert Fowler, Simon J. Gathercole, Juan Hernandez Jr., John S. Kloppenborg, Michael Labahn, Love L. Sechrest, Robert Wall, Catrin H. Williams, Britanny Wilson

QUOTATIONS IN JOHN

Studies on Jewish Scripture in the Fourth Gospel

Michael A. Daise

LONDON • NEW YORK • OXFORD • NEW DELHI • SYDNEY

T&T CLARK
Bloomsbury Publishing Plc
50 Bedford Square, London, WC1B 3DP, UK
1385 Broadway, New York, NY 10018, USA
29 Earlsfort Terrace, Dublin 2, Ireland

BLOOMSBURY, T&T CLARK and the T&T Clark logo
are trademarks of Bloomsbury Publishing Plc

First published in Great Britain 2020
Paperback edition first published 2021

Copyright © Michael A. Daise, 2020

Marilyn Dunn has asserted her right under the Copyright, Designs and
Patents Act, 1988, to be identified as Author of this work.

For legal purposes the Acknowledgements on pp. xii–xiii constitute
an extension of this copyright page.

All rights reserved. No part of this publication may be reproduced or
transmitted in any form or by any means, electronic or mechanical,
including photocopying, recording, or any information storage or retrieval
system, without prior permission in writing from the publishers.

Bloomsbury Publishing Plc does not have any control over, or responsibility for,
any third-party websites referred to or in this book. All internet addresses given
in this book were correct at the time of going to press. The author and publisher
regret any inconvenience caused if addresses have changed or sites have
ceased to exist, but can accept no responsibility for any such changes.

A catalogue record for this book is available from the British Library.

A catalog record for this book is available from the Library of Congress.

ISBN: HB: 978-0-5676-8179-9
PB: 978-0-5677-0210-4
ePDF: 978-0-5676-8180-5
eBook: 978-0-5676-8183-6

Series: Library of New Testament Studies, 2513-8790, volume 610

Typeset by Integra Software Services Pvt. Ltd.

To find out more about our authors and books visit
www.bloomsbury.com and sign up for our newsletters.

*To Mary Frances Daise,
whose love of the ancient world
gave vocation to her son.*

CONTENTS

List of Tables	x
Acknowledgements	xii
Editorial Notes	xiv

INTRODUCTION			1
A.	New lenses for a long-standing issue		1
B.	The continued relevance of historical-critical and theological questions		4
	1.	Criticism of the historical-critical/theological approach	4
	2.	An *apologia* for the traditional approach	5
		a. The criticisms point by point	5
		b. Lingering exegetical and theological issues	7
		c. Quotation clusters and literary structures	9
		d. Broader theological implications	11
	3.	This work	12
C.	Guiding assumptions		13
	1.	The versions cited by John	13
		a. Confirming the Septuagint	13
		b. Expecting the Hebrew Bible	19
	2.	Texts from the Judaean desert	20
	3.	Mediating sources	26
	4.	Hypotheses for Johannine anomalies	26

Part I
ISAIAH, JESUS AND THE JEWS

Chapter 1

ISAIAH 40:3, A CALL TO BELIEVE			31
A.	Quotations of Isaiah and Jesus's public ministry		31
B.	The Johannine rendering of Isaiah 40:3 (John 1:23)		32
	1.	The text	33
	2.	The version cited	34
	3.	The anomalies	37
		a. Two deviations from the LXX	37
		b. Hypotheses on the deviations	39

	C.	Isaiah 40:3: An embodied appeal to believe		45
		1. Problems in hypotheses on the anomalies		45
			a. Freed	46
			b. Menken and Williams	47
			c. Schuchard	50
		2. Wisdom as believing		50
			a. 'Making straight' (εὐθύνειν) as wisdom	53
			b. 'Making straight' (εὐθύνειν) as believing	56
		3. Summary		66

Chapter 2
ISAIAH 53:1 AND ISAIAH 6:10, AN OBSTRUCTION TO FAITH — 67

	A.	John 12:37-41: An Isaianic *inclusio*		68
		1. Ascriptions to Isaiah in the immediate context		68
		2. Ascriptions to Isaiah in the Book of Signs		69
	B.	The Johannine renderings		70
		1. The Johannine rendering of Isaiah 53:1 (John 12:38)		70
			a. The text	70
			b. The version cited	70
		2. The Johannine rendering of Isaiah 6:10 (John 12:40)		72
			a. The text	72
			b. Version(s), anomalies and referents	73
	C.	Isaiah 53:1/6:10: The call to believe obstructed		97
		1. Isaiah 53:1: A lament over unbelief		97
			a. 'Our report'	98
			b. 'The arm of the Lord'	106
			c. Summary	108
		2. Isaiah 6:10: Belief obstructed		108
			a. Isaiah 6:10 and the Jews' unbelief	108
			b. Isaiah's apocalyptic vision	110
			c. Summary	124
	D.	Conclusion: The Isaianic *inclusio*		124

Part II
THE DISCIPLES, THE SPIRIT AND THE SCRIPTURES

Chapter 3
PSALM 69:10, THE PROMISE OF A NEW TEMPLE — 127

	A.	Quotations with 'remembrance' formulae		127
		1. An earlier arrangement: 'Remembrance' quotations as a piece		129
		2. A *'geistgewirkte Erinnern'*		132
	B.	The Johannine rendering of Psalm 69:10		133
		1. The texture of the quotation		134
			a. The version cited	134
			b. Anomalies and hypotheses	136

	2.	The import of the quotation		141
		a.	'Consume' as 'reprisal'?	141
		b.	Prolepsis of a new sanctuary	144

Chapter 4
PSALM 118:25-26 AND ZECHARIAH 9:9, THE RESTORATION OF THE UNITED MONARCHY   157
  A. A 'remembrance' *inclusio*   157
  B. The Johannine renderings   157
      1. The texture of the quotations   157
          a. Psalm 118:25-26 (John 12:13)   157
          b. Zechariah 9:9 (John 12:15)   167
      2. Version, anomalies and import of the quotations   178
          a. Starting points   178
          b. The major anomalies   184
          c. The import of the quotations   196
  C. Conclusions   198
      1. The putative tradition   198
      2. The 'remembrance' *inclusio*   198

Part III
CHIASMUS AND THEOLOGY

Chapter 5
CONCLUSIONS   203
  A. The *chiasmus*   203
  B. The theology   205
      1. John's debt to apocalypticism   205
      2. Theological corollaries   206
          a. Christology   206
          b. Soteriology   206
          c. Eschatology   207
          d. Ecclesiology and pneumatology   210
  C. Epilogue   211

Appendices   212
Bibliography   215
Ancient Sources Index   227
Modern Authors Index   245

LIST OF TABLES

1	Psalm 69:10a in the HB, LXX and John	14
2	Linguistic arguments for LXX *Vorlagen*	14
3	Maarten Menken and the Judaean desert texts, 1985–2009 (*BHS* 1967/77)	23
4	Andreas Obermann and the Judaean desert texts, 1996 (*BHS²* 1983)	24
5	Isaiah 40:3 in the HB, LXX and John	33
6	Isaiah 40:3 in the HB, LXX and the Synoptic gospels	37
7	LXX sapiential texts and John 1:23	40
8	The Synoptic midrash on Elijah	51
9	John as Elijah in Matthew and Luke	51
10	1QS ix 19-21 and sapiential texts	54
11	Isaiah 53:1 in the HB, LXX and John	70
12	Isaiah 6:10 in the HB, LXX and John	72
13	LXX allusions in John 9:39	79
14	LXX texts and τυφλοῦν at John 12:40a	79
15	Early Christian texts and πωροῦν at John 12:40b	81
16	Personal pronouns in LXX Isaiah 6:10 and John 12:40	83
17	LXX texts and νοεῖν at John 12:40d	84
18	HB/LXX Isaiah 44:18 and νοεῖν at John 12:40d	85
19	Anomalies in John 12:40/Isaiah 6:10 from a LXX *Vorlage*	95
20	LXX Isaiah 6:9-10, Mark 8:17-18 and John 12:40	96
21	Exodus 4:1-9 and the numbered signs performed by Jesus	103
22	Isaiah 53:1 and Isaiah 6:10 as prophetic lament and divine reply	113
23	4QDibre Ha-Meʾorotᵃ (4Q504) 18 2-4	117
24	4QDibre Ha-Meʾorotᵃ (4Q504) 18 2-3 and Deuteronomy 29:3	118
25	Jesus's entry into Jerusalem and temple cleansing in John (John 12:12-16/John 2:13-22)	131
26	Psalm 69:10 in the HB, LXX and John	134
27	Psalm 69:22 and John 19:28	135
28	Psalm 69:5 and John 15:25	136
29	Psalm 69 in John and cognate literature	138
30	Deuteronomy 32:19-22, Psalm 69:10a and John 2:17	145
31	'Destroying' and 'building' the sanctuary in early Christian literature	147

32	Psalm 118:25-26 in the HB, LXX and John	161
33	Assimilated passages for 'Hosanna'	162
34	'Hosanna' (ὡσαννά) in Matthew and Mark	163
35	Assimilated texts for 'king of Israel' (John 12:13/Psalm 118:25-26)	166
36	Zechariah 9:9 in the HB, LXX and John	167
37	Assimilated texts for 'fear not'	170
38	Assimilated texts for 'your king comes'	174
39	'A foal of his donkey' and Genesis 49:11	178
40	'Hosanna' (ὡσαννά) in the Synoptic gospels	179
41	Zechariah 9:9 in Matthew and John	180
42	Zephaniah 3 and the call of Nathanael	190

ACKNOWLEDGEMENTS

This work is a highly revised portion of a mémoire written under Fr Marie-Émile Boismard at the École biblique et archéologique française de Jérusalem in 1998–99. I wrote it primarily to furnish context for a doctoral dissertation on John 7:37–39 that I was writing simultaneously under James Charlesworth; and given the thoroughgoing work of Maarten J.J. Menken and Bruce G. Schuchard on its issue (quotations in the Fourth Gospel), I had no intention of publishing it. When I was encouraged by Boismard to do so, nonetheless, several years later, I began considering ways I might modify the piece in light of ongoing discussion on the Jewish scriptures in John; and having alighted upon the quotation clusters in the Book of Signs, I found (what I think has been) a way forward and have expanded the work accordingly.

I am indebted to the École biblique, as well as the Catholic Biblical Association, for inviting me to give lectures on this material in Jerusalem as Catholic Biblical Association Visiting Professor a decade after writing the mémoire. Special thanks here go to Fr Luc Devillers, o.p., second reader of the mémoire, and Fr Adam Kubiś, who attended those lectures and assimilated some of their observations into his own work, *The Book of Zechariah in the Gospel of John* (2012). At points throughout this piece I engage Adam critically, but this only indicates how much his deliberations on these issues have helped my own. Also critical for my thinking on this project has been my interaction with colleagues in the Catholic Biblical Association Task Force on 'The Use of the Old Testament in the Gospel of John', particularly the insights offered by Gregory Glazov relative to Chapter 3.

I am deeply honoured to have this work accepted for the Bloomsbury series Library of New Testament Studies and extend my warmest gratitude to Chris Keith and the editorial board for their gracious reception of it. Sincerest thanks also go to the staff of Earl Gregg Swem Library at the College of William & Mary, for furnishing such ample and timely bibliographical resource; to Dominic Mattos and Sarah Blake at Bloomsbury Publishing, for such patient and supportive editorial guidance; to Gopinath Anbalagan and the production team, for such careful attention to detail in preparing the manuscript for publication; to PJHeim, for furnishing the indices; and to my wife, Leslie, for being the reason I want do this in the first place. I hope my efforts for this monograph will in some way yield a return (not necessarily financial!) for all the investment these colleagues, friends and family have made in it. And I do hope its discourse will by some means enrich its readers.

I am advised to close on a less romantic note. The third-party copyrighted material displayed in the pages of this book is done on the basis of fair use for the purposes of teaching, criticism, scholarship or research only, in accordance with international copyright laws, and is not intended to infringe upon the ownership rights of the original owners.

Michael Daise
Feast of the Presentation of the Lord
2019

EDITORIAL NOTES

All translations of non-English texts, ancient and modern, are by the author. Editions of non-biblical texts and of biblical texts from Judaean desert manuscripts are cited in footnotes with their first usage. As for editions of biblical texts, the Masoretic text (MT) is drawn from Karl Elliger and Wilhelm Rudolph, eds., *Torah, Nevi'im uKethuvim: Biblia Hebraica Stuttgartensia*, 2nd rev. ed. (Stuttgart: Deutsche Bibelgesellschaft, 1983); the New Testament, from Barbara Aland et al., eds., *Novum Testamentum Graece*, 28th rev. ed. (Stuttgart: Deutsche Bibelgesellschaft, 2012). And regarding the Septuagint (LXX), where available it is drawn from *Septuaginta: Vetus Testamentum Graecum auctoritate Societatis Litterarum Gottingensis editum* (Göttingen: Vandenhoeck & Ruprecht, 1931–[2006]); where not available in that series, from Alfred Rahlfs, ed., *Septuaginta: Id est Vetus Testamentum graece iuxta LXX interpretes*, 2nd ed., 2 vols. (Stuttgart: Deutsche Bibelgesellschaft, 1979). Further, when a single translation is presented to represent both HB and LXX versions of a passage, it is drawn from the HB with the operative LXX terms inserted next to the Hebrew.

With regard to terminology, a note on two matters which have been subject to debate: one concerns the authorship of the Fourth Gospel – that is, whether it was done by a single evangelist or (the inclination here) by the evangelist followed by one or more redactors; the other concerns the group which in the narrative is called οἱ Ἰουδαῖοι – more specifically, whether that term speaks of the Jews at large, Jewish leadership, Judaeans only or some combination of these groups at any given *locus*. Inasmuch as neither is at issue in this study, the first will simply be designated as 'the evangelist' or 'John', with the understanding that these terms designate the last tradent(s) responsible for the text as we have it; the second will simply be translated as 'the Jews'.

And three smaller items. First, throughout the shorthand family[1] and family[13] is used for the Ferrar groups headed by codices 1 and 13, respectively – this, per Kirsopp Lake, *Codex 1 of the Gospels and Its Allies*, vol. 7/3 of *Texts and Studies: Contributions to Biblical and Patristic Literature*, ed. J. Armitage Robinson (Cambridge: Cambridge University Press, 1902), vi. Second, references to Psalms will be given by their HB (not LXX) chapter and verse numbers, even when the LXX text is under discussion. And third, taking a cue from David Rensberger's review of Bruce Schuchard, *Scripture within Scripture*, the detailed textual discussion of this inquiry will be accompanied by ample representations of the texts in question; cf. Rensberger, Review of *Scripture within Scripture: The Interrelationship of Form and Function in the Explicit Old Testament Citations in the Gospel of John*, by Bruce G. Schuchard, *JBL* 113 (1994): 345–46.

INTRODUCTION

A. New lenses for a long-standing issue

Quotations in John have attracted considerable attention over the last century and a half. Though fewer than their Synoptic counterparts,[1] they have been the subject of no less than five monographs,[2] four major book

---

1. Using appendices in the New Testament edition of Westcott and Hort, C.K. Barrett counted 124 quotations for Matthew, 70 for Mark, 109 for Luke and 27 for John; 'The Old Testament in the Fourth Gospel', *JTS* 48 (1947): 155 (Bent Noack misreads Barrett's count to include allusions; *Zur johanneischen Tradition: Beiträge zur Kritik an der literarkritischen analyse des vierten Evangeliums*, Det Laerde selskabs skrifter: Teologiske Skrifter 3 [København: Rosenkilde Og Bagger, 1954], 72, 72n180). The NA^{28} numbers for designated quotations run lower, but still show quotations in John to be less than those in the Synoptics. Counting the biblical passages considered to have been quoted (even if some occur several times in the same book or others are merged in polyvalent citations), the marginal notes have Matthew at 88, Mark at 48, Luke at 38, John at 21; and the appendix 'Loci citati vel allegati' has Matthew at 84, Mark at 46, Luke at 36 and John at 21. Criteria for defining quotations, of course, differ among editions and exegetes; and, as the numbers for the NA^{28} margins vis-à-vis appendix show, the Nestle-Aland tools for identifying them are not always consistent (see, for instance, the concerns about NA^{26} cited by Jaime Clark-Soles, *Scripture Cannot Be Broken: The Social Function of the Use of Scripture in the Fourth Gospel* [Leiden: E.J. Brill, 2003], 223n33). Even so, John's numbers run well below those of the other canonical gospels.

2. Edwin D. Freed, *Old Testament Quotations in the Gospel of John*, NovTSup 11 (Leiden: E.J. Brill, 1965); Bruce G. Schuchard, *Scripture within Scripture: The Interrelationship of Form and Function in the Explicit Old Testament Citations in the Gospel of John*, SBLDS 133 (Atlanta, GA: Scholars Press, 1992); Maarten J.J. Menken, *Old Testament Quotations in the Fourth Gospel: Studies in Textual Form*, ed. Maarten J.J. Menken, CBET 15 (Kampen: Kok Pharos, 1996); Andreas Obermann, *Die christologische Erfüllung der Schrift im Johannesevangelium: Eine Untersuchung zur johanneischen Hermeneutik anhand der Schriftzitate*, WUNT 2/83 (Tübingen: J.C.B. Mohr [Paul Siebeck], 1996); and treating only the quotations from John 1:23 to John 12:15, Ruth Sheridan, *Retelling Scripture: 'The Jews' and the Scriptural Citations in John 1:19–12:15*, BibInt 110 (Leiden/Boston: E.J. Brill, 2012).

sections[3] and myriad articles.[4] Their enduring allure may be due to several stimuli which have kept interest alive over the years: the textual data brought to light with the discovery of Judaean desert texts;[5] the prospect that anomalies in

3. August H. Franke, *Das alte Testament bei Johannes: Ein Beitrag zur Erklärung und Beurtheilung der johanneischen Schriften* (Göttingen: Vandenhoeck & Ruprecht's Verlag, 1885), 255–316; Günter Reim, *Jochanan: Erweiterte Studien zum alttestamentlichen Hintergrund des Johannesevangeliums* (Hessdorf-Hannberg: Eigenverlag des Autors/Erlangen: Der Verlag der Ev.-Luth. Mission, 1995; 1st part is repr. of *Studien zum alttestamentlichen Hintergrund des Johannesevangeliums*, SNTSMS 22 [London/New York: Cambridge University Press, 1974]), 1–96; Clark-Soles, *Scripture Cannot Be Broken*, 207–315; and, treating three references to Zechariah (John 7:38/Zech 14:8; John 12:15/Zech 9:9; and John 19:37/Zech 12:10), Adam Kubiś, *The Book of Zechariah in the Gospel of John*, EBib, New series 64 (Pendé: J. Gabalda et Cie, 2012), 27–315.

4. Given his prolific and pioneering contribution to this matter, it may be appropriate to note that most of the chapters in Maarten J.J. Menken's *Old Testament Quotations in the Fourth Gospel* (note 2) are revised versions of individual articles published between 1985 and 1996 and that to these now may be added seven more: 'Jezus tegenover de Farizeeën in het vierde evangelie: Joh. 8,12–20', in *Jodendom en vroeg christendom: continuïteit en discontinuïteit. Opstellen van leden van de Studiosorum Novi Testamenti Conventus*, ed. Tjitze Baarda, Henk Jan de Jonge and Maarten J.J. Menken (Kampen: Kok Pharos Publishing House, 1991), 103–17; Maarten J.J. Menken, 'The Quotations from Zech 9,9 in Mt 21,5 and in Jn 12,15', in *John and the Synoptics*, ed. Adelbert Denaux, BETL 101 (Leuven: Leuven University Press, 1992), 571–78; Maarten J.J. Menken, 'The Use of the Septuagint in Three Quotations in John: Jn 10,34; 12,38; 19,24', in *The Scriptures in the Gospels*, ed. C.M. Tuckett, BETL 131 (Louvain: Leuven University, 1997), 367–93; Maarten J.J. Menken, 'Vertaling als interpretatie: Twee citaten uit Jesaja in het vierde evangelie (Joh 12,38,40)', in *Exegeten aan het werk: Vertalen en interpreteren van de bijbel. Opstellen van leden van het Bijbels Werkgenootschap St. Hiëronymus*, ed. H.M. Welzen (Brugge/'s Hertogenbosch/Tabor: Katholieke Bijbelstichting, 1998), 35–43; Maarten J.J. Menken, 'Observations on the Significance of the Old Testament in the Fourth Gospel', *Neot* 33 (1999): 125–43; Maarten J.J. Menken, 'Interpretation of the Old Testament and the Resurrection of Jesus in John's Gospel', in *Resurrection in the New Testament: Festschrift J. Lambrecht*, ed. R. Bieringer, V. Koperski and B. Lataire, BETL 165 (Dudley, MA: Peeters, 2002), 189–205; and Maarten J.J. Menken, 'The Minor Prophets in John's Gospel', in *The Minor Prophets in the New Testament*, ed. Steve Moyise and Maarten J.J. Menken, LNTS 377 (London: T&T Clark, 2009), 79–96.

Reviews of research on the quotations have been made by Obermann, *Die christologische Erfüllung der Schrift im Johannesevangelium*, 3–33; Sheridan, *Retelling Scripture*, 12–37; and Alicia D. Myers, 'Abiding Words: An Introduction to Perspectives on John's Use of Scripture', in *Abiding Words: The Use of Scripture in the Gospel of John*, ed. Alicia D. Myers and Bruce G. Schuchard, RBS 81 (Atlanta, GA: SBL Press, 2015), 2–18.

5. The first to bring Judaean desert texts to bear on John's quotations was Freed (*Old Testament Quotations in the Gospel of John*), who in some ways modulated into a Johannine key what his *Doktorvater*, Krister Stendahl, did in Matthew; cf. *The School of St. Matthew and Its Use of the Old Testament*, Uppsala universitet: Nytestamentliga seminar, Acta 20 (Uppsala: C.W.K. Gleerup, Lund, 1954).

John's quotations betray his usage of Jewish exegetical techniques;[6] the awareness that John's use of quoted scripture would have had formative effects on his community;[7] or the insight that, as one type of 'hypertext' within the Fourth Gospel, quotations from a single biblical book share *intratextual* relationships with other types of references from that same book – allusions, echoes and the like.[8] But perhaps a more fundamental reason lay beneath the 'staying power' of this sub-discipline, namely, that John's quotations furnish a gateway into the Fourth Gospel itself. That is to say, narrow a set of data as they are, John's quotations provide an apt means of entering the broader world of his narrative and, as such, perpetually entice exegetes to look again at their dynamics.

Until the mid-1990s (culminating in the work of Maarten J.J. Menken, Bruce G. Schuchard and Andreas Obermann), exegesis on John's quotations was done with historical-critical and theological questions in view – some ten of them, in fact:

1. How many (that is, which) *loci* in the Fourth Gospel are to be counted as quotations?
2. What segments of the Fourth Gospel's text represent those quotations?
3. What bearing do introductory formulae have on these references?
4. What biblical passages are cited?
5. From what versions (and/or media) have they been drawn – HB,[9] LXX, Synoptics, *testimonia, targumim* – and what do those sources indicate about the evangelist's provenance?
6. How do the Johannine renderings compare with their source texts and original contexts?
7. How can differences between the Johannine renderings and their source texts be explained?
8. What implications do the quotations carry for the Fourth Gospel's narrative, composition history and theology?
9. How does the Johannine interpretation of these passages (and its method) compare with cognate understandings?
10. And what do these quotations signal about the evangelist's awareness of the Jewish scriptures?[10]

These questions continue to be addressed, perhaps most saliently in the endeavour of William Randolph Bynum to revisit the quotation of Zechariah 12:10 at John 19:37 in light of the *Greek Minor Prophets Scroll* from Naḥal

---

6. Menken, *Old Testament Quotations in the Fourth Gospel*, 13–14.
7. Clark-Soles, *Scripture Cannot Be Broken*, 1, 207–08.
8. Kubiś, *Book of Zechariah in the Gospel of John*, 13–16.
9. The abbreviation HB (for Hebrew Bible) is used rather than MT (for Masoretic Text) so as to account for the non-Masoretic textual attestations found among the Judaean desert texts.
10. Most of these questions are rehearsed by Reim, *Jochanan*, 1–3.

Ḥever.[11] From Obermann on, however, the queries have by and large been issued from new vantage points – hermeneutical, social-scientific, semiotic. Alongside his concern for the Fourth Gospel's theology, Obermann, himself, focused his attention on the evangelist's hermeneutical premises and methodological appropriation of scripture[12]; Jaime Clark-Soles has examined how those quotations (and Jesus's words) would have helped fashion Johannine Christianity – 'the way John uses Scripture to do something for and to his community'[13]; Ruth Sheridan has explored how the quotations are employed rhetorically to construct 'the Jews' as narrative characters in John 1-12[14]; and, along a different line, Adam Kubiś has traced how John's quotations from Zechariah carry meaning relative to both their *Rezeptionsgeschichte* (intertextuality) and their relations with other references in the narrative (intratextuality), be they allusions and echoes to Zechariah or quotations from other biblical books.[15]

B. The continued relevance of historical-critical and theological questions

1. Criticism of the historical-critical/theological approach

Advocates of the new approaches have rightly stated the need for new questions to be posed, and two, Sheridan and Kubiś, have gone so far as to doubt the continued relevance – even inherent value – of the earlier approach. Together they issue five reasons for their reservations:

---

11. *The Fourth Gospel and the Scriptures: Illuminating the Form and Meaning of Scriptural Citation in John 19:37*, NovTSup 144 (Leiden: E.J. Brill, 2012), entire, but see especially pp. 5–6, 52–58, 89–90, 168–69.

12. *Die christologische Erfüllung der Schrift im Johannesevangelium*, 35. Building upon the ideas of Ernst Fuchs and Klaus Berger – that quotations are vitally discursive (having an '*Anredecharakter als lebendiger Rede*') and create alien occurrences (each, a '*Moment des Fremden*') in the Johannine text – Obermann explores how such features affect their function and performance in the narrative (pp. 64–69).

13. *Scripture Cannot Be Broken*, 1–3, 8–9 (quotation p. 1).

14. *Retelling Scripture*, 6, 46–48.

15. *Book of Zechariah in the Gospel of John*, 13–16, 20–25. A similar approach to that of Kubiś is applied to the Fourth Gospel's quotations of Isaiah in an unpublished dissertation written by Pawel Rytel-Adrianik for St. Cross College, Oxford; 'Use of Isaiah in the Fourth Gospel in Comparison to the Synoptics and Other Places in the New Testament' (Ph.D. diss., St. Cross College, University of Oxford, 2013). Both Sheridan and Myers mark the shift in approaches to have begun with Obermann and to turn on an interest in how the quotations function within the Fourth Gospel's narrative; Sheridan, *Retelling Scripture*, 26–37; Myers, 'Abiding Words', 15–18. The interest in intertextuality by Kubiś and Rytel-Adrianik, however, broadens that shift to include the way those quotations mediate meaning from passages outside the narrative.

(1) that the range of biblical passages covered by the quotations is too slim to yield a thesis about John's overall use of the Jewish scriptures;
(2) that the 'insufficient distinctions'[16] used to define quotations over against other types of references (allusions, echoes) have prevented any consensus about the scope of data to be examined;
(3) that the writings from which John drew his quotations cannot be equated with a fixed Hebrew canon, which is assumed to have existed by exegetes looking for 'an OT "source text"';
(4) that the several text types and translations of the HB known to have existed in the first century CE imply that anomalies in the Fourth Gospel's quotations may, in fact, be accurate renderings of variant textual traditions;
(5) and that the vestiges of orality in the Fourth Gospel's written text suggest that the evangelist quoted 'from memory rather than from a written source', thereby making the search for scriptural source texts an 'exercise in futility'.[17]

2. An apologia *for the traditional approach*

a. *The criticisms point by point*

The approach taken here, however, like that of Bynum, builds on the more traditional questions asked of the quotations, particularly those addressed by Menken and Schuchard. And the case for doing so rests on four factors.

First, the five arguments against doing so (just listed) can be disputed on their own terms. Regarding (1) above, the scope of a project (in this case, quotations in John) need not address all aspects of a larger issue (John and the Jewish scriptures) to make a significant contribution to it. For (2), inasmuch as the number and *loci* of quotations in John represent one of the ten questions posed by the traditional approach, disagreement among exegetes is to be expected.[18] Put another way, the

---

16. Kubiś, *Book of Zechariah in the Gospel of John*, 14.
17. Sheridan, *Retelling Scripture*, 24–25 (quotations p. 25); the second quotation here is Sheridan citing Paul J. Achtemeier, 'Omne Verbum Sonat: The New Testament and the Oral Environment of Late Western Antiquity', *JBL* 109 (1990): 27. For these five criticisms, numbers (1) and (2) are issued by Kubiś, *Book of Zechariah in the Gospel of John*, 13–15; numbers (3) through (5), by Sheridan, *Retelling Scripture*, 22–25 (quotation in [3] p. 23). For point (4), Sheridan closely follows Craig A. Evans, 'From Prophecy to Testament: An Introduction', in *From Prophecy to Testament: The Function of the Old Testament in the New*, ed. Craig A. Evans (Peabody, MA: Hendrickson, 2004), 5.
18. Kubiś brings this disagreement into relief by listing the number of *loci* thought to be quotations in John by six exegetes: François-Marie Braun, Freed, Reim, Schuchard, Menken and Obermann; *Book of Zechariah in the Gospel of John*, 14n8. His example can be pressed further by dividing the number of quotations fully agreed upon (13) by the number proposed (23) among those who have treated the topic in some depth (see Appendix I). Doing so shows that full agreement exists only for some 57 per cent of suggested quotations (specifically, those at John 1:23; 2:17; 6:31, 45; 10:34; 12:15, 38, 40; 13:18; 15:25; 19:24,

scope of quotations in John is not an a priori to be assumed but a conclusion to be sought. Consequently, the disparity that exists among scholars over their number does not reflect 'insufficient' criteria so much as it does healthy debate.[19]

For (3), it is not clear that all exegetes working historical-critically on the quotations have assumed a fixed, universal Hebrew canon, such as Sheridan alleges.[20] And even were this so, the issue becomes moot if the search for sources has been conducted through the gamut of Second Temple literature.[21] More to the point, however, most of the books to which discernible quotations in John can be

---

36-37). That number can be raised to 65 per cent, if the three quotations proposed by only one exegete each (John 1:45; 12:41; 20:9) are removed. Even so, the ratio of agreement to disagreement by no means reflects a consensus.

19. After reviewing proposed criteria for determining allusions and echoes, Kubiś, himself, later concedes that 'the detection and analysis of scriptural references in any biblical text will always remain a *subjective* enterprise' (italics original). Then, quoting Marko Jauhiainen, he writes, 'the best approximation to objectivity is the normal scholarly debate to which all interpretations are subjected'; *Book of Zechariah in the Gospel of John*, 21; Jauhiainen, *The Use of Zechariah in Revelation*, WUNT 2/199 (Tübingen: Mohr Siebeck, 2005), 34.

The question of which *loci* in John represent quotations is compounded by the complex relationships that occur between quotations, allusions and introductory formulae. References introduced by formulae span a gamut, from verbatim re-presentations of single verses (e.g. John 10:34/Ps 82:6; John 12:38/Isa 53:1; John 19:24/Ps 22:19) to midrashic summaries of many passages (e.g. John 7:42 with any or all of 1 Sam 16:18; 17:12, 58; 20:6; 2 Sam 7:12; 22:51; 1 Kgs 1:48; 2:33; Jer 23:5; 33:22, 25-26; Micah 5:1; Pss 18:51; 89:4-5, 30, 36-37; 1 Chron 17:11; see, for instance, Menken, *Old Testament Quotations in the Fourth Gospel*, 16–17). Further, some alleged formulae may not introduce specific biblical passages at all: phrases that could be read as introductory formulae at John 7:38; 17:12; and 19:28, for instance, may, in fact, serve as adverbial modifiers referencing all of scripture in general. Or the passages to which some formulae refer are cited elsewhere in the gospel narrative: the phrase 'that the scripture might be fulfilled' at John 17:12, for example, if taken as an introductory formula, may refer to the quotation of Ps 41:10 at John 13:18. Moreover, certain formulae introduce *logia* of Jesus rather than verses of the Bible (John 18:8-9 and possibly John 17:12; cf. John 6:39 – on this, see Clark-Soles, *Scripture Cannot Be Broken*, 221–22, 294–310). And several references unaccompanied by formulae so closely approximate biblical passages as to defy separate categorization from references which are introduced by such formulae: here (to anticipate discussion below), compare John 12:13/Ps 118:25-26 with the verbatim re-presentations of single verses listed above.

20. Obermann, for instance, assumes not a fixed canon but a 'circle of Jewish writings' (*Kreis jüdischer Schriften*), by which he means Jewish works 'whose affiliation to the writings recognized as holy and used in worship was, in part, not yet established'; *Die christologische Erfüllung der Schrift im Johannesevangelium*, 36n196; cf. 40n10.

21. Discussions of the quotations that include Qumran texts and *targumim* suggest that this kind of wider search has to some degree been done; and to the extent it has not, further discussion requires an extension (not abandonment) of that approach.

traced would have been part of the emerging Hebrew canon in any case.[22] Regarding (4), anomalies in the Johannine quotations may, indeed, be accurate renderings of alternate textual traditions and translations, but this by no means implies that the search for those referents should cease. Translations have, in fact, been routinely canvassed to explain those anomalies, albeit with no precise correspondence yet found.[23] And, far from summoning a halt to the search for sources, the new text types discovered among Judaean desert texts call for further work to be done on their ramifications for the text forms of John's quotations. Finally on (5), the prospect that anomalies in the Fourth Gospel's quotations reflect the evangelist citing from memory (rather than from written texts)[24] in no way renders a search for their sources an 'exercise in futility'. As Schuchard has replied to Paul Achtemeier (on which Clark-Soles's criticism here depends), 'even if John cited from memory, his citations do, in fact, represent precise and therefore perceptible recollections of a specific textual tradition.'[25] As such, they – no less than quotations drawn from written sources – allow (if not plead for) historical-critical exploration.

b. Lingering exegetical and theological issues
A second reason for pursuing historical-critical and theological questions lies in the state of discussion on them. Several issues raised by those questions remain open to debate and beg for new hypotheses. A case in point (to be developed in Chapter 3) is the future tense 'will consume' in the quotation of Psalm 69:10 at

---

22. If the discernible sources of all Johannine quotations suggested by exegetes (Appendix I) are categorized under the three sections of the HB and the Apocrypha/Pseudepigrapha, the books cited by John readily fit (Appendix II): Exodus, Numbers and Deuteronomy from Torah; 2 Samuel, Isaiah, Ezekiel, Micah and Zechariah from the Prophets; and Psalms, Proverbs and Nehemiah/2nd Esdras from the Writings. The only outlier is the possible reference to *Psalms of Solomon* at John 15:25. Suggestive here is the observation by Timothy H. Lim that, despite their diversity, many collections of authoritative scriptures prior to the fixed Hebrew canon shared the books that would ultimately be included in that canon: 'the five books of Moses or Pentateuch ... [a] core of prophetical books (e.g., Samuel-Kings, the Minor Prophets) and psalms ...'; *The Formation of the Jewish Canon*, Anchor Yale Bible Reference Library (New Haven: Yale University Press, 2013), 185.

23. *Targumim* were sought to explain New Testament (and thereby Johannine) quotations as early as Eduard Böhl, *Die alttestamentlichen Citate im Neuen Testament* (Wien: Wilhelm Braumüller, 1878), xvi–xvii, xix; see the comments by Georg Richter, 'Die alttestamentlichen Zitate in der Rede vom Himmelsbrot Joh 6, 26-51a', in *Studien zum Johannesevangelium*, ed. Josef Hainz; Biblische Untersuchungen 13 (Regensburg: Verlag Friedrich Pustet, 1977), 207–08, 254; first publ. in *Schriftauslegung: Beiträge zur Hermeneutik des Neuen Testamentes und im Neuen Testament*, ed. Josef Ernst (Paderborn: Verlag Ferdinand Schöningh, 1972). A more recent treatment can be found in Günter Reim, 'Targum und Johannesevangelium', in *Jochanan*, 334–47, particularly pp. 336–37, 341–43; first publ. in *BZ* 27 (1983).

24. Among other advocates of this explanation are Noack, *Zur johanneischen Tradition*, 84–85; and Charles Goodwin, 'How Did John Treat His Sources'? *JBL* 73 (1954): 61–75.

25. *Scripture within Scripture*, xvii.

John 2:17. Where the HB and LXX read that verb as a preterite, 'Zeal for your house has consumed me (אכלתני/κατέφαγέν με)', John renders it as a future, 'Zeal for your house will consume me (καταφάγεταί με)'. The long-standing hypothesis for this variance asserts that it signals Jesus's temple cleansing as the ultimate cause of his demise. 'Zeal for your house will consume me' is understood to mean that Jesus's ardour for the temple in John 2 provoked a reprisal that would kill him by John 19.[26] That thesis, itself, however, labours under at least two problems, which bid for further attention. First, it burdens the verb 'consume' with a sense it does not usually carry: 'to experience reprisal' rather than 'to possess the emotions'. And second, it lacks support from the Johannine narrative. The reaction to Jesus's temple cleansing at John 2:18-22 does not entail a desire to kill him. And, conversely, the expression of such a desire elsewhere in the gospel is provoked by other factors: his healing on the Sabbath, his declared parity with God, his potential provocation of Rome and his claim to royalty.[27] Further, this anomaly might be better addressed through two other hypotheses, yet unexplored (or under-explored as explanations to it). One is that Psalm 69:10 has been merged with Deuteronomy 32:19-22, a passage which, like Psalm 69:10, juxtaposes the verbs 'to become/make zealous' (לקנא/[παρα]ζηλοῦν) with the imperfect/future tenses of the verb 'to consume' (ותאכל/καταφάγεται). The other is that the preterite has been made future because Jesus's 'zeal' towards the Jerusalem temple in John 2 is proleptic of a 'zeal' he will display for a metaphorized temple later in the narrative, either by raising 'the sanctuary of his body' (asserted at John 2:19-21), by 'preparing' his

---

26. This hypothesis has been notably argued by C.H. Dodd, *The Interpretation of the Fourth Gospel* (Cambridge: Cambridge University Press, 1953), 301; C.H. Dodd, *Historical Tradition in the Fourth Gospel* (Cambridge: Cambridge University Press, 1963), 158. And among major commentators advocating it are Rudolf Bultmann, *The Gospel of John: A Commentary*, trans. G.R. Beasley-Murray, R.W.N. Hoare and J.K. Riches (Philadelphia: Westminster, 1971), 124; trans. of *Das Evangelium des Johannes* with the Supplement of 1966 (Göttingen: Vandenhoeck & Ruprecht, 1964); Rudolf Schnackenburg, *The Gospel according to St John*, trans. Kevin Smyth, Cecily Hastings, Francis McDonagh, David Smith, Richard Foley, s.j. and G.A. Kon, 3 vols. (New York: Crossroad, 1990), 1:347; trans. of *Das Johannesevangelium*, 4 vols., HThKNT 4/1-2 (Freiburgh: Herder, 1965–1975); Raymond E. Brown, *The Gospel according to John*, 2 vols., AB 29-29A (Garden City, NY: Doubleday, 1966/1970), 1:124; Marie-Émile Boismard and Arnaud Lamouille, *L'Évangile de Jean*, vol. 3 of *Synopse des quatre évangiles en français* (Paris: Éditions du Cerf, 1977), 109. To these one may add Menken, '"Zeal for Your House Will Consume Me" (John 2:17)', in *Old Testament Quotations in the Fourth Gospel*, 40–41; first publ. in *Broeder Jehosjoea, opstellen voor Ben Hemelsoet: bij zijn afscheid als hoogleraar in de exegese van het Niewe Testament van de Katholieke Theologische Universiteit te Utrecht*, ed. D. Akerboom et al. (Kampen: Kok Pharos Publishing House, 1994); and Schuchard, *Scripture within Scripture*, 30n67.

27. John 5:16-18; 7:1, 19-25; 8:57-59; 10:31-33; 11:45-53; 18:33-38; 19:1-22. For these points, see, for instance, C.K. Barrett, *The Gospel according to St. John*, 2nd ed. (Philadelphia: Westminster Press, 1978), 199, 201; as well as the concession to them by Schnackenburg, who holds the dominant view; *Gospel according to St John*, 1:355.

'Father's house' for the disciples (promised at John 14:1-2) or by both – each done at his resurrection. Such further possibilities attend other issues raised by conventional exegetical and theological questions and, as such, suggest those queries ought not yet be abandoned.

c. Quotation clusters and literary structures

Third, some quotations in John share lexical and thematic features that suggest they should be examined as clusters rather than as discrete units; and this, in turn, invites a reapplication of historical-critical and theological questions on a larger scale. Particularly, three quotations are the only ones whose introductory formulae explicitly ascribe them to Isaiah[28]; three are the only ones cast as being 'remembered' (ἐμνήσθησαν) by Jesus's disciples[29]; and each of these groupings forms an *inclusio* within the Book of Signs which, when combined with the other, produces a *chiasmus* to Jesus's public ministry in John.[30] All have been treated individually – though, owing to its features, John 12:13/Psalm 118:25-26 less so[31]; and the affinities that create these groupings have not been lost on exegetes.[32] Their full ramifications, however, have yet to be teased out, and this implies a continued relevance (and need) for the older questions that have driven this area of research.

---

28. John 1:23/Isa 40:3; John 12:38/Isa 53:1; and John 12:40/Isa 6:10.

29. John 2:17/Ps 69:10; John 12:13/Ps 118:25-26; and John 12:15/Zech 9:9.

30. A third cluster also merits further attention but lies outside the scope of this work: four quotations share the factor of having been fulfilled during Jesus's crucifixion: John 19:23-24/Ps 22:19; John 19:28-30/Pss 42:3 (?); 63:2 (?); 69:22 (?); John 19:36/Exod 12:10 (?), 46 (?); Num 9:12 (?); Ps 34:21 (?); and John 19:37/Zech 12:10.

31. For different reasons, the reference to Ps 118:25-26 at John 12:13 has been disqualified as a quotation (and so omitted from consideration as one) by Franke, *Das alte Testament bei Johannes*, 256–57; François-Marie Braun, *Les grandes traditions d'Israël et l'accord des Écritures selon le Quatrième Évangile*, vol. 2 of *Jean le théologien*, EBib (Paris: J. Gabalda et C\ie, 1964), 3–4, 8; Menken, *Old Testament Quotations in the Fourth Gospel*, 11–13; Schuchard, *Scripture within Scripture*, xiv, 76n31; and Sheridan, *Retelling Scripture*, 105–06 (see Appendix I). A full discussion, with arguments to the contrary, is developed in Chapter 4. Further, because its verbatim re-presentation of the LXX presents no anomalies to text form, the quotation of Isa 53:1 at John 12:38 was initially of no interest to Menken; *Old Testament Quotations in the Fourth Gospel*, 14–15. It was, however, taken up later by him, along with two other verbatim quotations; 'The Use of the Septuagint in Three Quotations in John: Jn 10,34; 12,38; 19:24', 382–86.

32. Perhaps the most salient of these explorations has been made on the three Isaianic quotations by Catrin H. Williams, '"He Saw His Glory and Spoke of Him": The Testimony of Isaiah and Johannine Christology', in *Honouring the Past and Shaping the Future: Religious and Biblical Studies in Wales. Essays in Honour of Gareth Lloyd Jones*, ed. Robert Pope (Leominster: Gracewing, 2003), 53–80; Catrin H. Williams, 'Isaiah in John's Gospel', in *Isaiah in the New Testament*, ed. Steve Moyise and Maarten J.J. Menken (London: T&T Clark, 2005), 101–16; and Catrin H. Williams, 'The Testimony of Isaiah and Johannine Christology', in *'As Those Who Are Taught': The Interpretation of Isaiah from the LXX to the SBL*, ed. Claire Matthews McGinnis and Patricia K. Tull, SymS 27 (Atlanta, GA: Society of Biblical Literature, 2006), 107–24.

To be more specific – and to forecast the horizon of this work – these six quotations carry three dynamics that invite further work. First, the formulae attending them carry one or the other of two features found nowhere else in John and, as such, sort those quotations into two groups of three: those at John 1:23; 12:38; and 12:39-40 are the only quotations explicitly ascribed to Isaiah; those at John 2:17 and 12:12-16 (as well as the formula for Jesus's *logion* at 2:19-22) are the only quotations which indicate that their fulfilment was 'remembered' by the disciples. Second, these Isaianic and 'remembrance' groupings are, themselves, split within the narrative, so that each brackets the Book of Signs as an *inclusio*: the Isaianic quotations do this across chapters 1 and 12; the 'remembrance' quotations, across chapters 2 and 12. Inasmuch as the components of *inclusios* (or *epanalepsis*) resonate with one another to convey overarching themes for the narrative that passes between them,[33] so it is with these between the beginning and end of Jesus's public ministry. The Isaianic quotations, it will be argued, show the Jews to have been called by, yet kept from, that ministry; that is, the Jews are (a) initially summoned to 'make straight the way of the Lord', (b) ultimately resistant to that call and (c) fundamentally found to have been impaired (by 'the ruler of this world') from responding as they should have. The 'remembrance' quotations, by contrast, show Jesus's disciples to have been illumined to a new order established by that ministry; that is, by Spirit-wrought recollection of scripture they are given insight into two of Jesus's gestures: (1) that his action in the temple anticipated his establishment of a new dynasty and (2) that his entrance into Jerusalem authorized him to do this as king over the reunited monarchy.

Finally, these two brackets of quotation clusters are positioned within the Book of Signs in a 'specular or "mirrorlike"' A-B-B′-A′ arrangement.[34] While the Isaianic quotations are the first (John 1:23) and last two (John 12:38, 40) explicit citations in John 1–12, the 'remembrance' quotations are the second (John 2:17) and second-to-last two (John 12:13, 15-16) in those chapters. Thus, the 'remembrance' *inclusio* is immediately tucked within the Isaianic one, rendering the two into a

---

Further, the 'memory language' common to the quotations at John 2:17, 19-22; 12:12-16 has been recognized by Clark-Soles, *Scripture Cannot Be Broken*, 294–95; and the four quotations fulfilled during Jesus's crucifixion were noted by Richard Morgan, 'Fulfillment in the Fourth Gospel: The Old Testament Foundations', *Int* 11 (1957): 157.

33. See Arthur Quinn and Lyon Rathbun, 'Epanalepsis', in *Encyclopedia of Rhetoric and Composition: Communication from Ancient Times to the Information Age*, ed. Theresa Enos (New York/London: Garland Publishing, 1996), 228; Heiner Peters, 'Epanalēpsis', in *Encyclopedia of Rhetoric*, ed. Thomas O. Sloane (Oxford: Oxford University Press, 2001), 250–51; Arthur Quinn and Lyon Rathbun, 'Inclusio', in *Encyclopedia of Rhetoric and Composition*, 346. E.W. Bullinger identifies *inclusio* instead with *epanadiplosis*, to which he ascribes the same definition that Quinn, Rathbun and Peters (above) give to *epanalepsis*: 'the repetition of the same Word or Words at the beginning and end of a Sentence'; *Figures of Speech Used in the Bible Explained and Illustrated* (1898; repr., Grand Rapids, MI: Baker Book House, 1968), 245–49 (quotation p. 245).

34. José Antonio Mayoral, 'Chiasmus', in *Encyclopedia of Rhetoric*, 89.

chiastic sequence – an 'introverted correspondence' of subjects, wherein the first matches up with the last and the second with the penultimate.[35] Inasmuch as such a structure brings the theme of its inner bracket into relief against that of its outer, it creates an even starker contrast between the two messages conveyed by the *inclusios*: over against the Jews being angelologically blinded to the significance of Jesus's signs (Isaianic *inclusio*) stands the disciples being pneumatologically illumined to the import of Jesus's gestures ('remembrance' *inclusio*).

d. Broader theological implications
Finally, the fourth factor for building on the more traditional questions asked of John's quotations, namely, that their theological implications can be teased out further. In part (as articulated above), this concerns conclusions about those implications which are open to debate. John the Baptist's recitation of Isaiah's 'make straight the way of the Lord', for instance,[36] has been variously interpreted as an admonition to live ethically (made by John to the people),[37] an exhortation to testify to Jesus (made to John by God),[38] an invitation to follow wisdom (made by John to the people)[39] and a commission to announce 'the coming of Jesus' (made to John by God).[40] Taking cognate interpretations of Isaiah 40:3 and the broader Johannine narrative into account, however,[41] John's words in this instance arguably convey something quite different: an appeal to believe, issued by John to the populace. More specifically (but to be developed fully below), as Luke interprets John's message to include a call to believe,[42] so the fourth evangelist seems to do with John's preaching in the Fourth Gospel, given two assertions the evangelist makes elsewhere in the narrative: (1) that John came 'in order that all might believe (ἵνα ... πιστεύσωσιν) through him'[43] and (2) that after many people at Bethany beyond the Jordan recalled that 'everything John said about this man (Jesus) was true', they consequently 'believed (ἐπίστευσαν) in him (Jesus) there'.[44]

But further, this matter concerns broader theological implications which emerge when the quotations are engaged as clusters. When the narratives embodied in

---

35. Bullinger, *Figures of Speech Used in the Bible*, 374–79 (quotation p. 374).
36. John 1:23/Isa 40:3.
37. Freed, *Old Testament Quotations in the Gospel of John*, 2–3, 6–7.
38. Menken, '"I Am the Voice of One Crying in the Wilderness ... " (John 1:23)', in *Old Testament Quotations in the Fourth Gospel*, 26–28, 30–31, 33, 35; first publ. in *Bib* 66 (1985).
39. Schuchard, *Scripture within Scripture*, 6–15.
40. Williams, '"He Saw His Glory and Spoke of Him": The Testimony of Isaiah and Johannine Christology', 58–61 (quotation p. 60); Williams, 'Isaiah in John's Gospel', 103–104; Williams, 'The Testimony of Isaiah and Johannine Christology', 109–111.
41. Cf. 1QS viii 14 (= 4QS^e iii 4-5 [frgs 2a ii, 3a-c]); ix 19-21 (=4QS^b xviii 3-4 [frgs 6a i, 6b]; 4QS^d viii 4-5 [frgs 4a ii, 4c-f]; 4QS^e iii 19 [frgs 2a ii, 3a-c]; iv 1-2 [frgs 4a-d]); 4QTanh 1-2 i 6-7; Matt 3:3; Mark 1:2-3; Luke 1:76; 3:4-6.
42. Acts 19:3-4.
43. John 1:7.
44. John 10:41-42.

the Isaianic and 'remembrance' *inclusios* are synthesized into a *chiasmus* and translated into theological categories, they elucidate and challenge assumptions on an array of issues in theological taxonomy; and on such a prospect, they merit revisitation through a traditional theological lens. How does Jesus's crucifixion, for instance, weigh against his incarnation when his death is necessary to remove cosmic impairment of human perception (christology)? What texture does such a removal bring to the Johannine concept of 'salvation' (soteriology)? What factors change in the Johannine soteriological landscape once that removal has taken place (eschatology)? That is, are the conditions and dynamics of mission the same at the end of the Book of Glory as they were at the beginning of the Book of Signs? How does John conceive the identity of believers if Jesus is understood to have united the northern and southern kingdoms and set them as a temple 'in spirit and truth', heralding his new dynasty (ecclesiology)? And how are the members of that church epistemologically distinguished from the 'blindness' befalling their peers when Spirit-wrought recollection affords them insight into Jesus's life after the crucifixion (pneumatology)?

3. This work

In light of these four factors (now argued), this work revisits quotations in John from an historical-critical and theological vantage point, examining the two clusters of quotations delineated above in three studies. The first two (covering chapters 1–4) examine the exegetical issues raised by the quotations, with a view towards distilling the themes resonating between each *inclusio*. The third (chapter 5) synthesizes the stories resonating from these *inclusios* into the overarching narrative of the *chiasmus* they form, then from that narrative distils implications spanning the five spheres of theological thought listed above: christology, soteriology, eschatology, ecclesiology and pneumatology. With regard to the narrative of the *chiasmus*, it will be concluded that the failing 'closure' brought to Jesus's public ministry in the Isaianic *inclusio* points to the triumphant 'anticipation' of his death and resurrection inherent in the 'remembrance' *inclusio*: Jesus, who, as Moses, is attested to the Jews but thwarted in that effort by 'the ruler of this world' (the Isaianic quotations) emerges also as David, who ousts that figure through his passion and restores the divided monarchy by 'raising the sanctuary of his body' (the 'remembrance' *inclusio*). As for the theological implications of that *chiasmus*, it will be suggested (a) that in John Jesus's death is as crucial to his purpose as is his incarnation (christology); (b) that this death entails removing the perceptual impairment to humanity caused by the devil (soteriology); (c) that this removal, in turn, changes the soteriological landscape so as to free the Jews/world from the devil's thrall and shed the need for signs or (perhaps even) election (eschatology); (d) that the collective of believers created by this removal serves as both the prophetic fulfilment of a reunited monarchy and the shrine raised to signal it (ecclesiology); and (e) that, after the resurrection, this collective, itself, becomes pneumatologically privy to the deeper import of Jesus's public ministry (pneumatology).

C. Guiding assumptions

Among the methodological considerations guiding these studies, four so suffuse the discussion as to merit preliminary articulation here. One concerns the biblical versions used by John; another, the data from the Judaean desert texts; a third, the prospect of intermediary sources (between the Jewish scriptures and John); and the last, acceptable hypotheses for deviations in the Fourth Gospel's quotations.

1. The versions cited by John

One of the questions conventionally asked of quotations in John concerns the type of textual traditions they reflect. As it was put above (for quotations whose referents can be reasonably discerned), from what versions have these references been drawn? The Hebrew Bible? The LXX? *Testimonia*? *Targumim*? For several quotations the answer seems self-evident: they follow the LXX verbatim (or nearly so) and, thus, appear to have been cited from that version.[45] The issue, however, is more complex on four counts: (1) the LXX versions of the several quotations just noted follow the HB verbatim and, thereby, allow the possibility that John cited the Hebrew directly, coincidentally using the same Greek wording as the LXX; (2) at least two other quotations are drawn from passages whose HB and LXX forms differ dramatically, and in John they appear to be closer to the former (HB) than to the latter (LXX)[46]; (3) four further quotations do not precisely align with either version and betray features that could arguably be traced to each[47]; and, (4) inasmuch as a number of Johannine anomalies may reflect polyvalent citations – in which the base text quoted has been conflated with elements from one or more other passages[48] – questions arise as to whether or not the assimilated texts are taken from the same textual tradition as the major one cited: Hebrew with Hebrew, Greek with Greek.

a. Confirming the Septuagint

Steering the discussions of this issue as it arises for each quotation are two working suppositions, both of which address the complexities just listed: the first concerns (1) above, the degree to which the LXX is to be expected when the LXX of a passage cited follows the HB verbatim; the second concerns (2)–(4) above, essentially, the degree to which the HB is to be expected at all in John's quotations and, if so, whether the two versions are ever conflated in a single reference.

With regard to (1), when John's rendering by and large follows the LXX on a passage in which the LXX does the same with the HB, it is assumed here to

---

45. John 10:34/Ps 82:6; John 12:13/Ps 118:25-26 (the precise correspondence occurs with Ps 118:26a); John 12:38/Isa 53:1; John 19:24/Ps 22:19.
46. John 13:18/Ps 41:10; John 19:37/Zech 12:10.
47. John 6:45/Isa 54:13; John 8:17/Deut 17:6 (?); 19:15; John 12:15/Zech 9:9; John 12:40/Isa 6:10.
48. John 1:23/Isa 40:3; John 2:17/Ps 69:10; John 6:31/Exod 16:4 (?), 15 (?); Ps 78:24 (?); Neh 9:15/2 Esd 19:15 (?); John 15:25/Pss 35:19 (?); 69:5 (?); *Pss. Sol.* 7:1 (?).

have been drawn from the LXX unless compelling textual evidence to the contrary dictates otherwise. Thus, for instance, where John's quotation of Psalm 69:10a at John 2:17 matches the LXX word-for-word save for its anomalous future tense verb, it is assumed to have been drawn from that version, even though the LXX, itself, follows the HB with the same precision (Table 1).

Table 1 Psalm 69:10a in the HB, LXX and John

HB Psalm 69:10a	LXX Psalm 69:10a	John 2:17/Psalm 69:10a
כי-קנאת ביתך אכלתני	ὅτι ὁ ζῆλος τοῦ οἴκου σου κατέφαγέν με	ὁ ζῆλος τοῦ οἴκου σου καταφάγεταί με
For zeal for your house has consumed me	For zeal for your house consumed me	Zeal for your house will consume me

The case for discerning a LXX *Vorlage* in such circumstances has been pressed further by some exegetes, particularly Menken, using criteria which turn on lexical and grammatical peculiarities in (or options for) Johannine parlance. It is argued that when a quotation in John reflects the language of the LXX but could also have been translated from the HB, it is more likely to have been drawn from the LXX if its wording includes morphology, vocabulary or grammar which is (a) unique to or rare in Johannine literature and/or (b) replaceable with other choices. The reasoning pivots on the idea that were John to translate directly from the Hebrew, he would use glosses and constructs that one could find elsewhere in Johannine writings or more prominently throughout the LXX and other Greek translations of the HB. Inasmuch as John does not do so in these cases, he is deemed more likely to have re-presented the LXX than to have translated the HB. A synopsis of the arguments (particularly made by Menken) is charted in Table 2.[49]

Winsome as these criteria are, however – and correct as they may be in any given case – they labour under at least two major problems (evident in Menken's arguments) which bid caution in accepting their results.

Table 2 Linguistic arguments for LXX *Vorlagen*

Quotation	Vocabulary or construct in HB	Vocabulary or construct in LXX and John	Reasoning
John 1:23/Isa 40:3	• קורא ([of one] calling)	• βοῶντος (of one calling)	• βοᾶν is a *hapax legomenon* to Johannine literature: elsewhere John indicates 'calling' with κράζειν (John 1:15; 7:28, 37; 12:44) or κραυγάζειν (John 11:43; 12:13; 18:40; 19:6, 12, 15) and could be expected to do so here if he were translating the HB.

49. The data for this table are drawn ad loc. from the exegetes in question. Where no name is given, that exegete is Menken – specifically, from his treatments of fifteen quotations

Quotation	Vocabulary or construct in HB	Vocabulary or construct in LXX and John	Reasoning
John 2:17/Ps 69:10	• בֵיתְךָ (for your house)	• τοῦ οἴκου σου (for your house)	• A Johannine gloss is more likely to have been οἰκία, since elsewhere John uses οἶκος 2x (John 2:16; 11:20) but οἰκία 5x (John 4:53; 8:35; 11:31; 12:3; 14:2).
	• אֲכָלָתְנִי (has consumed me)	• κατέφαγέν με/ καταφάγεταί με (consumed/will consume me)	• A Johannine gloss could rather have been either ἐσθίειν (per LXX Isa 10:17; 26:11; 30:27; cf. Heb 10:27; Jas 5:3) or e.g. καταναλίσκειν (per Symmachus).
John 6:31/ Exod 16:4 (?), 15 (?); Ps 78:24 (?); Neh 9:15/2 Esd 19:15 (?)			• No issue or argument of this type made.
John 6:45/Isa 54:13	• יהוה (of the Lord)	• θεοῦ (of God)	• John's use of κύριος (rather than θεός) for God at two other *loci* drawn from biblical passages (John 12.13/LXX Ps 118:25-26; John 12:38/LXX Isa 53:1) suggests he would have done the same here if translating the HB.
	• לִמּוּדֵי (taught)	• διδακτούς/ διδακτοί (taught)	• Διδακτός is a *hapax legomenon* to Johannine literature and used only at one other place in the LXX: 1 Macc 4:7.[50]
John 7:38/???			• No issue or argument of this type made.
John 7:42/???			• No issue or argument of this type made.
John 8:17/ Deut 17:6 (?); 19:15			• No issue or argument of this type made.

(Continued)

in *Old Testament Quotations in the Fourth Gospel*, as well as from the works listed in note 4. In the one case where an argument stems from other exegetes, their names and works (though not the page numbers of those works) are given in a footnote.

50. Cf. Barrett, *Gospel according to St. John*, 296; Schnackenburg, *Gospel according to St John*, 2:50–51. Curiously, Menken dissents from this deduction; see the further discussion below.

Quotation	Vocabulary or construct in HB	Vocabulary or construct in LXX and John	Reasoning
John 10:34/Ps 82:6	• אני־אמרתי (I said)	• ἐγὼ εἶπα (I said)	• A Johannine gloss is more likely to have been ἐγὼ εἶπον (per John 1:15, 30, 50; etc.).[51]
John 12:13/ Ps 118:25-26			• No issue or argument of this type made.
John 12:15/Zech 9:9			• No issue or argument of this type made.
John 12:34/ 2 Sam 7:16 (?); Ezek 37:25 (?); Ps 89:37(?)			• No issue or argument of this type made.
John 12:38/Isa 53:1	• נגלתה (it has been revealed)	• ἀπεκαλύφθη (it was revealed)	• A Johannine gloss is more likely to have been φανεροῦν (per John 1:31; 2:11; etc.).[52]
John 12:40/Isa 6:10			• No issue or argument of this type made
John 13:18/Ps 41:10			• No issue or argument of this type made
John 15:25/ Pss 35:19 (?); 69:5 (?); *Pss. Sol.* 7:1 (?)	• חנם (without cause/ Pss 35:19; 69:5)	• δωρεάν (without cause/ Pss 35:19; 69:5)	• A Johannine gloss could also have been ἀδίκως (LXX Prov 1:11), ἀναιτίως (Aquila on Ps 35:19; Symmachus on Ps 69:5), διὰ κενῆς (LXX Job 2:3) or μάτην (LXX Ps 35:7), particularly given the choice of ἀναιτίως made by Aquila and Symmachus for the two psalms which likely furnish the major sources of this quotation.

51. Here Menken takes a reading of εἶπον, found in A D M S Δ and elsewhere, to be a scribal alteration; *Old Testament Quotations in the Fourth Gospel*, 15n13.

52. In his discussion of this quotation Menken also observes that since both the LXX and John read the vocative 'Lord' (κύριε) where the HB has nothing, the Johannine rendering is best identified as a re-presentation of the LXX; *Old Testament Quotations in the Fourth Gospel*, 15. This point, however, does not turn on the criterion in question here. In this case, the issue is not a Greek translation choice for a Hebrew word or construct but a departure from the HB altogether, shared by both the LXX and John.

Introduction 17

Quotation	Vocabulary or construct in HB	Vocabulary or construct in LXX and John	Reasoning
John 19:24/Ps 22:19	• יחלקו (they divided)	• διεμερίσαντο (they divided)	• A Johannine gloss could also have been μερίζειν (e.g. 3 Kgdms 18:6), διαιρεῖν (e.g. LXX Isa 9:2) or διαδιδόναι (LXX Gen 49:27; cf. John 6:11).
	• בגדי (my garments)	• τὰ ἱμάτιά μου (my garments)	• A Johannine gloss could also have been στολή (e.g. LXX Gen 27:15).
	• לבושי (my clothing)	• τὸν ἱματισμόν μου/(my clothing)	• A Johannine gloss could also have been στολή (per above), and the order of the synonyms τὰ ἱμάτιά μου and τὸν ἱματισμόν μου could have been inverted.
	• יפילו גורל (they cast the lot)	• ἔβαλον κλῆρον (they cast the lot)	• A Johannine gloss could also have been λαγχάνειν (per Symmachus).
John 19:36/ Exod 12:10 (?), 46 (?); Num 9:12 (?); Ps 34:21 (?)			• No issue or argument of this type made.
John 19:37/ Zech 12:10			• No issue or argument of this type made.

First, Menken sometimes comes to conclusions about Johannine versus Septuagint parlance which overreach the scope of available data. At John 2:17/ Psalm 69:10, for instance, he argues that the evangelist would have rendered 'house' with οἰκία rather than οἶκος on the meagre grounds that apart from the quotation, οἰκία appears five times in the gospel[53] while οἶκος occurs only twice.[54] Similarly, at John 15:25/Pss 35:19 (?); 69:5 (?); *Pss. Sol.* 7:1 (?) Menken gives the words μισεῖν ('to hate') and δωρεάν ('without cause') dramatically different import for determining a LXX source for the quotation by appealing to nothing more than a slight difference in their LXX usage. Both terms are the most common Greek glosses used for their Hebrew counterparts in HB Psalm 35:19 and HB Psalm 69:5: μισεῖν translates לשנא some one hundred and twenty-seven times in the LXX[55] but shares that role with two other glosses – ἐχθρός[56] and ὑπεναντίος[57]; δωρεάν translates חנם twenty times in the LXX but shares that role with four other glosses – ἀδίκως, ἀναιτίως, διὰ κενῆς and μάτην.[58] Yet, because δωρεάν allows two translation

---

53. John 4:53; 8:35; 11:31; 12:3; 14:2.
54. John 2:16; 11:20; see '"Zeal for Your House Will Consume Me" (John 2:17)', 39.
55. One hundred and thirty-three out of one hundred and fifty-seven if translations of Hebrew Sirach are counted.
56. Menken gives Exod 23:5 and Ps 41:8 as examples.
57. Menken gives Gen 24:60 as an example.
58. Representative verses here are listed in Table 2.

options more than μισεῖν, and because one of those options (ἀναιτίως) was used by Aquila and Symmachus for Psalm 35:19 and Psalm 69:5, Menken regards μισεῖν to be 'irrelevant to the problem of the provenance of the quotation' but deems δωρεάν to 'tip the balance in favour of the LXX'.[59]

Second, Menken does not make uniform inferences from the lexical and grammatical features he observes. Put another way, he often draws opposite conclusions from the same (or similar) premises.

(1) At John 1:23/Isaiah 40:3, for instance, he identifies the verb βοᾶν as betraying the evangelist's use of the LXX, in part, because it is a *hapax legomenon* to Johannine literature (and, thus, he would argue, more likely to have been borrowed from the LXX than chosen by the evangelist). For several other quotations, however, Menken maintains that had the evangelist translated them from the HB, he would have drawn his vocabulary from the array of glosses used for each respective Hebrew term by the LXX and other Greek versions[60]; and yet βοᾶν, itself, is just such a gloss for the Hebrew לקרא of Isaiah 40:3. It is used to translate that verb (and its Aramaic equivalent) some thirty-eight times in the LXX; and, thus, on Menken's own terms (stated elsewhere), it may just as well represent a translation from the Hebrew as it does a carry-over from the Greek, despite its condition as a *hapax legomenon*.

(2) Conversely, Menken holds that the *hapax* διδακτός at John 6:45/Isaiah 54:13 and the *hapax* δωρεάν at John 15:25/Pss 35:19 (?); 69:5 (?); *Pss. Sol.* 7:1 (?) do not, in fact, indicate LXX *Vorlagen*. For δωρεάν, he simply asserts that it 'is not significant' for determining the version of the quotation[61]; for διδακτός, he contends (a) that it 'is an acceptable translation of למוד', (b) that it appears only once in the gospel because the evangelist had 'no other occasion' to employ it and (c) that its -τος ending matches Johannine preference.[62] But can it not be argued that at John 1:23/Isaiah 40:3 βοᾶν, like δωρεάν, 'is not significant' for determining the version of Isaiah being cited? Or that, like διδακτός, it 'is an acceptable translation of לקרא' and, likewise, appears only once in the gospel because the evangelist had 'no other occasion' to use it?

(3) Yet again, for some quotations Menken ascribes *hapax legomena* (or words used rarely in John) straight out to the evangelist as editorial or translation choices. To look again at John 1:23/Isaiah 40:3, Menken identifies another *hapax*, εὐθύνειν,

---

59. '"They Hated Me without Reason" (John 15:25)', in *Old Testament Quotations in the Fourth Gospel*, 142–43; see esp. p. 142n16. Bracketed here is the question of whether Menken fairly counts translation options: לשׂנא, for instance, is also rendered by ἔχθρα ('hatred') at LXX Sir 6:9, as well as by μισητός ('hateful') at LXX Prov 30:23 and LXX Sir 10:7, bringing its further translation options from two to four, equivalent to חנם.

60. In Table 2, see ἐσθίειν and καταναλίσκειν for John 2:17/Ps 69:10; ἀδίκως, ἀναιτίως, διὰ κενῆς and μάτην for John 15:25/Pss 35:19 (?); 69:5 (?); *Pss. Sol.* 7:1 (?); and μερίζειν, διαιρεῖν, διαδιδόναι, στολή and λαγχάνειν for John 19:24/Ps 22:19.

61. '"They Hated Me without Reason" (John 15:25)', 143n17.

62. John 9:30; 10:12-13; 18:15-16; 19:13, 23. For these premises, see '"And They Shall All Be Taught by God" (John 6:45)', in *Old Testament Quotations in the Fourth Gospel*, 72–73; first publ. in *ETL* 64 (1988). For the first of them Menken follows Freed (*Old Testament Quotations in the Gospel of John*, 18).

as having been adopted and merged into the quotation by John from a putative Septuagintal/pre-Aquilan recension.⁶³ And at John 13:18/Psalm 41:10 Menken classifies the *hapax* πτέρνα and the rare verb τρώγειν⁶⁴ as the evangelist's own choices for translating the Hebrew of that verse.⁶⁵

These (and like) factors suggest that, for Menken, such arguments function more as reference points for thought than as algorithms for calculation; and in that spirit this work will consider (but will by no means feel bound by) them as the study proceeds.

b. Expecting the Hebrew Bible

With regard to the use of the HB in John's quotations – (2) through (4) above – this study assumes a slightly modified form of the dynamic proposed by August Franke in the earliest extended treatment of the matter, 'Urtext und Septuaginta', in part three of *Das alte Testament bei Johannes*.⁶⁶ Franke argued not only that John used both versions but that he at points conflated the two, even in quotations evidently cited from the Greek. Bracketing references whose versions he believed were indeterminable⁶⁷ – and keeping in mind the possible brokerage of quotations through the Synoptics⁶⁸ – he ascribed most quotations to the LXX,⁶⁹ conceded two to the HB⁷⁰ and, on the basis of those two – as well as on the more allusive use of scripture throughout the rest of the gospel – he argued

---

63. "'I Am the Voice of One Crying in the Wilderness ... '" (John 1:23)', 22–25.

64. Τρώγειν is not a *hapax legomenon* to Johannine literature per se, but it is nearly so, appearing elsewhere in John (and in the entire New Testament) only four further times, at John 6:54, 56-58.

65. '"He Who Eats My Bread, Has Raised His Heel against Me" (John 13:18)', in *Old Testament Quotations in the Fourth Gospel*, 123–25, 128–38; first publ. in *JSNT* 40 (1990).

66. *Das alte Testament bei Johannes*, 282–93.

67. Franke ascribed the versional uncertainty of these references to either the free paraphrase (John 8:17/Deut 19:15 [cf. Num 35:30]; John 12:15/Zech 9:9; John 15:25/Ps 69:5), summarization (John 7:42; 12:34) or personalized language (John 7:38) employed by the evangelist; *Das alte Testament bei Johannes*, 283.

68. Several of the Fourth Gospel's citations have counterparts in Matthew, Mark and Luke; consequently, part of ascertaining the versions from which they were drawn involves weighing the HB and LXX texts, themselves, against possible Johannine dependence on the Synoptics (or putative earlier tradition). See the roles played by Mark 11:9 and Matt 21:5 in Franke's determination of the versions used for John 12:13/Ps 118:25-26 and John 12:15/Zech 9:9, respectively; *Das alte Testament bei Johannes*, 286, 288–89.

69. Franke divided these references into quotations that follow the LXX verbatim (John 10:34/Ps 82:6; John 12:38/Isa 53:1; John 19:24/Ps 22:19), quotations that deviate slightly from it (John 1:23/Isa 40:3; John 2:17/Ps 69:10; John 6:31/Exod 16:4; Ps 78:24; John 6:45/Isa 54:13; John 19:36/Exod 12:46 [cf. Num 9:12]; Ps 34:21) and the anomalous quotation of Isa 6:10 at John 12:40, which he ultimately regarded to yield 'no certain result' for the question; *Das alte Testament bei Johannes*, 283–84 (quotation p. 284).

70. John 13:18/Ps 41:10; John 19:37/Zech 12:10.

that the influence of the HB should be expected, even in passages whose main text was clearly drawn from the LXX.[71] This study takes such a dynamic (though not necessarily Franke's categorization of quotations) as its point of departure, making but one adjustment, namely, that where a quotation may be polyvalent, hypotheses will be preferred which align (rather than mix) the versions of the base and assimilated passages.[72]

2. Texts from the Judaean desert

When Edwin Freed revived research on the Fourth Gospel's quotations in 1965, he broke new ground by consulting several texts from Khirbet Qumran that had become available.[73] In part, this was to check the textual traditions they represent against the MT and LXX; in part, it was to draw exegetical inferences from the way they were interpreted in cognate settings.[74] Freed's endeavour was taken up by some of his successors, but at present it stands unfinished for two reasons. One is somewhat fortuitous: a chronological fissure between the agendas of each discipline. While the last wholesale effort to consult Judaean desert texts for the text forms of Johannine quotations dates to the publications of Menken

---

71. Franke, *Das alte Testament bei Johannes*, 284–90. Specifically, Franke argued HB influence in the quotations of (what he viewed to be) LXX Zech 9:9 at John 12:15 and LXX Isa 54:13 at John 6:45. By contrast to Franke's nuanced analysis, Roger Humann has suggested that (with the exception of John 2:17/Ps 69:10) the evangelist used the LXX where it conveys the meaning of the HB and that where it does not (John 13:18/Ps 41:10; John 19:37/Zech 12:10), he translated the Hebrew; 'The Function and Form of the Explicit Old Testament Quotations in the Gospel of John', *Lutheran Theological Review* 1 (1988–89): 39–42. Several quotations, however, show otherwise: (1) LXX Isa 54:13 diverges from the HB by reading 'taught of God' (διδακτοὺς θεοῦ) rather than 'taught of the Lord' (למודי יהוה), yet the evangelist follows the LXX reading (διδακτοὶ θεοῦ; John 6:45); similarly, (2) LXX Isa 6:10g differs from the HB by reading 'and I heal them' (καὶ ἰάσομαι αὐτούς) rather than 'and he heal them' (ורפא לו), yet the evangelist, again, appears to cite that version (καὶ ἰάσομαι αὐτούς; John 12:40); and conversely, (3) LXX Ps 41:10b follows the HB closely (HB אוכל לחמי הגדיל עלי עקב/LXX ὁ ἐσθίων ἄρτους μου, ἐμεγάλυνεν ἐπ' ἐμὲ πτερνισμόν), yet the evangelist has chosen to render the Hebrew with his own vocabulary (ὁ τρώγων μου τὸν ἄρτον ἐπῆρεν ἐπ' ἐμὲ τὴν πτέρναν αὐτοῦ; John 13:18) rather than cite the LXX.

72. This starting point, therefore, respectfully differs from the conclusion of Schuchard that 'there is in John's citations tangible evidence for the use of one and only one textual tradition, the OG' (Old Greek = 'the first Greek translation of the Bible'); *Scripture within Scripture*, xvii, xviin28.

73. 1QS iv 20-21; viii 14; ix 20; CD ii 12; 1QHª iv 37-38 (Suk[enik] xvii/frg 14 25-26); xii 12 (Suk iv/frg 43 11); xiii 25-26 (Suk v/frg 29 23-24); xv 9-10 (Suk vii 6-7); xvi 17 (Suk viii 16); xx 14-16 (Suk xii/frgs 54 & 60 11-13); Freed, *Old Testament Quotations in the Gospel of John*, 1, 22, 89, 104.

74. Freed, *Old Testament Quotations in the Gospel of John*, xii and *passim*.

and Obermann,[75] many *editiones principes* of those texts were not published until sometime after those years.[76] So, also, for several important reference works which facilitate such study.[77] One might expect, then, that the full scope of Judaean desert manuscripts has not yet been scanned for possible relevance to the text forms of John's quotations.

The second reason has been methodological. Even when parallels to the Fourth Gospel's quotations have been published and available, they have not always been taken into account by Johannine scholars working on those

---

75. This is not to dismiss the later work of Clark-Soles (2003) and Sheridan (2012), the two treatments of all (or a large swath of) the quotations subsequent to Menken and Obermann. It is only to indicate the last date at which the Judaean desert texts were broached with the questions in view here. Clark-Soles does, indeed, engage those texts (specifically, those from Qumran), but not with the same purpose (and, therefore, not with the same passages) in view. She is concerned with comparing the Qumran and Johannine uses of scripture for identity formation; and, as such, though she notes the quotation of Isa 40:3 at 1QS viii 14 (as showing the *Yaḥad* to be Torah centred) – and though she treats the implications of the citation formulae at Qumran relative to those in John – she, in fact, examines Qumran quotations of passages other than those found in the Fourth Gospel, cited in 1QpHab, 4QMMT and CD 1-8, 19-20; *Scripture Cannot Be Broken, passim* 66–135.

76. As a rough measure, both Menken's anthology of previously published articles and Obermann's monograph date to 1996; but from 1996 and 2009 have come to print some twenty-three further volumes of the *Discoveries in the Judaean Desert* (DJD) series, as well as Yigael Yadin's important *Masada VI. Yigael Yadin Excavations 1963–1965: Final Reports*, The Masada Reports (Jerusalem: Israel Exploration Society and The Hebrew University of Jerusalem, 1999). From 1996 to 2009 Menken has published (at least) seven further articles on the issue (see note 4), but these, themselves, have not addressed the gamut of new data available with the complete publication of Judaean desert texts.

The complex relationships between (a) the DJD series, (b) first editions published outside of it, (c) first editions published within it but redone and (d) preliminary editions are sorted out by Emanuel Tov in 'The *Discoveries in the Judaean Desert* Series: History and System of Presentation', in *The Texts from the Judaean Desert: Indices and an Introduction to the* Discoveries in the Judaean Desert *Series*, ed. Emanuel Tov, DJD 39 (Oxford: Clarendon Press, 2002), 3–8, 12–14, 17–18, 21–25.

77. Two of these tools appear in the 39th volume of the DJD series: Emanuel Tov, 'Categorized List of the "Biblical Texts"', in *The Texts from the Judaean Desert: Indices and an Introduction to the* Discoveries in the Judaean Desert *Series*, 165–83; and Eugene Ulrich, 'Index of Passages in the "Biblical Texts"', in *The Texts from the Judaean Desert: Indices and an Introduction to the* Discoveries in the Judaean Desert *Series*, 185–201. Two are the concordances provided for biblical texts from the Judaean desert and non-biblical texts from Qumran: Martin G. Abegg, Jr., ed., *The Dead Sea Scrolls Concordance. Volume One: The Non-Biblical Texts from Qumran*, 2 vols. (Leiden/Boston: E.J. Brill, 2003); Martin G. Abegg, Jr., ed., *The Dead Sea Scrolls Concordance. Volume Three: The Biblical Texts from the Judaean Desert*, 2 vols. (Leiden/Boston: E.J. Brill, 2010).

quotations.⁷⁸ Part of this is due to the scope of discoveries consulted. Attention has been paid to Khirbet Qumran, but the breadth of finds is much broader and for biblical attestations, in particular, includes texts from at least six other sites: Wadi Murabbaʿat, Naḥal Ḥever/(Seiyal), Masada, Wadi Sdeir, Naḥal Ṣeʾelim and Khirbet Mird.⁷⁹ Yet a noteworthy amount has been missed, even from the Qumran corpus itself. To chart just two examples – showing, in fact, both parts of this problem: the narrow scope of discoveries consulted and the Qumran texts missed – Tables 3 and 4 synchronize treatments of the quotations by Menken and Obermann with attestations in biblical manuscripts from the Judaean desert published in their first editions up to one year before each scholar's work came to print – that is, allowing for Menken and Obermann to have stopped research and put their works in press one year prior to their publication dates.⁸⁰ The number

78. This point is partially drawn from a preliminary report by Michael A. Daise, 'Quotations in John and the Judaean Desert Texts' (paper presented to the Johannine Literature section of the Society of Biblical Literature, International Meeting, University of St. Andrews, St. Andrews, Scotland, 7–11 July, 2013). Cf. also Daise, 'Quotations with "Remembrance" Formulae in the Fourth Gospel', in *Abiding Words: The Use of Scripture in the Gospel of John*, 77n7.

79. See Tov, 'Categorized List of the "Biblical Texts"', 179–83.

80. Assessing Menken's consultation of Judaean desert texts requires accounting for articles outside his 1996 anthology in which he either (a) treats quotations not included in that work or (b) later follows up on quotations which were included in that volume – particularly, John 8:17/Deut 17:6 (?); 19:15 (treated in 1991); John 10:34/Ps 82:6 (1997); John 12:38/Isa 53:1 (1997); John 19:24/Ps 22:19 (1997); John 12:38/Isa 53:1 and John 12:40/Isa 6:10 (1998); as well as John 12:15/Zech 9:9 and John 19:37/Zech 12:10 (2009); see the bibliography in note 4. In Table 3, each of these quotations is marked with the date of Menken's treatment in parentheses, and the available Judaean desert editions are accounted for up to one year before it.

Also accounted for in Tables 3 and 4 are the Judaean desert texts incorporated into the *Biblia Hebraica Stuttgartensia* (*BHS*) apparatuses used by Menken and Obermann. In his anthology Menken used the 1st edition of 1967/77 (*BHS*; see *Old Testament Quotations in the Fourth Gospel*, 9); Obermann, for his part, used the 2nd emended edition of 1983 (*BHS*²; see *Die christologische Erfüllung der Schrift im Johannesevangelium*, 431). Both editions would have included the manuscripts from Wadi Murabbaʿat, as well as (from Qumran) the texts published in DJD 1–5, 1QIsaiah^(a-b), *1QGenesis Apocryphon, 1QSefer ha-Milḥama, 4QPsalms*^b and fragments (some in preliminary editions) of 1-2 Samuel. Obermann's 2nd edition would have also included the texts published in DJD 6–7. For this, see ad loc. in the prolegomena of Karl Elliger and Wilhelm Rudolph, eds., *Torah, Neviʾim uKethuvim: Biblia Hebraica Stuttgartensia* (Stuttgart: Deutsche Bibelgesellschaft, 1977); and Karl Elliger and Wilhelm Rudolph, eds., *Torah, Neviʾim uKethuvim: Biblia Hebraica Stuttgartensia*, 2nd rev. ed. (Stuttgart: Deutsche Bibelgesellschaft, 1983). Menken does not cite the edition(s) he used in the articles listed in note 4. The differential between *BHS* and *BHS*², however, would have only affected a quotation which was not, in fact, treated in those articles (two phylactery attestations to Exod 12:46 relative to John 19:36), and so the matter is moot.

Table 3 Maarten Menken and the Judaean desert texts, 1985–2009 (*BHS* 1967/77)

Quotation in John	Judaean Desert Texts Referenced	Judaean Desert Texts Available
John 1:23/Isa 40:3	1QS viii 14; ix 19-20	• 1QIsa^a xxxiii 2-3 (Burrows 1950) 1QIsa^b xvi 24-25 (Suk 12 2-3; Sukenik 1955) 4QTanh 1-2 i 6-7 (DJD 5/1968)
John 2:17/Ps 69:10		
John 6:31/Exod 16:4 (?), 15 (?); Ps 78:24 (?); Neh 9:15/ 2 Esd 19:15 (?)		• Exod 16:4 4QpaleoGen-Exod^l 11 6-7 (DJD 9/1992) 4QpaleoExod^m xv 25 (DJD 9/1992) • Exod 16:15 1QExod 1 4-5 (DJD 1/1955)
John 6:45/Isa 54:13	CD xx 3-4	• 1QIsa^a xlv 12 (Burrows 1950) 1QH^a x 41 (Suk ii 39); xv 13, 17 (Suk vii 10, 14); xvi 37 (Suk viii 36; Sukenik 1955)
John 8:17/Deut 17:6 (?); 19:15 (1991)		
John 10:34/Ps 82:6 (1997)		
John 12:13/Ps 118:25-26	Not treated	
John 12:15/Zech 9:9 (2009)		
John 12:38/Isa 53:1 (1997–98)	1QIsa^a xliv 5	• 1QIsa^b xxiii 10 (Suk viii 10; Sukenik 1955) • 4QIsa^c 36-38 9 (DJD 15/1997)
John 12:40/Isa 6:10 (1998)		• 1QIsa^a vi 2-5 (Burrows 1950) • 4QIsa^f 11 1 (DJD 15/1997)
John 13:18/Ps 41:10	1QH^a xiii 25-26 (Suk v/frg 29 23-24)	
John 15:25/Pss 35:19 (?); 69:5 (?); *Pss. Sol.* 7:1 (?)		
John 19:24/Ps 22:19 (1997)		
John 19:28/Pss 42:3 (?); 63:2 (?); 69:22 (?)	Not treated	• 1QH^a xii 12 (Suk iv/frg 43 11)
John 19:36/Exod 12:10 (?), 46 (?); Num 9:12 (?); Ps 34:21 (?)		• Exod 12:10 4QpaleoGen-Exod^l 7 ii 25-26 (DJD 9/1992) • Exod 12:46 4QpaleoGen-Exod^l 9 6 (DJD 9/1992) 4QExod^c v (frgs 32i, 33i) 14 (DJD 12/1994) 4QDeut^j x 1 (DJD 14/1995) 4QPhyl A verso 47-48 (DJD 6/1977) 4QPhyl M recto 2-3 (DJD 6/1977) 8QPhyl 17-25 (DJD 3/1962) XQPhyl 1 2-3 (Yadin 1969)
John 19:37/Zech 12:10 (2009)		

Table 4 Andreas Obermann and the Judaean desert texts, 1996 (BHS^2 1983)[81]

Quotation in John	Judaean Desert Texts Referenced	Judaean Desert Texts Available
John 1:23/Isa 40:3	1QS iv 2; viii 13-14; ix 19-20 4QTanh 1-2 i 6-7	• 1QIsa^a xxxiii 2-3 (Burrows 1950) 1QIsa^b xvi 24-25 (Suk 12 2-3; Sukenik 1955)
John 2:17/Ps 69:10		
John 6:31/ Exod 16:4 (?), 15 (?); Ps 78:24 (?); Neh 9:15/ 2 Esd 19:15 (?)		• Exod 16:4 4QpaleoGen-Exod^l 11 6-7 (DJD 9/1992) 4QpaleoExod^m xv 25 (DJD 9/1992) • Exod 16:15 1QExod 1 4-5 (DJD 1/1955)
John 6:45/Isa 54:13	CD xx 3-4 1QH^a x 41 (Suk ii 39); xv 13, 17 (Suk vii 10, 14); xvi 37 (Suk viii 36)	• 1QIsa^a xlv 12 (Burrows 1950)
John 8:17/Deut 17:6 (?); 19:15	Not treated	• Deut 19:15 4QDeut^{k2} 1 9 (DJD 14/1995)
John 10:34/Ps 82:6		
John 12:13/Ps 118:25-26		
John 12:15/Zech 9:9		
John 12:38/Isa 53:1	1QIsa^a xliv 5 1QIsa^b xxiii (Suk viii) 10	
John 12:40/Isa 6:10	1QIsa^a vi 2-5 4QIsa^f 11 1 (Isa 6:9)	
John 13:18/Ps 41:10	1QH^a xiii 25-26 (Suk v/frg 29 23-24)	
John 15:25/Pss 35:19 (?); 69:5 (?); *Pss. Sol.* 7:1 (?)		
John 19:24/Ps 22:19		
John 19:28/Pss 42:3 (?); 63:2 (?); 69:22 (?)	• Ps 69:22 1QH^a xii 12 (Suk iv/frg 43 11)	
John 19:36/ Exod 12:10 (?), 46 (?); Num 9:12 (?); Ps 34:21 (?)		• Exod 12:10 4QpaleoGen-Exod^l 7 ii 25-26 (DJD 9/1992) • Exod 12:46 4QpaleoGen-Exod^l 9 6 (DJD 9/1992) 4QExod^c v (frgs 32i, 33i) 14 (DJD 12/1994) 4QDeut^j x 1 (DJD 14/1995) 4QPhyl A verso 47-48 (DJD 6/1977) 4QPhyl M recto 2-3 (DJD 6/1977) 8QPhyl 17-25 (DJD 3/1962) XQPhyl 1 2-3 (Yadin 1969)
John 19:37/Zech 12:10		

81. Among references which Obermann deems 'allusions' rather than 'quotations' are several whose language runs so close to the biblical texts in question that they are included here.

of untreated attestations per work (right-hand columns of each table) signals how much available cognate material was not engaged (or at least not presented as such) (see Tables 3 and 4).[82]

This gap in research has begun to be closed, particularly by the work of Bynum and Kubiś on John 19:37/Zechariah 12:10. Both engage the attestation of Zechariah 12:10 in the Qumran Minor Prophets manuscripts.[83] And, as noted above, Bynum goes so far as to infer the source of John's citation to be the *Greek Minor Prophets Scroll* from Naḥal Ḥever (*8ḤevXIIgr*) or a textual tradition similar to it.[84] Bynum insists, in fact, that 'the most glaring inadequacy' in scholarly discussion of this quotation 'is the lack of attention to the Dead Sea Scrolls (DSS) discoveries in the Twelve and the implications of those discoveries for Johannine citation of the Scriptures'.[85]

This work will continue such a task, citing all available attestations of the quotations being treated. At points this will yield some suggestive new data.[86] But it should be said that even when it does not – and the attestations merely follow readings in the MT or LXX – the endeavour is still worth doing, if only to confirm that various Johannine anomalies are better ascribed to the evangelist's theological purposes than to alternate textual traditions.

---

82. In the interests of simplicity page numbers for each attestation cited by Menken and Obermann in Tables 3 and 4 are ad loc. Publications of *editiones principes* in the DJD series are identified by volume number and date. The three editions published outside that series are Millar Burrows, ed., with John C. Trevor and William H. Brownlee, *The Dead Sea Scrolls of St. Mark's Monastery*, 2 vols. (New Haven, CT: American Schools of Oriental Research, 1950–51); E.L. Sukenik, ed., *The Dead Sea Scrolls of the Hebrew University* (Jerusalem: Magnes Press, 1955); and Yigael Yadin, *Tefillin from Qumran (X Q Phyl 1-4)* (Jerusalem: Israel Exploration Society and the Shrine of the Book, 1969).

83. 4QXII^e 18 4-5; *editio princeps* by Russell E. Fuller, '4QXII^e (Pl. XLVII)', in *Qumran Cave 4: X, The Prophets*, DJD 15 (Oxford: Clarendon Press, 1997), 257–65. Cf. Bynum, *Fourth Gospel and the Scriptures*, 40–41, 79, 104, 144–45; Kubiś, *Book of Zechariah in the Gospel of John*, 117–18, 157–62.

84. *8ḤevXIIgr* does not attest to Zech 12:10 but is conjectured to have done so (or to represent a tradition which had done so) by Bynum, developing an earlier suggestion from Robert Hanhart: see the reference to Bynum in note 83 and cf. Robert Hanhart, introduction to *The Septuagint as Christian Scripture: Its Prehistory and the Problem of Its Canon*, by Martin Hengel, trans. Mark E. Biddle, OTS (Edinburgh: T&T Clark, 2002), 6–7. More cautious on this prospect is Kubiś, *Book of Zechariah in the Gospel of John*, 173, 180–81.

85. *Fourth Gospel and the Scriptures*, 5.

86. Of particular interest (to be developed below) is the reading 'you have smeared over[their eyes' ([ותשע]עיניהמה) in *4QDibHam^a* (4Q504) 18 4 for MT Isa 6:10 'smear over their eyes' (ועיניו השע) – this, in relation to the quotation of Isa 6:10 at John 12:40, published as early as 1982 by Maurice Baillet but not yet discussed in the literature on Johannine quotations; '4Q504 Paroles des Luminaires (i) (Pl. XLIX-LIII)', in *Qumrân Grotte 4: III (4Q482–4Q520)*, DJD 7 (Oxford: Clarendon Press, 1982), 165.

3. Mediating sources

Another question put to John's quotations concerns intermediary sources, whether any of the texts had somehow been brokered to the evangelist through *testimonia* or peer Christian literature. Since the quotation of Isaiah 40:3 at John 1:23 occurs also in the Synoptics, for instance, has the fourth evangelist cited it indirectly from one of their texts (rather than directly from the Jewish scriptures)? Or since the quotation of Psalm 69:10 at John 2:17 has a parallel in Paul at Romans 15:3, could both have been cited from a collection of apologetic 'proof texts' (rather than each from Psalm 69, itself)?[87]

The prospect of *testimonia* is, in fact, treated under the next guiding assumption: inasmuch as their existence at this early a date is putative, they are deemed less preferable as exegetical explanations than extant sources (and so, in the end, are not entertained). As for cognate Christian writings, two further considerations. First, since proving John's dependence on them requires a broader study in itself, discussion will mark where such a prospect is plausible but will not argue further – for or against. And second, since the fourth evangelist doubtless had access to (or at least knowledge of) large swaths of scripture,[88] a mediating source will not be deemed the beginning and end of his citation process: it may simply have served as a catalyst for him to 'search the scripture' directly and draw afresh from its original context.[89]

4. Hypotheses for Johannine anomalies

Finally, two matters are assumed regarding sources proposed for anomalies in the Fourth Gospel's quotations: (1) that a hypothesis which traces an anomaly to an extant source is to be preferred over one that traces it to a putative one; and, following the lead of Menken, (2) that an anomaly which cannot be traced to any extant source is best ascribed to the style or exegetical methods (and thereby *Tendenz*)[90] of the fourth evangelist (or redactor).[91] Often such anomalies have

---

87. *Testimonia* were brought to the fore of exegetical discussion by J. Rendel Harris in the early twentieth century and have been revived as a possibility more recently by Martin Albl; Harris, *Testimonies*, 2 vols. (Cambridge: Cambridge University Press, 1916–1920); Albl, *And Scripture Cannot be Broken: The Form and Function of the Early Christian Testimonia Collections*, NovTSup 96 (Leiden: E.J. Brill, 1999).

88. At the very least this is made clear by Barrett in his 1947 article on the matter: 'The Old Testament in the Fourth Gospel', 155–69.

89. This seems to have been the case with Luke, who likely cites Isa 40:3 because he found it in Mark and perhaps Matthew but expands it to include Isa 40:4-5; cf. Matt 3:3; Mark 1:2-3; Luke 3:4-6.

90. Menken distinguishes between exegetical techniques, which legitimate a textual change, and the evangelist's motivation, which induces him to make such a change; *Old Testament Quotations in the Fourth Gospel*, 19.

91. Menken's commitment to prefer Johannine redaction over putative sources was first noted (and followed) by Schuchard (*Scripture within Scripture*, xiv–xvi; cf. David Rensberger, review of *Scripture within Scripture: The Interrelationship of Form* and

been explained (as mentioned above) by appeal to alleged texts or to mental processes in the evangelist. The deviations that occur between the quotation at John 6:31 and any of its candidate passages, for instance, have been accredited to unidentified Jewish *haggadoth*[92]; differences in the quotation at John 13:18 from HB Psalm 41:10 have been assigned to a conjectured Aramaic *Vorlage*[93]; the third person 'they will look on him, whom' (εἰς ὅν) for the HB first person 'they will look on me, whom' (אלי את אשר) at John 19:37/Zechariah 12:10 has been attributed to a proto-Theodotionic Greek recension[94]; and divergences in sundry quotations have been put down to the evangelist's creativity or defective memory.[95] Intriguing in this regard is the suggestion of Bent Noack that, since the deviations in the Johannine quotations seem proportional to the complexity of the verses being cited, the evangelist's lapses were due to his inability to recall the more intricate passages he had in mind.[96]

Function in the Explicit Old Testament Citations in the Gospel of John by Bruce G. Schuchard, *JBL* 113 [1994]: 346) then articulated by Menken, himself, in the introduction to his later collection of earlier articles (*Old Testament Quotations in the Fourth Gospel*, 13–14). Such a position, however, was anticipated by both Franke and Humann: Franke argued that alleged Greek translations contemporary with the LXX 'belong ... exclusively to fantasy'; Humann assumed that the form of a quotation in John 'is always appropriate to the context in which it is used in the Gospel and serves to reinforce the meaning intended by the evangelist' – see Franke, *Das alte Testament bei Johannes*, 285; Humann, 'The Function and Form of the Explicit Old Testament Quotations in the Gospel of John', 39.

Menken, himself, though, has not entirely followed this rule, allowing εὐθύνατε (for LXX ἑτοιμάσατε) at John 1:23/Isa 40:3 to have derived from an alleged pre-Aquilan recension of Isaiah and (anticipated by Schnackenburg) tracing the christological 'they will look on him (εἰς ὅν)' for HB 'they will look on me (אלי)' at John 19:37/Zech 12:10 to an unidentified Christian *testimonium*; Menken, '"I Am the Voice of One Crying in the Wilderness ... " (John 1:23)', 22–25; Menken, '"They Shall Look on Him Whom They Have Pierced" (John 19:37)', in *Old Testament Quotations in the Fourth Gospel*, 171–78, 185; first publ. in *CBQ* 55 (1993); cf. Rudolf Schnackenburg, 'Das Schriftzitat in Joh 19,37', in *Ergänzende Auslegungen und Exkurse*, vol. 4 of *Das Johannesevangelium*, HThKNT 4/4 (Freiburg: Herder, 1984), 167–68; first publ. in *Wort, Lied und Gottesspruch: Beiträge zu Psalmen und Propheten. Festschrift für Joseph Ziegler*, ed. Josef Schreiner, FB 2 (Würzburg: Echter Verlag, 1972).

92. The candidate passages for this quotation, circumscribed by Richter, are Exod 16:4; 16:15; Ps 78:24; Neh 9:15/2 Esd 19:15; 'Die alttestamentlichen Zitate in der Rede vom Himmelsbrot Joh 6,26-51a', 202. For theories tracing deviations to Jewish *haggadoth*, pp. 211–29.

93. Noack, *Zur johanneischen Tradition*, 78n191.

94. Brown, *Gospel according to John*, 2.938.

95. So, for instance, Noack and Goodwin; see note 24.

96. *Zur johanneischen Tradition*, passim 72–85. Noack distinguished between citations that display a close proximity to the LXX (John 2:17/Ps 69:10; John 10:34/Ps 82:6; John 12:38/Isa 53:1; John 19:24/Ps 22:19) and those which are so free as to suggest 'that for the citations John had no written text before him' (p. 82).

Any or all of these inferences may be correct, but in the interests of due caution they (and theories like them) will be weighed less favourably than hypotheses based on existing data. More specifically, proposals that turn on putative sources will be deemed less preferable than proposals grounded on extant ones; and elements that cannot be traced to any extant source (biblical or peritestamental[97]) will be attributed to the editorial activity of the Fourth Gospel's author(s).

---

97. The term 'peritestamental', coined by Émile Puech, will be used for all non-canonical and non-rabbinic Jewish and Christian texts of the Second Temple and early rabbinic periods. Further on this term, see Kubiś, *Book of Zechariah in the Gospel of John*, 24n42.

Part I

ISAIAH, JESUS AND THE JEWS

Chapter 1

ISAIAH 40:3, A CALL TO BELIEVE

A. Quotations of Isaiah and Jesus's public ministry

Three quotations in John are the only ones explicitly ascribed to Isaiah. The first is the citation of Isaiah 40:3 at John 1:23, where, responding to queries about his identity, John replies, 'I am "a voice of one calling in the wilderness, 'Make straight the way of the Lord'", *as Isaiah the prophet said*.'[98] The second and third are the quotations of Isaiah 53:1 at John 12:38 and Isaiah 6:10 at John 12:40, both cited by the evangelist to interpret the Jews' unbelief at the end of Jesus's public ministry:

> But though he had done so many signs before them,
> they were not believing in him,
> *that the word of Isaiah the prophet might be fulfilled*, which he said,
> 'Lord, who has believed our report?
> And to whom has the arm of the Lord been revealed'?
>
> For this reason they were not able to believe,
> *for again Isaiah said*,
> 'He has blinded their eyes
> and hardened their heart,
> lest they see with the eyes
> and discern with the heart,
> and turn, and I heal them.'[99]

---

98. Following a comment by George D. Kilpatrick, Reim suggests that besides introducing John's words, the ἔφη ('he said') which immediately precedes them also serves as a second introductory formula to Isa 40:3; *Jochanan*, 4, 4n18. Such a reading, however, creates a redundancy with the formula that ends John's words ('He [Isaiah?] said … as Isaiah the prophet said') and, as such, is better abandoned for the plain sense of the text: 'he said' is the evangelist introducing the words of John; 'as the prophet Isaiah said' is John introducing the words of Isaiah.

99. Isaiah is also cited between these quotations, Isa 54:13 at John 6:44-45. This inquiry, however, turns on the *inclusio* formed by the explicit ascriptions to Isaiah at John 1:23 and John 12:37-41; and since no such formula appears at John 6:45, that reference will be considered in discussion but not given the detailed textual attention furnished for the other three.

The evangelist closes these last two quotations by tying them to Isaiah's vision of divine glory in Isaiah 6, the same chapter from which the second of the citations was drawn: 'These things Isaiah said, because (or when) he saw his glory and spoke about him.'[100]

These quotations form an *inclusio* to chapters 1–12 which unfolds as a commentary on the Jews' responsibility and response to Jesus's public ministry; and in this chapter and the next (Part I) they will be engaged with a view towards offering alternate hypotheses to the exegetical problems they raise and teasing out the theological import of this literary structure which they create: John 1:23/Isaiah 40:3 in the present chapter; John 12:38/Isaiah 53:1 and John 12:40/Isaiah 6:10 in Chapter 2. The endeavour will conclude that, as an *inclusio*, these quotations bring closure to the Book of Signs by unfolding as (1) a call to believe in Jesus, (2) a lament that no one had and (3) a disclosure that the insight needed to do so had been cosmically obstructed.

B. *The Johannine rendering of Isaiah 40:3 (John 1:23)*

The quotation of Isaiah 40:3 at John 1:23 is placed in the mouth of John the Baptist and functions as the obliging part of his answer to a query about his identity. The passage in which it occurs is labelled 'the testimony of John',[101] and it turns on questions put to him by priests and Levites sent from Jerusalem by the Jews – particularly, the Pharisees. When they first ask him 'Who are you'?, John replies thrice in the negative. He denies he is the Christ and successively answers 'no' to further suggestions that he is Elijah or 'the prophet'. When they ask him again who he is, if not these three, he holds forth by 'making' Isaiah 40:3ab 'his own' (*zu eigen macht*)[102]:

---

100. John 12:41. This provenance for John 12:41 is deduced, in part, because it is the context from which the second quotation is drawn, but also because its reference to Isaiah seeing 'his glory' is matched in targumic and Septuagintal paraphrases of Isaiah 6: *Tg. Isa.* 6:1 reads 'the glory of the Lord' (ית יקרא דייי); *Tg. Isa.* 6:5, 'the royal (shekinah) glory of the king of ages' (ית יקר שכינת מלך עלמיא); and LXX Isa 6:1, 'the house was full of his glory (πλήρης ... τῆς δόξης αὐτοῦ)'. The text for *Targum of the Prophets* is Alexander Sperber, ed., *The Latter Prophets according to Targum Jonathan*, vol. 3 of *The Bible in Aramaic Based on Old Manuscripts and Printed Texts* (Leiden: E.J. Brill, 1962).

On the reading 'because' or 'when' at John 12:41, the first (ὅτι) is attested in P[66] P[75] ℵ A B L Θ Ψ 1 33 579 Sinai lectionary 844; the second (ὅτε), in D K Γ Δ family[13] 565 700 892 1241 1424 and the majority of manuscripts; and a third (ἐπεί), either 'since' or 'when', is attested in W. The UBSGNT committee has preferred the first as the *lectio difficilior*; cf. Bruce M. Metzger, *A Textual Commentary on the Greek New Testament*, 2nd ed. (Stuttgart: Deutsche Bibelgesellschaft/United Bible Societies, 1994), 203.

101. John 1:19-23.

102. Obermann, *Die christologische Erfüllung der Schrift im Johannesevangelium*, 107. In his redaction critical look at this passage Ernst Haenchen has suggested that while the priests' first question (σὺ τίς εἶ) is pointedly pitched to check John's claims about messianic

He (John) said,
'I am "a voice of one calling in the wilderness,
'Make straight the way of the Lord'",
as Isaiah the prophet said.'[103]

1. The text

The HB, LXX and Johannine renderings of this verse are shown in Table 5.[104]

Table 5 Isaiah 40:3 in the HB, LXX and John

HB Isaiah 40:3[105]	LXX Isaiah 40:3	John 1:23
קול קורא במדבר פנו דרך יהוה ישרו בערבה מסלה לאלהינו	φωνὴ βοῶντος ἐν τῇ ἐρήμῳ ἑτοιμάσατε τὴν ὁδὸν κυρίου, εὐθείας ποιεῖτε τὰς τρίβους τοῦ θεοῦ ἡμῶν·	ἐγὼ φωνὴ βοῶντος ἐν τῇ ἐρήμῳ· εὐθύνατε τὴν ὁδὸν κυρίου,
A voice is/of one calling 'In the wilderness prepare the way of the Lord; make straight in the desert a highway for our God.'	A voice of one calling in the wilderness, 'Prepare the way of the Lord; make straight the paths of our God.'	I am 'a voice of one calling in the wilderness, "Make straight the way of the Lord"'…

figures (Elijah, the prophet and the Christ), the second (τίς εἶ) allows his own self-definition and sets up the quotation; *John 1–2*, ed. and trans. Robert W. Funk, 2 vols., Hermeneia (Philadelphia: Fortress, 1984), 1:145.

103. John 1:23.

104. For attestations of biblical passages in texts from the Judaean desert (in this table and other similar tables below), four protocols will be followed. (1) All *loci* from biblical (as opposed to apocryphal or sectarian) texts will be 'ad loc.' in the documents cited. (2) Passages found in non-biblical texts will only be included if they appear to be quotations (and, thus, represent textual traditions external to the documents in which they are cited); that is, since the purpose here is to log possible text types circulating in the first century, allusions (such as 1QS ix 19-21 on Isa 40:3) will not be listed (even though they may later be discussed for the interpretations they yield). (3) Such passages (whether from biblical or non-biblical manuscripts) will be listed, even if only part of the verse(s) in question is extant or cited in the Judaean desert manuscripts. And (4) peculiar features in these texts will only be noted if they suggest a meaning other than the one implied in corresponding MT renderings; that is, peculiarities are not listed if their variance from the MT is only orthographic or morphological (including methods of representing the tetragrammaton).

105. Besides the MT, Isa 40:3 is attested in 1QIsa[a]; 4QIsa[b]; 1QS viii 14 (= 4QS[e] iii 4-5 [frgs 2a ii, 3a-c]); 4QTanh 1-2 i 6-7. On Isa 40:3b, following an allusion to this colon in line 4, 4QS[e] is reconstructed by Philip Alexander and Geza Vermes to read the tetragrammaton as האמת, 'pr[epare the way of the Truth …' (פ]נו דרך האמת); '4Q259. 4QSerekh ha-Yaḥad[e]', in *Qumran Cave 4. XIX: Serekh Ha-Yaḥad and Two Related Texts*, DJD 26 (Oxford: Clarendon Press, 1998), ad loc. and pp. 146–47. And regarding Isa 40:3c, (a) 1QIsa[a] adds a ו before ישרו:

2. The version cited

The version cited is almost certainly the LXX. The LXX, itself, diverges from the HB in one, possibly two, respects; and, save for the verb εὐθύνατε, John's rendering follows suit: like the LXX, it reads 'Lord' (κύριος) for the tetragrammaton; and, if the ambiguous קוֹל קוֹרֵא was intended as a predication ('a voice calls'), the Fourth Gospel, like the LXX, takes those words instead as a genitive construct – φωνὴ βοῶντος, 'a voice of one calling'. A Hebrew *Vorlage* could (and to some extent has) be(en) argued on two grounds: that since Aquila independently translated קוֹל קוֹרֵא as a genitive construct (albeit with different vocabulary – φωνὴ καλοῦντος), so might the evangelist have done; and that since εὐθύνατε can plausibly be explained as a translation of ישרו in HB Isaiah 40:3c,[106] the rest of the lines quoted could similarly be explained as a translation of HB Isaiah 40:3ab.[107] Following the guiding assumption used here, however, neither of these prospects (nor their combination) marshal a case compelling enough to offset the verbal agreement that occurs between John 1:23 and the LXX, and this leaves it more probable that the evangelist has re-presented the Greek rather than translated the Hebrew.

The case for a LXX source has been pressed further by Schuchard and Menken, but on premises that are open to question. Schuchard argues on the grounds of syntax and original context: (a) like LXX Isaiah 40:3 (over against the HB), he contends, the evangelist adjoins the phrase 'in the wilderness' to the phrase 'a voice

---

'*and* make straight (וישרו) in the desert …' – see Eugene Ulrich and Peter W. Flint, eds., *Qumran Cave 1. II: The Isaiah Scrolls*, 2 vols., DJD 32 (Oxford: Clarendon Press, 2010), ad loc.; and (b) in 4QTanh the singular imperative ישר published by John Allegro in the *editio princeps* was corrected to the (MT) plural ישרו by John Strugnell in his notes on that volume – John M. Allegro, ed., '176. Tanḥûmîm', in *Qumrân Cave 4. I (4Q158-4Q186)*, DJD 5 (Oxford: Clarendon Press, 1968), ad loc.; John Strugnell, 'Notes en marge du volume V des « Discoveries in the Judaean Desert of Jordan »', *RevQ* 7 (1970): 230.

106. So, C.F. Burney, *The Aramaic Origin of the Fourth Gospel* (Oxford: Clarendon Press, 1922), 114–15.

107. Freed has outlined (though not necessarily endorsed) this case by noting that εὐθύνειν as well as cognates κατευθύνειν, εὐθύς and εὐθής serve as glosses for לישר (and its cognates) in the LXX; *Old Testament Quotations in the Gospel of John*, 4–5. For the issue at hand, לישר in the piel is translated thrice with κατευθύνειν (Prov 9:15; 15:21; 2 Chr 32:30) and once with εὐθύς (Isa 45:13); and in the hiphil (carrying a similar causative force) it is also translated once with κατευθύνειν (Ps 5:9). Less convincing for a Hebrew *Vorlage* is the case by Freed that HB Isa 40:3 was likewise deemed a fulfilled prophecy by the Qumran sectarians, citing 1QS viii 14; ix 19-20 (*Old Testament Quotations in the Gospel of John*, 2–3). In the LXX εὐθύνειν never translates לפנות. And, though the Qumran interpretation of this verse is critical for understanding the Johannine rendering (as is argued below), a similar reading between the two (Isa 40:3 as fulfilled prophecy) does not require a similar version (the HB) to have been used by both.

of one calling' (syntax)[108]; and, (b) echoing LXX Isaiah 40:2 (over against its HB counterpart), the evangelist depicts priests hearing (and presumably reporting) John's salvific declaration of Isaiah 40:3 to Jerusalem (context)[109] – that is to say, Schuchard argues that if the pericope surrounding the quotation echoes LXX Isaiah 40, the quotation, itself, is likely drawn from that same version.[110] Both of these premises, however, have been rightly questioned by Menken, who observes (a) that since John does not cite Isaiah 40:3c – which could better indicate the syntax of 'in the wilderness' – the role of that phrase at John 1:23 is uncertain[111]; and (b) that had the evangelist wished to portray the priests in John 1 on the basis of LXX Isaiah 40:2, he would not have included Levites along with them: 'And this is the testimony of John, when the Jews from Jerusalem sent priests *and Levites* to ask him, "Who are you"'?[112]

Menken's own case for a LXX (or, as he entertains, pre-Aquilan[113]) source turns on vocabulary – specifically (as noted above), the verb βοᾶν in John's rendering

108. At Isa 40:3c the LXX omits the phrase 'in the desert' (בערבה), which in the HB stands parallel to the phrase 'in the wilderness' (במדבר) at Isa 40:3b. This, in turn, frees the phrase 'in the wilderness' to modify the phrase 'a voice of one calling' (which comes before it) rather than the verb 'prepare' (which comes after it). The fourth evangelist does not cite Isa 40:3c, but Schuchard maintains that this same syntax was his 'almost certain intention' nonetheless; *Scripture within Scripture*, 3–4 (quotation p. 4); followed by Obermann, *Die christologische Erfüllung der Schrift im Johannesevangelium*, 93–94.

109. John 1:19, 24; *Scripture within Scripture*, 4–5. In the LXX (but not in the HB) the divine commission to issue a salvific message to Jerusalem in Isa 40:2 is specifically given to priests – 'Priests (ἱερεῖς), speak to the heart of Jerusalem …'.

110. Schuchard's thoughts on this second of the two premises are ascribed to lectures given at Union Theological Seminary, Richmond, by Matthias Rissi in 1987; see *Scripture within Scripture*, 4n18.

111. See note 108

112. John 1:19; Menken, "'I Am the Voice of One Crying in the Wilderness … ' (John 1:23)", 23n6.

113. It has been suggested by Menken, speculating on work done by Dominique Barthélemy, (a) that εὐθύ<νατε> for ישרו at Isa 40:3c in Aquila (manuscript 86) was drawn from a putative recension of the LXX which had been corrected towards the MT and (b) that this same *Vorlage* was shared by the fourth evangelist; "'I Am the Voice of One Crying in the Wilderness … ' (John 1:23)", 24–25; cf. Barthélemy, *Les devanciers d'Aquila: première publication intégrale du texte des fragments du Dodécaprophéton trouvés dans le désert de Juda, précédée d'une étude sur les traductions et recensions grecques de la Bible réalisées au premier siècle de notre ère sous l'influence du rabbinat palestinien*, VTSup 10 (Leiden: E.J. Brill, 1963). This scenario has rightly been questioned, however, given the differences between the two renderings in the rest of the quotation – particularly, Aquila's φωνὴ καλοῦντος for the Fourth Gospel's φωνὴ βοῶντος; Freed, *Old Testament Quotations in the Gospel of John*, 6; followed by Schuchard, *Scripture within Scripture*, 6, 6n26. It has also been dismissed by Obermann on the grounds that the Fourth Gospel's quotation does not include Isa 40:3c (and, therefore, ישרו); *Die christologische Erfüllung der Schrift im Johannesevangelium*, 95n18. But this begs the question, since the issue concerns whether εὐθύνατε represents a blending of that line with Isa 40:3b, which is cited.

of the verse. Since that verb is a *hapax legomenon* to Johannine literature, he contends, and since John elsewhere expresses 'calling' with the verbs κράζειν[114] or κραυγάζειν,[115] βοᾶν is more likely to have been imported from the LXX than to have been used as a gloss for לקרא.[116] As argued above, however, Menken's approach to this matter labours under several difficulties[117]: specifically for this quotation, (1) he fails to note that the verb in the quotation which he does ascribe to the evangelist (εὐθύνειν) is also a *hapax legomenon* to Johannine literature; (2) he elsewhere declines to read *hapax legomena* as indicators of a LXX source[118]; (3) his inferences about the evangelist's preference for κράζειν or κραυγάζειν overreach the (relatively meagre) data available on Johannine parlance[119]; and (4) he does not consider that, like other terms he lists as more probable translation choices for the evangelist, βοᾶν, itself, was generously used as a LXX gloss for לקרא (and, so, could furnish an apt option for the evangelist's own rendering of the Hebrew).

A LXX source for the quotation may perhaps increase the likelihood that the verse was brokered by the Synoptic gospels, which likewise cite the passage.[120] Partly supporting Synoptic agency is that like the Fourth Gospel, they too ascribe the verse explicitly to Isaiah: in Mark, 'As it is written in Isaiah the prophet'; in Matthew, 'For this is that which was spoken through Isaiah the prophet, saying ...'; and in Luke, 'As it is written in the book of the words of Isaiah the prophet'.[121] Added to this, however, is that, even more evidently than John, the Synoptics draw the verse from the LXX. Like John 1:23, they follow LXX Isaiah 40:3ab in its one or two departures from the HB: the use of 'Lord' for 'Yahweh' and the phrase 'a voice of one calling' for the (possible) Hebrew original, 'a voice is calling'. But further (and unlike John 1:23), they include LXX Isaiah 40:3c, which differs dramatically from

---

114. John 1:15; 7:28, 37; 12:44.

115. John 11:43; 12:13; 18:40; 19:6, 12, 15.

116. Menken, "'I Am the Voice of One Crying in the Wilderness ... ' (John 1:23)', 23; followed by Schuchard, *Scripture within Scripture*, 3; and Obermann, *Die christologische Erfüllung der Schrift im Johannesevangelium*, 93.

117. See the section *a. Confirming the Septuagint* in the Introduction.

118. Specifically noted in the Introduction are διδακτός at John 6:45/Isa 54:13 and δωρεάν at John 15:25/Pss 35:19 (?); 69:5 (?); *Pss. Sol.* 7:1 (?).

119. This point was made in the Introduction by referencing Menken's discussion of οἰκία and οἶκος (both 'house') relative to John 2:17/Ps 69:10, as well as his examination of μισεῖν ('to hate') and δωρεάν ('without cause') relative to John 15:25/Pss 35:19 (?); 69:5 (?); *Pss. Sol.* 7:1 (?). The same can apply, however, to κράζειν and κραυγάζειν relative to John 1:23/Isa 40:3 – the first appears just four times in John; the second, six (see Table 2).

120. In Mark the quotation is part of a compound citation that includes Exod 23:20, as well as Mal 3:1; and, akin to Luke (which cites Isa 40:3-5), uncial W extends the quotation in Mark to Isa 40:8. Moreover, a likely allusion to Isa 40:3b appears in Zechariah's prophecy on John the Baptist at Luke 1:76: see Table 9.

121. Mark 1:2-3; Matt 3:3; Luke 3:4-6.

the Hebrew[122]: here they diverge from the LXX by reducing the phrase 'paths of our God' (τὰς τρίβους τοῦ θεοῦ ἡμῶν) to 'his paths' (τὰς τρίβους αὐτοῦ)[123]; but, like the LXX (and over against the HB), they omit the phrase 'in the desert' (בערבה) and gloss the singular 'highway' (מסלה) with the plural 'paths' (τὰς τρίβους) (Table 6).

Table 6 Isaiah 40:3 in the HB, LXX and the Synoptic gospels

HB Isaiah 40:3	LXX Isaiah 40:3	Synoptic gospels
קול קורא במדבר פנו דרך יהוה ישרו בערבה מסלה לאלהינו	φωνὴ βοῶντος ἐν τῇ ἐρήμῳ ἑτοιμάσατε τὴν ὁδὸν κυρίου, εὐθείας ποιεῖτε τὰς τρίβους τοῦ θεοῦ ἡμῶν·	φωνὴ βοῶντος ἐν τῇ ἐρήμῳ ἑτοιμάσατε τὴν ὁδὸν κυρίου, εὐθείας ποιεῖτε τὰς τρίβους αὐτοῦ·
A voice is/of one calling, 'In the wilderness prepare the way of the Lord; make straight in the desert a highway for our God.'	A voice of one calling in the wilderness, 'Prepare the way of the Lord; make straight the paths of our God.'	A voice of one calling in the wilderness, 'Prepare the way of the Lord; make straight his paths.'

That the Synoptics deviate somewhat from LXX Isaiah 40:3c may indicate that they played no role in the Fourth Gospel's use of that verse.[124] That both they and John 1:23 by and large follow the LXX, however – and that all four explicitly ascribe the verse to Isaiah – supports the prospect that they may, in fact, have mediated the passage to the fourth evangelist.

3. The anomalies

a. Two deviations from the LXX

On the premise, then, that the quotation was drawn from the LXX, it carries two anomalies: one, syntactical; one, lexical. The syntactical is created by the personal pronoun ἐγώ. To put the verse in the mouth of John, the evangelist inserts it before the phrase φωνὴ βοῶντος; and this, in turn, changes the role of that construct from nominative absolute (as it functions in the biblical, at least LXX, version[s]) to the predicate of a nominal sentence: 'I (*am*) a voice of one calling …'[125] The lexical anomaly, for its part, is the use of εὐθύνειν for ἑτοιμάζειν, that is, reading 'make straight' (εὐθύνατε) rather than 'prepare (ἑτοιμάσατε) the way of the Lord'. The

---

122. See note 108.

123. An exception among NT texts is Codex Bezae, which reads 'paths of your God' (τὰς τρίβους τοῦ θεοῦ ὑμῶν) at Mark 1:3 and 'your paths' (τὰς τρίβους ὑμῶν) at Luke 3:4. 'His paths' (τὰς τρίβους αὐτοῦ) is also attested in LXX 309 534 566, but this is likely a scribal attempt to align the LXX with the Synoptic reading; cf. *Septuaginta* (J. Ziegler), ad loc. (apparatus).

124. For Franke, as an example, this discrepancy was grounds to reject Synoptic mediation in favour of *testimonia*; *Das alte Testament bei Johannes*, 259.

125. The insertion likely also accounts for the introductory formula following (rather than preceding) the quotation; see Reim, *Jochanan*, 4.

exhortation, itself, is a metaphor drawn from the practice of engineers levelling a route to be travelled by a dignitary[126]; and this variance (like anomalies in other quotations) has raised two interwoven but discrete questions for exegetes. What does the verb reflect textually? And what does it signify theologically? The first of these is at issue here; and, assuming εὐθύνατε is not a translation of the Hebrew,[127] it has been ascribed to a merger of Isaiah 40:3ab with one or more of an array of proposed passages.[128] One is close at hand: Isaiah 40:3c, 'make straight (יִשְּׁרוּ/ εὐθείας ποιεῖτε) the paths of our God', where εὐθύνατε is deemed either a gloss for לְיַשֵּׁר in the HB or a conflation of εὐθείας ποιεῖτε in the LXX[129] – the latter possibly evoked by its similar phonation.[130] The other proposed passages are some thirteen

---

126. See Craig S. Keener, *The Gospel of John: A Commentary*, 2 vols. (Peabody, MA: Hendrickson, 2003), 1:437–38, 438n78.

127. If the quotation (or this part of it) was translated by the evangelist from the HB, εὐθύνατε may not, in fact, reflect an anomaly but simply represent the evangelist's choice to translate לִפְנוֹת. So, for instance, Reim, who allows the possibility that the evangelist quoted most of the verse from the LXX but rendered פְּנוּ directly from the Hebrew with this verb; *Jochanan*, 5 – here, following a similar case for the Synoptic quotations of the verse by Krister Stendahl, *The School of St. Matthew and Its Use of the Old Testament*, 50–52. Inasmuch as the rest of the verse was doubtless drawn from the LXX, however – and that εὐθύνατε is never employed to translate לִפְנוֹת in the LXX – εὐθύνατε most likely signals a second way in which John's rendering differs from its *Vorlage*.

128. Conflation is commonly assumed in work on the Fourth Gospel's quotations; that is, anomalies are often ascribed to a citation protocol that blends two or more biblical passages on the basis of shared features between them. As Schuchard has pointed out, Menken associates this method with rabbinic *middoth* – particularly, *gezerah shavah*. Just as the rabbis juxtaposed texts in their *midrashim* based on similarities between them, so has John done: but, where the rabbis did so in the commentaries which followed their *lemmata*, the fourth evangelist is presumed to have done so in the *lemmata* themselves. See Schuchard, *Scripture within Scripture*, xiv-xv, xvn21; Menken, *Old Testament Quotations in the Fourth Gospel*, 13–14.

129. Noted (though not endorsed) by Freed, who traces it as early as Origen's suggestion that the evangelist sought to 'abridge' (ἐπιτέμνειν) the two cola (*Comm. Jo.* 6:24; text: Erwin Preuschen, *Der Johanneskommentar*, vol. 4 of *Origenes Werke*, GCS 2 [Leipzig: J.C. Hinrichs'sche Buchhandlung, 1903]); cf. *Old Testament Quotations in the Gospel of John*, 6, 6n2. In support of this solution Menken attributes the merger to a pre-70 CE use of the 22nd *middah* associated with R. Eliezer b. Jose ha-Gelili: דבר שחברו מוכיח עליו (perhaps, 'a word whose counterpart determines [its import]'); "'I Am the Voice of One Crying in the Wilderness … '" (John 1:23)', 25; cf. Hermann L. Strack and Günter Stemberger, *Introduction to the Talmud and Midrash*, trans. and ed. Markus Bockmuehl, 2nd ed. (Minneapolis, MN: Fortress Press, 1991), 31; trans. of *Einleitung in Talmud und Midrasch*, 7th ed. (München: C.H. Beck'sche Verlagsbuchhandlung [Oscar Beck], 1982).

130. So, Barrett (*Gospel according to St. John*, 173), but tempered by Obermann's observation that any phonetic resemblance would have had to work in tandem with a linguistic-semantic connection; *Die christologische Erfüllung der Schrift im Johannesevangelium*, 95n20.

LXX sapiential texts which employ εὐθύνειν or a cognate, sometimes with ὁδός (which likewise appears in LXX Isaiah 40:3 and John 1:23) (Table 7).[131]

b. Hypotheses on the deviations

As for the second question raised for exegetes – What do these anomalies signify? – hypotheses have been disproportionate between the two, the first (ἐγώ) being largely overlooked while the second (εὐθύνατε) has enjoyed several involved proposals. Regarding the first, ἐγώ, its insertion, of course, 'transforms the quotation into the content of the Baptist's self-testimony'[132] and identifies John with the herald of Deutero-Isaiah who 'proclaims God's message of imminent salvation and the universal disclosure of his glory'.[133] More to the point of the evangelist's motive, however, it has been observed that the resulting nominal sentence conforms to the evangelist's style[134]; that the consequent equation of John with Isaiah's herald serves the evangelist's christological wish to show 'that the Baptist himself realizes the superiority of Jesus'[135]; and that, given the use of 'I am' formulae in sapiential discourse, it serves 'as part of a larger scheme which purposes to portray the Baptist as the consummate disciple of Wisdom (= Jesus)'.[136]

131. Barrett, *Gospel according to St. John*, 173; followed by Freed, *Old Testament Quotations in the Gospel of John*, 4–5; Humann, 'The Function and Form of the Explicit Old Testament Quotations in the Gospel of John', 45n49; and, particularly, Schuchard, *Scripture within Scripture*, 11–12. Menken traces εὐθύνατε to Isa 40:3c, but allows for Sir 2:6; 37:15; and 49:9 as a 'secondary inducement for the change'; '"I Am the Voice of One Crying in the Wilderness ... " (John 1:23)', 25n12. The vocabulary shared between these LXX texts and John 1:23 has also been used to argue the other way round, namely, that since the passage(s) merged with Isa 40:3 would have come from a Greek (rather than Hebrew) text, it would be more likely that the primary passage cited (Isa 40:3) did the same; so Schuchard, *Scripture within Scripture*, 11, 11n42, 14–15.

132. Williams, '"He Saw His Glory and Spoke of Him": The Testimony of Isaiah and Johannine Christology', 58.

133. Williams, 'Isaiah in John's Gospel', 102.

134. Following the discussions on unemphatic personal pronouns in Moulton and Colwell, Freed here cites the ἐγώ εἰμί passages, as well as John 1:27; 4:14; 11:27; *Old Testament Quotations in the Gospel of John*, 3, 3nn4–5; cf. James H. Moulton, *Prolegomena*, vol. 1 of *A Grammar of New Testament Greek*, 3rd ed. (Edinburgh: T&T Clark, 1908), 85–86; Ernest Colwell, *The Greek of the Fourth Gospel: A Study of Its Aramaisms in the Light of Hellenistic Greek* (Chicago: Chicago University Press, 1931), 51–55.

135. Freed, *Old Testament Quotations in the Gospel of John*, 3–4, 4n2 (quotation p. 4). Obermann has argued that since Isa 40:3 was not the subject of any known biblical or Jewish expectation, its identification with John here by the inserted ἐγώ should not be taken as fulfilled prophecy; *Die christologische Erfüllung der Schrift im Johannesevangelium*, 107n99. Given the pivotal role played by Isa 40:3 in Qumran literature (see note 105), however, could it not have been attached to the figure of John in polemic against this sectarian *raison d'être* – if not by the fourth evangelist, then at least by the Synoptic evangelists?.

136. Schuchard, *Scripture within Scripture*, 12n45.

Table 7 LXX sapiential texts and John 1:23

John 1:23
He said, 'I am "a voice of one calling in the wilderness, 'make straight the way (εὐθύνατε τὴν ὁδόν) of the Lord'", as Isaiah the prophet said.'

LXX Isaiah 40:3
A voice of one calling in the wilderness, 'Prepare the way (τὴν ὁδόν) of the Lord; make straight the paths of our God.'

LXX Proverbs 4:25-26	LXX Proverbs 9:14-15
Let your eyes look to what is level, and your eyelids nod to what is just. Make level tracks for your feet, and make straight your ways (τὰς ὁδούς σου κατεύθυνε).	She sat at the doors of her house, upon a stool, openly in the streets, calling to those passing by and to those making straight in their ways (κατευθύνοντας ἐν ταῖς ὁδοῖς αὐτῶν).

LXX Proverbs 13:13a	LXX Proverbs 15:21
For a deceitful son nothing will be good, but for a wise slave there will be unhindered business, and his way shall be made straight (κατευθυνθήσεται ἡ ὁδὸς αὐτοῦ).	The paths of the undiscerning lack wits, but the thoughtful man proceeds by making straight (κατευθύνων).

LXX Proverbs 20:24	LXX Proverbs 29:27
Steps are made straight (εὐθύνεται) for a man by the Lord. How, then, might a mortal discern his ways (τὰς ὁδοὺς αὐτοῦ)?	An abomination to the righteous is an unjust man, but an abomination to the lawless is a way that makes straight (κατευθύνουσα ὁδός).

LXX Sirach 2:2	LXX Sirach 2:6
Make straight (εὔθυνον) your heart and persevere, and do not act hastily in a time of trial.	Believe him and he will assist you; Make straight your ways (εὔθυνον τὰς ὁδούς σου) and hope in him.

LXX Sirach 6:17	LXX Sirach 37:15
He who fears the Lord will make straight (εὐθυνεῖ) his friendship, because, as he is, so also is his neighbour.	And above all these things beg the Most High, that he may make straight your way (ἵνα εὐθύνῃ ... τὴν ὁδόν σου) in truth.

LXX Sirach 38:10	LXX Sirach 39:24
Put away error and make straight (εὔθυνον) (your) hands, and from all sin purify the heart.	His ways (αἱ ὁδοὶ αὐτοῦ) are straight (εὐθεῖαι) for the scrupulous, (and) thus stumbling blocks for the lawless.

LXX Sirach 49:8-9
It was Ezekiel, who saw a view of glory, which he showed him on the chariot of the cherubim. For, indeed, he (God) recalled enemies in the storm, to do good to those who make straight (their) ways (τοὺς εὐθύνοντας ὁδούς).

As for the second anomaly, εὐθύνατε, it has given rise to two kinds of proposals. One assigns it to factors outside the evangelist's own design: that his memory lapsed[137] or that his concern was limited to the first part of the quotation, 'a voice of one calling in the wilderness', with little thought given to the line in question.[138] The other, by contrast, assumes the verb reflects the evangelist's intention and, more specifically, ties it to his conception of the Baptist's mission. Among exegetes focused on the quotations it is argued along three different lines by four figures: Freed, Menken (followed by Catrin Williams) and Schuchard.

For Freed (initially), εὐθύνειν was used to blend the quotation into John's profile as an 'ethical and moral' (rather than apocalyptic and eschatological) precursor to Jesus. In both the Fourth Gospel and the Synoptic gospels, Freed maintains, John is cast as a 'precursor' to Jesus. But, where in the Synoptics he plays that role as an apocalyptic and eschatological figure, in the Fourth Gospel he does so as an 'ethical and moral' one; that is, in the Fourth Gospel John does not warn of a baptism 'with fire' (as in Matthew and Luke),[139] but instead witnesses to the light.[140] The verb ἑτοιμάζειν, contends Freed, 'was too ineffective' to depict such a profile, so the evangelist replaced it with εὐθύνειν, drawn from one or more of the wisdom texts listed in Table 7.[141]

For Menken, followed by Williams, the change was made to harmonize the quotation with John's profile as a contemporaneous witness (rather than penultimate precursor) to Jesus. Menken reads εὐθύνατε as a merger of LXX Isaiah 40:3ab with a conflation of εὐθείας ποιεῖτε at LXX (or pre-Aquilan) Isaiah 40:3c[142]; and he contends that the exhortation 'make straight the way of the Lord' articulates not John's message to the people (something John says to the populace) but his commission from God (something John does for Jesus). That is to say, unlike the case in the Synoptic gospels, where the admonition 'prepare the way of the Lord' can reflect either John's role relative to Jesus, his message relative to

---

137. Burney, *Aramaic Origin of the Fourth Gospel*, 114; J.H. Bernard, *Critical and Exegetical Commentary on the Gospel according to St. John*, 2 vols., ICC (Edinburgh: T&T Clark, 1928), 1: 38.

138. Schnackenburg, *Gospel according to St John*, 1:291–92; Reim, *Jochanan*, 5.

139. Matt 3:11-12; Luke 3:15-16.

140. Cf. John 1:6-9; 3:19-21; 8:12; 12:35-36, 46; cf. 11:9-10.

141. *Old Testament Quotations in the Gospel of John*, 2–3, 6–7 (quotations pp. 6–7). Freed supports an ethical connotation for εὐθύνειν by noting such meaning in its cognate εὐθύς at Acts 13:10 (Paul to the magician Bar-Jesus): 'will you not stop perverting the straight ways (τὰς ὁδοὺς ... τὰς εὐθείας) of the Lord'? (p. 6n4). Later, however, he adopted the proposal offered by Menken; Edwin D. Freed, 'Jn 1,19-27 in Light of Related Passages in John, the Synoptics, and Acts', in *The Four Gospels 1992. Festschrift Frans Neirynck*, ed. F. van Segbroek, 3 vols., BETL 100 (Leuven: Leuven University-Peeters, 1992), 3:1959; see Menken, '"I Am the Voice of One Crying in the Wilderness ... " (John 1:23)', 33n32.

142. '"I Am the Voice of One Crying in the Wilderness ... " (John 1:23)', 23–25.

the people or both,[143] in the Fourth Gospel, for Menken, it can only be the former. Menken concedes that by virtue of his exhortations for baptism and reform John is somewhat depicted in the Fourth Gospel as urging people to 'make straight' the way for Jesus.[144] But this call is stated indirectly, Menken argues[145]; and throughout John's public ministry in the Fourth Gospel he issues no explicit admonition to the people but 'solely speaks about Jesus'.[146] As such, Menken concludes, despite the 'slight anomaly' that this commission to an individual is issued with an imperative in the plural (εὐθύνατε), the clause 'make straight the way of the Lord' at John 1:23 articulates what John is to do vis-à-vis Jesus, not what he is to say vis-à-vis the Jews.[147]

It is this commission, continues Menken, that requires the verb ἑτοιμάζειν to be removed in the quotation, because the task to which John is being called has him acting not as Elijah coming prior to Jesus but as a 'witness' running concurrent with him. Unlike the Synoptic gospels, where John is Elijah[148] and completes that role by the time Jesus appears,[149] the Fourth Gospel has John as a 'witness',[150] who denies being Elijah[151] and who, while emerging publicly prior to Jesus,[152] fulfils his role during (not before) the beginning of Jesus's ministry; that is, in the Fourth Gospel John continues to baptize and testify after Jesus is baptized.[153] The semantics

---

143. In the Synoptic gospels, Menken observes, John is depicted as 'preparing' the way for Jesus himself by virtue of (1) the tandem application to him of Mal 3:1, 'Behold, I send my messenger before your face, who will prepare your way' (Mark 1:2; cf. Matt 11:10; Luke 7:27) and (2) the clear statement to this effect in the Lukan infancy narrative, which also alludes to Mal 3:1 and Isa 40:3: 'for you will go before in the presence of the Lord to prepare his ways' (Luke 1:76); see Menken, "'I Am the Voice of One Crying in the Wilderness … ' (John 1:23)", 28–29.

144. For such a portrayal of John, Menken cites Matt 3:1-2, 4-12; Mark 1:4-8; Luke 3:1-3, 7-18; "'I Am the Voice of One Crying in the Wilderness … ' (John 1:23)", 28–29.

145. Here, citing John 1:25-26, 28, 31, 33.

146. "'I Am the Voice of One Crying in the Wilderness … ' (John 1:23)", 29.

147. "'I Am the Voice of One Crying in the Wilderness … ' (John 1:23)", 29.

148. This is articulated directly in Matt 11:13-14; 17:10-13; Mark 9:11-13; and it is implied in the identification of John with Mal 3:1 (Mark 1:2; Matt 11:10; Luke 7:27), which, in turn, connotes Elijah by its connection to Mal 3:23; Menken, "'I Am the Voice of One Crying in the Wilderness … ' (John 1:23)", 28–29, 33–34. The full Synoptic midrash is set out below in this chapter, under Excursus, *'Preparing' (ἑτοιμάζειν) and the Synoptic John*.

149. In Matthew and Mark, Menken notes, John's ministry ends with Jesus's baptism and his imprisonment launches Jesus's ministry (Matt 3:13-17; 4:12; Mark 1:9-11, 14). In Luke John is jailed before Jesus is baptized (Luke 3:19-22; cf. Acts 13:24-25; 19:4); Menken, "'I Am the Voice of One Crying in the Wilderness … ' (John 1:23)", 30–31.

150. Citing John 1:26, 29-37; 3:27-30.

151. John 1:21.

152. John 1:15, 27; 3:28; cf. 1:30.

153. John 1:29-37; 3:22-24, 27-30; Menken, "'I Am the Voice of One Crying in the Wilderness … ' (John 1:23)", 31.

1. Isa 40:3, A Call to Believe

of ἑτοιμάζειν, according to Menken, do not convey such a profile. Rather, with an indirect object – which Menken takes to be the genitive 'of the Lord'[154] – ἑτοιμάζειν signifies a preparation which is complete by the time that indirect object arrives:

> The verb ἑτοιμάζειν, used with an explicit or implicit indirect object, often has this connotation: a subject A prepares something for an indirect object B, and only when it is ready, B may come there where A already is, to use what has been prepared, to partake in it, and the like. In such instances, A precedes B in time at a certain place and accomplishes his task of preparing before B appears there.[155]

While apt for the Synoptic gospels, writes Menken, ἑτοιμάζειν is not so for the Fourth Gospel; and it was for this reason, he concludes, that the evangelist replaced it with εὐθύνειν:

> The connotation of ἑτοιμάζειν which has been described above, made it impossible for John to use it in his quotation from Isa. 40:3, because it did not fit in with his picture of the relationship between Jesus and John the Baptist ... It seems then that the change of ἑτοιμάσατε into εὐθύνατε introduced by the fourth evangelist in his quotation from Isa. 40:3 was motivated by the preoccupation to make John the Baptist not so much the precursor of Jesus as a witness contemporaneous with Jesus.[156]

Williams follows Menken entirely: that εὐθύνατε is a conflation of εὐθείας ποιεῖτε in LXX Isaiah 40:3c; that the exhortation 'make straight the way of the Lord' is directed to John from God (not from John to the people); and that ἑτοιμάζειν was removed because it connotes a completed preparation that mischaracterizes John's relation to Jesus in the Fourth Gospel – that is, because in the Fourth Gospel John is not Elijah and his ministry continued alongside (rather than ended with) the beginning of Jesus's ministry.[157] Williams presses further, however, by supporting Menken's case along two lines. One of these does not treat εὐθύνατε per se but is important nonetheless for Williams's overall conception of the exhortation. She notes the 'conundrum' in Menken's hypothesis that the exhortation issued to John has its imperative in the plural (εὐθύνατε); and, though she does not hope to resolve it, she seeks to ameliorate it by defining the exhortation more explicitly in light of John's profile in the Fourth Gospel's narrative, that is, 'by considering

---

154. Menken makes this deduction on the parallelism that occurs between a genitive and a dative indirect object accompanying ἑτοιμάζειν at LXX Job 38:25: 'Who prepared a course for gusty rain (ὑετῷ λάβρῳ), and a way for turbulences (κυδοιμῶν)'?; "'I Am the Voice of One Crying in the Wilderness ... " (John 1:23)', 28.
155. Menken, "'I Am the Voice of One Crying in the Wilderness ... " (John 1:23)', 26.
156. Menken, "'I Am the Voice of One Crying in the Wilderness ... " (John 1:23)', 28, 33.
157. "'He Saw His Glory and Spoke of Him": The Testimony of Isaiah and Johannine Christology', 58–59; Williams, 'Isaiah in John's Gospel', 103; Williams, 'The Testimony of Isaiah and Johannine Christology', 109–10.

its role in relation to the broader presentation of the Baptist and his testimony in the opening narrative sections of the Gospel in its present form'.[158] Doing so, she follows Menken again by reading the phrase 'way of the Lord' as a subjective (rather than objective) genitive, 'the Lord's way'[159]; and, accordingly, she sees the Baptist's activity in the broader narrative as announcing the coming of that 'way': by his declaration of Jesus as 'the lamb of God'[160]; by his 'repeated references ... to Jesus as the one who comes (ὁ ἐρχόμενος) after him'[161]; by his 'witness' on Jesus's behalf[162]; and by his introduction of (the otherwise unknown) Jesus to the public.[163] Such an 'exclusive focus on Jesus in the testimony and activity of John the Baptist', concludes Williams, implies 'that Isaiah 40:3 is here subjected to christological interpretation'; and this, in turn, supports Menken's view that the exhortation is issued to John (not from him), despite its plural verb.[164]

Williams's second line of support for Menken does broach εὐθύνατε directly, particularly by suggesting two further premises for the inadequacy of ἑτοιμάζειν: first, that John's acknowledgement of Jesus's pre-existence[165] 'also rules out his role as a forerunner' (and, thereby, further renders the language of 'preparing' inept); second, that, since in the gospel's opening episodes John had only the beginning of Jesus's ministry in view (not the end), he could 'only claim to make straight, not prepare beforehand, the way of the Lord'.[166]

Finally, Schuchard. For him, ἑτοιμάσατε was replaced by εὐθύνατε to merge Second Isaiah's exodus soteriology with a sapiential call to follow Jesus as Wisdom. With Menken, Schuchard sees John in the Fourth Gospel as a witness contemporary with Jesus, not the forerunner Elijah; and, with Menken, he ascribes the removal of ἑτοιμάζειν to the association of that verb with Elijah.[167] With Freed, however

---

158. '"He Saw His Glory and Spoke of Him": The Testimony of Isaiah and Johannine Christology', 60.

159. '"He Saw His Glory and Spoke of Him": The Testimony of Isaiah and Johannine Christology', 60; cf. Menken, '"I Am the Voice of One Crying in the Wilderness ... " (John 1:23)', 30.

160. John 1:29.

161. John 1:15, 27; cf. 1:30.

162. John 1:29-34, 36.

163. John 1:26, 31, 33; '"He Saw His Glory and Spoke of Him": The Testimony of Isaiah and Johannine Christology', 60-61 (quotations p. 60).

164. '"He Saw His Glory and Spoke of Him": The Testimony of Isaiah and Johannine Christology', 60. This argument is repeated to some degree in Williams, 'Isaiah in John's Gospel', 103-04; and Williams, 'The Testimony of Isaiah and Johannine Christology', 110-11.

165. Cited is John 1:30; cf. John 1:15.

166. '"He Saw His Glory and Spoke of Him": The Testimony of Isaiah and Johannine Christology', 59, 62; Williams, 'Isaiah in John's Gospel', 105-06; Williams, 'The Testimony of Isaiah and Johannine Christology', 109-10, 112.

167. *Scripture within Scripture*, 9-10. Schuchard does not, however, read ἑτοιμάζειν to carry the complex lexical significance which Menken gives it, namely, the completion of preparation prior to the arrival of the one expected (p. 10).

(and against Menken), he traces εὐθύνατε to a blend of Isaiah 40:3 with the LXX sapiential texts listed above[168]; and for him that merger supplies the hermeneutical key to the exhortation. He reads 'make straight the way of the Lord' as being issued both to John (from God) and from John (to the populace) – thus, both converging with and diverging from Freed and Menken.[169] And, based on the association of the *Logos* with divine wisdom in the Prologue, he interprets εὐθύνατε in that exhortation to portray the Baptist as a disciple of this sapiential *Logos*, calling others to be the same.[170] Since Second Isaiah (from which Isaiah 40:3 is drawn) elsewhere alludes to the exodus,[171] the phrase 'way of the Lord', argues Schuchard, connotes a metaphorized wilderness sojourn, a symbolic 'way' through the desert.[172] To 'make' that way 'straight' (εὐθύνειν), however, is to see Jesus as christologized Wisdom and follow him as such. For Schuchard, John in the Fourth Gospel is 'the quintessential witness to the Logos', who 'speaks in a manner reminiscent of a disciple of Wisdom'.[173] As such, the inserted 'I' (ἐγώ) casts John as beckoning the populace unto wisdom[174]; and to 'make straight (εὐθύνατε) the way of the Lord' is 'to see in Jesus the way of Wisdom as well, to be conformed to Wisdom, to become a disciple of Wisdom, and to find in the way of Wisdom the way to salvation'.[175]

C. Isaiah 40:3: An embodied appeal to believe

1. Problems in hypotheses on the anomalies

The full import of Isaiah 40:3 in the Fourth Gospel turns on more than its anomalies. Those anomalies do, however, play a critical role in the quotation's meaning; and, inasmuch as the hypotheses on them (outlined above) stand open to challenge, they will first be revisited as an initial step towards a more rounded appreciation of the verse.

It should be noted that εὐθύνατε may, indeed, be unintentional, as some have suggested: a misquotation from memory or a 'throw away' part of the verse to which the evangelist was indifferent. This becomes less likely, however, to the degree the verb reflects a plausible source used for theological purposes; and, building particularly on the contribution by Schuchard, such a case can be

---

168. *Scripture within Scripture*, 11, 14–15.
169. *Scripture within Scripture*, 10–11. Schuchard takes issue with Menken for having 'overlooked the fact that εὐθύνατε is a second person plural imperative'. He allows that verb nonetheless to be directed in some sense also towards John, when he prefaces that comment with the assertion that for the evangelist '*more* than the Baptist's testimony alone "makes straight" the way of the Lord' (both quotations p. 10, italics added).
170. *Scripture within Scripture*, 11–14.
171. Citing Isa 43:14-21, particularly Exod 14:21-22 at Isa 43:16 (and cf. Isa 11:16; 51:10).
172. *Scripture within Scripture*, 13, 13n48.
173. Schuchard, *Scripture within Scripture*, 11–12.
174. Schuchard, *Scripture within Scripture*, 12n45.
175. *Scripture within Scripture*, 13–14 (quotation p. 14).

made here: 'make straight' arguably signals a sapiential soteriology, wherein the evangelist has drawn from Proverbs and/or Sirach to characterize faith in Jesus as 'wisdom'.

a. Freed

The explanations for εὐθύνατε (recounted above) labour under several problems, particularly those proposed by Freed, Menken and Williams. For Freed, the difficulties number four – three to be treated here; the last to be done below, because its resolution by Schuchard forges a way forward on the overall meaning of the quotation.

First, by setting 'ethical and moral' over against 'apocalyptic and eschatological' Freed creates a false dichotomy. Apocalyptic Judaism no less than non-apocalyptic Judaism had its rights and wrongs, albeit in its own key; and since Freed's distinction turns partly on the view that εὐθύνατε represents a merger of Isaiah 40:3 with the texts from LXX Proverbs and LXX Sirach listed in Table 7, it would be more accurate (as Schuchard later has done) to speak of John in the Fourth Gospel as a 'sapiential' (rather than 'ethical') figure. Second, by appealing to the cognate interpretation of Isaiah 40:3 at Qumran, Freed, in fact, undermines his case for εὐθύνειν at John 1:23. Elsewhere in his discussion Freed contends that, like the fourth evangelist, the Qumran sectarians gave Isaiah 40:3 an 'ethical and moral' sense; and to buttress his claim he references the *Serekh ha-Yaḥad* at two junctures where the verse is referenced: the quotation of it at 1QS viii 14-16, where it is interpreted as a call to 'midrash Torah'; and the allusion to it at 1QS ix 19-21, where it is interpreted as defining the *heilsgeschichtliche* 'period' in which the sectarians perceived themselves to be living.

> As it is written, 'In the wilderness prepare (פנו) the way of ••••,
> make straight in the desert a highway for our God'.
> This is the study of Torah, which he commanded by the hand of Moses,
> to act according to all that has been revealed age by age,
> and according to that which the prophets have revealed by his holy spirit.[176]

> This is the age to prepare (פנות) the way to the wilderness,
> (and) to teach them everything that has been discovered to do in this age
> (and) to separate oneself from every person (who) has not removed his way from all unrighteousness.[177]

---

176. 1QS viii 14-16. Text for the *Serekh ha-Yaḥad* (here and elsewhere): James H. Charlesworth with Henry W.L. Rietz, eds., *The Rule of the Community and Related Documents*, vol. 1 of *The Dead Sea Scrolls: Hebrew, Aramaic, and Greek Texts with the English Translations*, PTSDSSP 1 (Tübingen: J.C.B. Mohr [Paul Siebeck]/Louisville: Westminster John Knox, 1994).

177. 1QS ix 19-21. For the English words in parentheses, see note 205 on the composite rendering of these lines in Table 10.

In both instances, however, the 'ethical and moral' sense which Freed is claiming to be expressed is articulated without altering the verb in question. Both the quotation at 1QS viii and the allusion at 1QS ix employ לפנות: 'in the wilderness prepare (פנו) the way of ••••'; 'this is the time to prepare (פנות) the way to the wilderness'. Inasmuch as the Greek equivalent of לפנות is ἑτοιμάζειν, Freed weakens (if not altogether cancels) his explanation for εὐθύνατε at John 1:23, since he argues that to achieve this same 'ethical and moral' sense for John in the Fourth Gospel, the evangelist had to discard ἑτοιμάσατε, because it 'was too ineffective to express Jn's thought'.[178] Here one might ask: If the Qumran sectarians could give Isaiah 40:3 an 'ethical and moral' sense without changing its wording in the Hebrew, why was it necessary for the fourth evangelist to replace 'prepare' with 'make straight' to do the same in the Greek?

Finally, by taking εὐθύνατε to cast John as an 'ethical and moral figure' Freed invests the verb with a meaning that is not supported by its context. It is to be expected that the import of a quotation which defines John's ministry in the Fourth Gospel will be matched in the narrative by features which reflect it. But, if the replacement of 'prepare' with 'make straight' is meant to connote John as an 'ethical and moral' precursor to Jesus, it finds no corroboration in the rest of the story. John is 'testimony ... to the light'; the one who baptizes 'in water'; the one who facilitates Jesus's 'manifestation' to the world; the 'friend of the bridegroom', who 'decreases' as Jesus 'increases'; the one who 'did no sign' but spoke truth.[179] He is not, however, a model or advocate for a moral life; and this puts in question whether εὐθύνατε was meant to identify him as such. As Menken writes (contra Freed's position), 'I do not see what there is specifically "ethical" or "moral" in what John the Baptist does and says according to the Fourth Gospel. Compared with the Synoptics, esp. Matthew and Luke, the moral element of the message of the Baptist is reduced to almost nothing in John.'[180]

b. Menken and Williams

The proposal by Menken and Williams, for its part, carries three difficulties. The first concerns the reason for which ἑτοιμάσατε was removed. By insisting that it denotes a preparation (by John) that must be completed by the time its indirect object (Jesus) arrives Menken invests it with a fixed nuance that it does not necessarily carry. As much has been suggested by Schuchard, who asserts that though John does complete his work before Jesus appears in the Synoptic gospels, that sequence does not turn on the verb ἑτοιμάζειν, nor does it preclude ἑτοιμάζειν from denoting a preparation by people other than John after Jesus arrives.[181] And the point could be pressed further by appeal to lexical semantics. Linguists have noted that a word's meaning in any given passage depends not on an innate denotation

---

178. Freed, *Old Testament Quotations in the Gospel of John*, 6.
179. John 1:6-8, 15, 26, 29, 31, 35-36; 3:29-30; 5:33, 35; 10:41.
180. Menken, '"I Am the Voice of One Crying in the Wilderness ... " (John 1:23)', 33n32.
181. Schuchard, *Scripture within Scripture*, 10.

which it carries within itself but on the context in which it has been placed and the way it is elsewhere used by the author who penned it.[182] That meaning, in turn, is ascertained not (primarily) by examining instances in which other authors have employed it, as Menken has done,[183] but by investigating other settings in which the author in question has applied it. For ἑτοιμάζειν, it is only used twice in Johannine literature, at John 14:2-3; and there it does align with the import Menken assigns to it: Jesus goes 'to prepare a place' (ἑτοιμάσαι τόπον) for his disciples, and he will not return to take them there until that 'preparation' is complete.[184] Since it is only used these two times by the evangelist, however, it runs against the same problem that attends some of Menken's arguments on the implications of unique, rare or replaceable linguistic features for LXX *Vorlagen*, namely, that the data are too meagre to draw such complex and nuanced conclusions about its import in the Fourth Gospel. Menken may be correct; and well taken is Williams's supporting observation that in the Fourth Gospel, unlike the Synoptics, John knows Jesus as existing 'before him' and, therefore, does not function as his 'forerunner'.[185] Such an inference, however, lacks sufficient evidence to confirm it and remains open to question.

The second difficulty turns on the assumption of the first and concerns the *locus* to which Menken traces εὐθύνατε. By taking it as a conflation of εὐθείας ποιεῖτε in LXX Isaiah 40:3c, he effectively recreates the problem he presumed to resolve. The colon in question, LXX Isaiah 40:3c, stands in synonymous parallelism with the one cited, LXX Isaiah 40:3b: in the Greek, 'paths' (τὰς τρίβους) is synonymous with 'way' (τὴν ὁδόν); 'of our God' (τοῦ θεοῦ ἡμῶν) is synonymous with 'of the Lord' (κυρίου); and, accordingly, 'make straight' (εὐθείας ποιεῖτε) is synonymous with 'prepare' (ἑτοιμάσατε).[186] Inasmuch as, for Menken, 'prepare' (ἑτοιμάσατε) was removed because its meaning did not serve the evangelist's purposes, one might ask how that problem is solved by replacing it with its synonym 'make straight' (εὐθείας ποιεῖτε) in the following line. To say, as Menken effectively does, that 'make straight' (εὐθύνειν) allowed a concurrence between John and Jesus while 'prepare' (ἑτοιμάζειν) did not sets Isaiah 40:3bc into a synthetic (rather than synonymous) parallelism, and at the very least this requires further explanation.

---

182. Moises Silva, *Biblical Words and Their Meanings: An Introduction to Lexical Semantics*, rev. and exp. ed. (Grand Rapids, MI, 1994), 138–48.

183. Menken, '"I Am the Voice of One Crying in the Wilderness ... " (John 1:23)', 26–28.

184. Menken, '"I Am the Voice of One Crying in the Wilderness ... " (John 1:23)', 28.

185. '"He Saw His Glory and Spoke of Him": The Testimony of Isaiah and Johannine Christology', 59; Williams, 'The Testimony of Isaiah and Johannine Christology', 109–10.

186. In the HB the grammar connecting the roadway to God differs slightly: 'a highway *for* our God' (מסלה לאלהינו) at Isa 40:3c over against 'the way *of* the Lord' (דרך יהוה) at Isa 40:3b. Due to its inclusion of the phrase 'in the desert' (בערבה) at Isa 40:3c, however, the HB also draws synonymity (where the LXX does not) between that phrase and the phrase 'in the wilderness' (במדבר) at Isa 40:3b.

The third difficulty in Menken's proposal concerns the recipient of the exhortation 'make straight the way of the Lord'; and a pivotal factor here is an overlooked aspect of the other anomaly in the quotation, the insertion of ἐγώ before Isaiah 40:3a. Menken insists that, despite its plural form, the imperative εὐθύνατε is addressed to John (not issued from him) and articulates his role in the narrative relative to Jesus, not his message relative to the people. But, while such a scenario is arguable in the Synoptics (both for ἑτοιμάσατε and its parallel, εὐθείας ποιεῖτε),[187] the inserted ἐγώ at John 1:23 precludes it from being so in the Gospel of John. Its presence specifically identifies John as 'a' or 'the voice' of the one uttering the admonition: 'He said, "*I am 'a/the voice* of one calling in the wilderness, "Make straight the way of the Lord""'; and this being the case, John cannot also be the recipient of that exhortation. To read it so creates the incongruous image of John issuing a message to himself: 'I am "a voice of one calling (to myself!) in the wilderness, 'Make straight the way of the Lord"'.

The 'conundrum' of this plural imperative for Menken's position is addressed by Williams, who attempts to ameliorate it by underscoring the christological focus of John's activity in the narrative[188]; and the critique made here is not to deny such. John is, indeed, 'the one sent before' Jesus, who baptizes in water 'that he (Jesus) might be manifested to Israel'. Accordingly, John announces Jesus as 'the one who comes after me' and identifies him to the public by attesting that he is 'the lamb of God, who takes away the sin of the world', the one on whom the Spirit has descended and remained, 'the one who baptizes in the Holy Spirit' (to John's baptism in water) and (perhaps) 'the Son of God'.[189] The ἐγώ preceding the quotation, however, requires that John also issues a message to the people, epitomized in the quotation; and theologically this means that at John 1:23 Isaiah

---

187. In Matthew, Mark and Luke ἑτοιμάσατε and its parallel εὐθείας ποιεῖτε primarily represent John's message to the people. Elsewhere in the Synoptic narratives (unlike the case in the Fourth Gospel) John is portrayed as issuing a moral message to the multitudes. And further, if John does have a 'preparatory' role towards Jesus (alongside this message to the populace), it is accounted for by the verb κατασκευάζειν (for LXX ἐπιβλέπειν) in the Synoptic renderings of Mal 3:1, leaving ἑτοιμάσατε and εὐθείας ποιεῖτε free to represent (instead) John's exhortation to the people: 'This (John) is the one concerning whom it is written, "Behold, I send my messenger before your face, who will prepare your way (ὃς κατασκευάσει τὴν ὁδόν σου) before you"' (Mal 3:1/Matt 11:10; Luke 7:27); 'As it is written in Isaiah the prophet, "Behold, I send my messenger before your face, who will prepare your way (ὃς κατασκευάσει τὴν ὁδόν σου)"' (Mal 3:1/Mark 1:2-3).

188. '"He Saw His Glory and Spoke of Him": The Testimony of Isaiah and Johannine Christology', 59-61.

189. John 1:15, 26-27, 29-34, 36; 3:28. The uncertainty over 'the Son of God' turns on whether John 1:34 represents the testimony of John (as do vv. 29-33 before it) or that of the evangelist.

40:3 is not 'subjected to a christological interpretation', as Williams would have it, but endowed with a soteriological one.

c. Schuchard

Finally on Schuchard, the proposal he offers likely carries an inconsistency – particularly, between its interpretation of the verse and its conclusion about its source. Noting Second Isaiah's exodus imagery, Schuchard understands 'the way of the Lord' as a metaphorical wilderness sojourn, a figurative journey 'after the pattern of the "way" which God had made for the Jews as they marched out of Egypt'.[190] He also, however, traces the quotation to the LXX[191]; but while 'the way', indeed, runs through 'the wilderness' in the HB, it does not necessarily do so in the Greek. As noted above,[192] the LXX omits the parallel phrase 'in the desert' from Isaiah 40:3c and this frees the phrase 'in the wilderness' to modify 'a voice of one calling' which precedes it rather than 'make straight the way of the Lord' which follows it.

2. Wisdom as believing

Excursus: 'Preparing' (ἑτοιμάζειν) and the Synoptic John

A way forward for understanding both εὐθύνατε and the import of the quotation as a whole can be found along two lines: one is Schuchard's resolution of a fourth problem (yet to be noted) raised by Freed; the other is a missed element of John's profile in the Fourth Gospel. Before developing these matters, however, a further word on the evangelist's motive for removing ἑτοιμάσατε. If that verb was, indeed, excised because its Synoptic usage associated John with Elijah (as Menken, Schuchard and Williams have argued[193]), the dynamic by which it did so may lay in a further factor: the midrashic relationship into which Isaiah 40:3 is placed with two other biblical passages in the Synoptic gospels, Malachi 3:1 and Malachi 3:23-24.

'Prepare' (ἑτοιμάζειν) does not appear in the passage which predicts Elijah's coming, Malachi 3:23-24. Its connection to Elijah in the Synoptics comes rather through a collage in which, on the basis of shared vocabulary, Malachi 3:23-24 and Isaiah 40:3 are further blended with Malachi 3:1. Like Malachi 3:23 (which names Elijah), Malachi 3:1 speaks of someone being 'sent' by the Lord; and like Malachi 3:1, Isaiah 40:3 speaks of someone 'preparing the way' for the Lord (Table 8).

---

190. *Scripture within Scripture*, 13; cf. 13n48.
191. *Scripture within Scripture*, 3–5, 14–15.
192. Note 108.
193. On the assumption that εὐθύνατε translates HB פנו, Reim contends the quotation does, in fact, resonate with Elijah – that it is a later insertion, designed to recast John as such and inserted at John 1:23 to correct the Fourth Gospel towards the Synoptics; *Jochanan*, 5–6, 9–10. His proposal falters, however, on the fact (observed in note 127) that nowhere in the LXX is εὐθύνειν used for לפנות.

Table 8 The Synoptic midrash on Elijah

Isaiah 40:3	Malachi 3:1	Malachi 3:23
A voice is/of one calling 'In the wilderness prepare the way of the Lord (פנו דרך יהוה); make straight in the desert a highway for our God.' (HB)	Behold, I am sending (שלח) my messenger and he prepares a way (ופנה-דרך) before me; and suddenly the Lord (האדון) whom you seek will come to his temple ... (HB)	Behold, I am sending (שלח) you Elijah the prophet before the coming of the day of the Lord (יום יהוה), great and dreaded ... (HB)
A voice of one calling in the wilderness, 'Prepare the way of the Lord (ἑτοιμάσατε τὴν ὁδὸν κυρίου); make straight the paths of our God.' (LXX)	Behold, I am sending (ἐξαποστέλλω) my messenger, and he will attend a way (ἐπιβλέψεται ὁδόν) before my face; and the Lord (κύριος) whom you seek will suddenly come to the sanctuary ... (LXX)	And behold, I am sending (ἀποστέλλω) you Elias the Thesbite before the great and manifest day of the Lord (ἡμέραν κυρίου) comes ... (LXX)

Table 9 John as Elijah in Matthew and Luke

Matthew	Luke
For this is that which was spoken through Isaiah the prophet, saying, 'A voice of one calling in the wilderness, "Prepare the way of the Lord (ἑτοιμάσατε τὴν ὁδὸν κυρίου); make straight (εὐθείας ποιεῖτε) his paths"'. (Matthew 3:3)	And indeed, you, child, will be called a prophet of the Most High; for you will go before in the presence of the Lord to prepare his ways (ἑτοιμάσαι ὁδοὺς αὐτοῦ). (Luke 1:76)[104]
	As it is written in the book of the words of Isaiah, the prophet, 'A voice of one calling in the wilderness, "prepare the way of the Lord (ἑτοιμάσατε τὴν ὁδὸν κυρίου); make straight (εὐθείας ποιεῖτε) his paths ..."' (Luke 3:4-6)
This (John) is the one concerning whom it is written, 'Behold, I send my messenger before your face (Exodus 20:23), who will prepare your way (κατασκευάσει τὴν ὁδόν σου) before you' (Malachi 3:1). (Matthew 11:10)	This (John) is the one concerning whom it is written, 'Behold, I send my messenger before your face (Exodus 20:23), who will prepare your way (κατασκευάσει τὴν ὁδόν σου) before you' (Malachi 3:1). (Luke 7:27)

194. This allusion runs into one of the difficulties that disqualifies 1QS iv 2-3 as a reference to Isa 40:3; that is, it employs vocabulary from that verse ('prepare' [ἑτοιμάζειν] and 'way' [ὁδός]), but sets the latter term in the plural ('his ways' [ἑτοιμάσαι ὁδοὺς αὐτοῦ]), as do some of the wisdom texts thought to be merged with Isa 40:3 (see Table 7 and the discussion of 1QS iv 2-3 below in this chapter, under *a. 'Making straight' (εὐθύνειν) as wisdom*). Since in this Lukan verse, however, the 'ways' which John is to 'prepare' designate the ministry of Jesus (rather than his own life course), the reference here lies closer to Isa 40:3 than does the allusion at 1QS iv 2-3 and so may be included as a Synoptic use of that verse.

In Matthew and Luke, Isaiah 40:3 and Malachi 3:1 (along with Exodus 23:20) appear in different pericopes but resonate with each other across the narrative between them: Isaiah 40:3, in the Matthean and Lukan introductions to John; Malachi 3:1 (with the LXX ἐπιβλέπειν replaced by κατασκευάζειν), in Jesus's later commentary on John (see Table 9).

In Mark the same two verses are juxtaposed in a single passage, the opening introduction to John (again alongside Exodus 23:20 and again with the LXX ἐπιβλέπειν replaced by κατασκευάζειν):

As it is written in Isaiah the prophet,
'Behold, I send my messenger before your face (Exodus 23:20),
who will prepare your way (κατασκευάσει τὴν ὁδόν σου/Malachi 3:1).
A voice of one calling in the wilderness,
"prepare the way of the Lord (ἑτοιμάσατε τὴν ὁδὸν κυρίου);
make straight (εὐθείας ποιεῖτε) his paths"' (Isaiah 40:3).[195]

And in Luke's birth narrative all three verses are blended in Gabriel's prophecy about John (once again, with the LXX ἐπιβλέπειν replaced by κατασκευάζειν):

And he (John) will turn many of the sons of Israel to the Lord their God.
And he will go before in his presence in the spirit and power of Elijah,
to turn the hearts of fathers to children (Malachi 3:23),
and the disobedient toward the wisdom of the righteous,
to prepare (ἑτοιμάσαι/Isaiah 40:3) for the Lord a people made ready (κατεσκευασμένον/Malachi 3:1).[196]

In such combinations the words in one passage can become associated with the themes in the other two. And so in the Synoptics – the 'sending' ([ἐξ]ἀποστέλλειν) of Elijah to 'prepare' (κατασκευάζειν) before 'the great and manifest day of the Lord' in Malachi 3:1 and 3:23 begins to connote the 'preparing' (ἑτοιμάζειν) and 'making straight' (εὐθείας ποιεῖν) the 'way of the Lord' in Isaiah 40:3; and, conversely, the 'preparing' (ἑτοιμάζειν) and 'making straight' (εὐθείας ποιεῖν) the 'way of the Lord' in Isaiah 40:3 does the same with Elijah being 'sent' ([ἐξ]ἀποστέλλειν) to 'prepare' (κατασκευάζειν) before 'the great and manifest day of the Lord' in Malachi 3:1 and 3:23. If, then, the fourth evangelist was defining John apart from Elijah (over against the Synoptics), this dynamic, too, may have rendered ἑτοιμάζειν ill-suited for the quotation. Through Synoptic cross-pollination Isaiah's 'prepare' had come to connote Malachi's Elijah.[197]

---

195. Mark 1:2-3.
196. Luke 1:16-17.
197. The unsuitability of ἑτοιμάζειν would have been all the more pronounced if, as Franke argued, the evangelist consulted the Hebrew even when citing the Greek. Where the LXX reads ἑτοιμάζειν in Isa 40:3 and ἐπιβλέπειν in Mal 3:1, the HB reads לפנות in both; see Table 8, as well as Franke's position in the Introduction, under *b. Expecting the Hebrew Bible*.

a. 'Making straight' (εὐθύνειν) as wisdom

That said, why εὐθύνατε instead? That is, if the evangelist removed 'prepare' to distance John from Elijah, what did he mean to communicate by inserting 'make straight' in its place? A way forward is forged by Schuchard's development of the sapiential model espoused by Freed; and it should be said, first, that this model is to be preferred on two grounds. One is that compared to the alternative – the conflation of εὐθείας ποιεῖτε at LXX Isaiah 40:3c – it is the more elegant solution: εὐθύνειν (or its cognate κατευθύνειν) appears (without the need for such alteration) in twelve of the thirteen sapiential passages in view; and in eight of them it occurs in tandem with ὁδός.[198] If the merger arises from shared vocabulary, the wisdom texts lie closer to the verb now found in John 1:23 than does LXX Isaiah 40:3c. The other reason is that a supporting scenario occurs in the *Serekh ha-Yaḥad* from Qumran. It is well known that Isaiah 40:3 is referenced at least twice in 1QS: a straight quotation at *1QSerekh ha-Yaḥad* viii 14 and an allusion at *1QSerekh ha-Yaḥad* ix 19-21, with their parallels.[199] Unnoticed, however, are two further factors which similarly show an association being made between Isaiah 40:3 and the wisdom texts under review here.

The first is the language at *1QSerekh ha-Yaḥad* iv 2-3. These lines open a section describing proper sectarian behaviour, 'the spiritual foundations for the sons of truth in the world'[200]; and, though they have been identified by Obermann as an allusion to HB Isaiah 40:3,[201] their vocabulary (while dovetailing Isaiah 40:3) is more plausibly traced to one of the sapiential texts in question. The lines speak of 'ways' (דרכים) and 'making straight' (ליישר), but not of 'a voice calling' (קול קרא), a 'wilderness' (מדבר), a 'desert' (ערבה), 'the Lord' (יהוה) or 'God' (אלהים); and, as such, the passage forms a closer match with HB Proverbs 4:25-26:

> These are their ways (דרכיהן) in the world: to illumine the heart of a man,
> to make straight (ולישר) before him all the ways (כול דרכי) of true
> righteousness, and to instill fear in his heart for the judgments of God ...[202]

> Let your eyes look forward,
> and let your eyelids make straight (יישרו) before you;
> level a track for your feet,
> and all your ways (וכל-דרכיך) will be established.[203]

The second factor is that the language at the end of the allusion to Isaiah 40:3 at 1QS ix 19-21 arguably echoes several of those same wisdom texts and thereby betrays an association between them similar to the one contemplated for John 1:23. The directive in these lines commands the Maskil to teach his disciples 'to

---

198. LXX Prov 4:25-26; 9:14-15; 13:13a; 20:24; 29:27; LXX Sir 2:6; 37:15; 49:8-9. See Table 7.
199. See note 41.
200. 1QS iv 2-6; quotation, line 6.
201. *Die christologische Erfüllung der Schrift im Johannesevangelium*, 94n7.
202. 1QS iv 2-3.
203. HB Prov 4:25-26.

separate (themselves) from every person (who) has not turned his way from all unrighteousness (ולוא הסר דרכו מכול עול)', and two aspects of that charge are noteworthy: first, the terms for 'turning' (לסור) and 'unrighteousness' (עול) occur within or just before and after HB Proverbs 4:24-27; 9:14-16; 29:27; second, for the singular 'his way' (דרכו) in 1QS and 4QS^b the recensions 4QS^{d-e} read the plural 'his ways' (דרכיו), such as is found in HB Proverbs 4:24-27 (albeit with a second-person singular pronominal suffix) (Table 10).[204]

Table 10 1QS ix 19-21 and sapiential texts

1QS ix 19-21 and its recensions	
This is the age to prepare the way to the wilderness (פנות הדרך למדבר), (and) to teach them (give them mastery in) everything that has been discovered to do in this age (בעת הזואת) (and) to separate oneself from every person (who) has not removed his way(s) (הסר דרכו\יו) from all unrighteousness.[205]	
HB Proverbs 4:24-27	**HB Proverbs 9:14-16**
Remove (הסר) from yourself crookedness of mouth; and deviance of lips put far from you. Let your eyes look forward, and let your eyelids make straight (יישרו) before you; level a track for your feet, and all your ways (וכל-דרכיך) will be established. Do not turn right or left; remove (הסר) your foot from evil.	She sits at the doorway of her house, upon a seat at the heights of the city; to call (לקרא) to those passing along the way (דרך), making straight (המישרים) their paths. The one who is simple turns aside (יסר) to her.
HB Proverbs 29:27	
An abomination to the righteous is the man of unrighteousness (איש עול); and an abomination to the wicked is the straight of way (ישר-דרך).	

204. See ad loc. in Philip Alexander and Geza Vermes, eds., '4Q258. 4QSerekh ha-Yaḥad^d', in *Qumran Cave 4. XIX: Serekh Ha-Yaḥad and Two Related Texts*; and apparently (as reconstructed) in Alexander and Vermes, '4Q259. 4QSerekh ha-Yaḥad^e'. Alexander and Vermes, in fact, press the matter further and suggest that the so-called singular reading דרכו in 1QS and 4QS^b may, itself, 'be the plural spelled defectively'; '4Q259. 4QSerekh ha-Yaḥad^e', 151; and cf. Philip Alexander and Geza Vermes, eds., '4Q256. 4QSerekh ha-Yaḥad^b', in *Qumran Cave 4. XIX: Serekh Ha-Yaḥad and Two Related Texts*, 58.

205. 1QS ix 19-21; 4QS^b xviii 3-4; 4QS^d viii 4-5; and 4QS^e iii 19-iv 2. The translation is a composite: terms in parentheses are attested in some but not all of the manuscripts. Further, readings in two of the recensions are not represented. The first is a ו preceding לוא הסר in 1QS, which renders the text 'and to separate oneself from every person; and he has not removed his way from all unrighteousness'. In the 4Q parallels the ו is replaced by אשר and, according to Alexander and Vermes, this reading is to be preferred, 'since ולוא in 1QS must, in context, anomalously be taken as equivalent to אשר לוא': 'and to separate oneself from every person (who) has not removed his way from all unrighteousness' – see

This scenario does not precisely match that of the Fourth Gospel. The sapiential allusion at 1QS iv 2-3 is not conflated with Isaiah 40:3, as is being contemplated for John 1:23. Nor is the purpose of the wise behaviour being advocated christological (or even messianic). Like the Fourth Gospel, however, the passages do show the sectarians to have used vocabulary common to both Isaiah 40:3 and wisdom texts to articulate their mission for the Lord (Isaiah) and their conduct in the world (Proverbs); and, inasmuch as this occurs in a group that was cognate to the Johannine community, it lends a second line of support to the prospect that the fourth evangelist has done the same.

If this sapiential model, then, is adopted, it raises a more basic question for John 1:23/Isaiah 40:3 – What does it now mean? That is, how does this merger between Isaiah 40:3 and these wisdom texts work? Answering this is difficult, because while Isaiah 40:3 calls for someone other than the Lord to make the Lord's way straight, the idea of one person 'straightening the ways' of another occurs in only one of the sapiential passages in question, LXX Proverbs 20:24, and there it concerns not a human 'making straight' the 'way' of the Lord, but the other way round – the Lord 'making straight' the 'ways' of a human:

Steps are made straight (εὐθύνεται) for a man by the Lord.
How, then, might a mortal discern his ways (τὰς ὁδοὺς αὐτοῦ)?[206]

Freed (who brought the model into view) offered no explanation, but Schuchard has pressed further to suggest the quotation now serves as a call to a sapiential discipleship which assists Jesus in his mission. That is (more specifically), Isaiah 40:3 at John 1:23 is now (a) a call to discipleship in wisdom (the sapiential texts) which (b) facilitates Jesus's return to the Father (Isaiah 40:3). The 'way of the Lord', contends Schuchard, is 'a path that returns (Jesus) ultimately to the Father'. All who respond to the exhortation become 'disciples of Wisdom'; and by doing so, those disciples assist Jesus in his return to the Father. 'Those who go with Jesus', he writes, 'facilitate his journey, and help him in accomplishing his purposes along the way "make straight the way of the Lord"'.[207]

'4Q258. 4QSerekh ha-Yaḥad^d', 119; and cf. Alexander and Vermes, '4Q256. 4QSerekh ha-Yaḥad^b', 58; Alexander and Vermes, '4Q259. 4QSerekh ha-Yaḥad^e', 151. The second reading not represented is a lacuna at 4QS^d viii 4, requiring the rendering ' ... in everything that has been discovered to do. In this age to separate oneself ...'; see Alexander and Vermes, '4Q258. 4QSerekh ha-Yaḥad^d', 116, 119.

206. Elsewhere among these passages other processes are in view: 'making straight' one's own 'way(s)' (LXX Prov 4:25-26; LXX Sir 2:6; 37:15; 49:8-9) or 'in' one's own 'ways' (LXX Prov 9:14-15); 'making straight' one's 'heart' (LXX Sir 2:2), one's 'friendship' (LXX Sir 6:17), one's 'hands' (LXX Sir 38:10); 'a way' being 'made straight' by wisdom (LXX Prov 13:13a) or, itself, 'making straight' (LXX Prov 29:27); 'making straight' as the conduct of thoughtfulness (LXX Prov 15:21); and the Lord's 'ways' being 'straight' for the scrupulous (LXX Sir 39:24).

207. Schuchard, *Scripture within Scripture*, 11-15 (quotations pp. 11-12, parenthetical note added for clarity).

b. 'Making straight' (εὐθύνειν) as believing

Hermeneutically, Schuchard's reading brings discussion of John 1:23/Isaiah 40:3 significantly forward: it furnishes a framework which begins to make sense of an Isaianic/sapiential polyvalence in the quotation. Theologically, however, it falters, inasmuch as it also assumes a synergism between Jesus and his followers that is foreign to the Fourth Gospel. As much has been noted by Menken in the revised version of his article on this quotation, completed after Schuchard's work: 'it is difficult', he writes, 'to see how, in John's gospel, others can help Jesus in this journey by making his way straight'.[208] And it can be noted further that far from being aided by those who respond to his ministry, Jesus in the Fourth Gospel, in fact, fulfils his mission on his own – at points despite (not with the help of) his disciples. When he is believed by many at the first Passover (John 2), for instance, he chooses not to entrust himself to them, because he knows 'what was in humanity'.[209] When he is sought by disciples at the second Passover (John 6) and 'believed' by pilgrims during the Festival of Tabernacles (John 7–8), he follows with discourses that cause many in the first group to stop following him[210] and that provoke those in the second group to attempt to stone him.[211] And, when he is assured by his closest disciples during the final Passover (John 13–19) that they are now persuaded he came from God, he retorts that they, in fact, do not yet believe; that they will soon 'be scattered, each to his own'; and that, with the exception of the Father, he goes to the cross alone.[212]

This challenge can be resolved, however – and Schuchard's sapiential reading maintained – by revisiting the quotation's context through cognate interpretations of the passage. Isaiah 40:3 is also cited in the Synoptic gospels and in Qumran literature; and when those *loci* are given further scrutiny and set against John 1:23, they bring into relief an aspect of John's ministry in the Fourth Gospel that more closely aligns the wisdom of εὐθύνατε with Johannine soteriology. Indeed, in light of cognate literature it can be argued that this wisdom, to which John summons the populace (per Schuchard), is, in fact, simply 'to believe in Jesus'. That is, to 'make straight (εὐθύνατε) the way of the Lord' is not to 'facilitate (Jesus') journey, and help him in accomplishing his purposes along the way', as Schuchard infers. Rather, like 'the work of God' to which Jesus refers in John 6:29, it is 'that you believe in him whom (the Father) has sent'.

(1) Cognate interpretations of Isaiah 40:3

The interpretations of Isaiah 40:3 in Qumran literature have no direct bearing on the meaning of John's rendering. They do, however, demonstrate the wide range of

---

208. Menken, '"I Am the Voice of One Crying in the Wilderness ... " (John 1:23)', 29n24.
209. John 2:23-25.
210. John 6:66.
211. John 8:59.
212. John 16:29-33; quotation, v. 32.

meanings attached to Isaiah's language in this verse, as well as the role context plays in determining those meanings; and so, before the (more relevant) treatments in the Synoptics are examined, those from Qumran are reviewed.

(a) Isaiah 40:3 at Qumran

Of four alleged references to Isaiah 40:3 in Qumran literature only two are accompanied by an interpretation: 1QS viii 14 and 1QS ix 19-21, with their parallels in other recensions.[213] 1QS iv 2-3, as previously noted, uses language found in Isaiah 40:3, but, in fact, likely alludes instead to Proverbs 4:25-26; and 4QTanhûmîm 1-2 i 6-7 does quote the verse, but appears in a catena of Isaianic passages on 'consolation'[214] which contains no specific commentary on them.

[1] 1QS viii 10-16: The study of Torah

At 1QS viii 10-16 HB Isaiah 40:3bc is interpreted as a call to study Torah in light of subsequent revelation disclosed to the sectarian community; and that interpretation appears in a commentary directly after the verse is quoted. The quotation, itself, comes amid instructions for a fifteen man 'council of the *Yahad*'[215]: after this group has acted 'for two years with integrity', it is to separate itself from the wider 'council of the men of the *Yahad*' and to be instructed in 'every word which is hidden from Israel yet discovered by the one who interprets (לאיש הדורש)'. As these men then form a '*Yahad*' among themselves, they are to separate themselves further 'from the midst of the dwelling of the men of unrighteousness'; and, to reinforce the authorization for that task, the directives cite HB Isaiah 40:3bc:

> When these are established (at the establishing of these) in the foundation of the *Yahad* for two years (of time) with integrity, they will separate themselves as holy amidst the council of the men of the *Yahad*. And with respect to any word which is hidden from Israel yet (which is) discovered by the one who interprets, let him not conceal it from these for fear of a relapsing spirit. And when these have become a *Yahad* in Israel (by these preparations), they will separate themselves from (the midst of) the dwelling of the men of unrighteousness, to walk to the wilderness to prepare there his way/the way of truth. As it is written, 'In the wilderness prepare the way of ••••/the truth(במדבר פנו דרך/....האמת); make straight in the desert a highway for our God (ישרו בערבה מסלה לאלוהינו)'.[216]

---

213. See note 41.
214. In this *locus* the quotation of Isa 40:3, itself, furnishes part of an excerpt which spans Isa 40:1-5a (4QTanh 1-2 i 4-9).
215. In other recensions this context (1QS viii 1–16) or a portion of it is found at 4QS^d vi (frgs 3a, 3b, 3c, 3d) 1–8 ; 4QS^e ii (frgs 2a i, 2b-d) 9–18 ; iii (frgs 2a ii, 3a-c) 1–6.
216. 1QS viii 10-14; cf. 4QS^e ii 18-iii 1-5. The translation is composite: words in parentheses are found in only one of the two recensions; and further, the rendering for 4QS^e iii 3 follows the textual development proposed by Alexander and Vermes, '4Q259. 4QSerekh ha-Yahad^e', 145–46.

Part of the sectarian interpretation of this verse is baked into the version and portion cited. By citing the Hebrew, in which (unlike the LXX) 'in the wilderness' at Isaiah 40:3b lies parallel to 'in the desert' at Isaiah 40:3c – and by omitting קול קורא at Isaiah 40:3a (to which 'in the wilderness' might otherwise be attached) – it ensures that 'the wilderness' and 'the desert' are the *loci* of the action being urged, not of 'a voice' which is 'calling'. 'Preparing' and 'making straight' are to be done 'in the wilderness' and 'in the desert'.[217]

Most of the sectarian interpretation, however, is stated explicitly in a commentary that immediately follows. In *pesher*-like fashion the next clause reads, 'this (the exhortation) is the study of Torah' (היאה/הואה מדרש התורה); and the next two lines assert that this 'midrash' involves observance (לעשות) and that Torah is to be learned through the lens of Spirit-wrought prophetic revelation:

This is the study of Torah (מדרש התורה), which he commanded by the hand of Moses, to act (לעשות) according to all that has been revealed age by age, and according to that which the prophets have revealed by his holy spirit.[218]

---

217. Because the site of Khirbet Qumran was, itself, situated in a barren region, the 'wilderness' at issue in the *Serekh ha-Yaḥad* has been thought to be literal, even if also metaphorical; see George J. Brooke, 'Isaiah 40:3 and the Wilderness Community', in *New Qumran Texts and Studies: Proceedings of the First Meeting of the International Organization for Qumran Studies, Paris 1992*, ed. George J. Brooke and Florentino García Martínez, STDJ 15 (Leiden: E.J. Brill, 1994), 117–32; James H. Charlesworth, 'Intertextuality: Isaiah 40:3 and the Serek Ha-Yaḥad', in *The Quest for Context and Meaning: Studies in Biblical Intertextuality in Honor of James A. Sanders*, ed. Craig A. Evans and Shemaryahu Talmon, BibInt 28 (Leiden: E.J. Brill, 1997), 206–18, 220–24; Sarianna Metso, 'The Use of Old Testament Quotations in the Qumran Community Rule', in *Qumran Between the Old and New Testaments*, ed. Frederick H. Cryer and Thomas L. Thompson, JSOTSup 290/Copenhagen International Seminar 6 (Sheffield: Sheffield Academic Press, 1998), 225. Debate has recently emerged, however, over whether this was the case. Reading the initial demonstrative pronoun which follows as masculine (הואה) rather than feminine (היאה) – as in 4QS^e iii 6 (frgs 2 a ii, 3a-c) over against 1QS viii 15 – Devorah Dimant has argued (a) that 'the study of Torah' is, in fact, depicted by the entirety of Isa 40:3 (not just the actions of 'preparing' and 'making straight') and (b) that, accordingly, the phrase 'in the wilderness' is (entirely) metaphor, not actual geography; 'Non pas l'exil au désert mais l'exil spirituel: l'interprétation d'Isaïe 40,3 dans la Règle de la Communauté', in *Qoumrân et le Judaïsme du tournant de notre ère: Actes de la Table ronde, Collège de France, 16 novembre, 2004*, ed. André Lemaire and Simon C. Mimouni, Collection de la REJ 39 (Paris: Peeters, 2006), 22, 25–35 (particularly pp. 28–29); first publ. in *Meghillot: Studies in the Dead Sea Scrolls* 2 (2004). In response, George Brooke agrees with the syntactical observation, but questions whether such a sweeping inference is necessary; 'The Place of Prophecy in Coming Out of Exile: The Case of the Dead Sea Scrolls', in *Scripture in Transition: Essays on Septuagint, Hebrew Bible, and Dead Sea Scrolls in Honour of Raija Sollamo*, ed. Anssi Voitila and Jutta Jokiranta, Supplements to the Journal for the Study of Judaism 126 (Leiden: E.J. Brill, 2008), 546–47.

218. 1QS viii 15-16.

[2] 1QS ix 12-21: The teaching of mission

At 1QS ix 19-21 (which has already been introduced) Isaiah 40:3 is paraphrased rather than quoted. It is given a related but different meaning than the quotation in 1QS viii – a call for 'the Maskil' (משכיל) to teach matters learned in his era of salvation history; and, once again, that interpretation is to be found in the context immediately following the reference. The allusion, itself, closes a series of directives to the Maskil concerned with 'ages' (העתים) in the sectarian *Heilsgeschichte*: God's dealings with humankind are understood to be arranged in a sequence of temporal phases, and these charges are intent on ensuring the Maskil lives and acts in accord with each.[219] They conclude by summing up the Maskil's tasks for the period at the time of writing; and this last phase, in particular, is framed in the language of Isaiah 40:3b.

This is the age (עת) to prepare the way to the wilderness (פנות הדרך למדבר),
(and) to teach them (give them mastery in) everything that has been discovered to do in this age (בעת הזואת) (and) to separate oneself from every person (who) has not removed his way(s) (דרכו\יו) from all unrighteousness.[220]

Unlike 1QS viii, the clauses which immediately follow these lines do not offer an explicit, *pesher*-like interpretation of Isaiah 40:3. They rather continue the summary of the Maskil's duties and purpose: specifically, he is 'to teach … everything that has been discovered to do in this age' and 'to separate oneself from every person (who) has not removed his way(s) from all unrighteousness'.[221] An implicit interpretation, however, might be gleaned from the first of these last two duties. That the Maskil was to teach 'everything that has been discovered to do in this age' implies a task similar to (though not precisely the same as) the one articulated at 1QS viii 10-16; that is (more precisely), for him to teach the

---

219. 1QS ix 12–21; in other recensions this context or a portion of it is found at 4QS^b xviii (frgs 6a i, 6b) 1–4; 4QS^d vii (frgs 4a i, 4b) 13; viii (frgs 4a ii, 4c-f) 1-5; 4QS^e iii (frgs 2a ii, 3a-c) 6-iv (frgs 4a-d) 2. Specifically (with respect to the 'ages'), the Maskil is 'to walk … according to that which is established age by age (עת ועת)'; 'to do the will of God according to all that is revealed from age to age (לעת בעת)'; 'to learn all the insight which has been discovered according to the command of the ages (לפי העתים) and the decree of the period (ואת חוק העת)'; 'to lay hold of the elect of the age (ובבחירי העת) according to the command of his will'; and 'to reprove … the elect of the way … according to that which is established for the age (כתכון העת)'; 1QS ix 12-15, 17-18.

220. 1QS ix 19-21. This rendering is the composite text constructed for Table 10. Sufficient language is present to trace the reference to Isa 40:3b – 'prepare' (לפנות), 'way' (דרך), 'wilderness' (מדבר). The forms and grammar of that vocabulary, however, are decidedly altered: Isaiah's imperative (פנו) is made an infinitive, 'to prepare' (פנות); Isaiah's anarthrous (דרך) is made an articular (הדרך); and Isaiah's locative phrase 'in the wilderness' (במדבר) is made the lative 'to the wilderness' (למדבר). As such, the reference is better defined as an allusion than a quotation.

221. 1QS ix 20-21.

observance of something 'discovered' in the current age (at 1QS ix) is not far removed from the council of the *Yaḥad* studying and observing Mosaic law through the lens of subsequent prophetic revelation (at 1QS viii).

Key to distinguishing this nuance may be the lative preposition (-ל), which precedes the term 'wilderness' in 1QS ix: where in 1QS viii the 'study of Torah' was to be done to prepare a way 'in the wilderness' (במדבר), as Isaiah has it, in this passage the instruction in 'everything that has been discovered' was to be done to prepare the way 'to the wilderness' (למדבר). Since the rubrics at 1QS viii 1-13 speak of a period of instruction for the council of the *Yaḥad* before they actually walk 'to the wilderness', (למדבר)[222] the two passages treated here may be addressing (and applying Isaiah 40:3 to) two stages of a larger process: 1QS viii, to the study of Torah 'in the wilderness'; 1QS ix, to preliminary instruction from the Maskil before going 'to the wilderness'. This would further imply that the students of the Maskil at 1QS ix are, in fact, the council of the *Yaḥad* introduced at 1QS viii.

If so, at 1QS ix Isaiah 40:3b was altered and given a slightly different interpretation than the quotation at 1QS viii. Where at 1QS viii the verbatim rendering served as a call for the council of the *Yaḥad* to study and observe Torah in light of subsequent prophecy, at 1QS ix its paraphrase issued a directive to the Maskil to instil observance of matters learned by the sectarians during his era of their salvation history.

(b) Isaiah 40:3 in the Synoptic gospels

[1] Matters covered, A recapitulation

In the Synoptic gospels Isaiah 40:3 is interpreted as a twofold call made by John the Baptist to Jews at large. One part of that call figures prominently in the Synoptic portrayal of John: a summons to repent and reform from sin. The other lies tacit, save for two cues in Matthew and Luke, and points to an overlooked element in the Fourth Gospel: an invitation to believe in Jesus.

Before examining these Synoptic *loci*, four of their features should be noted. All have been at least partially treated above, but they are worth a brief review – and in some cases a more complete exposition. The first is simply the passages in which Isaiah 40:3 appears: it is quoted in the introductions to John in all three Synoptics – in Mark, alongside Exodus 23:20 and Malachi 3:1; in Luke, in an extended excerpt spanning LXX Isaiah 40:3-5[223]; and in tandem with an allusion to Malachi 3:1, it is alluded to in Zechariah's prophecy on John in the Lukan birth narrative.[224] Second is the version cited. More evidently than the Fourth Gospel, the Synoptics cite the LXX. Their representation of Isaiah 40:3ab follows the LXX in its one or two departures from the HB. And, with the exception of reading 'his'

---

222. 1QS viii 13.
223. Matt 3:3; Mark 1:2-3; Luke 3:4-6.
224. Luke 1:76.

(αὐτοῦ) for 'of our God' (τοῦ θεοῦ ἡμῶν), it follows LXX Isaiah 40:3c (over against the HB) by omitting the phrase 'in the desert' (בערבה)[225] and glossing 'highway' (מסלה) with 'paths' (τὰς τρίβους).

Third, the admonitions 'prepare (ἑτοιμάσατε) the way of the Lord' and 'make straight (εὐθείας ποιεῖτε) in the desert the paths of our God'. To some degree (in the Synoptics) they represent John's message to the people: unlike the case in the Fourth Gospel, John is portrayed in Matthew, Mark and Luke as issuing such moral directives to the populace; and, if John also has a preparatory role towards Jesus, it is amply accounted for by the verb κατασκευάζειν from the Synoptic rendering of LXX Malachi 3:1 (and need not be expressed by LXX Isaiah 40:3). It should be noted further, however, that these admonitions may also intimate John's commission from God; that is, they may represent God's message to John as well as John's to the people, despite their plural imperatives. Such a scenario is more feasible in the Synoptics, where the quotations of Isaiah 40:3 are issued by the evangelists rather than John himself; and the use of ἑτοιμάζειν to depict John's preparatory work for Jesus at Luke 1:76 suggests that by the Synoptic cross-pollination of LXX Isaiah 40:3 with LXX Malachi 3:1 the terms ἑτοιμάσατε and εὐθείας ποιεῖτε (from LXX Isaiah 40:3) absorb the connotations of John's role vis-à-vis Jesus embodied in κατασκευάζειν (from the Synoptic rendering of LXX Malachi 3:1): 'and he will go before in his presence in the spirit and power of Elijah...to prepare (ἑτοιμάσαι/ Isa 40:3) for the Lord a people made ready (κατασκευασμένον/Mal 3:1)'.

Finally, the locative phrase 'in the wilderness'. On two grounds it designates the place from which the admonition is being issued, not (as in the Qumran reading) the location in which it was to be worked out. The first follows from the version cited: LXX Isaiah 40:3c does not read the phrase 'in the desert', which in its Hebrew counterpart runs parallel to the phrase 'in the wilderness' at Isaiah 40:3b. This untethers the phrase 'in the wilderness' at LXX Isaiah 40:3b from having to modify the exhortation 'prepare' which follows and allows it more readily to modify the phrase 'a voice of one calling' which precedes it. Thus, where the *Serekh ha-Yaḥad* reads 'In the wilderness prepare the way of the Lord', Matthew, Mark and Luke read, 'A voice of one calling in the wilderness, "Prepare the way of the Lord"'.

The second basis for 'the wilderness' designating the place from which the admonition is issued is context: aside from the quotation itself, the Synoptic evangelists concretely describe John as preaching and administering baptism 'in the wilderness'. Mark writes that 'John the Baptist was in the wilderness (ἐν τῇ ἐρήμῳ)'[226]; Matthew expands that to say he 'appeared ... proclaiming in the wilderness of Judaea (ἐν τῇ ἐρήμῳ τῆς Ἰουδαίας)'[227]; Luke has John growing up 'in the wilderness places' (ἐν ταῖς ἐρήμοις) until his manifestation to Israel and describes his ministry beginning when 'a word of God' came upon him 'in the wilderness (ἐν τῇ ἐρήμῳ)'[228]; and both Matthew and Luke have Jesus begin his later

225. See note 108.
226. Mark 1:4.
227. Matt 3:1.
228. Luke 1:80; 3:2.

tribute to John asking the crowds, 'What did you go out into the wilderness (εἰς τὴν ἔρημον) to see?'[229]

In sum, the Synoptics reference LXX Isaiah 40:3 four times: three as quotations; one as an allusion. They understand 'the wilderness' as the place from which Isaiah's admonition is issued. And, due to the ambiguity created by their association of LXX Isaiah 40:3 with LXX Malachi 3:1, they see John as both the agent and the recipient of that admonition.

[2] The import of the Synoptic quotations

[a] An exhortation to repentance and reform

As in the *Serekh ha-Yaḥad*, the interpretation of Isaiah 40:3 in the Synoptics is to be found in the broader contexts in which it is placed. But where at Qumran this occurred in explicit commentary or directives about the council of the *Yaḥad*, in Matthew, Mark and Luke it appears as further narrative descriptions of John's activities. More specifically (and, as Menken has rightly assumed[230]), since the part of the quotation in question is an exhortation ('prepare the way of the Lord'), Synoptic interpretation is to be found in further accounts of the message John urged upon the people.

Those accounts show him pressing for two responses. The most noticeable is repentance (including moral reform) in view of an imminent divine reckoning. John preaches this generally as he baptizes: he is described by Mark and Luke as declaring 'a baptism of repentance unto the forgiveness of sins'[231]; and his message in Matthew is summarized as, 'Repent, for the kingdom of heaven has come near.'[232] He also elaborates, in several ways: in Matthew and Luke (or for some, Q) he tells the crowds that in light of impending judgement, they are not to rest complacently in Abrahamic lineage but 'bear fruit worthy of repentance' – for Luke, this is spoken to everyone[233]; for Matthew, only to the Pharisees and Sadducees.[234] And in all three Synoptics he pronounces specific ways in which such reform is to be done: in Luke, among 'many other exhortations', he directs that those with two coats share with those who have none, that tax collectors collect no more than is owed and that soldiers stop extortion[235]; and in Matthew, Mark and Luke he reproves Herod Antipas for unlawfully marrying his brother's wife (as well as, in Luke, 'for all the evil things' he had done).[236]

---

229. Matt 11:7; Luke 7:24.
230. Menken, '"I Am the Voice of One Crying in the Wilderness ... " (John 1:23)', 29.
231. Mark 1:4; Luke 3:3; cf. Acts 10:36-37; 13:24.
232. Matt 3:2.
233. Luke 3:7-9.
234. Matt 3:7-10.
235. Luke 7:10-14, 18.
236. Matt 14:3-4; Mark 6:16-18; Luke 3:19-20.

1. Isa 40:3, A Call to Believe

[b] An exhortation to believe in Jesus

The second response for which John presses the people in the Synoptic gospels is belief in Jesus, who was coming soon after him. In most of the remaining Synoptic narrative on John this does not appear. Aside from urging repentance and reform, he is principally portrayed as announcing the arrival and identity of Jesus; that is, his message is christological, not soteriological. Jesus, he proclaims, is the 'mightier' one coming after him, 'the strap of whose sandals' he is 'not worthy to stoop to untie'[237]; the one who will baptize with the Holy Spirit (and, for Matthew and Luke, fire) for his baptism with water[238]; and the one who (again for Matthew and Luke) will split wheat from chaff in imminent judgement.[239]

At two junctures, however, John is cast as in some way urging people to believe. One is the close of Jesus's parable on the two sons in Matthew, where John's christological message is assumed to have some connection with faith (albeit, faith in his own word, not in Jesus per se). In articulating the two responses elicited by John's preaching, Jesus asserts that while the chief priests and elders did not 'believe' him, the tax collectors and prostitutes did:

> Jesus said to them, 'Truly I tell you, the tax collectors and prostitutes precede you into the kingdom of God. For John came to you in the way of righteousness and you did not believe him (οὐκ ἐπιστεύσατε αὐτῷ), but the tax collectors and prostitutes did believe him (ἐπίστευσαν αὐτῷ); and having seen (him), you had no change of heart later, so as to believe him (τοῦ πιστεῦσαι αὐτῷ).'[240]

The other *locus* – most relevant for John 1:23 – is Luke's portrayal of Paul's preaching to John's Ephesian disciples in Acts 19. Here John's message is expressly defined as including an invitation to 'believe'. When Paul is told by those disciples that they had only been baptized into John's baptism, he responds, 'John baptized a baptism of repentance for the people, speaking of the one coming after him – that is, of Jesus – that they might believe (ἵνα πιστεύσωσιν) in the one who was to come after him, that is, Jesus.'[241] The earlier, direct accounts of John speaking about 'the one coming after' him, of course, do not have him issuing an explicit appeal to 'believe' along with it.[242] That such an appeal emerges in this later account of Paul's preaching, however, signals that, at least for Luke, it was deemed implicit in that christological declaration.

---

237. Mark 1:7; cf. Matt 3:11; Luke 3:16; Acts 13:25.
238. Matt 3:11; Mark 1:8; Luke 3:16.
239. Matt 3:12; Luke 3:17.
240. Matt 21:31c-32.
241. Acts 19:3-4.
242. Matt 3:11; Mark 1:7.

In sum, the broader contexts of Matthew, Mark and Luke betray the Synoptic interpretation of Isaiah 40:3 to be twofold: in all three John is portrayed as summoning the Jews to repent and reform from sin in light of an imminent divine judgement; in Matthew and Luke he is also cast as bidding the Jews to believe in (the forthcoming) Jesus.

(2) The Fourth Gospel's interpretation of Isaiah 40:3

(a) A divine call embodied in John

Before examining the implications of these cognate interpretations for John 1:23, two matters on other aspects of Isaiah 40:3 as it appears in the Fourth Gospel: the locative phrase 'in the wilderness' and a further feature of the inserted ἐγώ.

The phrase 'in the wilderness' at John 1:23 likely serves as a metaphorical (rather than geographical) *locus* from which John is issuing his message. This follows from its broader, narrative context. Unlike the Synoptics (which explicitly describe John as preaching 'in the wilderness') or the *Serekh ha-Yahad* (which, pending the current debate, may have identified the phrase with Khirbet Qumran), the Fourth Gospel does not depict John or his constituents as appearing in such a setting. It places them at Bethany beyond the Jordan[243] and at Aenon near Salim[244]; and regardless of whether those sites were 'desert places' themselves, nothing is made of it in the narrative. Indeed, John's motive for choosing Aenon is not that he desired a setting that connoted some (redemptive) biblical motif, but only 'because there was much water there'.[245] If 'in the wilderness' connotes a salvific context, in the Fourth Gospel that setting (as Devorah Dimant is now pressing for the quotation in the *Serekh ha-Yahad*[246]) is figurative, not literal.

And regarding the ἐγώ inserted before the quotation, it carries two implications, yet unnoticed. The first is that it equates the 'voice' which is speaking with John himself. That is, by having John say '*I* am a voice of one calling in the wilderness', it identifies the 'voice' issuing the exhortation not (merely) with John's words but with his entire person (and thereby also his deeds). This identification has been (rightly) seen as a foil to Jesus as 'the Word',[247] but a second implication follows from it; namely, that if John is but 'a voice of one calling in the wilderness', the 'one calling' is, in fact, God. It is God who utters the appeal 'make straight the way of the Lord'; and that message is embodied in (not necessarily spoken by) the figure of John. Such a rendering fits hand-in-glove with the point just noted on reading the phrase 'in the wilderness' as a metaphorical rather than actual *locus*: and, if the two are taken together, they suggest that in the Fourth Gospel Isaiah's exhortation

---

243. John 1:28; 3:26; 10:40.
244. John 3:23.
245. John 3:23.
246. See note 217.
247. Bernard, *Critical and Exegetical Commentary on the Gospel according to St. John*, 1:38.

'make straight the way of the Lord' (whatever it may mean) is (a) issued by God (b) evocative of deliverance and (c) personified by John.

(b) A call to believe in Jesus
With regard to the exhortation, itself, if it is properly read as John's message to the people (not God's commission to John) – and if, following the cognate interpretations reviewed above, it is revisited in light of the broader portrait of John in the Fourth Gospel – it issues an appeal for the Jews to believe in Jesus. This is not, of course, stated outright in the text. But, as is the case with Matthew 21:31-32 and Acts 19:3-4, it can be inferred from the evangelist's depiction of John elsewhere in the narrative. Tacitly so at John 1:35-37, where, after John for a second time declares 'Behold, the lamb of God', the evangelist has two of John's disciples respond by following (that is, believing in) Jesus. More explicitly, however, it appears at two further junctures: John 10:41-42, where the evangelist writes that after many who come to Jesus at Bethany beyond the Jordan recall that 'everything which John said about this man was true', they 'believed in him (ἐπίστευσαν εἰς αὐτόν) there'; and the Prologue, where, in articulating the purpose of John's message, the hymn states pointedly, 'He came as a testimony, that he might testify concerning the light, that all might believe through him (ἵνα πάντες πιστεύσωσιν δι' αὐτοῦ).'[248]

Facilitating this inference is the implication of the inserted ἐγώ rehearsed above. By identifying the 'voice' of the quotation with John's person (rather than just his words), it suggests John's message is conveyed as much through what he is and does as it is through what he says; and this, in turn, allows for John's actions to urge faith, even though his words only tell of Christ. Otherwise put, John's (explicit) verbal testimony to Jesus is accompanied by his (implicit) behavioural bid to believe; and that bid aptly corresponds to Isaiah 40:3b, 'make straight the way of the Lord'.

When viewed in relation to Schuchard's reading of the quotation, this rendering resonates with its sapiential timbre but offers a theological significance more compatible with the Fourth Gospel's christology. With Schuchard, it follows Freed by tracing εὐθύνατε to LXX Proverbs and/or LXX Sirach; and with Schuchard, it understands 'make straight' as an invitation to live by wisdom. But where Schuchard interprets such living as a synergistic discipleship foreign to the Fourth Gospel's portrait of Jesus – a 'go(ing) with Jesus' that 'facilitate(s) his journey, and help(s) him in accomplishing his purposes along the way', this reading takes it simply as faith in Jesus. When asked in John 6 what one must do to 'work the works of God', Jesus answered that it was to believe in him: 'This is the work of God, that you believe in him whom he (the Father) sent.'[249] Reading John 1:23/ Isaiah 40:3 in light of its broader, narrative context has its exhortation advising the same: in 'make straight the way of the Lord' John is summoning the populace to the wisdom of faith.

---

248. John 1:7.
249. John 6:28-29.

3. Summary

In sum, the quotation of Isaiah 40:3 at John 1:23 is drawn from the LXX: it conflates the first two cola of that verse with one or more passages from LXX Proverbs or Sirach; and it makes that conflation a predicate by which John identifies his role in Johannine salvation history. By casting John specifically as 'a voice' of someone else 'calling in the wilderness', it conceives its exhortation 'make straight the way of the Lord' to be embodied in John's person but issued by God; by embellishing that exhortation with sapiential language, it bids the populace to greet Jesus with wisdom; and in the light of John's profile (portrayed elsewhere in the narrative) it conceives that wisdom to be faith. In short, 'I am "a voice of one calling in the wilderness, 'Make straight the way of the Lord'"' presents John as the personification of a divine appeal for the Jews to believe in Jesus.

Chapter 2

ISAIAH 53:1 AND ISAIAH 6:10, AN OBSTRUCTION TO FAITH

The quotations of Isaiah at John 12:38 and 12:40 are cited by the evangelist, not John; and, as noted in Chapter 1, they serve to elucidate the Jews' unbelieving response to Jesus's ministry. 'First', writes Barnabas Lindars, 'Isa 53.1 foretells the *fact* of unbelief. Then, in verse 40, Isa 6.10 provides the *reason* for unbelief.'[250] Otherwise put (as noted by C.H. Dodd), both answer to John 1:11b, 'and his own did not receive him'.[251]

More specifically, after Jesus issues a final admonition to 'believe in the light', then hides himself from the multitude,[252] the evangelist inserts two summary remarks on the Jews' reception of him. The first is that, despite the signs Jesus had performed among them, the Jews 'were not believing in him'.[253] The second is that this unbelief, in fact, fulfilled Isaiah 53:1 and is (somehow) explained by Isaiah 6:10.

> But, though he had done so many signs before them,
> they were not believing in him,
> that the word of Isaiah the prophet might be fulfilled, which he said,
> 'Lord, who has believed our report?
> And to whom has the arm of the Lord been revealed'? (Isaiah 53:1)
>
> For this reason they were not able to believe,
> that again Isaiah said,
> 'He has blinded their eyes
> and hardened their heart,
> lest they perceive with the eyes
> and discern with the heart,
> and turn, and I heal them.' (Isaiah 6:10)[254]

---

250. *The Gospel of John*, NCB (Greenwood, SC: Attic Press, Inc., 1972), 437 (italics original).
251. *Interpretation of the Fourth Gospel*, 380.
252. John 12:35-36.
253. John 12:37. In 'characteristically Johannine' style this sweeping statement is not absolute but qualified by the account of clandestine faith among Jewish authorities at John 12:42-43; see Barrett, *Gospel according to St. John*, 431.
254. John 12:37-40.

The evangelist closes by stating that Isaiah said these words in relation to an encounter with divine glory, doubtless his experience in the same chapter from which the second of the citations was drawn – Isaiah 6: 'These things Isaiah said, because he saw his glory and spoke about him.'[255]

A. John 12:37-41: An Isaianic inclusio

Like Isaiah 40:3 at John 1:23, the introductory formulae to these quotations explicitly ascribe them to Isaiah: for Isaiah 53:1, 'that *the word of Isaiah the prophet* might be fulfilled, which he said'; for Isaiah 6:10, 'that again *Isaiah said*'. This may be the work of the evangelist, perhaps to match the explicit ascription at John 1:23. But it may also have been assimilated from medial Christian sources: both quotations are cited by Paul, Matthew and Luke; and in each case they are similarly attributed specifically to Isaiah.[256] Given that the explicit ascription to Isaiah at John 1:23/Isaiah 40:3 may, itself, have been brokered to the evangelist through cognate sources,[257] the same must be allowed for Isaiah 53:1 and 6:10 at John 12:37-41; that is, their formulae may have been drawn from the same mediating source as they, themselves, were – the evangelist altering their language to suit his style and the new context.

1. Ascriptions to Isaiah in the immediate context

These formulae serve at least two functions in the narrative: one in the immediate context of John 12:37-41; one in the more extensive context of the Book of Signs. In their immediate context they join with John 12:41 to cast the quotations of Isaiah 53:1 and 6:10 as specific dialogue in Isaiah's throne room vision of divine glory. In the reference to that vision at John 12:41, the evangelist writes 'these things *Isaiah said*, because he saw his glory and spoke about him'. By similarly introducing their quotations with these same words – '*Isaiah said*' – the formulae in John 12:38 and 12:40 effectively tie those citations to that encounter and, thereby, invest them with a significance more pointed than just references to scripture. They are scripture, but through this threefold repetition of the verb 'said' they also become the very discourse spoken and received by Isaiah in that experience of divine glory:

---

255. John 12:41.
256. At Rom 10:16, Isa 53:1a with 'for Isaiah says'; at Matt 13:14-15, Isa 6:9-10 with 'for them is fulfilled the prophecy of Isaiah, which says'; and at Acts 28:25-27, Isa 6:9-10 with 'well did the Holy Spirit speak through Isaiah the prophet to your fathers, saying'.
257. See Chapter 1, under *2. The version cited*.

that the word of Isaiah the prophet might be fulfilled, *which he said* (ὃν εἶπεν) …
that again *Isaiah said* (εἶπεν) …
These things *Isaiah said* (εἶπεν), because he saw his glory and spoke about him.

2. Ascriptions to Isaiah in the Book of Signs

In the broader Book of Signs these introductory formulae also serve to create a thematic resonance between the quotations at John 12:37-41 and Isaiah 40:3 at John 1:23. They are the only formulae in John which ascribe their quotations explicitly to Isaiah; and since they do so at the opening and close of Jesus's public ministry, they form a figure of speech 'by addition' (*per adiectionem*) which brackets Jesus's public ministry.[258] Strictly speaking, the device in play is *epanalepsis*, 'the repetition of the beginning at the end'.[259] But while the dynamic captured by that term may operate at the micro level of clause or sentence,[260] it may also do so at the macro level of passage or complete work, as occurs here; and in such a case the more common designation is the Latin *inclusio*.[261]

*Inclusio*s or *epanalepsis* operate through some manner of interaction between their opening and concluding components, and they have been observed to do this in a number of ways: creating symmetry, bringing closure, evoking emotion, lending emphasis.[262] Their role in any given text, however, ultimately resides with the author's intent and broader context of the narrative; and, as such, it is best determined on a case-by-case basis. With regard to the Isaianic formulae in question here, more must be developed (below). *In nuce*, however, it can be said that the *inclusio* they form lies closest to the second function listed above, 'bringing closure', since its concluding elements (the quotations at John 12:37-40) furnish commentary on the effect of its beginning element (the quotation at John 1:23); that is, a 'call to believe' (Isaiah 40:3) is followed by a lament that no one has (Isaiah 53:1), coupled with an explanation as to why this was so (Isaiah 6:10).[263] Before this dynamic is teased out, the texts of both quotations will be examined for their wording, sources and deviations.

---

258. See Peters, 'Epanalēpsis', 250; Arthur Quinn and Lyon Rathbun, 'Figures of Speech', in *Encyclopedia of Rhetoric and Composition*, 269, 271; Heinrich F. Plett, 'Figures of Speech', in *Encyclopedia of Rhetoric*, 309, 311.

259. Peters, 'Epanalēpsis', 250.

260. Quinn and Rathbun, 'Epanalepsis', 228.

261. Peters, 'Epanalēpsis', 250.

262. Quinn and Rathbun, 'Epanalepsis', 228; Quinn and Rathbun, 'Inclusio', 346; Peters, 'Epanalēpsis', 250-51.

263. By virtue of another feature the introductory formulae at John 12:38, 40 launch a third trajectory in the Johannine narrative (ancillary to the concern here): they are the first of a series of constructs which introduce biblical references as having been 'fulfilled' (πληροῦν) or 'completed' (τελειοῦν): John 12:38-39; 13:18; 15:25; 17:12; 19:24, 28, 36-37; D. Moody Smith, 'The Setting and Shape of a Johannine Narrative Source', *JBL* 95 (1976): 237-38; Craig A. Evans, 'On the Quotation Formulas in the Fourth Gospel', *BZ* 26 (1982): 79-81.

B. The Johannine renderings

1. The Johannine rendering of Isaiah 53:1 (John 12:38)

a. The text
The HB, LXX and Johannine renderings of John 12:38/Isaiah 53:1 are as follows (Table 11).

Table 11 Isaiah 53:1 in the HB, LXX and John

HB Isaiah 53:1[264]	LXX Isaiah 53:1	John 12:38
מי האמין לשמעתנו וזרוע יהוה על-מי נגלתה	κύριε, τίς ἐπίστευσε τῇ ἀκοῇ ἡμῶν; καὶ ὁ βραχίων κυρίου τίνι ἀπεκαλύφθη;	κύριε, τίς ἐπίστευσεν τῇ ἀκοῇ ἡμῶν; καὶ ὁ βραχίων κυρίου τίνι ἀπεκαλύφθη;
Who has believed our report? And upon whom has the arm of the Lord been revealed?	Lord, who has believed our report? And to whom has the arm of the Lord been revealed?	Lord, who has believed our report? And to whom has the arm of the Lord been revealed?

b. The version cited
The version used is almost certainly the LXX. As was the case with Isaiah 40:3, the LXX of Isaiah 53:1 diverges from the HB at one, possibly two, places; and, notwithstanding its moveable -ν in ἐπίστευσεν, the Fourth Gospel follows it verbatim. The first may be the phrase designating the recipient of revelation in Isaiah 53:1b: 'to whom' (τίνι) over against 'upon whom' (על-מי) the 'arm of the Lord has been revealed'? For some textual witnesses there is no discrepancy here: LXX manuscript 88 aligns with the MT's 'upon whom' (על-מי) by making τίνι an object of the preposition ἐπί ('upon'); and conversely, 1QIsaiah[a-b] read the MT's 'upon whom' (על-מי) as 'to whom' (אל מי), thus coinciding with the sole τίνι in most LXX recensions.[265] The majority of MT and LXX manuscripts, however, read 'upon whom' (על-מי) and 'to whom' (τίνι), respectively; and inasmuch as the Fourth Gospel likewise reads 'to whom' (τίνι), it would follow the Greek over against the Hebrew. The second (and undeniable) LXX departure from the HB is

---

264. Besides the MT, Isa 53:1 is attested in 1QIsa[a]; 1QIsa[b]; and 4QIsa[c]. On Isa 53:1b, both 1QIsa[a] and 1QIsa[b] read אל מי ('to whom') for MT על-מי ('upon whom'); see Ulrich and Flint, *Qumran Cave 1. II: The Isaiah Scrolls*, ad loc.

265. Menken ascribes the alternate reading in 1QIsa[a] (and one might add 1QIsa[b]) to common scribal confusion of the two prepositions; 'The Use of the Septuagint in Three Quotations in John: Jn 10,34; 12,38; 19,24', 368–69. Given the Hebrew *Vorlagen* found for other LXX texts at Qumran, however, it may rather represent a genuine Hebrew textual tradition behind the LXX; see, for instance, James VanderKam and Peter Flint, *The Meaning of the Dead Sea Scrolls: Their Significance for Understanding the Bible, Judaism, Jesus, and Christianity* (New York: HarperSanFrancisco, 2002), 123–24. In such a scenario – with 1QIsa[a-b] reading 'to whom' (אל מי) – neither the LXX nor John would be diverging from the HB on this phrase.

2. Isa 53:1 and Isa 6:10, An Obstruction to Faith

its initial vocative, κύριε: 'Lord (κύριε), who has believed our report'? This has no counterpart in any known Hebrew tradition; and that the Fourth Gospel has the same tilts the evidence towards a Greek rather than Hebrew *Vorlage*.[266]

Menken has pressed further for a LXX source by arguing that the evangelist is more likely to have translated HB לגלות ('to reveal') with φανεροῦν rather than (the LXX) ἀποκαλύπτειν.[267] It has been noted in the Introduction, however, that such criteria require caution, and in this case that holds on three counts. Two were stated in (or follow from) the introductory discussion: first, that inferences about the evangelist's preferred translation choices presume more about Johannine idiom than extant data allow; second, that, on Menken's own criteria, ἀποκαλύπτειν, no less than φανεροῦν, would qualify as just such a choice. That is, for several other quotations Menken suggests that had the evangelist translated from the Hebrew, he would have drawn his vocabulary from glosses routinely used for the terms in question by the LXX and other Greek versions; and for לגלות and its Aramaic counterparts ἀποκαλύπτειν is used eighty-one times in the LXX.

The third consideration is the observation by Urban von Wahlde that ἀποκαλύπτειν and φανεροῦν are not synonyms and, therefore, that the evangelist may have chosen ἀποκαλύπτειν himself (rather than import it from the LXX), because its nuance of 'uncovering' (rather than 'manifesting') was more appropriate to the context.[268] To be sure, Menken enjoys more support here than in his similar argument at John 2:17 that the evangelist would have chosen οἰκία over οἶκος as a gloss for בית: the differential between the usage of those terms elsewhere in Johannine literature is two times (οἶκος) to five (οἰκία),[269] while that between the *hapax* ἀποκαλύπτειν and φανεροῦν is one to eighteen – for the latter, nine each in the Fourth Gospel and 1 John.[270] As von Wahlde continues, however, the evidence for John 12:38/Isaiah 53:1 on the whole 'is not compelling' and bids due caution.[271]

---

266. So, for instance, Goodwin, 'How Did John Treat His Sources'?, 62, 62n7; and Menken, 'The Use of the Septuagint in Three Quotations in John: Jn 10,34; 12,38; 19,24', 369. And the same observation is made for Paul's quotation of LXX Isa 53:1a at Rom 10:16 by J. Ross Wagner, *Heralds of the Good News: Isaiah and Paul 'in Concert' in the Letter to the Romans*, NovTSup 101 (Leiden: E.J. Brill, 2002), 179n181.

267. Menken, *Old Testament Quotations in the Fourth Gospel*, 15; Menken, 'The Use of the Septuagint in Three Quotations in John: Jn 10,34; 12,38; 19,24', 369.

268. *The Gospel and Letters of John*, 3 vols., ECC (Grand Rapids, MI: William B. Eerdmans, 2010), 3:309.

269. See Table 2.

270. John 1:31; 2:11; 3:21; 7:4; 9:3; 17:6; 21:1, 14; and cf. 1 John 1:2; 2:19, 28; 3:2, 5, 8; 4:9. Compare this ratio also with the evidence for Menken's cases on (a) κράζειν and κραυγάζειν relative to βοᾶν at John 1:23/Isa 40:3; and (b) the LXX uses of μισεῖν and δωρεάν relative to other terms employed for the respective Hebrew words they render at John 15:25/Pss 35:19 (?); 69:5 (?); *Pss. Sol.* 7:1 (?)—set out in the Introduction, under *a. Confirming the Septuagint*.

271. *Gospel and Letters of John*, 3:309.

Given that the first colon of LXX Isaiah 53:1 is also cited at Romans 10:16– and this, with an explicit ascription to Isaiah– its presence in the Fourth Gospel might have somehow been mediated through Paul. Were this the case, however, its citation in full at John 12:38 indicates that, though its use might have been catalysed by the apostle, its text was likely drawn directly from its biblical context.

2. The Johannine rendering of Isaiah 6:10 (John 12:40)

a. The text

As for John 12:40/Isaiah 6:10, the HB, LXX and Johannine renderings are as follows (Table 12).

Table 12 Isaiah 6:10 in the HB, LXX and John

HB Isaiah 6:10[272]	LXX Isaiah 6:10	John 12:40
השמן לב-העם הזה	ἐπαχύνθη γὰρ ἡ καρδία τοῦ λαοῦ τούτου,	τετύφλωκεν αὐτῶν
ואזניו הכבד	καὶ τοῖς ὠσὶν αὐτῶν βαρέως ἤκουσαν	τοὺς ὀφθαλμοὺς
ועיניו השע	καὶ τοὺς ὀφθαλμοὺς αὐτῶν ἐκάμμυσαν,	καὶ ἐπώρωσεν αὐτῶν
פן-יראה בעיניו	μήποτε ἴδωσι τοῖς ὀφθαλμοῖς	τὴν καρδίαν,
ובאזניו ישמע	καὶ τοῖς ὠσὶν ἀκούσωσι	ἵνα μὴ ἴδωσιν
ולבבו יבין	καὶ τῇ καρδίᾳ συνῶσι	τοῖς ὀφθαλμοῖς
ושב ורפא לו	καὶ ἐπιστρέψωσι καὶ ἰάσομαι αὐτούς.	καὶ νοήσωσιν τῇ καρδίᾳ,
		καὶ στραφῶσιν,
		καὶ ἰάσομαι αὐτούς.

Make the heart
    of this people fat,
and render their ears heavy,
and smear over their eyes,
lest they perceive
    with their eyes,
and with their ears hear,
and their heart understand,
and they turn back
    and he heal them.
	For the heart of this people grew fat,
	and with their ears they heard
	    in disgust,
	and their eyes they shut;
	lest they perceive with the eyes,
	and with the ears hear,
	and with the heart understand,
	and turn and I heal them.
		He has blinded their eyes
		and hardened their heart,
		lest they perceive
		    with the eyes
		and discern
		    with the heart,
		and turn,
		    and I heal them.

272. Besides the MT, Hebrew Isa 6:10 is attested in 1QIsa[a] and 4QIsa[f]. Regarding Isa 6:10a, 1QIsa[a] reads the hiphil imperative השם ('to make desolate') for MT השמן ('to make fat'): no final ן appears in the readable leather following מ, and 'medial' מ often serves as final ם in Qumran documents; Ulrich and Flint, *Qumran Cave 1. II: The Isaiah Scrolls*, ad loc. and 2:100. For Isa 6:10e, (a) 4QIsa[f] reads וב[אזנו] for MT ובאזניו, which may represent either an orthographic difference or a variant ('lest … they hear *with their ear*')— Patrick W. Skehan and Eugene Ulrich, eds., '4QIsa[f]', in *Qumran Cave 4. X: The Prophets*, ed. Eugene Ulrich et al., DJD 15 (Oxford: Clarendon Press, 1997), ad loc.; and (b) 1QIsa[a] reads the plural ישמעו for singular ישמע: given the singular subject 'this people' (העם הזה), both can be translated as 'lest ….they hear'; Ulrich and Flint, *Qumran Cave 1. II: The Isaiah Scrolls*, ad loc. Finally, with respect to Isa 6:10f, 1QIsa[a] and 4QIsa[f], along with a number of MT manuscripts, read [ו]בלבבו ('and with their heart understand') for ולבבו ('and their heart understand'); Ulrich and Flint, *Qumran Cave 1. II: The Isaiah Scrolls*, ad loc.; Skehan and Ulrich, '4QIsa[f]', ad loc.

b. Version(s), anomalies and referents

Determining the version cited in this quotation requires more than in the previous two on two counts: first, HB and LXX Isaiah 6:10 differ substantially; and second, the Johannine rendering both diverges from and resembles each – so much so that inquiring into its source is ineluctably coupled with distilling its anomalies. Accordingly, discussion will proceed by (1) clarifying the relationship of the Johannine rendering to the HB and LXX versions, then (2) canvassing hypotheses on the peculiar features of that rendering – theories on its anomalies, as well as its referents (particularly, the figures or entities acting in the third-person singular verbs at John 12:40ab and the first-person singular verb at John 12:40e).

(1) John 12:40 and the versions

To discuss the version(s) cited, the distinctions between HB and LXX Isaiah 6:10 will first be defined, after which the Fourth Gospel's rendering will be examined for its similarities to and differences from each.

On the LXX relative to the HB,[273] for HB Isaiah 6:10a (1) the hiphil singular imperative 'make fat' (השמן) becomes an aorist passive 'grew fat' (ἐπαχύνθη); (2) the accusative '*heart* of this people' (לב-העם הזה) reads as a nominative (ἡ καρδία τοῦ λαοῦ τούτου); and (3) the LXX links this verse causally with Isaiah 6:9 by inserting the postpositive γάρ after ἐπαχύνθη – that is, the people will 'hear yet not understand' and 'see yet not perceive' in Isaiah 6:9 because their heart 'grew fat', they 'heard with their ears in disgust' and 'shut their eyes' in Isaiah 6:10. For HB Isaiah 6:10b (4) the hiphil singular imperative 'render heavy' (הכבד) becomes the adverbially modified aorist plural 'heard in disgust' (βαρέως ἤκουσαν); and (5) the accusative 'and ... their ears' (ואזניו) becomes the instrumental dative 'and with their ears' (καὶ τοῖς ὠσὶν αὐτῶν). For HB Isaiah 6:10c (6) the hiphil singular imperative 'smear over' (השע) becomes the aorist plural 'they shut' (ἐκάμμυσαν). For HB Isaiah 6:10b-cg, (7) the singular pronominal suffixes, literally 'its'/'it' (לו/ועיניו/ואזניו), become the plural pronouns 'their'/'them' (αὐτῶν [twice]/αὐτούς). And for HB Isaiah 6:10d-f (8) the nouns 'eyes', 'ears' and 'heart' have no pronominal modifiers in the LXX; (9) with the exception of the third-person plural ישמעו in 1QIsaiah[a] (which is matched in the LXX), the third-person singular verbs 'see', 'hear', 'understand' and 'turn' become third-person plurals in the Greek; and specifically for HB Isaiah 6:10g (10) the third-person singular 'and he heal them' (ורפא לו) becomes first-person singular 'and I heal them' (καὶ ἰάσομαι αὐτούς). Finally, regarding HB Isaiah 6:10f, (11) the prepositional phrase '(and) with their heart' (בלבבו[ו]) in 1QIsaiah[a], 4QIsaiah[f] and a number of MT manuscripts is matched by the dative τῇ καρδίᾳ in the LXX – the nominative 'and their heart' (ולבבו) in most MT manuscripts, however, becomes the aforementioned instrumental dative in the Greek.

---

273. Accounts of the anomalies and hypotheses on the version of this quotation can also be found in Freed, *Old Testament Quotations in the Gospel of John*, 85–86; and Schuchard, *Scripture within Scripture*, 92–95. The alphabetized divisions of Isa 6:10 in this comparison represent the seven cola (a–g) as they appear in both the HB and the LXX.

Before comparing the Johannine rendering to each of these versions, it can be noted that in five respects it differs from both. (1) The two lines treating 'hearing' and 'the ears', Isaiah 6:10be, have been removed.[274] (2) The first two lines dealing with 'heart' and 'eyes' in Isaiah 6:10ac have been inverted, with the conjunction 'and' now lying before the former rather than the latter: this, in turn, reconfigures the original *chiasmus* of heart-eyes-eyes-heart (A-B-B'-A') into two parallel pairs, eyes-heart/eyes-heart (A-B-A'-B'). (3) The verbs used for 'smearing over'/'shutting'/'blinding' the eyes (השע/ἐκάμμυσαν/τετύφλωκεν) at Isaiah 6:10c and 'understanding'/'perceiving'/'discerning' with the heart (יבין/συνῶσι/νοήσωσιν) at Isaiah 6:10f are relocated from clause-last, where they are placed in the HB and LXX, to clause-first (or, for the verb νοήσωσιν, clause-second, after the conjunction καί). (4) The genitive 'of this people' in Isaiah 6:10a has been reduced to the plural (rather than singular) pronoun 'their' (αὐτῶν), which, together with the same plural pronoun (αὐτῶν) modifying 'eyes' for Isaiah 6:10c, precedes rather than follows the noun it modifies, making both of the terms 'eyes' and 'heart' (from Isaiah 6:10ac) clause-last in their respective cola.[275] And likewise (5) the phrase 'and (with) the(ir) heart' (ו[ב]לבבו/τῇ καρδίᾳ) at Isaiah 6:10f follows rather than precedes its verb, matching the phrase 'with the eyes' in John 12:40c as clause-last in its colon.[276]

When the Johannine rendering is compared with the LXX (factoring in the alterations just listed), four elements match: 'their eyes' (τοὺς ὀφθαλμοὺς αὐτῶν[277]) at LXX Isaiah 6:10c/John 12:40a, albeit with the pronoun coming before rather than after the noun; 'they perceive with the eyes' (ἴδωσι[ν] τοῖς ὀφθαλμοῖς) at LXX Isaiah 6:10d/John 12:40c, notwithstanding the moveable -ν in John; 'and with the heart' (καὶ τῇ καρδίᾳ) at LXX Isaiah 6:10f/John 12:40d, albeit with the dative noun coming after rather than before the verb; and perhaps most saliently 'and … and I heal them' (καὶ … καὶ ἰάσομαι αὐτούς) at LXX Isaiah 6:10g/John 12:40e.

Many elements, however, differ. Already mentioned are (1) the placement of αὐτῶν before rather than after τοὺς ὀφθαλμούς for LXX Isaiah 6:10c/John 12:40a and (2) the placement of τῇ καρδίᾳ after rather than before the verb νοήσωσιν for LXX Isaiah 6:10f/John 12:40d. Further, however, are (3) the third-person singular perfect 'he has blinded' (τετύφλωκεν) in place of the third-person plural aorist 'they shut' (ἐκάμμυσαν) for LXX Isaiah 6:10c/John 12:40a; (4) the active clause 'and he/it hardened (or maimed)[278] their heart' (with someone or something acting

---

274. LXX Isa 6:10e, however, is also omitted in 88^txt.

275. The αὐτῶν modifying τοὺς ὀφθαλμούς at LXX Isa 6:10c is absent from Vaticanus and 393.

276. On these features, see also Menken, "'He Has Blinded Their Eyes …'" (John 12:40)', in *Old Testament Quotations in the Fourth Gospel: Studies in Textual Form*, 105–06; first publ. in *BZ* 32 (1988).

277. This, notwithstanding the absence of the genitive personal pronoun in LXX Vaticanus and 393; see note 275.

278. Several witnesses to the Johannine text read πηροῦν rather than πωροῦν: ἐπήρωσεν in P^66 P^75 ℵ K W 579. The UBSGNT editorial committee views the change of verb as a scribal attempt to furnish a more fitting verb for τὴν καρδίαν; Metzger, *Textual Commentary on the Greek New Testament* (2nd ed.), 203.

2. Isa 53:1 and Isa 6:10, An Obstruction to Faith 75

upon the people's heart) in place of the passive 'for the heart of this people grew fat' (with the people's heart as subject) for LXX Isaiah 6:10a/John 12:40b; (5) ἵνα μή in place of μήποτε for LXX Isaiah 6:10d/John 12:40c; (6) the verbs τυφλοῦν ('blind'), πωροῦν ('harden')/πηροῦν ('maim') and νοεῖν ('discern'), respectively, in place of καμμύειν ('shut'), παχύνειν ('fatten') and συνιέναι ('understand') for LXX Isaiah 6:10acf/John 12:40abd; and, notwithstanding the correspondence in part of the textual tradition,[279] (7) the second aorist passive στραφῶσιν ('be turned'), with moveable -ν, in place of the aorist active of its compound ἐπιστρέψωσι ('turn') for LXX Isaiah 6:10g/John 12:40e.

Similarly with respect to the HB, four elements of the Johannine quotation roughly match: '(their) eyes' (ועיניו/αὐτῶν τοὺς ὀφθαλμούς) at Isaiah 6:10c/John 12:40a, albeit with the pronoun placed before rather than after (that is, suffixed to) the noun; 'lest (they) see/perceive with (their) eyes' (פן-יראה בעיניו/ἵνα μὴ ἴδωσιν τοῖς ὀφθαλμοῖς) at Isaiah 6:10d/John 12:40c, notwithstanding the absence of personal pronoun; 'and understand (or discern) with the heart' ([ו]בלבבו יבין/καὶ νοήσωσιν τῇ καρδίᾳ) at Isaiah 6:10f/John 12:40d – here reading [ו]בלבבו in 1QIsaiah[a], 4QIsaiah[f] and a number of MT manuscripts, and notwithstanding the absence of personal pronoun and placement of τῇ καρδίᾳ after rather than before its verb; and finally, 'and (they) turn' (ושב/καὶ στραφῶσιν) at Isaiah 6:10g/John 12:40e.

As with the LXX, however, many elements in the Fourth Gospel's rendering diverge from the HB. Besides the aforementioned relocations of (1) the personal pronoun αὐτῶν for Isaiah 6:10c/John 12:40a and (2) the phrase 'with the heart' for Isaiah 6:10f/John 12:40d, there are (3) the verb τυφλοῦν ('to blind') in place of hiphil להשע ('to smear over') for Isaiah 6:10c/John 12:40a; (4) the verb πωροῦν ('to harden') or πηροῦν ('to maim') in place of hiphil להשמין for Isaiah 6:10a/John 12:40b; (5) the person, number and mood of the verbs listed in (3) and (4) as third-person singular preterites rather than second-person singular imperatives; (6) the placement of the verb for 'blind' before rather than after the phrase 'their eyes' for Isaiah 6:10c/John 12:40a; (7) the reduction of the genitive phrase 'of this people' to the personal pronoun 'their' (αὐτῶν) for Isaiah 6:10a/John 12:40b; (8) the placement of that personal pronoun αὐτῶν before rather than after the noun it modifies for Isaiah 6:10a/John 12:40b (as is the case with Isaiah 6:10c/John 12:40a); (9) the lack of pronominal modifiers attending 'eyes' and 'heart' for Isaiah 6:10df/John 12:40cd; (10) the dative 'with the heart' (τῇ καρδίᾳ) instead of the

---

279. A number of New Testament manuscripts read some form of ἐπιστρέφειν instead of στρέφειν; and inasmuch as they coincide with readings in LXX manuscripts, it is suspected that they are scribal adaptations to those readings: (a) the aorist subjunctive ἐπιστρέψωσιν ('and they turn') for John (K L W Θ 1424) relative to the primary LXX reading (see Table 12); (b) the future indicative ἐπιστρέψουσιν ('and they [will] turn') for John (family[13]) relative to LXX Sinaiticus, Venetus and 26 62 90 93 147 456; and (c) aorist passive subjunctive ἐπιστραφῶσιν ('and they turn') for John (A D [second corrector] Γ Δ family[1] 565 700 892 1241 Sinai lectionary 844 and the majority of manuscripts) relative to LXX 301 534. On these readings as adaptations, see Menken, "'He Has Blinded Their Eyes ... '" (John 12:40)', 118n73.

nominative '(and) the heart' (וּלְבָבוֹ) for Isaiah 6:10f/John 12:40d, if one follows the reading of most MT manuscripts; (11) the first-person singular active 'and I heal' (καὶ ἰάσομαι) for the third-person singular active 'and he heal' (וְרָפָא) for Isaiah 6:10g/John 12:40e; and (12) the plural personal pronouns αὐτῶν/αὐτούς at John 12:40abe for the singular 'of this people' at Isaiah 6:10a and the singular pronouns וְעֵינָיו/לוֹ at Isaiah 6:10cg, albeit all plausibly to be translated as 'them'.

(2) Hypotheses

(a) On the anomalies

As the question of version for this quotation is interwoven with that of its anomalies, so also the hypotheses for each: a theory to address one ineluctably addresses the other. For both matters there is agreement on several items. Regarding the version, all concur that the last three words, καὶ ἰάσομαι αὐτούς, are drawn from the LXX. And with respect to the anomalies, all similarly agree that the omission of the lines treating 'ears' and 'hearing' (Isaiah 6:10be), as well as the inversion of Isaiah 6:10ac, is theologically keyed to the commentary at John 12:37 – that, 'though (Jesus) had done so many signs before (the Jews), they were not believing in him'. This comment casts 'unbelief' as a response to signs which are to be seen (rather than words which are to be heard); and, on the inference that 'belief' is synonymous to 'understanding' with the 'heart' – that is, that ἡ καρδία is 'the seat of faith'[280] – these two anomalies are seen as serving such a soteriology by (a) removing the role of 'hearing' from the process and (b) creating a sequence which accentuates the prerequisite of 'seeing' for *semeia*-faith – 'eyes'/'heart'/'eyes'/'heart'.[281]

Beyond these items, however, discussion is divided – on the version, on the anomalies and on the subjects of the verbs 'he has blinded', 'he hardened' and 'lest ... I heal them' (or, as John Painter has labelled them, 'the cause of obduracy' and 'the agent of healing').[282] Views on the version are of three kinds: those that trace the entire quotation to the LXX[283]; those that to some degree trace all but the last three words to the HB[284]; and those that, despite premises supporting

---

280. Menken, '"He Has Blinded Their Eyes ... "' (John 12:40)', 107–08 (quotation p. 107), citing John 14:1, 27, 29.

281. See, for instance, Boismard and Lamouille, *L'Évangile de Jean*, 328–29. Menken associates the inversion of these cola with *miqra mesuras*, the thirty-first *middah* of R. Eliezer b. Jose ha-Gelili; '"He Has Blinded Their Eyes ... "' (John 12:40)', 105n25; cf. Strack and Stemberger, *Introduction to the Talmud and Midrash*, 30.

282. 'The Quotation of Scripture and Unbelief in John 12.36b-43', in *The Gospels and the Scriptures of Israel*, ed. Craig A. Evans and W. Richard Stegner, JSNTSup 104/SSEJC 3 (Sheffield: Sheffield Academic Press, 1994), 435.

283. Franke, *Das alte Testament bei Johannes*, 283–84; Schuchard, *Scripture within Scripture*, 97, 100–06, 106n69.

284. Reim, *Jochanan*, 38; Menken, '"He Has Blinded Their Eyes ... "' (John 12:40)', 118–19; and cf. Lindars, *Gospel of John*, 438. Reim (more particularly) assigns the modifications to oral tradition (pp. 38–39).

2. Isa 53:1 and Isa 6:10, An Obstruction to Faith

either of the first two options, remain agnostic about the source.[285] Theories on the anomalies appeal to four factors: textual tradition, style, the assimilation of other passages and theological *Tendenz*. And proposals on the verb subjects identify the first-person speaker as either Jesus or God and the third-person actor as either Jesus, God, 'the ruler of this world', signs or Jesus's message.

To furnish an apt framework on which to evaluate this discussion, the viewpoints on version and anomalies will be organized around the latter; and, as such, they will first be rehearsed seriatim (as they unfold from John 12:40a-e), then followed by an account of the sundry referents proposed for 'the cause of obduracy' and 'the agent of healing'.

[1] 'He/It has blinded' and 'hardened' (John 12:40ab)

[a] Verb tenses

First, the verbs τετύφλωκεν and ἐπώρωσεν at John 12:40ab. The issues here concern (a) their tense, as preterites, and (b) the evangelist's choice to use these terms rather than those from (or more apt to) their biblical counterparts. On (a) tense, two explanations envision a LXX *Vorlage*. One, by Franke, suggests on two counts that these preterites lie closer to that version than to the HB: that, like the LXX, they are descriptive rather than directive; and that assuming the LXX verbs 'they shut' (ἐκάμμυσαν) and 'grew fat' (ἐπαχύνθη) imply a *passivum divinum*, these verbs at John 12:40ab likewise speak of God's direct action upon the people (rather than his mediated action through Isaiah).[286] A second explanation, offered by Craig Evans, proposes an assimilation of LXX Isaiah 29:10 (presumably into LXX Isaiah 6:10). That verse attests neither τυφλοῦν nor πωροῦν. It does, however, juxtapose the future tense of καμμύειν (employed in LXX Isaiah 6:10) with the perfect tense of ποτίζειν; and this, suggests Evans, may account for the perfect tense τετύφλωκεν at John 12:40a[287]:

Because the Lord has quenched you (πεπότικεν ὑμᾶς) with a spirit of slumber; and he will shut the eyes (καμμύσει τοὺς ὀφθαλμούς) of them, their prophets and their rulers – the ones who see the hidden matters.

---

285. So, it seems, John O'Rourke, 'John's Fulfillment Texts', *ScEccl* 19 (1967): 435–36; and Craig A. Evans, 'The Function of Isaiah 6:9-10 in Mark and John', *NovT* 24 (1982): 134–35. An exception is the proposal by Barrett and Evans that John 12:40/Isa 6:10 was drawn from *Targum Jonathan*; Barrett, 'The Old Testament in the Fourth Gospel', 167n2; Evans, op. cit., 134n48.

286. Franke, *Das alte Testament bei Johannes*, 284; cf. Schnackenburg, *Gospel according to St John*, 2:416. It is similarly argued by Painter that καὶ ἰάσομαι αὐτούς ('and I heal them') at LXX Isa 6:10g is a correct rendering of ורפא לו at HB Isa 6:10g, which he takes as a divine passive ('and it be healed to them'); 'The Quotation of Scripture and Unbelief in John 12.36b-43', 447.

287. 'The Function of Isaiah 6:9-10 in Mark and John', 134–35.

More influential has been the proposal assuming a Hebrew *Vorlage* by Charles F. Burney, namely, that in translating an unpointed Hebrew text, the evangelist (or a tradent before him) read the verbs as either infinitive absolutes or perfects rather than imperatives: הַשְׁמֵן (as 'making fat') or הִשְׁמִין ('he has made fat') for הַשְׁמֵן ('make fat'); הָשֵׁעַ ('smearing over') or הָשֵׁעַ – possibly הֵשַׁע – ('he has smeared over') for הָשַׁע ('smear over').[288] Tied to this hypothesis is the observation made by Freed and Günter Reim that to make such an alteration from the HB, the evangelist would have theologically believed that the commission given to Isaiah had now been accomplished in the ministry of Jesus.[289]

[b] Word choice

Regarding (b) the choice of the verbs τυφλοῦν and πωροῦν/πηροῦν, the first, τυφλοῦν, has been ascribed to three factors, none of them exclusive of the others. One would have been a secondary consideration – aesthetics, namely, that the τ, φ and λ of the verb assonate well with ὀφθαλμός at John 12:40.[290] More decisive would have been the second and third, the evangelist's theology and his assimilation of other texts. For the evangelist's theology, τετύφλωκεν is thought to be carrying over the metaphor used for Jesus's eschatological judgement in the story of his healing the man born blind at John 9. As in the quotation, the ideas of 'blindness' and 'healing' in that chapter are juxtaposed – there using the cognate τυφλός.[291] Further, at John 9:39, as at John 12:40/Isaiah 6:10, the language of 'sight' and 'blindness' becomes metaphorical for the salvation and judgement effected during Jesus's public ministry; and that language itself (it is alleged) is traceable to one, perhaps two, LXX passages with lexical affinities to LXX Isaiah 6:10 – LXX Isaiah 6:9, just prior to LXX Isaiah 6:10, and LXX Isaiah 29:18 (Table 13).[292]

---

288. *Aramaic Origin of the Fourth Gospel*, 120–21; followed by Reim, *Jochanan*, 38; Freed, *Old Testament Quotations in the Gospel of John*, 85, 87; Menken, '"He Has Blinded Their Eyes ... " (John 12:40)', 110.

Burney's explanation has been challenged by Schuchard, who asks why the evangelist would translate the first verb as a perfect (τετύφλωκεν) and the second as an aorist (ἐπώρωσεν) if read both in the Hebrew as perfects, particularly given the parallelism in which they are set; *Scripture within Scripture*, 96 – somewhat anticipating Schuchard is O'Rourke, 'Explicit Old Testament Citations in the Gospels', 435–36. Menken has countered that the evangelist (or a putative Greek source used by him) constructs similar sequences of verbs in different tenses elsewhere and would simply have done the same in rendering HB Isa 6:10ac; Menken, '"He Has Blinded Their Eyes ... " (John 12:40)', 110, citing John 3:32; 6:31-32; 8:38, 42; 12:46-47; 14:25-26; 17:2; 18:20-21.

289. Freed, *Old Testament Quotations in the Gospel of John*, 87; Reim, *Jochanan*, 39.

290. Menken, '"He Has Blinded Their Eyes ... " (John 12:40)', 111–12, 112n53, citing further examples of assonance at John 9:32; 10:21; 11:37.

291. John 9:1-2, 13, 17-20, 24-25, 32, 39-41.

292. Evans, 'The Function of Isaiah 6:9-10 in Mark and John', 136; Menken, '"He Has Blinded Their Eyes ... " (John 12:40)', 111-12.

Table 13 LXX allusions in John 9:39

LXX Isaiah 6:9	LXX Isaiah 29:18	John 9:39
And he (the Lord) said, 'Go and say to this people, "You will hear by listening, but by no means understand; and you will see by observing (βλέποντες βλέψετε) but by no means perceive (οὐ μὴ ἴδητε)"'.	And on that day the deaf will hear words of a book; and the eyes of the blind (οἱ … ὀφθαλμοὶ τυφλῶν), in the darkness and mist, will see (βλέψονται).	And Jesus said, 'For judgment I came into this world, that those who do not see (οἱ μὴ βλέποντες) may see (βλέπωσιν) and those who see (οἱ βλέποντες) may become blind (τυφλοί)'.

As for the assimilation of outside texts, it has been suggested that τετύφλωκεν reflects a merger of LXX Isaiah 6:(9-)10 with one or more of several LXX passages which similarly attest τυφλοῦν or a cognate, sometimes alongside other terms found in that verse (Table 14).[293]

Table 14 LXX texts and τυφλοῦν at John 12:40a

John 12:40
He has blinded (τετύφλωκεν) their eyes (τοὺς ὀφθαλμούς) and hardened their heart, lest they perceive (ἴδωσιν) with the eyes (τοῖς ὀφθαλμοῖς) and discern with the heart, and turn, and I heal them.
LXX Isaiah 6:9-10
And he (the Lord) said, 'Go and say to this people, "You will hear by listening (ἀκοῇ ἀκούσετε), but by no means understand; and you will see by observing (βλέποντες βλέψετε) but by no means perceive (οὐ μὴ ἴδητε)". For the heart of this people grew fat, and with their ears (τοῖς ὠσίν) they heard (ἤκουσαν) in disgust, and their eyes (τοὺς ὀφθαλμούς) they shut; lest they perceive with the eyes (ἴδωσι τοῖς ὀφθαλμοῖς), and with the ears hear (τοῖς ὠσὶν ἀκούσωσι), and with the heart understand, and turn and I heal them'.

(Continued)

293. Freed, *Old Testament Quotations in the Gospel of John*, 87–88; Evans, 'The Function of Isaiah 6:9-10 in Mark and John', 134–35, 138; Craig A. Evans, *To See and Not Perceive: Isaiah 6.9-10 in Early Jewish and Christian Interpretation*, JSOTSup 64 (Sheffield: Sheffield Academic, 1989), 131–32; Roman Kühschelm, *Verstockung, Gericht und Heil: Exegetische und bibeltheologische Untersuchung zum sogenannten 'Dualismus' und 'Determinismus' in Joh 12, 35-50*, BBB 76/Athenäum Monographien: Theologie (Frankfurt am Main: Anton Hain, 1990), 129; Menken, '"He Has Blinded Their Eyes … " (John 12:40)', 111-12; cf. Schuchard, *Scripture within Scripture*, 102–03, 103n51.

LXX Job 29:1-3, 15	LXX Wisdom of Solomon 2:21
And having referred still to the exordium, Job said, 'Who would place me in a month of earlier days, over which God kept me; as when his lamp used to shine above my head, when by his light I went forth amid darkness … I was the eye of the blind (ὀφθαλμὸς … τυφλῶν), the foot of the lame.'	These things, they (the ungodly) reckoned but were misled, for their wickedness blinded (ἀπετύφλωσεν) them.
LXX Isaiah 42:18-20	**LXX Isaiah 43:8**
You deaf, hear (ἀκούσατε); and blind (οἱ τυφλοί), look up, so as to perceive (ἀναβλέψατε ἰδεῖν)! And who is blind (τυφλός), other than my children? And deaf, other than those who lord over them? Indeed, the servants of God's slaves have been blinded (ἐτυφλώθησαν). You perceived (εἴδετε) more frequently, but did not observe; your ears (τὰ ὦτα) were opened, but you did not hear (οὐκ ἠκούσατε).²⁹⁴	And I led out a blind (τυφλόν) people; and their eyes (ὀφθαλμοί) are likewise blind (τυφλοί); and, having ears (τὰ ὦτα), they are deaf!
LXX Isaiah 56:9-10	
All you wild animals of the fields, come; eat, all you wild animals of the wood. Perceive (ἴδετε) that all have been made blind (ἐκτετύφλωνται); they have not learned to think. All are speechless dogs; they will not be able to howl, dreaming in bed, loving to sleep.	

On πωροῦν or πηροῦν, however close their semantic ranges,²⁹⁵ it should first be noted that some read the latter as original: 'he has *maimed* (ἐπήρωσεν) their heart.'²⁹⁶ On that assumption the verb choice has been explained as a translation from the HB, in either of two ways: a direct rendering of השמ ('to make desolate')

294. This passage is particularly favoured by Schuchard on the grounds that the full chapter of Isaiah 42 echos themes common to the Fourth Gospel: that God's chosen servant bears the Spirit and brings judgement (Isa 42:1, 3); that this servant is a light to the Gentiles, who opens their eyes and is an object of their trust (Isa 42:4, 6-7); that God promises to give his glory (Isa 42:8), his fulfilment (Isa 42:9) and his peace (Isa 42:13); and that God will turn darkness to light for the blind (Isa 42:16); *Scripture within Scripture*, 103n50.

295. Brown, for instance, suggests their near synonymity; *Gospel according to John*, 1:483-84.

296. A case for this verb has particularly been made by Menken: against the UBSGNT editorial committee's judgement that ἐπήρωσεν reflects a scribal attempt to furnish a more fitting verb for τὴν καρδίαν (see note 278), Menken appeals to the early attestation of the reading (P⁶⁶,⁷⁵) and argues that the widespread metaphorical use of ἐπώρωσεν in early Christian literature (often with καρδία) renders the movement more likely to go the other way, that is, that a scribe altered πηροῦν to πωροῦν; '"He Has Blinded Their Eyes … " (John 12:40)', 103-04, 104n24, citing Mark 3:5; 6:52; 8:17; Rom 11:7, 25; 2 Cor 3:14; Eph 4:18;

in the textual tradition represented by 1QIsaiah[a297] or a semantic parallel to (the evangelist's choice of) τετύφλωκεν at John 12:40a, both verbs signalling a stop to the operations in question – the 'eyes' (τυφλοῦν) and the 'heart' (πηροῦν).[298]

As for πωροῦν, it is explained along two lines. One, offered by Freed and Schuchard, is that it reflects a conflation with LXX Job 17:7: 'For my eyes have been hardened (πεπώρωνται ... οἱ ὀφθαλμοί μου) from anger; I am greatly hemmed in by all.'[299] The other is that, given the wide use of πωροῦν and its noun form πώρωσις ('hardening') with καρδία in cognate Christian literature, it reflects an assimilation of an early Christian formulation – if not from those writings themselves, then (it is thought) from *testimonia* (Table 15).[300]

Table 15 Early Christian texts and πωροῦν at John 12:40b

Mark 3:5	Mark 6:51-52
And looking around at them with anger, grieved at the hardening of their heart (ἐπὶ τῇ πωρώσει τῆς καρδίας αὐτῶν), (Jesus) said to the man, 'Stretch out your hand' ...	And (Jesus) climbed up to them in the boat and the wind dropped. And they were entirely astonished in themselves, for they did not understand (οὐ ... συνῆκαν) about the loaves, but their heart was hardened (αὐτῶν ἡ καρδία πεπωρωμένη).
Mark 8:17	**Romans 11:7**
And apprehending, Jesus said to them, 'Why are you discussing that you have no bread? Do you not yet discern (νοεῖτε) or understand (συνίετε)? Is your heart hardened (πεπωρωμένην ... τὴν καρδίαν ὑμῶν)'?	What then? That which Israel seeks it did not attain. The elect attained, but the rest were hardened (ἐπωρώθησαν) ...

Herm. *Mand.* 4.2.30:1; 12.4.47:4; Theophilus *Autol.* 2.35. Schuchard, for his part, allows for ἐπήρωσεν to be original, but faults Menken's premises for assuming an intentional (rather than inadvertent) scribal alteration, citing the Sinaiticus reading ἐπήρωσεν for ἐπλήρωσεν at Acts 5:3; *Scripture within Scripture*, 93n11; cf. Metzger, *Textual Commentary on the Greek New Testament* (2nd ed.), 285; and somewhat anticipating the UBSGNT committee, Barrett, *Gospel according to St. John*, 432.

297. Considered by Jan de Waard, *A Comparative Study of the Old Testament in the Dead Sea Scrolls and in the New Testament*, STDJ 4 (Leiden: E.J. Brill, 1965), 7-8.

298. Menken, '"He Has Blinded Their Eyes ... " (John 12:40)', 112-13. Schuchard entertains (though does not endorse) πηροῦν as a merger of LXX Isa 6:10 with LXX Job 17:7, reading the variant πεπήρωνται (Sinaiticus [added] and Alexandrinus, as well as 543 575 620 637 644 [corrected]) for πεπώρωνται—'For my eyes have become maimed (πεπήρωνται) from anger...'; *Scripture within Scripture*, 103n54.

299. Freed, *Old Testament Quotations in the Gospel of John*, 87-88; Schuchard, *Scripture within Scripture*, 103-04.

300. Franke, *Das alte Testament bei Johannes*, 284; Evans, 'The Function of Isaiah 6:9-10 in Mark and John', 135; Schuchard, *Scripture within Scripture*, 103-04, 103n52.

Romans 11:25	2 Corinthians 3:14
For I do not wish you to be unaware, brothers, of this mystery, lest you be wise among yourselves, that a hardening in part (πώρωσις ἀπὸ μέρους) has happened to Israel until the fullness of the Gentiles arrives.	But their minds were hardened (ἐπωρώθη); for to this very day the same veil remains upon the reading of the old covenant, not being lifted because (only) in Christ is it brought to naught.
Ephesians 4:17-18	**Hermas, *Mandate* 4.2.30:1**[301]
Therefore this I say and testify in the Lord, that you no longer walk as the Gentiles walk, in the futility of their mind – being darkened in thought, alienated from the life of God because of the ignorance that is in them, because of the hardness of their heart (τὴν πώρωσιν τῆς καρδίας αὐτῶν).	I asked him again, saying, 'Since the Lord deemed me worthy that you dwell with me always, allow me still a few words, since I understand nothing and my heart has been hardened (ἡ καρδία μου πεπώρωται) from my prior deeds.'
Hermas, *Mandate* 12.4.47:4	
But for those who have the Lord on the lips, yet whose heart has been hardened (τὴν δὲ καρδίαν αὐτῶν πεπωρωμένην) and who are far from the Lord, these commandments are harsh and arduous.	

[2] 'Their eyes', 'their heart' (John 12:40ab)
The questions here concern the two genitive personal pronouns αὐτῶν at John 12:40ab: specifically, (a) the use of the second of these (at John 12:40b) as a substitute for 'of this people' in both HB and LXX Isaiah 6:10a; (b) the placement of both pronouns before (rather than after) the substantives they modify at John 12:40ab, again as otherwise occurs in HB and LXX Isaiah 6:10ac; and (c) the absence of such genitive pronouns modifying the substantives in John 12:40cd. The first of these – (a) the reading 'their heart' for 'the heart of this people' – has been attributed to the evangelist's soteriological predilection to employ ὁ λαός for affirmative rather than negative assessments. It is proposed that while the evangelist uses specific social labels to denounce unbelief – Pharisees, for instance, or chief priests[302] – he employs the term 'people' only to forecast salvation.[303] Since at John 12:40 he is doing the former (denouncing unbelief), he removed that term, it is believed, by abbreviating the HB/LXX reading to αὐτῶν.[304]

---

301. Text: Michael W. Holmes, ed. and trans., *The Apostolic Fathers: Greek Texts and English Translations*, 3rd ed. (Grand Rapids, MI: Baker Academic, 2007).
302. John 9 (*passim*); 12:42.
303. John 11:50; 18:14.
304. Rudolf Schnackenburg, 'Joh 12,39-41. Zur christologischen Schriftauslegung des vierten Evangelisten', in *Ergänzende Auslegungen und Exkurse*, 147–48; first publ. in *Neues Testament und Geschichte: Historisches Geschehen und Deutung im Neuen Testament: Oscar Cullmann zum 70. Geburtstag*, ed. Heinrich Baltensweiler and Bo Reicke (Zürich: Theologischer Verlag/Tübingen: Mohr, 1972); followed by Menken, '"He Has Blinded Their Eyes ... " (John 12:40)', 114; and Schuchard, *Scripture within Scripture*, 104.

As for (b), the placement of the possessive pronouns before their substantives at John 12:40ab, this has been traced to the evangelist's style. On the grounds of several grammatical studies, it is alleged that John tends to make such inversions of expected word order when the genitives of personal pronouns are used attributively: Menken counts this occurring fifty-six out of three hundred and twelve times in the Fourth Gospel – ten out of twelve times with the word ὀφθαλμός; five out of five with the word καρδία.[305] And with regard to (c), the absence of such pronouns at John 12:40cd, it has been noticed by Schuchard that, preceded as it is by the presence of personal pronouns at John 12:40ab, this absence creates a sequence in John 12:40a-d that matches the respective LXX cola; that is, allowing for the contraction of τοῦ λαοῦ τούτου at LXX Isaiah 6:10a into αὐτῶν at John 12:40b, the two cola at LXX Isaiah 6:10ac (and their counterparts at John 12:40ab) carry genitive modifiers to 'heart' and 'eyes', while the two cola at LXX Isaiah 6:10df (and their counterparts at John 12:40cd) do not (Table 16).[306]

Table 16 Personal pronouns in LXX Isaiah 6:10 and John 12:40

LXX Isaiah 6:10	John 12:40
ἐπαχύνθη γὰρ ἡ καρδία τοῦ λαοῦ τούτου …	τετύφλωκεν αὐτῶν τοὺς ὀφθαλμοὺς
καὶ τοὺς ὀφθαλμοὺς αὐτῶν ἐκάμμυσαν,	καὶ ἐπώρωσεν αὐτῶν τὴν καρδίαν,
μήποτε ἴδωσι τοῖς ὀφθαλμοῖς …	ἵνα μὴ ἴδωσιν τοῖς ὀφθαλμοῖς
καὶ τῇ καρδίᾳ συνῶσι …	καὶ νοήσωσιν τῇ καρδίᾳ …
For the heart of this people grew fat …	He has blinded their eyes,
and their eyes they shut;	and hardened their heart,
lest they perceive with the eyes …	lest they perceive with the eyes,
and with the heart understand …	and discern with the heart …

Menken has countered that the absence of genitive pronouns at John 12:40cd is rather due to the evangelist's preference for elision. The Fourth Gospel, he notes, is replete with instances in which the evangelist has omitted possessive personal pronouns that would otherwise be expected.[307] So also here: the evangelist is translating from the HB, Menken argues, not adjusting the LXX; and, in accord with his own style, he includes the genitive personal pronouns for HB Isaiah 6:10ac but leaves them out for HB Isaiah 6:10df.[308]

305. Menken, "'He Has Blinded Their Eyes … '" (John 12:40), 113–14; following Edwin A. Abbott, *Johannine Grammar* (London: Adam and Charles Black, 1906), 414–25; Eduard Schweizer, *Ego eimi … : Die religionsgeschichtliche Herkunft und theologische Bedeutung der johanneischen Bildreden, zugleich ein Beitrag zur Quellenfrage des vierten Evangeliums*, FRLANT 56/N.F. 38 (Göttingen: Vandenhoeck & Ruprecht, 1939), 99; and Eugen Ruckstuhl, *Die literarische Einheit des Johannesevangeliums: Der gegenwärtige Stand der einschlägigen Forschungen*, NTOA 5 (Freiburg, Schweiz: Universitätsverlag/Göttingen: Vandenhoeck & Ruprecht, 1987), 223–24. Menken, himself, is followed by Schuchard, *Scripture within Scripture*, 104.

306. Schuchard, *Scripture within Scripture*, 97.

307. John 6:5; 7:30, 44; 11:41, 44; 13:10; 19:30; 20:20.

308. Menken, "'He Has Blinded Their Eyes … '" (John 12:40), 115, 115n63.

[3] 'Lest ... they discern with the heart and turn' (John 12:40c-e)
Finally, hypotheses on John 12:40c-e concern four components: (a) the negative conjunction ἵνα μή, (b) the verb νοεῖν, (c) the dative τῇ καρδίᾳ and (d) the verb στρέφειν. The conjunction ἵνα μή ('lest') is understood in either of two scenarios: as an alteration of LXX μήποτε or as a translation of HB פן. It has, in part, been assigned to the evangelist's style, inasmuch as it occurs frequently in the gospel.[309] But it has also been ascribed by Menken to the evangelist's theological concern. He observes that where μήποτε can serve as a negative conjunction ('lest'), an interrogative particle ('whether maybe') or an adverb ('perhaps'), ἵνα μή can only serve as the first of these – that is, to articulate the rationale of an action; and so, he argues, it was more apt than μήποτε to convey the evangelist's belief that the 'blinding' and 'hardening' described in this quotation were done with the express purpose of obstructing the capacity to believe.[310]

Regarding (b) νοεῖν ('to discern'), akin to some of the explanations for τυφλοῦν and πωροῦν, it has been accounted for as reflecting a merger between Isaiah 6:10 (also embracing Isaiah 6:9) and one or more other passages that share its vocabulary and themes. An array of *loci* have been suggested from the LXX – some which, like John 12:40d, pair νοεῖν with ἡ καρδία (Table 17).[311]

Table 17 LXX texts and νοεῖν at John 12:40d

John 12:40
He has blinded their eyes (τοὺς ὀφθαλμοὺς) and hardened their heart (τὴν καρδίαν), lest they perceive with the eyes (τοῖς ὀφθαλμοῖς) and discern with the heart (νοήσωσιν τῇ καρδίᾳ), and turn (στραφῶσιν), and I heal them.
LXX Isaiah 6:9-10
And he (the Lord) said, 'Go and say to this people, "You will hear by listening, but by no means understand; and you will see by observing (βλέποντες βλέψετε), but by no means perceive". For the heart (ἡ καρδία) of this people grew fat, and with their ears they heard in disgust, and their eyes (τοὺς ὀφθαλμοὺς αὐτῶν) they shut; lest they perceive with the eyes (τοῖς ὀφθαλμοῖς), and with the ears hear, and with the heart (τῇ καρδίᾳ) understand, and turn (ἐπιστρέψωσι) and I heal them'.

309. Gilbert van Belle and Menken count it occurring some eighteen-to-nineteen times in John; van Belle, *Les parenthèses dans l'Évangile de Jean: Aperçu historique et classification. Texte grec de Jean*, SNTA 11 (Leuven: Leuven University Press, 1985), 139; cf. Menken, "'He Has Blinded Their Eyes ... ' (John 12:40)", 116; and see Schuchard, *Scripture within Scripture*, 104–05, 105n61.
310. Menken, "'He Has Blinded Their Eyes ... ' (John 12:40)", 116; following Schnackenburg, *Gospel according to St John*, 2:415, 531n14.
311. See the lists in Schuchard, *Scripture within Scripture*, 105, 105nn65-66; and Menken, "'He Has Blinded Their Eyes ... ' (John 12:40)", 117–18.

1 Kingdoms 4:20	LXX Proverbs 16:23
And at her moment (of birth) she (Eli's daughter-in-law) was dying; and the women attending her said to her, 'Fear not, for you have borne a son.' But she did not answer; and her heart did not discern (οὐκ ἐνόησεν ἡ καρδία αὐτῆς).	The heart (καρδία) of the wise will discern (νοήσει) the (words) from his own mouth; and on the lips he will carry prudence.
LXX Job 33:23	**LXX Isaiah 32:6**
If there be a thousand lethal angels, no one of them will hurt him, if he discerns with the heart to turn (ἐὰν νοήσῃ τῇ καρδίᾳ ἐπιστραφῆναι) to the Lord, (if he) declares to a person reproof against himself and brings his naïveté into relief ...	For the stupid will speak stupid things, and his heart will discern (ἡ καρδία αὐτοῦ ... νοήσει) idle things, to accomplish lawlessness and speak error toward the Lord – to scatter souls that are famished and to render destitute souls that are thirsty.
LXX Isaiah 44:18	**LXX Isaiah 47:7**
They have not learned to think, because they were obstructed from seeing with their eyes (τοῦ βλέπειν τοῖς ὀφθαλμοῖς αὐτῶν) and discerning with their heart (τοῦ νοῆσαι τῇ καρδίᾳ αὐτῶν).	And you (Babylon) said, 'I shall be ruler forever.' You did not discern (οὐκ ἐνόησας) these things in your heart (ἐν τῇ καρδίᾳ σου); nor did you remember the last things.

Along this line (of a conflated text), pointed arguments have particularly been made for Isaiah 44:18 – from the LXX by Schuchard; and from the HB by Menken (Table 18).[312]

Table 18 HB/LXX Isaiah 44:18 and νοεῖν at John 12:40d

John 12:40	
He has blinded their eyes (τοὺς ὀφθαλμούς) and hardened their heart (τὴν καρδίαν), lest they perceive with the eyes (τοῖς ὀφθαλμοῖς) and discern with the heart (νοήσωσιν τῇ καρδίᾳ), and turn, and I heal them.	
HB Isaiah 6:9-10	**LXX Isaiah 6:9-10**
And he said, 'Go, and you shall say to this people, "Keep hearing, but do not understand (ואל־תבינו); Keep seeing (וראו ראו), but do not perceive (ואל־תדעו)". Make the heart (לב) of this people fat, and render their ears heavy, and smear over their eyes (ועיניו), lest they see with their eyes (פן־יראה בעיניו), and with their ears hear, and their heart understand (ולבבו יבין), and they turn back and he heal them'.	And he (the Lord) said, 'Go and say to this people, "You will hear by listening, but by no means understand; and you will see by observing (βλέποντες βλέψετε), but by no means perceive". For the heart (ἡ καρδία) of this people grew fat, and with their ears they heard in disgust, and their eyes (τοὺς ὀφθαλμοὺς αὐτῶν) they shut; lest they perceive with the eyes (τοῖς ὀφθαλμοῖς), and with the ears hear, and with the heart (τῇ καρδίᾳ) understand, and turn and I heal them'.

312. Schuchard, *Scripture within Scripture*, 105; Menken, "'He Has Blinded Their Eyes ...' (John 12:40)", 117–18.

HB Isaiah 44:18	LXX Isaiah 44:18
They do not perceive (לא ידעו), nor do they understand (ולא יבינו); For their eyes are blocked from seeing (מראות עיניהם); and their hearts from considering (מהשכיל לבתם).	They have not learned to think, because they were obstructed from seeing with their eyes (τοῦ βλέπειν τοῖς ὀφθαλμοῖς αὐτῶν) and discerning with their heart (τοῦ νοῆσαι τῇ καρδίᾳ αὐτῶν).

Both Schuchard and Menken note the similarities of this passage to Isaiah 6:9-10 in vocabulary and sentiment. And Schuchard adds that themes in the rest of LXX Isaiah 44 appear elsewhere in the Fourth Gospel: that the Lord (as with Jesus in the Fourth Gospel) is God, creator, king of Israel, source of living water, sender of the Spirit and the one who calls witnesses to testify; and that, despite the blindness of the people, this Lord will come as redeemer to blot out sin as darkness, give glory and lay the foundation for a temple.[313] The debate over the version rather turns on the HB counterpart to the LXX gloss νοεῖν. Since it is (the hiphil of) לשכל rather than לבין (the verb in HB Isaiah 6:10), Schuchard sees LXX Isaiah 44:18 as the *Vorlage* assimilated into John 12:40.[314] But since that verb was translated by the LXX with νοεῖν, Menken sees a precedent set for the fourth evangelist to follow suit and argues, instead, that the evangelist conflated HB מהשכיל into Isaiah 6:10 and, following the lead of the LXX, translated it as νοήσωσιν.[315]

The dative (c) τῇ καρδίᾳ ('with the heart'), which follows νοήσωσιν, aligns with the LXX and has been explained as reflecting it. It also, however, corresponds to [ו]בלבבו in 1QIsaiah[a] and 4QIsaiah[f], as well as a number of MT manuscripts and ובליבהון in *Targum Jonathan*; and, as such, has been identified by Menken as a translation from a Hebrew text.[316] And as for (d) στρέφειν ('to turn'), it has been explained along two lines. One, once again, is as a conflation of LXX Isaiah 6:10 with one or more other texts – in this case, passages which couple στρέφειν ('to turn') with ἰᾶσθαι ('to heal')[317]:

> Wherever he should turn (στραφῇ), the ungodly vanishes;
> but the households of the righteous stand fast.
> The mouth of the quick-witted is lauded by a man;
> but the slow of heart is scorned ...
> There are those who, while speaking, hurt with a dagger;
> but the tongues of the wise heal (ἰῶνται).[318]

313. Cited by Schuchard are all or portions of LXX Isa 44:2-3, 6, 8, 22-24, 28, each paired to a theme; *Scripture within Scripture*, 77–78, 78n36, 105n64.

314. *Scripture within Scripture*, 105n65.

315. "'He Has Blinded Their Eyes ... ' (John 12:40)", 117–18.

316. Menken, "'He Has Blinded Their Eyes ... ' (John 12:40)", 116–17. The correspondence with 1QIsa[a] had been noticed (though not developed) by O'Rourke, 'Explicit Old Testament Citations in the Gospels', 436.

317. Noted, but not advocated, by Schuchard, *Scripture within Scripture*, 105n68.

318. LXX Prov 12:7-8, 18.

As a door turns (στρέφεται) on its pivot,
so is a procrastinator on his bed ...
As those who being healed (οἱ ἰώμενοι) propose theories to people,
and as the one who first comes upon the theory will stumble,
so are all who ambush their own friends,
and when they are found out, they say, 'I acted jesting'.[319]

The other line of explanation is the evangelist's preference for *verba simplicia*, particularly in aorist passives[320] – and this by two scenarios: either his alteration of the LXX compound ἐπιστρέψωσι[321] or his preferred gloss for HB ושׁב.[322]

(b) On the referents

[1] 'The agent of healing'

The first-person speaker in the quotation has been entertained as God (with Jesus as the third-person actor).[323] It is more broadly thought, however, to be Jesus, encountered by Isaiah in pre-incarnate form.[324] This primarily rests on an inference about the Johannine sense of divine glory. At John 12:41 Isaiah is said to have uttered Isaiah 6:10 in the context of seeing the 'glory' of God (not God himself); and since elsewhere in Johannine literature Jesus is cast as the one who elucidates this (otherwise unseen) God,[325] it is surmised that the 'glory' in question at John 12:41 was, in fact, Jesus and that he is the one speaking at John 12:40e.[326]

Also supporting this reading have been two further premises. One is grammatical: that the referent to the personal pronouns depicting the person seen by Isaiah at John 12:41 is one and the same with the referent to the personal pronoun at John 12:42, whose antecedent is clearly Jesus.

---

319. LXX Prov 26:14, 18-19.
320. John 1:38; 20:14-16; so, Schnackenburg, *Gospel according to St John*, 2:415.
321. Schuchard, *Scripture within Scripture*, 105-06 (inferred from his broader discussion).
322. Menken, '"He Has Blinded Their Eyes ... "' (John 12:40)', 118.
323. Such a reading may follow from (or be reflected in) part of the textual tradition for John 12:41, wherein Isaiah is more specifically depicted as seeing 'the glory of (his) God' (τὴν δόξαν τοῦ θεοῦ [αὐτοῦ]): in D Θ family[13] 1; and see Painter, 'The Quotation of Scripture and Unbelief in John 12.36b-43', 435–37.
324. Consensus on this view was observed by Franklin W. Young, 'A Study of the Relation of Isaiah to the Fourth Gospel', *ZNW* 46 (1955): 215–16. As Painter notes, the term 'pre-existent' is somewhat misleading when applied to the man 'Jesus'; 'The Quotation of Scripture and Unbelief in John 12.36b-43', 436n1. More apt, perhaps, is 'pre-incarnate', that is, before 'the Word became flesh'.
325. John 1:18; 5:37; 6:46.
326. See Schnackenburg, *Gospel according to St John*, 2:416–17; Schuchard, *Scripture within Scripture*, 98n30.

These things Isaiah said, because he saw his glory (τὴν δόξαν αὐτοῦ) and spoke about him (περὶ αὐτοῦ). Nevertheless, however, many of the rulers believed in him (ἐπίστευσαν εἰς αὐτόν); but because of the Pharisees, they were not confessing, lest they be put out of the synagogue.[327]

The second premise is thematic: the correspondence between the 'healing' envisioned by the first-person speaker and the healing signs performed by Jesus in the Fourth Gospel, particularly given the use of ἰᾶσθαι at John 4:47 and John 5:13: 'When (the royal official) heard that Jesus had come from Judaea into Galilee, he departed to him and was asking that he might go down and heal (ἰάσηται) his son …'; 'And the one who had been healed (ἰαθείς) did not know who it was, for Jesus had turned away …'[328]

[2] 'The cause of obduracy'
As for the figure (or entity) acting in the third-person verbs at John 12:40ab, there is an array of conjectural possibilities,[329] but considered hypotheses number five: one requiring God to be the first-person speaker – Jesus; four allowing Jesus to be the first-person speaker – God, 'the ruler of this world', signs and Jesus's message (that is, the 'report' of Isaiah 53:1 at John 12:38).

[a] Jesus
The case for Jesus as the third-person figure principally argues that he is the most likely antecedent in the quotation's context. As Judith Lieu has put it (partly dovetailing an earlier line of reasoning by Bruce Hollenbach), 'It is Jesus who has done the signs (37), Jesus who is most probably the "Lord" of the quotation from Isa 53.1 (38) and Jesus whose glory Isaiah saw (41).'[330] This position is buttressed by Hollenbach, who draws an analogy with the

---

327. John 12:41-42; see Painter, 'The Quotation of Scripture and Unbelief in John 12.36b-43', 446n1.

328. Schnackenburg, *Gospel according to St John*, 2:416; Schuchard, *Scripture within Scripture*, 98n30.

329. Aside from the options about to be outlined, Painter considers the possibilities of Isaiah or the evangelist (with Jesus as the first-person figure); 'The Quotation of Scripture and Unbelief in John 12.36b-43', 435–37. A further review (with critique) of views on this issue is offered by Schuchard, *Scripture within Scripture*, 98–100.

330. Judith M. Lieu, 'Blindness in the Johannine Tradition', *NTS* 34 (1988): 85–86 (quotation p. 86, parenthetical numbers are verse references in her text); cf. Bruce Hollenbach, 'Lest They Should Turn and Be Forgiven: Irony', *BT* 34 (1983): 313, 317–18. Lieu cites Freed for this view, but it should be noted that Freed posits this in a passing comment – '(or probably Jesus in Jn)' – and also entertains God as the figure; *Old Testament Quotations in the Gospel of John*, 87 (cf. p. 84). Cf. also F.F. Bruce, *The Gospel of John: Introduction, Exposition, and Notes* (Grand Rapids, MI: William B. Eerdmans, 1983), 271–72.

purpose of Jesus's parables in Mark 4:10-12, where a conflation of Isaiah 6:9-10 is also cited:

> And when he was alone, those around him with the Twelve were asking him about the parables. And he was saying to them, 'To you has been given the mystery of the kingdom of God, but for those outside everything is in parables, so that, "they will see by observing, but not perceive; and hear by listening, but not understand; lest they turn and it be forgiven them"'. (Isaiah 6:9-10)

As those parables were expressly spoken by Jesus 'to conceal (his) teachings from "those outside"', reasons Hollenbach, so in the Fourth Gospel Jesus's public ministry was designed by him to do the same to the Jews. Inasmuch as Isaiah 6:9-10 is cited to make this point in Mark, he concludes, it stands to reason that the same holds at John 12:40 and, therefore, that Jesus is the one who 'blinds' and 'hardens' in John.[331]

[b] God
The dominant view holds this third-person actor to be God, the Father of Jesus; and it rests on a perceived alignment of this figure with either of two theological currents in the Fourth Gospel: divine determinism or the *theologia crucis*. For determinism, as argued by Rudolf Schnackenburg, an obstruction by God at John 12:40ab is the negative aspect of his sovereign role in the *ordo salutis*. Just as believers are considered to be 'of God' and 'belonging to the Father',[332] and to have been 'drawn', 'taught' and 'given' by him to Jesus,[333] so unbelievers are deemed to have become such because they were 'blinded' and 'hardened' by God against Jesus. This is, in fact, understood to be manifest at John 9:39 (noted above for the word choice τυφλοῦν[334]), where Jesus articulates the adjudicatory purpose of his commission:

> For judgment I came into this world,
> that (ἵνα) those who do not see may see
> and those who see may become blind (τυφλοί).

Inasmuch as the Son is sent by the Father – and inasmuch as the ἵνα-clause used to state the Son's effect on the world in this verse 'expresses the divine

---

331. 'Lest They Should Turn and Be Forgiven: Irony', 316–18 (quotation p. 316). Hollenbach further contends that the quotation is to be read as an ironic expression of the Jews' impenitence, not a literal articulation of divine determinism.
332. John 8:47; 17:6.
333. John 6:37, 39, 44-45, 65; 10:29; 17:2, 6, 9; 18:9; cf. 10:4, 27.
334. See above in this chapter, under *[b] Word choice*.

will'³³⁵ – the blindness produced by Jesus, in this view, is deemed to be caused by God.³³⁶

For the *theologia crucis*, argued by Evans, it is similarly understood that the obstruction caused by God is effected through (not over against) Jesus's ministry. The impetus for this obstruction, however, is not the sovereignty of the Father but the glorification of Christ. Inasmuch as Jesus's glorification in the Fourth Gospel occurs through the cross,³³⁷ it is argued, the Father facilitates that end by preventing the Jews from believing and, thus, provoking the opposition that would get him there.³³⁸

[c] 'The ruler of this world'

An extensive case has been made by Painter that the subject of these third-person verbs is 'the ruler of this world', depicted at John 12:31; 14:30; and 16:11.³³⁹ The logical flow of Painter's discussion is at points difficult to follow.³⁴⁰ From what can be distilled, however – and based on his outline of the argument – he appeals to four lines of evidence: the gospel context, the anomalies of the quotation (which he regards as 'the evangelist's changes'), the Judaic context (particularly, its 'dualistic worldview') and the Alexandrian exegetical school.³⁴¹

For context, Painter makes three observations: (a) that the quotations are preceded by the arrival of Jesus's 'hour' as the moment for casting out 'the ruler of this world'³⁴²; (b) that those quotations are also preceded and followed by exhortations in which Jesus metaphorically casts belief and unbelief as coming to 'the light' and succumbing to 'darkness', respectively³⁴³; and (c) that in the Fourth Gospel 'the ruler of this world' is 'the power of darkness' and, so, presumably is in view within Jesus's metaphorical use of light and darkness.³⁴⁴ For this last point he

---

335. John 1:7; 3:16-17; 6:38; 7:32 (?); 12:47; 18:37.

336. Schnackenburg, *Gospel according to St John*, 2:259, 262-74, 415-16 (quotation p. 259), which draws from his excursus, 'Personal Commitment, Personal Responsibility, Predestination and Hardening' (pp. 259–74). Following Schnackenburg is Menken, '"He Has Blinded Their Eyes ... " (John 12:40)', 119–20.

337. John 17:1.

338. 'The Function of Isaiah 6:9-10 in Mark and John', 136–38.

339. 'The Quotation of Scripture and Unbelief in John 12.36b-43', 439–58. In this essay Painter primarily engages the excursus by Schnackenburg listed in note 336.

340. After reviewing the macro- and micro-contexts of John 12:37-41, for instance, Painter seems to forecast that 'the immediate and broader contexts in the Gospel... suggest and alternative view' to God as 'the cause of obduracy', as if those contexts had not yet been broached; 'The Quotation of Scripture and Unbelief in John 12.36b-43', 446; cf. pp. 440–446.

341. For these terms, specifically, 'The Quotation of Scripture and Unbelief in John 12.36b-43', 439.

342. John 12:31.

343. John 12:35-36a, 44-46.

344. 'The Quotation of Scripture and Unbelief in John 12.36b-43', 442–43, 450–51. Elsewhere – in fact, within his treatment of the Alexandrian school – Painter adds (a) that Jesus's metaphorical discourse in these passages is also preceded by a sentiment akin to Jesus's Gethsemane prayer in the Synoptics (John 12:27) and (b) that at Luke 22:53 Jesus also associates the 'hour' with 'the power of darkness': 'this is your hour and the domain (ἡ ἐξουσία) of darkness' (p. 457).

observes that the verb τυφλοῦν appears in only two other New Testament *loci* and that in both cases it describes the activity of either the devil himself or imagery associated with him: 'the god of this age' in 2 Corinthians 4:3-4; 'darkness' in 1 John 2:11, respectively:

And even if our gospel is veiled, it is veiled to those who are perishing,
in whose case the god of this age blinded the minds of the unbelievers
(ὁ θεὸς τοῦ αἰῶνος τούτου ἐτύφλωσεν τὰ νοήματα τῶν ἀπίστων),
so as not to see the light of the gospel of the glory of Christ,
who is the image of God.

But the one who hates his brother is in darkness, and in darkness he walks;
and he does not know where he goes, for the darkness blinded his eyes
(ὅτι ἡ σκοτία ἐτύφλωσεν τοὺς ὀφθαλμοὺς αὐτοῦ).[345]

For the anomalies, Painter notes (d) that the changes of tense, person and voice (presumably in John 12:40ab relative to John 12:40e) accentuate 'the opposition between the one who has blinded and hardened and the one who would heal'; and (e) that the choice of τυφλοῦν replaces verbs which depict a temporary obstruction of sight ('smear over'/'shut') with one that depicts (what was deemed to be) an 'incurable' one.[346] For the Judaic context, he contends (f) that, like the Qumran sect (particularly as expressed in 1QS iii 13–iv 26), the Fourth Gospel's monotheism appears in tandem with a cosmic dualism which allows 'the power that blinded and prevented people from believing' to be 'the power of darkness'.[347] And for the Alexandrian school, he notices (g) that such was the reading of Origen and Cyril of Alexandria.[348]

[d] Signs
Since the singular verbs at John 12:40ab can take a neuter plural nominative, it has also been argued that their subject is Jesus's signs (σημεῖα) themselves. The idea is thought by Evans to coincide (in some way) with Deuteronomy 29:1-3:

345. 'The Quotation of Scripture and Unbelief in John 12.36b-43', 449–50.
346. 'The Quotation of Scripture and Unbelief in John 12.36b-43', 446–51; quotations pp. 446, 448.
347. 'The Quotation of Scripture and Unbelief in John 12.36b-43', 456.
348. For Origen, John 12:40ab refers 'to the evil one' of 2 Cor 4:3-4; *Fr. Jo.* 92 (text: Preuschen, *Der Johanneskommentar*); for Cyril of Alexandria, God 'gave place' for the Jews 'to suffer blindness under the devil'; *Commentariorum in Joannem Continuatio: Librorum VII et VIII Fragmenta* (PG 74:96-97) – 'The Quotation of Scripture and Unbelief in John 12.36b-43', 456–57; and cf. Maurice F. Wiles, *The Spiritual Gospel: The Interpretation of the Fourth Gospel in the Early Church* (Cambridge: Cambridge University Press, 1960), 109. On p. 439 Painter inadvertently lists Cyril of Alexandria as Clement of Alexandria. A cogent overview of the issues surrounding the debate between God or the devil as 'the cause of obduracy' is offered by Jürgen Becker, *Das Evangelium nach Johannes*, 2 vols., 3rd ed., ÖTK 4/1-2 = Gütersloher Taschenbücher Siebenstern 505–506 (Gütersloh: Gerd Mohn, 1991), 1:477–78.

Moses called to all Israel and said to them,
'You have seen all that the Lord did before your eyes in the land of Egypt,
to Pharaoh, to all his servants and to all his land, the great ordeals which your eyes have seen, the signs (האתת/τὰ σημεῖα) and those great wonders.
But the Lord has not given you a heart to know, nor eyes to see nor ears to hear to this day'.[349]

It could be further supported, suggests Painter, by considering the obstructive role played by two other ostensibly soteriological media: the proclamation of Isaiah (as commissioned in Isaiah 6) and the parables of Jesus (as set out in Mark 4). That is, as Isaiah's commission was to 'make fat', 'render heavy' and 'smear over', and as Jesus's parables were to prevent 'perception' and 'understanding', so also (in this model) Jesus's signs in the Fourth Gospel were designed to 'blind' and 'harden'.[350]

[e] The message of Jesus
Finally – also on the grounds that this third-person actor could be an entity rather than a person – it has been argued by Schuchard that this actor is the 'report' (ἡ ἀκοή) referenced in Isaiah 53:1 at John 12:38, that is, that the factor which blinded the eyes and hardened the hearts of the Jews was the message of Jesus itself. Schuchard's basis is twofold: first, that in the Fourth Gospel Jesus's judgement upon the world is not enacted directly, but results from the provocation of his preaching[351]; and second, that such a dynamic aligns with Isaiah 6, where 'it is the content of the prophet's proclamation that causes offense and thus "blinds" the people of God'.[352]

(3) Proposal on the anomalies: A reworked LXX Vorlage
As with the anomalous quotation of Isaiah 40:3 at John 1:23, so here: these ambiguities and deviations require two related but different questions to be addressed. How can they explained textually? And what do they signify theologically? More specifically for this quotation: From what sources (including version) can they best be explained? And what message have they been designed to convey?

(a) 'He hardened' or 'he maimed'?
To begin with the first – the version and anomalies – it is at the start noted that the second verb in the reference is almost certainly ἐπώρωσεν ('he hardened'), not

---

349. *To See and Not Perceive*, 134–35.

350. 'The Quotation of Scripture and Unbelief in John 12.36b-43', 437–38; cf. Isa 6:9-10 and Mark 4:11-12. Painter suggests this premise but does not advocate the model. His appeal to the concealing purposes of Isaiah's message (in the HB) and Jesus's parables (in Mark 4) coincides with part of Hollenbach's case for Jesus as the third-person actor in the quotation, recounted above in this chapter, under *[a] Jesus*.

351. Cited are John 3:17-18, 20; 4:42; 5:24-25; 6:45, 60; 8:43, 47; 9:39; 10:3-4, 16, 27; 12:47.

352. *Scripture within Scripture*, 100–01 (quotation p. 101).

ἐπήρωσεν ('he maimed'). The latter cannot be sustained, either as a gloss for השם ('make desolate') in 1QIsaiah^a (de Waard) or as a semantic sibling for τετύφλωκεν ('he has blinded') at John 12:40a (Menken). On ἐπήρωσεν as a gloss for השם, two observations. First, given the propensity of Qumran biblical texts to assimilate sectarian (or at least 'intentional' non-biblical) terminology into themselves,[353] it is likely that the reading השם is just that, and, therefore, that it reflects a parochial text to which the evangelist would not have been privy – all the more so, given the use of that verb in the sectarian *1QHodayot^a* xv 5-6 (Suk vii 2-3) amid six terms which, themselves, dovetail HB Isaiah 6:10 – 'smear over' (לשע), 'eyes' (עינים), 'see' (לראות), 'ears' (אזנים), 'hear' (לשמע) and 'heart' (לבב):

שעו עיני מראות
רע ואוזני משמוע דמים
השם לבבי ממחשבת רוע ...

My eyes have been smeared over from seeing
evil, my ears from (hearing of) bloodshed,
my heart has been made desolate from evil design ...[354]

Second, even were this not the case, πηροῦν does not gloss לשם in the LXX and, therefore, is unlikely to reflect such a reading.

As for ἐπήρωσεν as an apt semantic partner to τετύφλωκεν, there is no evidence of such suitability,[355] while, to the contrary, there is evidence for the suitability of ἐπώρωσεν. Paul employs the two in close proximity, both with the noun τὰ νοήματα ('minds'), to depict the 'hardening' and 'blinding' of Israelites and unbelievers, respectively:

Having, then, such hope, we act with much boldness; not as Moses used to put a veil upon his face, that the sons of Israel not gaze into the close of something

---

353. This phenomenon was seen early in Qumran studies; so, Dominique Barthélemy, 'Le grand rouleau d'Isaïe trouvé près de la Mer Morte', *RB* 57 (1950): 546–49. Now see Corrado Martone, 'Sectarian Variant Readings and Sectarian Texts in the Qumran Corpus and Beyond: Reflections on an Elusive Concept', in *Ricercare la sapienza di tutti gli antichi (Sir. 39,1): Miscellanea in onore di Gian Luigi Prato*, ed. Marcello Milani and Marco Zappella, Supplementi alla Rivista biblica 56 (Bologna: Edizioni Dehoniane Bologna, 2013), 393–400; and Corrado Martone, 'Creative Reception: The Bible and Its Interpretations at Qumran' (paper presented at 'The Reception of Jewish Scripture in Early Judaism and Christianity', Università degli Studi di Napoli 'L'Orientale', Naples, 12–15 June 2017). The term 'intentional' for non-biblical (but not necessarily sectarian) insertions into biblical texts is drawn from the 2013 article by Martone (p. 395).

354. Text: Hartmut Stegemann with Eileen Schuller, eds., *1QHodayot^a*, DJD 40 (Oxford: Clarendon Press, 2009).

355. Πηροῦν does not occur in the New Testament, nor does it appear with τυφλοῦν in the LXX: πηροῦν is used at LXX Job 17:7 and LXX 4 Macc 18:21; τυφλοῦν at LXX Tob 7:7; Wis 2:21; and LXX Isa 42:19.

being brought to naught. But their minds were hardened (ἐπωρώθη τὰ νοήματα αὐτῶν); for to this very day the same veil remains upon the reading of the old covenant, not being lifted because (only) in Christ is it brought to naught.[356]

And even if our gospel is veiled, it is veiled to those who are perishing,
in whose case the god of this age blinded the minds of the unbelievers
(ὁ θεὸς τοῦ αἰῶνος τούτου ἐτύφλωσεν τὰ νοήματα τῶν ἀπίστων),
so as not to see the light of the gospel of the glory of Christ,
who is the image of God.[357]

On these grounds, the second colon of the quotation almost certainly reads 'and he hardened their heart'.

(b) The LXX and Mark

As for the version cited (and, consequently, the anomalies which attend it), the quotation is most aptly explained as a reference to LXX Isaiah 6:10 which has been reworked by (a) adjusting some elements to the evangelist's style, (b) assimilating Mark 8:17-18 (or a tradition akin to it) and (c) importing Johannine cosmic vocabulary.

Regarding the LXX *Vorlage*, the last three words, καὶ ἰάσομαι αὐτούς, speak for themselves; and the Greek base for a good deal that comes before has been soundly argued by Schuchard,[358] namely:

(1) that, like the LXX (and unlike the HB), possessives modify 'eyes' and 'heart' in (the equivalent of) Isaiah 6:10ac (John 12:40ab) but not in (the equivalent of) Isaiah 6:10df (John 12:40cd);
(2) that the differing tenses of the first two verbs – perfect (τετύφλωκεν) and aorist (ἐπώρωσεν), respectively – do not follow the parallelism expected if they were translations of the two perfect tenses in their corresponding cola (הֵשַׁע/הָשַׁע and הַשְׁמֵן);
(3) that neither of those two first verbs in John is used in the LXX to translate their Hebrew counterparts: τυφλοῦν for שׁע ל ; πωροῦν for לשׁמן;
(4) and that the quotation of Isaiah 53:1 at John 12:38 is, itself, from the LXX and would have been attracted to LXX Isaiah 6:10 through the relationship of its 'report' (ἀκοή) to the same term in LXX Isaiah 6:9 (and one might add, to its cognate ἀκούειν in that same verse): 'And he (the Lord) said, "Go and say to this people, 'You will hear by listening (ἀκοῇ ἀκούσετε), but by no means understand; and you will see by observing but by no means perceive'"'.

---

356. 2 Cor 3:12-14.
357. 2 Cor 4:3-4. The proximity of these verbs in both John 12:40 and Paul's discourse on 'the god of this age' will be argued (below) to have implications for 'the cause of obduracy' in the quotation; see below in this chapter, under *[1] The criticisms point by point*.
358. *Scripture within Scripture*, 96–97, 101–06, 106n69.

It was noted above that the first two of these premises have been assigned by Menken to style (either of the evangelist or of a putative Greek source translating from the Hebrew), particularly on the grounds that elsewhere in the narrative the author (a) routinely omits possessive pronouns (contrary to premise 1)[359] and (b) varies tenses between two verbs in close proximity (contrary to premise 2).[360] Neither of these criticisms, however, bear up under closer examination. For (a), if the evangelist preferred to elide pronouns, one would expect him to have done so for those at John 12:40ab, as well; as it is, the pattern of two pronominal possessives followed by two omissions aligns with the LXX and suggests that this is the source being used. And for (b), none of the data for tense variation mustered by Menken[361] represents a translation of Hebrew verbs in parallelism, as would be the case if the evangelist were translating HB Isaiah 6:10 at John 12:40.

Assigning these features, then, to the LXX, there remain (1) five anomalies that can be ascribed to style, adaptation or emphasis (italicized in Table 19)[362] and (2) three differences of word choice (underlined in Table 19): τετύφλωκεν ('he has blinded') for LXX ἐκάμμυσαν ('they shut'); ἐπώρωσεν ('he hardened') for LXX ἐπαχύνθη ('grew fat'); and νοήσωσιν ('lest … they discern') for LXX συνῶσι ('lest … they understand').

Table 19 Anomalies in John 12:40/Isaiah 6:10 from a LXX *Vorlage*

LXX Isaiah 6:10	John 12:40
ἐπαχύνθη γὰρ ἡ καρδία τοῦ λαοῦ τούτου,	τετύφλωκεν αὐτῶν τοὺς ὀφθαλμοὺς
καὶ τοῖς ὠσὶν αὐτῶν βαρέως ἤκουσαν	καὶ ἐπώρωσεν αὐτῶν τὴν καρδίαν,
καὶ τοὺς ὀφθαλμοὺς αὐτῶν ἐκάμμυσαν,	ἵνα μὴ ἴδωσιν τοῖς ὀφθαλμοῖς
μήποτε ἴδωσι τοῖς ὀφθαλμοῖς	καὶ νοήσωσιν τῇ καρδίᾳ,
καὶ τοῖς ὠσὶν ἀκούσωσι	καὶ στραφῶσιν, καὶ ἰάσομαι αὐτούς.
καὶ τῇ καρδίᾳ συνῶσι	
καὶ ἐπιστρέψωσι καὶ ἰάσομαι αὐτούς.	

For (2), Schuchard explains the word differences as a conflation of LXX Isaiah 6:10 with three texts: LXX Isaiah 42:18-20 for τυφλοῦν; LXX Job 17:7 for πωροῦν; and (with Menken) LXX Isaiah 44:18 for νοεῖν (all accounted for above).[363] Here it is argued, instead, that those choices reflect two editorial decisions: one (accounting for τυφλοῦν) depends on the identity of the third-person actor and

---

359. See note 307.
360. "'He Has Blinded Their Eyes … '" (John 12:40)", 110.
361. See note 288.
362. Specifically, the reduction of LXX 'of this people' (τοῦ λαοῦ τούτου) to 'their' (αὐτῶν); the placement of the two pronouns (αὐτῶν) at John 12:40ab/Isa 6:10ac prior to the nouns they modify; the declension of nominative ἡ καρδία in the LXX as an accusative (τὴν καρδίαν); ἵνα μή for LXX μήποτε; and the *verba simplicia* στραφῶσιν for LXX ἐπιστρέψωσι.
363. *Scripture within Scripture*, 102–05; cf. Menken, "'He Has Blinded Their Eyes … '" (John 12:40)", 117–18.

will be developed within that discussion below; the other (accounting for πωροῦν and νοεῖν) is, as some have suggested, the assimilation of Mark 8:17-18 (or a tradition akin to it). Given that Mark is in Greek, it aligns with the criterion set out above for anomalies by conflation, namely, that where a quotation may be polyvalent, hypotheses will be preferred which align (rather than mix) the versions of the base and assimilated passages.[364]

Mark 8:17-18 carries both these verbs in a setting with close thematic and lexical ties to LXX Isaiah 6:10 and John 12:40, particularly if one takes into account the vocabulary of LXX Isaiah 6:9. More specifically, (a) Mark 8:17-18 makes reference to Jeremiah 5:21 which, like Isaiah 6:9, speaks of eyes that do not see and ears that do not hear; (b) apart from πωροῦν and νοεῖν, those verses share six terms with LXX 6:9-10 (and so are an apt candidate for conflation with that passage) – 'eyes' (ὀφθαλμοί), 'see' (βλέπειν), 'ears' (ὦτα), 'hear' (ἀκούειν), 'heart' (καρδία) and 'understand' (συνιέναι); and (c) the use of συνιέναι and νοεῖν as synonyms in those verses could account for the evangelist's replacement of the former (read in the LXX) with the latter (at John 12:40d) (Table 20).

Table 20 LXX Isaiah 6:9-10, Mark 8:17-18 and John 12:40

John 12:40	
He has blinded their eyes (αὐτῶν τοὺς ὀφθαλμοὺς) and hardened their heart (ἐπώρωσεν αὐτῶν τὴν καρδίαν), lest they perceive with the eyes (τοῖς ὀφθαλμοῖς) and discern with the heart (νοήσωσιν τῇ καρδίᾳ), and turn, and I heal them.	

LXX Isaiah 6:9-10	Mark 8:17-18
And he (the Lord) said, 'Go and say to this people, "You will hear by listening (ἀκοῇ ἀκούσετε), but by no means understand (οὐ μὴ συνῆτε); and you will see by observing (βλέποντες βλέψετε), but by no means perceive". For the heart (ἡ καρδία) of this people grew fat, and with their ears (τοῖς ὠσὶν αὐτῶν) they heard (ἤκουσαν) in disgust, and their eyes (τοὺς ὀφθαλμοὺς αὐτῶν) they shut; lest they perceive with the eyes (τοῖς ὀφθαλμοῖς), and with the ears hear (τοῖς ὠσὶν ἀκούσωσι), and with the heart understand (τῇ καρδίᾳ συνῶσι), and turn and I heal them'.	And apprehending, Jesus said to them, 'Why are you discussing that you have no bread? Do you not yet discern (νοεῖτε) or understand (συνίετε)? Is your heart hardened (πεπωρωμένην ... τὴν καρδίαν ὑμῶν)? "Having eyes (ὀφθαλμούς), do you not see (οὐ βλέπετε)? And having ears (ὦτα), do you not hear (οὐκ ἀκούετε)"? (Jeremiah 5:21) And do you not remember'?

As such – and setting aside τετύφλωκεν at this juncture – the quotation of Isaiah 6:10 at John 12:40 is perhaps most elegantly understood as a reference to

364. See the section *b. Expecting the Hebrew Bible* in the Introduction.

the LXX[365] which has been reworked by adjustment to the evangelist's style and the assimilation of Mark 8:17-18 (or a tradition akin to it).[366] As is the case with Isaiah 40:3 at John 1:23, such a LXX base text lends itself to the prospect that John's quotation of this verse was catalysed by Synoptic usage. LXX Isaiah 6:9-10 is cited (nearly) verbatim by two of the Synoptics: Matthew, to explain the cryptic dynamic in Jesus's parables[367]; Luke, to indict the Roman Jewish diaspora for obstinacy.[368] And one or both of those quotations appear to be expanding on a condensed, modified reference to those same verses in Mark, which is also employed to explain the cloaking effect of Jesus's parables.

ἵνα βλέποντες βλέπωσιν καὶ ἴδωσιν,
καὶ ἀκούοντες ἀκούωσιν καὶ μὴ συνιῶσιν,
μήποτε ἐπιστρέψωσιν καὶ ἀφεθῇ αὐτοῖς.

... in order that 'observing, they might see but not perceive,
and listening, they might hear but not understand,
lest they turn and it be forgiven them'.[369]

That John's quotation can be traced to the same version does not require but does lend itself to the possibility that its presence here is somehow related to its usage in those cognate texts.

C. Isaiah 53:1/6:10: The call to believe obstructed

Now the second question raised by the anomalies in Isaiah 6:10 at John 12:40 – What do they signify theologically? That is (more broadly), what theological note is being sounded as these deviations combine with Isaiah 53:1 at John 12:38?

1. Isaiah 53:1: A lament over unbelief

To begin with Isaiah 53:1, in the *inclusio* formed by the introductory formulae this quotation picks up John's exhortation of Isaiah 40:3 at John 1:23 and bewails the subsequent lack of response to it. If John's call, 'make straight the way of the Lord',

---

365. Here, supporting Edwyn Clement Hoskyns, *The Fourth Gospel*, ed. Francis Noel Davey, 2nd ed. (London: Faber & Faber, Ltd., 1947), 428–29.

366. This, contra the case by Bultmann that (a) the quotations of Isa 53:1 and Isa 6:10 in this passage are drawn from different versions and that (b) while the latter was crafted by the evangelist, the former was assimilated from a Semeia Source; *Gospel of John*, 452n2.

367. Matt 13:13-15.

368. Acts 28:24-28. Bracketing variants to the NA[28] texts and choices to use moveable –ν, differences are (a) the rendering (Acts) or choice to include (Matthew) the Lord's commission at LXX Isa 6:9a and (b) the absence of αὐτῶν after τοῖς ὠσίν in Matt 13:15b and Acts 28:27b (both = LXX Isa 6:10b) – though it is furnished for Matthew by ℵ C 33 892 1241.

369. Mark 4:11-12; the portion cited is only from v. 12.

was a call to believe at the beginning of Jesus's public ministry, Isaiah's cry, 'who has believed our report', is a lament that no one had done so by the end of that ministry.

a. 'Our report'

(1) The testimony to Jesus

A way in to appreciating this lament is furnished by two of its phrases: 'our report' in its first colon; 'arm of the Lord' in the second. The first, 'our report', includes a cognate to ἀκούειν: ἀκοή. It denotes something spoken that is heard (not something done that is seen); and, if it carries significance in this quotation, it doubtless refers to the testimony which had been given to Jesus up to this point. At issue, however, is that this word has been deemed by some irrelevant to the evangelist's purpose in citing this verse; and so, before it can be teased out for its implications, its importance for the quotation must be established.

The problem emerges from the accentuation of Jesus's 'signs' in John 12:37-41. At John 12:37 the Jews' unbelief is set over against the 'signs' they saw, not the words they heard; and, as noted above, there is wide agreement that this 'ocular' soteriology (if you will) accounts for two major anomalies in the quotation of Isaiah 6:10 at John 12:40: the removal of the cola on 'ears' and 'hearing' (Isaiah 6:10be) and the inversion of Isaiah 6:10ac to form a thematic sequence of 'eyes'/'heart'/'eyes'/'heart'. Given such a *Tendenz* enveloping John 12:38, it has been supposed that the import of the quotation lay in its second colon (on 'the arm of the Lord') and that, if its first colon carries any significance, it is to be found in something other than its language of belief in a 'message': to raise the general question of faith, perhaps[370], or to underscore the issue of signs in the second colon.[371]

(a) Testimony and signs in the Fourth Gospel

Such a view, however, is predicated upon a wooden reading of John 12:37 – and, behind it, a misconstrual of the way Jesus's signs relate to testimony in the Fourth Gospel. To be sure, 'believing' in light of Jesus's 'signs' (σημεῖα) or 'works' (ἔργα)[372] is described and endorsed throughout the gospel: at places those signs could

---

370. Painter, 'The Quotation of Scripture and Unbelief in John 12.36b-43', 443-44; Menken, '"He Has Blinded Their Eyes ... " (John 12:40)', 108; Menken, 'The Use of the Septuagint in Three Quotations in John: Jn 10,34; 12,38; 19,24', 383.

371. Robert T. Fortna, *The Fourth Gospel and Its Predecessor: From Narrative Source to Present Gospel* (Philadelphia: Fortress, 1988), 138. The view is noted, but not endorsed, by Schuchard, *Scripture within Scripture*, 88–89.

372. The semantic overlap between 'signs' (σημεῖα) and 'works' (ἔργα), with cognates, appears saliently in two passages: John 6:30, where Jesus's interlocutors ask him, 'What sign (σημεῖον) do you do, then, that we might see and believe you? What do you work (ἐργάζῃ)'?; and John 9:3-4, 16, where the healing initially called a 'work' by Jesus is later called a 'sign' by the crowds who witness it – 'Jesus answered, "Neither this man nor his parents sinned, but (this has occurred) that the works of God (τὰ ἔργα τοῦ θεοῦ) might be manifested in him. We must work the works (ἐργάζεσθαι τὰ ἔργα) of him who sent me, while it is day" ... (But) others (over against the Pharisees) were saying, "How can a sinful man perform such signs (τοιαῦτα σημεῖα)"'?

be 'reported' and 'heard'[373] or 'written' and 'read'[374], but the first and expected dynamic surrounding them is that they were done to be 'seen' and 'believed'.[375] Closer scrutiny, however, shows that such belief from seeing signs is brooked in the Fourth Gospel only by concession, what Marie-Émile Boismard called the 'apologetic function' of signs.[376] Signs – as much as they are endorsed – serve only as a divine reinforcement for those who will not believe words; and, as such, they always operate in tandem with the message. At two junctures this is intimated: Jesus's retort to the royal official at Cana (already noted), where his opening

373. John 12:18.
374. John 20:30-31.
375. Jesus's disciples first 'believed (ἐπίστευσαν) in him' after 'the beginning of his signs' (ἀρχὴν τῶν σημείων) at Cana (John 2:11). Many 'believed (ἐπίστευσαν) in his name' at the first Passover, 'beholding his signs (αὐτοῦ τὰ σημεῖα) which he was doing (John 2:23)'. Jesus tells the royal official at Cana plainly, 'Unless you see signs and wonders (σημεῖα καὶ τέρατα), you will not believe (οὐ μὴ πιστεύσητε/John 4:48)'. When he heals that official's son, the official 'believed (ἐπίστευσεν) and his whole household' and the deed is registered as 'the second sign (δεύτερον σημεῖον) Jesus did' after travelling from Judaea to Galilee (John 4:53-54). The multitude at the Sea of Galilee 'was following him' because its participants were 'beholding the signs (τὰ σημεῖα) which he was doing upon the sick (John 6:2)'; and after 'seeing the sign (σημεῖον)' of their own miraculous feeding, they declare, 'This is truly the prophet which comes into the world (John 6:14)'. When they pursue Jesus for more bread the next day, they are chided by him for not doing so 'because (they) saw signs (σημεῖα/John 6:26)'; and in response to that scolding they retort, 'What sign (σημεῖον) do you do, then, that we might see and believe you (ἴδωμεν καὶ πιστεύσωμέν σοι/John 6:30)'?

Further, during the Festival of Tabernacles 'many of the people believed (ἐπίστευσαν) in him', asking, 'the Christ, when he comes, will not perform more signs (σημεῖα) than this one has, will he (John 7:31)'? At that same festival the man born blind is healed 'that the works of God (τὰ ἔργα τοῦ θεοῦ) might be manifested in him'; and, when he is later asked by Jesus where his allegiance now lies, he confesses 'Lord, I believe (πιστεύω/John 9:3-4, 38)'. During the Dedication Jesus tells his critics that though 'the works' (τὰ ἔργα) he does in his Father's name bear witness to him, they 'do not believe' (οὐ πιστεύετε) because they are not of his sheep (John 10:25-26); and he further appeals to them, saying, 'if I am not doing the works of my Father (τὰ ἔργα τοῦ πατρός μου), do not believe me (μὴ πιστεύετέ μοι), but if I am doing so, even though you do not believe me (κἂν ἐμοὶ μὴ πιστεύητε), believe the works (τοῖς ἔργοις), that you may know and continue to know that the Father is in me and I in the Father (John 10:37-38)'. After Jesus raises Lazarus, he is deemed a threat by the chief priests and Pharisees because he 'performs many signs (σημεῖα)' and, thus, if left unchecked, 'every one will believe (πιστεύσουσιν) in him (John 11:47-48)'. And during the Farewell Discourse Jesus urges his disciples to accept his reciprocal abiding in the Father by exhorting them either to 'believe me' (πιστεύετέ μοι) or to 'believe because of the works themselves (διὰ τὰ ἔργα αὐτὰ πιστεύετε/John 14:10-11)'.

376. *Moses or Jesus: An Essay in Johannine Christology*, trans. B.T. Viviano (Minneapolis, MN: Fortress Press/Leuven: Peeters Press, 1993), 57; trans. of *Moïse ou Jésus: Essai de christologie johannique*, BETL 84 (Leuven: Uitgeverij Peeters and Leuven University Press, 1988).

conjunction 'unless' (ἐὰν μή) betrays disappointment over having to perform such works to evoke faith – 'Unless (ἐὰν μή) you see signs and wonders (σημεῖα καὶ τέρατα), you will not believe (οὐ μὴ πιστεύσητε)'[377]; and the people's response to John's testimony at Bethany, where, after recalling that 'John did no sign (σημεῖον)', they note nonetheless that everything he said about Jesus was 'true' and 'believed (ἐπίστευσαν) in him there'.[378]

It is articulated quite markedly, however, at two other *loci*: specifically, in Jesus's dialogues at the Dedication and the Farewell Discourse, where he encourages his critics and disciples to believe because of his works only if they cannot do because of his words:

> If I am not doing the works of my Father (τὰ ἔργα τοῦ πατρός μου),
> do not believe me (μὴ πιστεύετέ μοι), but if I am doing so,
> even though you do not believe me (κἂν ἐμοὶ μὴ πιστεύητε),
> believe the works (τοῖς ἔργοις), that you may know and continue to know that the Father is in me and I in the Father.[379]

> Do you not believe (οὐ πιστεύεις) that I am in the Father and the Father is in me?
> The words (τὰ ῥήματα) that I speak to you I do not say from myself;
> but the Father who abides in me does his works (τὰ ἔργα αὐτοῦ).
> Believe me (πιστεύετέ μοι), that I am in the Father and the Father in me.
> But, if not, believe because of the works themselves (διὰ τὰ ἔργα αὐτὰ πιστεύετε).[380]

(b) A Mosaic christology

This dynamic may, in fact, reflect a Moses typology. Such has been argued for segments of the Fourth Gospel by Boismard in his work *Moses or Jesus: An Essay in Johannine Christology*.[381] His case is not without difficulties; and it is unnecessarily restricted to three passages in which signs occur. It is suggestive, however, of the way σημεῖα function in the Fourth Gospel and, if modified, applicable to John 12:37-41.

---

377. John 4:48.
378. John 10:41-42.
379. John 10:37-38.
380. John 14:10-11. A further instance could be Jesus's resurrection appearance to Thomas, where he issues a beatitude on those who believe on the basis of testimony rather than sight: 'Jesus said to him, "Because you have seen me (ἑώρακάς με) have you believed (πεπίστευκας)? Blessed are those who have not seen and have believed (οἱ μὴ ἰδόντες καὶ πιστεύσαντες/John 20:29)"'. It is argued below, however (Chapter 5, *(1) The medium for encountering signs*), that this arrangement reflects a theological shift which occurs with Jesus's death and resurrection (and so does not represent the relation of 'signs' to 'faith' in the Book of Signs).
381. *Moses or Jesus*, 42–59.

Boismard notes that three episodes involving Jesus's signs are marked 'beginning', 'second' and 'third': the turning of water into wine; the healing of the royal official's son; and the furnishing of the large catch of fish[382]:

(1) The turning of water into wine (John 2:11)
Ταύτην ἐποίησεν ἀρχὴν τῶν σημείων ὁ Ἰησοῦς ἐν Κανὰ τῆς Γαλιλαίας καὶ ἐφανέρωσεν τὴν δόξαν αὐτοῦ ...

This did Jesus as a beginning of the signs in Cana of Galilee and manifested his glory ...

(2) The healing of the royal official's son (John 4:54)
Τοῦτο δὲ πάλιν δεύτερον σημεῖον ἐποίησεν ὁ Ἰησοῦς ἐλθὼν ἐκ τῆς Ἰουδαίας εἰς τὴν Γαλιλαίαν.

This, again, did Jesus as the second sign when he had come from Judaea into Galilee.

(3) The furnishing of the large catch of fish (John 21:14)
Τοῦτο ἤδη τρίτον ἐφανερώθη Ἰησοῦς τοῖς μαθηταῖς ἐγερθεὶς ἐκ νεκρῶν.

This was now the third (time) Jesus was made manifest to his disciples, after he was raised from the dead.

All occur in Galilee; and Boismard contends that, in a putative source (in which they were all contiguous), they echoed the three miracles given to Moses to prove his commission from the Lord in Exodus 4:1-9. 'Moses had to perform three "signs" in order to authenticate his mission to the Hebrews, so must Jesus himself perform three "signs" in Galilee in order to be "manifested" as the Messiah sent by God.'[383]

Boismard builds on earlier redaction critics, who have suggested that initially the first two,[384] and ultimately all three pericopes,[385] were once of a piece. Where the earlier exegetes identified this tradition as part of the so-called Semeia Source, however, Boismard hesitates to go so far.[386] To support his own case for this source, he argues several points about features of the text that could otherwise suggest a different scenario[387]:

---

382. John 2:1-12; 4:46-54; 21:1-14. Because Boismard argues for specific grammatical readings of the numbering formulae for each of these episodes, the English translation is based upon B.T. Viviano's translation of his work; *Moses or Jesus*, 44 (cf. p. 50).
383. *Moses or Jesus*, 55.
384. Julius Wellhausen, *Das Evangelium Johannis* (Berlin: G. Reimer, 1908), 13–14.
385. Friedrich Spitta, *Das Johannes-Evangelium als Quelle der Geschichte Jesus* (Göttingen: Vandenhoeck & Ruprecht, 1910), 63–70; and Hans-Peter Heekerens, *Die Zeichen-Quelle der johanneischen Redaktion: Ein Beitrag zur Entstehungsgeschichte des vierten Evangeliums*, SBS 113 (Stuttgart: Katholisches Bibelwerk, 1984), in its entirety.
386. *Moses or Jesus*, 42, 46.
387. For the following, *Moses or Jesus*, 43–55.

(1) that, to align the second pericope with the end of the first (which has Jesus traveling to Capernaum[388]), the original tradition had Jesus heal the royal official's son from Capernaum, not Cana;
(2) that, to align the numbering language of the second pericope with that of the first,[389] its feminine demonstrative pronoun (ταύτην) must be understood as an original neuter accusative (τοῦτο), later attracted to the case of the feminine noun (ἀρχήν) it now modifies;
(3) that, (similarly) to align the numbering formula of the second pericope with that of the first, the terms δεύτερον σημεῖον in that formulation must be read as adjective and noun, respectively, in apposition to the preceding τοῦτο: 'This, again, did Jesus as the second sign …';
(4) that the post-resurrection miraculous draft of fish in John 21 has been re-situated from its location in the original source (also shared by Luke) at the beginning of Jesus's ministry[390];
(5) and that the admonition Jesus received from his brothers to make pilgrimage to Judaea at John 7:3-4 originally furnished the narrative bridge between the second and third signs.

From these premises Boismard arrives at a source that closes each pericope with similar formulae: all begin with demonstrative pronouns; their sequence is registered with 'a continuous enumeration'; the first two formulae refer to 'signs' (σημεῖα); and the first and third speak of Jesus in some way manifesting (φανεροῦν) himself.[391] Boismard then compares these formulae with the three miracles Moses received to validate his commission by the Lord at Exodus 4:1-9 and concludes that this source was designed to present Jesus as the prophet like Moses foretold in Deuteronomy 18:18-19. Like Exodus 4:1-9, Jesus's miracles in the Fourth Gospel are called 'signs'; like Exodus 4:1-9, the first two of those signs are numbered; and like Exodus 4:1-9, these signs serve the 'apologetic function' of proving his divine commission (see Table 21).[392]

As already noted, this thesis is not without its vulnerabilities. At points it requires inferred readings that are not attested in the textual tradition: that Jesus healed the royal official's son from Capernaum rather than Cana; that the feminine demonstrative ταύτην at John 2:11 had originally been the neuter τοῦτο. Further, the symmetry of its numbering formulae only holds if other features in each are ignored. The full second formula, for instance, asserts that this was the second sign

---

388. John 2:12, 'After this, he went up to Capernaum – he, his mother, his brothers and his disciples – and there they remained not many days.'

389. John 2:11; 4:54. For this and the next point made by Boismard, see the Greek and English translations of these formulae represented above.

390. Boismard understands this miraculous draft of fish tradition as specifically reflected in John 21:1-4, 6, 8, 11, and he sees its source also reflected in Luke 5:1-11; *Moses or Jesus*, 46–48.

391. *Moses or Jesus*, 50–52 (quotation p. 51).

392. *Moses or Jesus*, 55–59.

2. Isa 53:1 and Isa 6:10, An Obstruction to Faith

Table 21 Exodus 4:1-9 and the numbered signs performed by Jesus

Exodus 4:1-9[393]	Numbered signs performed by Jesus
Then Moses responded and said, 'But suppose they will not believe me or listen to my voice; for they will say, "The Lord has not appeared to you"'? The Lord said to him, '... If they will not believe you or listen to the voice of the first sign (האת הראשון/τοῦ σημείου τοῦ πρώτου), they will believe the voice of the next one (האת האחרון/τοῦ σημείου τοῦ ἐσχάτου). And if they will not believe even these two signs (לשני האתות האלה/τοῖς δυσὶν σημείοις τούτοις) or listen to your voice, you shall draw from the water of the Nile and pour onto the dry ground; and the water which you take from the Nile will become blood on the dry ground'.	• The turning of water into wine (John 2:11) This did Jesus as a beginning of the signs (ἀρχὴν τῶν σημείων) ... • The healing of the royal official's son (John 4:54) This, again, did Jesus as the second sign (δεύτερον σημεῖον) ... • The furnishing of the large catch of fish (John 21:14) This was now the third (time) (τρίτον) Jesus was made manifest to his disciples ...

Jesus performed 'when he had come from Judaea to Galilee', indicating a southern itinerary which was not to have occurred in this source.[394] And the third formula, for its part, makes no explicit mention of a 'sign' and could simply be read to be counting the miraculous catch of fish as Jesus's third resurrection appearance to the disciples: 'This was now the third (time) Jesus was made manifest to his disciples, after he was raised from the dead.' Boismard, with redaction critics, assumes that the noun to be supplied to the ordinal τρίτον is σημεῖον.[395] But, if one just counts Jesus's post-resurrection manifestations to the male disciples, it quite readily can refer to them – signs or no.[396] Finally, Boismard's argument that the verb φανεροῦν at John 21:14 connotes a messianic 'manifestation' more appropriate to Jesus's public ministry than to his resurrection appearances appeals at one point to *Psalms of Solomon* 18:5 which, while carrying the theme, does not, in fact, attest the term: 'May God purify Israel for the day of mercy in blessing, for the day of selection in the raising up (ἐν ἀνάξει) of his Christ.'[397]

The gist of Boismard's proposal, however, can still apply – that is, in a broader, less exacting mode, without the requirement that Jesus's signs number three, that they unfold seriatim or that they were done only in Galilee. Not just three, but all

---

393. These three works of power are also called 'signs' (אותות/σημεῖα) at Exod 4:17, 28, 30; LXX Exod 7:9.

394. Here one might especially note that Boismard explicitly builds his case by focusing only on 'the first part of the formulas'; *Moses or Jesus*, 44; cf. page 50.

395. *Moses or Jesus*, 45–46; cf. Robert T. Fortna, *The Gospel of Signs: A Reconstruction of the Narrative Source Underlying the Fourth Gospel*, SNTSMS 11 (Cambridge: Cambridge University Press, 1970), 103–04; as well as the references to Spitta and Heekerens in note 385.

396. The first (John 20:19-23), second (John 20:26-29) and third (John 21:1-14).

397. *Pss. Sol.* 18:5; *Moses or Jesus*, 48–49. Text: Robert B. Wright, ed., *The Psalms of Solomon: A Critical Edition of the Greek Text*, Jewish and Christian Texts in Contexts and Related Studies 1 (New York: T&T Clark, 2007).

of Jesus's works of power in the Fourth Gospel are, of course, called 'signs'. Correspondingly, more than three of Moses's works of power in the exodus story are dubbed the same: 'sign' (אות/σημεῖον) is used for all the plagues he performed upon Egypt,[398] sometimes with the term 'wonders'[399]; and it is also employed for the gamut of miracles Moses performed in the wilderness[400] – including Israel's worship at Sinai, the designed result of his commission.[401] Coupled with the major Johannine christological theme of Jesus as 'the one sent' from the Father,[402] it is arguable that this aspect of Moses typology seen by Boismard lies beneath the whole of Jesus's public ministry to the Jews in the Fourth Gospel. The full array of σημεῖα in the Fourth Gospel may plausibly reflect Jesus as a new Moses, sent by the Father to deliver and lead the Ἰουδαῖοι, so that for Jesus to plead with Philip, 'Believe me ... but, if not, believe because of the works themselves', is antitypical of the Lord saying to Moses, 'If they will not believe you or listen to the voice of the first sign, they will believe the voice of the next one.'[403]

Such a typology confirms the evidence from the Johannine narrative recounted above that 'signs' in the Fourth Gospel do not operate separately from 'testimony'. It suggests rather that they serve as a divine concession to reinforce 'testimony' for those who will not believe (as they should) on words alone: in Exodus 4 the אותות/σημεῖα do so to validate Moses's (verbal) claim that he had been sent by the Lord; in the Fourth Gospel the σημεῖα do so to validate Jesus's (verbal) claim to have been sent by the Father. And to return to the issue at hand, this lends a nuance to John 12:37 relative to 'our report' that is often missed. When the evangelist remarks, 'But, though he had done so many signs before them, they were not believing in him', he is not articulating a stilted 'σημεῖα soteriology', in which faith is expected to have been evoked solely from 'seeing' Jesus's 'signs'. Rather, he is accentuating the depth of the Jews' unbelief in 'testimony' by underscoring the extent of divine concession made to persuade them otherwise. Its import is that even though the Jews' disinclination to 'believe' from 'words' was compensated by Jesus with such a great apologetic manifestation of 'signs', they still remained unbelieving. Or to paraphrase, 'But, although Jesus had accommodated the evidence the Jews needed to believe his message by backing it up with so many signs, the Jews were still not responding.' The 'report' is still in view; it is just implicit in ('baked into') the language of 'signs'.

On this score the 'report' of Isaiah 53:1 at John 12:38 does carry significance. Jesus's signs were to validate his message; and the question, 'Lord, who has believed

---

398. Exod 7:3; 8:19; 10:1-2; 11:9-10 [LXX only]; Deut 4:34; 6:22; 7:19; 11:3; 26:8; 29:1-3; 34:10-12; Josh 24:17 [HB only]; Pss 78:42-43; 105:26-27; 135:8-9; Wis 10:15-16; LXX Sir 45:3.

399. Note John 4:48, 'Unless you see signs and wonders (σημεῖα καὶ τέρατα), you will not believe.'

400. Num 14:11, 22; 26:10 [LXX only]; Deut 29:1-3.

401. Exod 3:12.

402. John 4:34; 5:23-24, 30, 37; 6:38-39, 44; 7:16, 28, 33; 8:16, 18, 26, 29; 9:4; 12:44-45, 49; 13:20; 14:24; 15:21; 16:5; 20:21.

403. John 14:10-11; Exod 4:8.

our report'?, asserts that the Jews' refusal to believe the one (his signs) signals a (prior) refusal to believe the other (his words).[404]

(2) Isaiah, John, God and Moses
Inasmuch as this lament of Isaiah 53:1 is being uttered by Isaiah, the possessive 'our' which modifies that 'report' certainly includes him, as a proleptic witness to Jesus's public ministry. But it likely embraces other voices from the Book of Signs, as well, that have now joined Isaiah in this testimony. Jesus, to be sure, who throughout his ministry testified to himself.[405] And taking into account the *inclusio* with John 1:23 created by the Isaianic introductory formulae, John, also.[406] As Alicia Myers has put it, with John's quotation of Isaiah 40:3 at John 1:23, 'John's voice is fully blended into that of Isaiah as part of the narrative's larger presentation of Jesus as the consistent subject of scripture'[407]; and this would certainly include the quotation of Isaiah 53:1 at John 12:38. Moreover, to John's testimony there might be added several others still: those of the Father (through the works given to Jesus),[408] of Moses (through the scripture),[409] of the Johannine editors or community,[410] of the multitude who witnessed the raising of Lazarus (if

---

404. This observation does not dismiss the consensus explanation of the two anomalies in John 12:40 tied to John 12:37 (see above in this chapter, under *(a) On the anomalies)*. It does, however, modify it. The removal of the cola treating 'ears' and 'hearing' (Isa 6:10be) still reflects a focus on 'seeing' to 'believe', but it also reflects the evangelist's characteristic economy, inasmuch as the theme of hearing is already present in Isa 53:1a at John 12:38. In his argument for a LXX *Vorlage* to John 12:40/Isa 6:10, Schuchard notes that ἀκοή occurs in LXX Isa 6:9 (ἀκοῇ ἀκούσετε) and suggests that its presence there is what led the evangelist to insert LXX Isa 53:1 before Isa 6:10 at John 12:38-40 (see above in this chapter, under *(b) The LXX and Mark)*. One might press further and suggest that Isa 53:1 is meant to stand in for Isa 6:9 at John 12:38-40 and that, by its reading of ἀκοή for ἀκούειν, the motif of faith by hearing in Isa 6:9-10 has been retained in these two quotations. Similarly, the inversion of the *chiasmus* into the sequence 'eyes'/'heart'/'eyes'/'heart' still represents the process by which signs would otherwise have evoked faith (had the Jews not been 'blinded' and 'hardened'). That process, however, is conceived only to be at issue because the sequence 'ears'/'heart' (embodied now in Isa 53:1a) had failed.

405. John 3:32-33; 8:13-18; cf. John 18:37.
406. Cf. John 1:6-8, 15, 19, 32-34; 3:26; 5:33-35.
407. 'A Voice in the Wilderness: Classical Rhetoric and the Testimony of John (the Baptist) in John 1:19-34', in *Abiding Words: The Use of Scripture in the Gospel of John*, 132.
408. John 5:31-32, 36-38; 8:17-18; 10:25.
409. John 5:39-40, 45-47.
410. This, if one takes the collective 'we' at John 3:11 to include either of these groups: 'Truly I say to you', replies Jesus to Nicodemus, 'we speak what we know and testify to what we have seen, and you do not receive our testimony'. Similar is the suggestion by Hoskyns that the 'report' includes the later transmission of Jesus's teaching through the disciples' *kerygma* (John 17:20); *The Fourth Gospel*, 428. The connection between John 3:11 and 'our report' at John 12:38/Isa 53:1 is noted by Schuchard, *Scripture within Scripture*, 88n14; cf. also John 21:24.

only temporarily)[411] and, though stated later, of the Beloved Disciple.[412] At the very least, Jesus, John, the Father and Moses may be joining Isaiah in the testimony to Jesus articulated as 'our report'.[413]

b. 'The arm of the Lord'

As to the second phrase, 'arm of the Lord' in the next colon, it creates a foil to the unbelief lamented in the first colon. As a metaphor, it signifies 'divine strength' or 'power'; and given the reference to 'so many signs' at John 12:37, its intended referent is likely not the 'report' to which Isaiah refers in the previous colon[414] but the σημεῖα Jesus had just performed through his public ministry. This is amply supported in the Book of Signs, wherein Jesus's 'signs' and 'works' are depicted as being (in some way) a disclosure of divine reality. The language elsewhere is not identical to that of John 12:38/Isaiah 53:1b, inasmuch as ἀποκαλύπτειν in that quotation is a *hapax legomenon* to Johannine literature. The idea, however, is: the 'signs' Jesus performs during his public ministry make deity visible to those who see them.[415]

Reading 'arm of the Lord' this way sets the assertion in the second colon of the quotation over against that of the first; and (in reverse order) it reiterates the

---

411. John 12:17. Also testifying to Jesus in John 1-12 is the Samaritan woman – to other Samaritans (John 4:39); but, since the quotation of Isa 53:1 at John 12:38 is specifically lamenting the unbelief of the Jews, she may not strictly be in view for 'our report'.
412. John 19:35; 21:24.
413. So similarly Obermann, *Die christologische Erfüllung der Schrift im Johannesevangelium*, 227-28.
414. As Bultmann would have it; *Gospel of John*, 453n1.
415. In one respect these signs disclose the divine nature of Jesus: his 'first sign' of changing water to wine at Cana 'manifested (ἐφανέρωσεν) his glory' (John 2:11); and his brothers equate doing his works (σοῦ τὰ ἔργα ἃ ποιεῖς) before his disciples with being 'in the open' (ἐν παρρησίᾳ) rather than acting 'in secret' (ἐν κρυπτῷ), that is, with 'manifesting himself (φανέρωσον σεαυτόν) to the world' (John 7:3-4). Primarily, however, Jesus's signs disclose the Father and his power. Jesus 'did' (ποιεῖ) what he saw the Father doing (ποιῇ/John 5:19) and, so, 'worked the works' (ἐργάζεσθαι τὰ ἔργα) of him who sent him (John 9:4) and 'did the works (ποιῶ τὰ ἔργα) of (his) Father' (John 10:37). He 'worked' (ἐργάζομαι) on the Sabbath because the Father was 'working' (ἐργάζεται) on that day (John 5:17); his healing of the man born blind made 'the works of God (τὰ ἔργα τοῦ θεοῦ) manifest (φανερωθῇ)' in that man (John 9:3); and so by performing such signs he 'showed' (ἔδειξα) the Jews 'many good works (πολλὰ ἔργα καλά) from the Father' (John 10:32). As such, the Father was in essence 'doing his works' (ποιεῖ τὰ ἔργα αὐτοῦ) while abiding in Jesus (John 14:10); and this allowed the Jews to 'know and continue to know' (γνῶτε καὶ γινώσκητε) the reciprocal indwelling that occurred between the two – 'that the Father is in me and I in the Father' (John 10:37-38) – so that to see the one (Jesus) was to see the other (the Father/John 14:10-11). By doing 'the works (τὰ ἔργα) ... which no one else did' Jesus enabled the world to 'see (ἑωράκασιν) and hate' both him and his Father (John 15:24). Indeed, through Jesus's 'signs' (σημεῖα) Nicodemus becomes aware that God is 'with him' (John 3:2).

sentiment just expressed at John 12:37. Both cola of Isaiah 53:1 are rhetorical questions, posed as queries but, in fact, asserting implicit answers to those queries. The implied answer to Isaiah 53:1a, 'who has believed our report'?, is 'no one'; and, if 'arm of the Lord' means Jesus's signs, the implied answer to Isaiah 53:1b, 'to whom has the arm of the Lord (signs) been revealed'?, is the opposite – everyone, since by chapter 12 all had seen Jesus's signs. This requires the conjunction καί at Isaiah 53:1b to carry adversative rather than copulative force[416]; and, though the two cola lie syntactically in synonymous parallelism, they semantically relate in antithetical parallelism. Paraphrased, with the rhetorical questions transformed into their implied assertions, the quotation gives the following sense:

Lord, no one has believed our report.
Yet (καί) to everyone has the arm of the Lord been revealed.

The commentary at John 12:37 had essentially made this same declaration, albeit with the idea of 'signs' preceding (rather than following) 'unbelief'. And so, at John 12:38/Isaiah 53:1 that commentary is repeated in an Isaianic key, creating a (small) thematic *chiasmus* between them[417]:

A   But though he had done so many *signs* before them,
B   they *were not believing* in him,
    that the word of Isaiah the prophet (Isaiah 53:1) might be fulfilled, which he said,
B' 'Lord, *who has believed* our report?
A' And to whom has *the arm of the Lord* been revealed'?

Put another way, the quotation at John 12:38 'seconds' the commentary at John 12:37 and is likely brought in by the evangelist as a proof-text for it.[418]

416. See Herbert Weir Smyth, *Greek Grammar*, ed. Gordon M. Messing, rev. ed. (Cambridge, MA: Harvard University Press, 1956), 650–651.
417. Also noting this is Menken, despite his stance that the first colon of the quotation speaks of faith in general (rather than faith in Jesus's message); 'The Use of the Septuagint in Three Quotations in John: Jn 10,34; 12,38; 19,24', 386; cf. p. 383.
418. From John 6:26 it might be argued that Jesus's works of power were not seen as 'signs' per se and, therefore, that 'the arm of the Lord' (as 'signs') had not been revealed to anyone. There the multitude who had been miraculously fed by the Sea of Galilee (John 6:5-13) – and who had deduced Jesus's miraculous crossing of the sea (John 6:22) – are scolded by Jesus as if they had nonetheless not seen σημεῖα: 'Truly I say to you, you seek me, not because you saw signs (σημεῖα), but because you ate of the loaves and were satisfied.' Were this the case, Isa 53:1b at John 12:38 would be semantically (as well as syntactically) related to Isa 53:1a in synonymous (rather than antithetical) parallelism. Jesus's admonition in this instance, however, does not deny that the multitude had seen his signs as 'signs'; it simply reproves them for following him on other grounds: 'because you ate of the loaves and were satisfied'; see also on this, Painter, 'The Quotation of Scripture and Unbelief in John 12.36b-43', 447–48.

c. Summary

In sum, the quotation of Isaiah 53:1 at John 12:38 is drawn verbatim from the LXX; and in its Johannine context it depicts Isaiah lamenting the Jews' unbelief to 'the Lord'. By being explicitly ascribed to Isaiah (through its introductory formula) it is rhetorically connected with two other *loci* in the Book of Signs: the allusion to Isaiah's throne room vision at John 12:41 and (by *inclusio*) the quotation of Isaiah 40:3 at John 1:23. And its two cola serve two ends in that broader narrative: the first (Isaiah 53:1a) picks up the call to faith embodied in John (as the 'voice' of Isaiah 40:3) and mourns the lack of response to it over the course of Jesus's public ministry; the second (Isaiah 53:1b) repeats the evangelist's own commentary on that unbelief at John 12:37 in reverse order, forming a *chiasmus* across the two by setting the Jews' lack of faith over against the divine power used to persuade them otherwise.

2. Isaiah 6:10: Belief obstructed

a. Isaiah 6:10 and the Jews' unbelief

(1) 'For this reason they could not believe' (John 12:39)

The quotation of Isaiah 6:10, for its part, is cited to give further commentary on the Jews' unbelief. It has been suggested by some that it elucidates the effect of that unbelief, that is, that the 'blinding' and 'hardening' at John 12:40 represent God's response to the unbelief at John 12:37.[419] Two grammatical factors at John 12:39, however, require that it be understood differently – that is, as the cause of that unbelief:

> διὰ τοῦτο οὐκ ἠδύναντο πιστεύειν, ὅτι πάλιν εἶπεν Ἡσαΐας·
>
> For this reason they were not able to believe, that again Isaiah said ...

First is the tense of δύνασθαι relative to the tense of ἐπίστευον at John 12:37. Like ἐπίστευον, it is imperfect (ἠδύναντο); and, inasmuch as (with the negative οὐκ) it expresses the Jews' inability to believe, it thereby asserts that such inability existed at the time they were not believing (not as a later consequence of that unbelief). That is, in the evangelist's mind, it was not that the Jews cannot believe now because they did not believe then. Rather, they did not believe then because they could not do so at the time.

> But though he had done so many signs before them,
> they were not believing (οὐκ ἐπίστευον) in him ...
> For this reason they were not able to believe (οὐκ ἠδύναντο πιστεύειν) ...

---

419. For instance, Paul A. Rainbow, *Johannine Theology: The Gospel, The Epistles and the Apocalypse* (Downers Grove, IL: IVP Academic, 2014), 138, 142n75, 288.

2. Isa 53:1 and Isa 6:10, An Obstruction to Faith

The second factor at John 12:39 is the construct 'for this reason ... that/because' (διὰ τοῦτο ... ὅτι). Based on usage elsewhere in the gospel, had the prepositional phrase appeared alone (without ὅτι), it might refer to any number of antecedents subsequent or prior to it in the text.[420] In the Fourth Gospel, however, whenever διὰ τοῦτο is followed by a causal or noun clause introduced by ὅτι, its antecedent is always that clause[421]:

And for this reason (διὰ τοῦτο) the Jews were persecuting Jesus,
that/because (ὅτι) he was doing these things on Sabbath.[422]

For this reason (διὰ τοῦτο), therefore, the Jews were seeking all the more to kill him, that/because (ὅτι) he was not only breaking the Sabbath, but also calling God his own Father, making himself equal to God.[423]

The one who is from God hears the words of God.
For this reason (διὰ τοῦτο) you do not hear,
that/because (ὅτι) you are not from God.[424]

For this reason (διὰ τοῦτο) the Father loves me,
that/because (ὅτι) I lay down my life, that I may take it again.[425]

For this reason (διὰ τοῦτο) the crowd greeted him,
that/because (ὅτι) they heard that he had done this sign.[426]

For John 12:39, such syntax makes the antecedent of διὰ τοῦτο the ὅτι clause which follows it[427]; and this, in turn, renders the 'reason' for which the Jews could not believe to be Isaiah's declaration in Isaiah 6:10, as reworked by the evangelist:

For this reason (διὰ τοῦτο) they were not able to believe,
that/because (ὅτι) again Isaiah said,
'He has blinded their eyes
and hardened their heart,

---

420. So John 1:31; 6:63-65; 7:21-22 (the majority or variant punctuation); 9:22-23; 12:27; 13:11; 15:19; 16:15; 19:11 (at John 6:65; 9:22-23; 13:11; 16:15 a subsequent ὅτι occurs but introduces discourse).
421. Thus, supporting Bernard, *Critical and Exegetical Commentary on the Gospel according to St. John*, 2:450; and Barrett, *Gospel according to St. John*, 431.
422. John 5:16.
423. John 5:18.
424. John 8:47.
425. John 10:17.
426. John 12:18.
427. Painter arrives at this conclusion on the more subjective premise that the alternative antecedent to διὰ τοῦτο, John 12:38/Isa 53:1, 'gives no explanation for the unbelief in the face of Jesus' signs'; 'The Quotation of Scripture and Unbelief in John 12.36b-43', 444.

> lest they perceive with the eyes
> and discern with the heart,
> and turn, and I heal them.'

Taken with the contemporaneous imperfects οὐκ ἐπίστευον and οὐκ ἠδύναντο πιστεύειν at John 12:37 and 12:39, this syntax casts the quotation of Isaiah 6:10 as elucidating the cause (not the consequence) of the Jews' unbelief. Where the quotation of Isaiah 53:1 at John 12:38 issues a prophetic lament over that unbelief, the quotation of Isaiah 6:10 at John 12:40 will divulge the reason for its occurrence.

(2) Metaphorical blindness

That reason, as the quotation of Isaiah 6:10 has it, is the impairment of mental (or what might be called 'inner') perception. The third-person actor is described as 'blinding the eyes' and 'hardening the heart' of the Jews, 'lest they perceive with the eyes and discern with the heart'; but on at least two grounds this 'blinding' cannot be taken as literal. One, noted by Painter, is that the 'hardening of the heart' is not so (suggesting that the 'blinding' in the prior colon follows suit).[428] The other is that there is no denial in the Fourth Gospel's narrative that the Jews had literally heard Jesus's words and seen his signs. The argument that might be made to the contrary from John 6:26, as shown above, breaks down upon closer examination.[429] As such, the 'blinding' which disabled the Jews from believing must be figurative, designating the impairment of an inner capacity to perceive; and it is that debilitation which is said in these quotations to have prevented the Jews from believing in Jesus during his public ministry.

b. Isaiah's apocalyptic vision

(1) Jesus as 'agent of healing'

To pick up now the question of the first-person speaker and third-person actor (reviewed above), two of the premises for Jesus as "the agent of healing' weaken under scrutiny: Painter's argument that the antecedent to the phrase 'his glory' (τὴν δόξαν αὐτοῦ) at John 12:41 is one and the same with the antecedent to the phrase 'in him' at John 12:42 (and so, Jesus); and Schnackenburg's observation that the 'healing' associated with the first-person speaker corresponds thematically (and in two cases, lexically) with Jesus's healing signs.[430] Contrary to Painter, the reference to Jesus at John 12:42 may, in fact, pick up from the reference to him at John 12:37, leaving the quotations in between (John 12:38-40) to function as an excursus, with different referents to its personal pronouns:

---

428. 'The Quotation of Scripture and Unbelief in John 12.36b-43', 448.
429. Note 418.
430. See above in this chapter, under *[1] 'The agent of healing'*; cf. the use of ἰᾶσθαι at John 4:47; 5:13.

But though he had done so many signs before them,
they were not believing in him (οὐκ ἐπίστευον εἰς αὐτόν) ...
Nevertheless, however, many of the rulers believed in him (ἐπίστευσαν εἰς αὐτόν);
but because of the Pharisees, they were not confessing, lest they be put out of the synagogue.

In such a reading, the antecedent of 'his glory' at John 12:41 could differ from that of 'in him' at John 12:42.

And on the point made by Schnackenburg, where the 'healing' in Jesus's signs is presented as literal,[431] the 'healing' of the first-person speaker is likely figurative; as hearts are not literally hardened in the quotation, nor eyes (which have seen signs) literally blinded, so the clause 'lest ... I heal them' is more apt to be metaphor than actual cure. As such, the import of the clause 'and I heal them' at John 12:40e is somewhat removed from the actual healing done by Jesus in the narrative and, so, does not necessarily connote him as its speaker.

That said, the weight of evidence nonetheless favours Jesus as the first-person speaker, 'the agent of healing'. In part, this is due to three weaknesses in the case for Jesus as third-person actor. Two are the arguments posed by Lieu and Hollenbach: specifically, their (mutual) observation that Jesus is the most likely antecedent to the quotation; and the inference by Hollenbach that as Jesus's parables in Mark were designed 'to conceal (his) teachings from "those outside"', so his public ministry in the Fourth Gospel was calculated to do the same with the Jews to whom he appealed.[432] Against the first, it is missed by Lieu and Hollenbach that Jesus can just as well serve as antecedent to the first-person speaker as he might to the third-person actor (and so be 'the agent of healing' rather than 'the cause of obduracy'). And against the second, there is a noteworthy difference in the means by which people are kept from perceiving in Mark (and the Synoptics), on one hand, and John, on the other. Where in the former it is done by the genre of Jesus's teaching (parables),[433] in the latter it is done by the impairment of metaphorical senses ('blinding' and 'hardening'); and at the very least this summons caution in using the one (Mark) to interpret the other (John).

Further, to contemplate Jesus as the third-person actor requires the first-person speaker to be either God or Isaiah, and neither are probable. Were it God, the quotation would cast God as wishing to heal while Jesus obscures; and, if the Johannine narrative suggests anything, it is that those roles are the other way round: it is the Father who 'draws', 'teaches' and 'gives' some,[434] while Jesus invites all. Were it Isaiah, by contrast, the quotation would set the prophet in a station that is unlikely to have been endorsed by the evangelist. In LXX Isaiah 6:10g, 'lest ... I heal them', it is the Lord who would heal; and, even if the 'salvation' meant by this metaphor could be done by a human (which is open to question), it is doubtful the evangelist would have reassigned words originally spoken by God to a prophet.

431. John 4:46-54; 5:1-9; 9:1-7.
432. See above in this chapter, under *[a] Jesus*.
433. Mark 4:10-12; cf. also Matt 13:10-15; Luke 8:9-10.
434. See note 333.

Most forceful for Jesus as the first-person speaker, however, is the premise most cited: the christological connotation of the commentary at John 12:41, recounted above.[435] Inasmuch as Jesus is the manifestation of the Father in the Fourth Gospel, he is 'the glory' of God. Thus, for Isaiah to have seen 'his glory' at John 12:41 was for him to have encountered the pre-incarnate Jesus as a disclosure of God; and such a scenario readily suggests that the speaker in Isaiah 6:10 was that same pre-incarnate Jesus, addressing the prophet.[436] This position can, in fact, be construed in a slightly different key. The sentiment of Isaiah 'seeing his glory' at John 12:41 is not far removed from that of the authorial 'we' at John 1:14 'beholding' the glory of Christ. The verbs differ – 'see' (ὁρᾶν) at John 12:41; 'behold' (θεᾶσθαι) at John 1:14; but the idea is the same:

These things Isaiah said, because he saw his glory (εἶδεν τὴν δόξαν αὐτοῦ) and spoke about him.[437]

And the Word became flesh and dwelt among us;
and we beheld his glory (ἐθεασάμεθα τὴν δόξαν αὐτοῦ),
glory (δόξαν) as of the only begotten from the Father, full of grace and truth.[438]

If the two can be equated, then, the import of the commentary at John 12:41 slightly shifts. Isaiah would not have seen Jesus as 'the glory' of another – that is, of God. He would have seen Jesus's own 'glory' in pre-incarnate form, similar to the way the Johannine authors would later behold that 'glory' in incarnate form.[439]

In either case, the christological import of the commentary at John 12:41, coupled with the problems attending Jesus as third-person actor, strongly suggests that Jesus is the first-person speaker in the quotation: 'lest I heal them' is Jesus speaking, as 'the agent of healing'.

(a) Prophetic lament and divine reply

With Jesus as this first-person speaker, two further aspects of these quotations come into relief. The first is that, taken together, they cast Isaiah and the pre-incarnate Christ in a trope of prophetic and apocalyptic literature: the despairing prophet and the consoling deity. The vocative 'Lord', which opens the quotation of LXX Isaiah 53:1, begins an address from Isaiah to that first-person figure; and the first-person clause 'lest I heal them', which closes the quotation of Isaiah 6:10, frames the entirety of that verse as a response to the questions posed by Isaiah in that first quotation. Inasmuch as this 'agent of healing' in Isaiah 6:10 is the

---

435. Above in this chapter, under *[1] 'The agent of healing'*.
436. See Schnackenburg, *Gospel according to St John*, 2:416–17.
437. John 12:41.
438. John 1:14. The interrelationship between the two texts is noted by Brown, *Gospel according to John*, 1:487.
439. It should be said that Schnackenburg's case for the first view stated (that Isaiah saw Jesus as God's glory) allows for this second view, as well; see the reference in note 436.

pre-incarnate Jesus, the two quotations operate as a dialogue between the two figures; and inasmuch as Isaiah mourns unbelief and Jesus explains his inability to 'heal', this conversation is modelled on the classic scenario of a downcast prophet grieving his circumstances to the Lord and the Lord (or emissary) revealing why those circumstances are so (Table 22).[440]

Table 22 Isaiah 53:1 and Isaiah 6:10 as prophetic lament and divine reply

Verse	Quotation	Speaker	Discourse
Isaiah 53:1	Lord, who has believed our report? And to whom has the arm of the Lord been revealed?	Isaiah to the Lord	Lament over the condition of the people
Isaiah 6:10	He has blinded their eyes and hardened their heart, lest they perceive with the eyes and discern with the heart, and turn, and I heal them.	The Lord to Isaiah	Explanation for the condition of the people

Noticing this scenario between the quotations, Ernst Haenchen breaks out of commentary into homily:

> We are therefore not the first and only ones who have had a dismal experience with our preaching, but come in a long line of bitterly disappointed proclaimers who are forced to cry out to God because nobody listens.[441]

(b) Signs as 'the arm of the Father'

The second aspect of the quotations to come into relief with Jesus as the first-person speaker concerns the second reference to 'the Lord' in the quotation of Isaiah 53:1 at John 12:38 – specifically, in the phrase 'arm of the Lord' at Isaiah 53:1b. In the LXX, which is cited, this designation reads awkwardly, because the Greek translator has inserted a vocative 'Lord' at the beginning of the verse: Isaiah addresses 'the Lord' in the first colon ('Lord, who has believed our report'?) yet speaks to that 'Lord' about 'the arm of (another?) Lord' in the second colon ('and to whom has the arm of the Lord been revealed'?). If Isaiah is addressing the pre-incarnate Jesus, however – as the first-person speaker in Isaiah 6:10 at John 12:40 – this awkwardness could be resolved in the Johannine rendering by understanding this second reference to 'the Lord' as speaking of 'the Father'. Such a reading is certainly allowed by the evangelist's binitarianism. And, inasmuch as the phrase 'arm of the Lord' designates Jesus's σημεῖα, it fits snugly with the Fourth Gospel's insistence that the 'signs' or 'works' performed by Jesus were given him by the Father.[442]

---

440. Such a reading means that the assertions 'Isaiah said' in the introductory formulae and John 12:41 (see above in this chapter, under *1. Ascriptions to Isaiah in the immediate context*) do not (merely) refer to the words verbalized by Isaiah in the conversation. They refer, rather, to his transmission of the whole experience, that is, of both voices in that encounter.
441. *John 1–2*, 2:101.
442. John 5:31-32, 36-38.

(2) 'The ruler of this world' as 'the cause of obduracy'

As for 'the cause of obduracy', the weight of evidence favours 'the ruler of this world' as that figure. Hypotheses for 'signs' and 'the report' of Isaiah 53:1 clash with the syntax required at John 12:39; and, though the case for 'God' can to some degree withstand critique – and even finds cognate support from Qumran – it must give way to 'the devil', when the language of John 12:40 is revisited in its broader Johannine (and early Christian) context.

(a) Rival hypotheses

[1] Signs and Jesus's message

On 'signs' or Jesus's 'message' as the third-person actor,[443] both models have attracted critique. Against the appeal to Deuteronomy 29:1-3 (for 'signs'), Painter has observed that this passage rather supports 'the Father' as this figure: 'it is not the signs of Moses that produced obduracy', he writes, 'but God who withholds the understanding'.[444]

> Moses called to all Israel and said to them,
> 'You have seen all that the Lord did before your eyes in the land of Egypt,
> to Pharaoh, to all his servants and to all his land, the great ordeals which your eyes have seen, the signs (האתת/τὰ σημεῖα) and those great wonders. But *the Lord has not given you a heart to know, nor eyes to see nor ears to hear to this day*'.

And against the appeal to ἀκοή at John 12:38/Isaiah 53:1 (for Jesus's 'message'), Menken has contended that this term is too remote from the verbs at John 12:40ab to serve as the antecedent to their subjects.[445]

More conclusive, however, is that neither proposal can be sustained against the grammatical and syntactical relationships which operate between John 12:39 and John 12:37-38, discussed above.[446] The contemporaneous imperfects 'they were not able to believe' (οὐκ ἠδύναντο πιστεύειν) at John 12:39 and 'they were not believing' (οὐκ ἐπίστευον) at John 12:37 indicate that the Jews' inability to believe was present at the time they had the opportunity to do so; and the trajectory of the construct 'for this reason ... that/because' (διὰ τοῦτο ... ὅτι) at John 12:39 specifies the cause of that unbelief to be the 'blinding' and 'hardening' of Isaiah 6:10 at John 12:40. This means that the 'blinding' and 'hardening' that incapacitated the Jews from believing had already occurred by the time they were hearing 'the report' and seeing Jesus's 'signs'; and, as such, neither medium could serve as the cause of that impairment. In a word, neither Jesus's 'signs' nor his 'message' could have provoked the Jews to 'obduracy', because that obduracy was the cause of their unbelief in them.

---

443. For the arguments under critique here, see *[d] Signs* and *[e] The message of Jesus*, above in this chapter.
444. 'The Quotation of Scripture and Unbelief in John 12.36b-43', 437; cf. Evans, *To See and Not Perceive*, 134–35.
445. '"He Has Blinded Their Eyes ... " (John 12:40)', 109–10.
446. See *(1) 'For this reason they could not believe' (John 12:39)*, above in this chapter.

[2] God

[a] Answers to criticisms
The consensus view that God the Father is the third-person actor, for its part, has also come under criticism, but not all of it stands up to scrutiny. Two arguments, offered by Schuchard, are readily countered: specifically, that since the Father has committed all judgement to the Son,[447] God, himself, does not judge (and, so, would not have 'blinded' or 'hardened'); and that since the first-person speaker in LXX Isaiah 6:10g is (and remains) 'God', reading 'God' also as the third-person actor requires 'an original Old Testament passage containing a grammatical impossibility: "He (God) blinded ... and I (God) heal them"'.[448] On the first – that God, himself, does not judge – one might first question whether 'blinding' and 'hardening' are 'judgement' per se. Could they not rather represent the creation of conditions that would lead to condemnation at such an event? Even if they are 'judgement', however, the Father may indeed be said to have committed such to the Son at John 5:22, 26-27, but the fluid expression of Johannine theological concepts cautions against taking these statements as hard-and-fast doctrine: at John 8:50b, for instance, the Father is also the one who 'seeks and judges'. And further, even taking the Father's delegation of judgement into account, the judgement enacted by Jesus is in any case done according to the Father's will, so that, in fact, the two judge in tandem:

> I cannot do anything from myself. As I hear I judge; and my judgment is righteous, because I do not seek my will but the will of the one who sent me.[449]

> And even if I judge, my judgment is true; for I am not alone, but I and the Father who sent me.[450]

And as to the second criticism – the 'grammatical impossibility' of God as first-person speaker and third-person actor – this can be resolved simply by noting that the evangelist understood deity in binitarian terms: for the evangelist, Jesus no less than the Father is God; consequently, Jesus can speak as the figure in John 12:40e/Isaiah 6:10g while the Father acts as the figure in John 12:40ab/Isaiah 6:10ac.[451]

---

447. John 5:22, 26-27.
448. *Scripture within Scripture*, 98–99 (quotation p. 99, parentheses original). In an *argumentum ex silentio* Schuchard buttresses the first premise by noting that of all the references which the evangelist makes to Psalm 69 (John 2:17/Ps 69:10; John 15:25/Ps 69:5 [?]; John 19:28/Ps 69:22 [?]), he does not cite the psalmist's call at LXX Ps 69:24 for 'the eyes' of his enemies to 'be darkened, so as not to see' (σκοτισθήτωσαν ... τοῦ μὴ βλέπειν); p. 98n29.
449. John 5:30.
450. John 8:16.
451. See also Menken, who suggests that in making this argument Schuchard 'has apparently not seen the distinction of persons in the quotation with sufficient clarity'; '"He Has Blinded Their Eyes ... " (John 12:40)', 120n80.

A third criticism of this view, issued by Painter (following Josef Blank), is more telling, but still problematic – namely, that with Jesus as the first-person speaker, such activity on the part of the Father 'would strain the Johannine view that God and Jesus act as one'.[452] To this it can be conceded that the Fourth Gospel is, indeed, clear that the Father and Son work in harmony, if not in unison[453]; and that such solidarity appears breached if the one 'blinds' and 'hardens', while the other attempts to 'heal'. That 'breach', however, does not disappear if God is not the third actor at John 12:40. As Schnackenburg has observed (and as is noted above), elsewhere in the gospel we are told that while Jesus is calling all, the Father 'draws', 'teaches' and 'gives' him only some[454]; and this, in turn, suggests that, unless the evangelist has been logically inconsistent, the mode in which the Father and Son work 'as one' somehow includes both agendas: a mission to save those who would 'turn' and a decision to 'draw' a select few to do so. Such a mode, in fact, seems indicated in the *loci* which assert that even Jesus, who otherwise would 'heal' all, himself chooses only some (albeit one of them 'a devil').[455] And, under the different metaphor of Good Shepherd, it is this very combination (of calling all while drawing some) that forms the context in which Jesus declares 'I and the Father are one'. Of all the people to whom Jesus preaches, only his sheep hear his voice; and these, in turn, are those given him by the Father:

> The works which I do in my Father's name, these testify concerning me. But you do not believe, because *you are not of my sheep. My sheep hear my voice*; and I know them and they follow me, and I give them eternal life. And they will by no means ever perish, and no one will seize them from my hand. *My Father, who gave them to me*, is greater than all, and no one can seize from the Father's hand. *I and the Father are one*.[456]

For the question at hand, this means theologically that God as third-person actor in the quotation would not necessarily set him at cross-purposes with Jesus as first-person speaker.

[b] Support from a cognate text: 4QDibre Ha-Me'orot^a (4Q504)18 2-4

It should further be noted that reading God as 'the cause of obduracy' finds support from a yet unnoticed cognate text: *4QDibre Ha-Me'orot^a* (4Q504)18 2-4, a

---

452. 'The Quotation of Scripture and Unbelief in John 12.36b-43', 436; and at least allowing this possibility, Josef Blank, *Krisis: Untersuchungen zur johanneischen Christologie und Eschatologie* (Freiburg im Breisgau: Lambertus-Verlag, 1964), 304–05.

453. John 5:19-20, 30; 17:4-5.

454. See note 333.

455. 'Jesus answered them, "Did I not choose you, the Twelve"'? (John 6:70ab); 'I am not speaking about all of you; I know whom I chose' (John 13:18ab); 'You did not choose me, but I chose you and appointed you, that you might go and bear fruit …' (John 15:16a-c); 'If you were of the world, the world would love its own; but, because you are not of the world, but I chose you out of the world, for this reason the world hates you' (John 15:19).

456. John 10:25c-30 (italics added).

sectarian (or more likely proto-sectarian) work from Khirbet Qumran, published in 1982 by Maurice Baillet (Table 23).[457]

Table 23 *4QDibre Ha-Me'orot*[a] (4Q504) 18 2-4

נ[תתה להמה לב[לדעת]
[ועינים] לראות ואוזנ[ים לשמוע]
[לאחרון ותשע [עיניהמה]
He has g]iven them a heart [to know]
[and eyes] to see and ear[s to hear] …
] for the following one, and you have smeared over [their eyes]

Significant for the third-person actor at John 12:40 are two features of this fragment. The first is that, as reconstructed by Baillet, line 4 reads as a reworking of Isaiah 6:10c similar to that in John 12:40a. The verb ותשע is a second-person singular hiphil imperfect of לשע, 'to smear over'. As a consecutive following the perfect tense נ]תתה in line 2, it would be rendered as a preterite, 'you have smeared over'; and on that score – as well as on the fact that it is preceded in lines 2-3 with language similar to the sentiment in Isaiah 6:10 – Baillet has reconstructed the text which would have followed as [עיניהמה], 'their eyes', and designated the line as a reference to that verse. If he is correct, it attests to a reading of Isaiah 6:10 which, like the Fourth Gospel, (a) conceives the 'smearing over of the eyes' as having already occurred (not as something commanded to the prophet) and, presuming the second-person addressee is the Lord, (b) regards the figure who did this 'smearing over' to be God. That is, 'And you (Lord) have smeared over [their eyes]' is cognate support for God the Father at John 12:40 as 'the cause of obduracy'.

The second feature of this fragment relative to John 12:40a is that similar to the Fourth Gospel it associates this reworked Isaiah 6:10 with Moses's 'signs' in the exodus saga. The lines which immediately precede that reference read, 'He has g]iven them a heart [to know and eyes] to see and ear[s to hear] …' Their language appears to reflect a different biblical passage, juxtaposed to Isaiah 6:10 in a florilegium or catena, likely based on shared vocabulary: 'heart' (לב), 'eyes' (עינים), 'ears' (אזנים), 'see' (לראות), 'hear' (לשמע); and for this (among more remote possibilities[458]) Baillet particularly suggests Deuteronomy 29:3 as a source 'which

---

457. '4Q504 Paroles des Luminaires (i) (Pl. XLIX-LIII)', 165. On the origins of the document, it was deemed pre-sectarian by Baillet (p. 137); and (perhaps on different grounds) this seems to be followed by Devorah Dimant, 'The Qumran Manuscripts: Contents and Significance', in *Time to Prepare the Way in the Wilderness: Papers on the Qumran Scrolls*, ed. Devorah Dimant and Lawrence H. Schiffman, STDJ 16 (Leiden: E.J. Brill, 1995), 40n42. The possibility of a sectarian provenance, however, is left open by Esther G. Chazon, 'Is *Divrei ha-Me'orot* a Sectarian Prayer'?, in *The Dead Sea Scrolls: Forty Years of Research*, ed. Devorah Dimant and Uriel Rappaport, STJD 10 (Leiden: E.J. Brill/Jerusalem: Magnes Press/Hebrew University: Yad Izhak Ben-Zvi, 1992), 15–17.

458. Ezek 12:2; Pss 115:5-6; 135:16-17; Qoh 1:8; and the aforementioned *1QH*[a] xv 5-6 (Suk vii 2-3).

seems to permit the restorations and suggest the short lines'.[459] This requires the negative particle לוא to be inferred prior to נ[תתה in line 2 (which does not appear in Baillet's transcription) (Table 24).

Table 24 *4QDibre Ha-Me'orot*[a] (4Q504) 18 2-3 and Deuteronomy 29:3

4QDibre Ha-Me'orot[a] (4Q504) 18 2-3	Deuteronomy 29:3
לוא נ[תתה להמה לב]לדעת[[ועינים] לראות ואוזנ]ים לשמוע]	ולא־נתן יהוה לכם לב לדעת ועינים לראות ואזנים לשמע עד היום הזה
He has not g]iven them a heart [to know] [nor eyes] to see nor ear[s to hear] …	But the Lord has not given you a heart to know, nor eyes to see nor ears to hear to this day.

Outside of morphology, the only differences between the two passages are (a) the absence of 'Lord' as subject in the fragment, (b) the addition of a resumptive object suffix to the verb לנתן in the fragment and (c) a difference in the 'person' of the indirect object – second person in Deuteronomy; third person in *4QDibre Ha-Me'orot*[a] – similar, perhaps, to the kind of changes that occur for Isaiah 6:10 in *4QDibre Ha-Me'orot*[a] 18 4.

Significant here is that, in its broader context, Deuteronomy 29:3 is part of the Torah motif of Mosaic 'signs' and, as such (following the discussion above[460]), forms part of the 'type' to Jesus's σημεῖα in the Fourth Gospel. Coming at the end of Moses's ministry to the first generation of Israelites, it conveys the idea that through all their wandering, the Lord had prevented them from perceiving the significance of Moses's 'signs'; and, consequently (as well as curiously), it has been thought by exegetes to lie beneath John 12:37. 'John 12:37', writes Schuchard, 'also appears to have been constructed in order to suggest that Jesus, the prophet like Moses, was no more successful in persuading Israel than was his predecessor'[461]:

> Moses called to all Israel and said to them,
> 'You have seen all that the Lord did before your eyes in the land of Egypt, to Pharaoh, to all his servants and to all his land, the great ordeals which your eyes have seen, the signs (האתת/τὰ σημεῖα) and those great wonders. But the Lord has not given you a heart to know, nor eyes to see nor ears to hear to this day'.[462]

> But though he had done so many signs (σημεῖα) before them, they were not believing in him.[463]

---

459. '4Q504 Paroles des Luminaires (i) (Pl. XLIX-LIII)', 165.
460. See in this chapter *(b) A Mosaic christology*.
461. Schuchard, *Scripture within Scripture*, 89n17, citing Deut 29:1-3 and following Brown, *Gospel according to John*, 1.485-86; Barrett, *Gospel according to St. John*, 430; and Robert Kysar, *John*, ACNT (Minneapolis, MN: Augsburg, 1986), 201-02. It was noted above, in fact, that Deut 29:1-3 was appealed to by Evans to argue for 'signs' as 'the cause of obduracy' and that, in a critique of Evans's position, it was understood by Painter as instead espousing 'God' as that cause; see in this chapter *[d] Signs* and *[1] Signs and Jesus's message*.
462. Deut 29:1-3.
463. John 12:37.

Juxtaposed as these lines in *4QDibre Ha-Me'orot*[a] are to a reworking of Isaiah 6:10 which (a) casts obduracy as having already occurred and (b) traces that act to God, they suggest that the quotation of Isaiah 6:10 at John 12:40 has done the same (and, therefore, that God is its 'cause of obduracy'). Both *4QDibre Ha-Me'orot*[a] 18 2-4 and John 12:37-41 bring Isaiah 6:10 to bear on the Israelite/Jewish failure to discern the significance of divinely wrought 'signs': since in the former that failure is the Lord's doing, in the latter, it can be argued, it must be the Father's.

In sum, the consensus view that God is 'the cause of obduracy' at John 12:40 remains viable: it withstands the critique which has been issued against it; and it finds cognate support in a text from Qumran.

(b) Further on 'the ruler of this world'
This notwithstanding, a more telling argument can be made for 'the ruler of this world' as the third-person actor. This hypothesis, too, has been subject to several criticisms: specifically, (a) that such a figure is too removed from the original meaning of Isaiah 6; (b) that, as can be inferred from 1QS iii 13-iv 1, the devil's effect on people in the Fourth Gospel occurs under the permission (or at the behest) of God (thus making this theory collapse into God as the third-person actor); (c) that 'a negative determination to unbelief by God' (such as would occur if the Father were the third-person actor) appears in biblical and cognate literature, as well as elsewhere in the Fourth Gospel[464] (and, thereby, should be expected at John 12:40); and (d) that, though τυφλοῦν is used to depict 'darkness' as 'blinding' at 1 John 2:11 (implied in Painter's case for this reading), it cannot be assumed to reflect that activity for 'the ruler of this world' in the Fourth Gospel – that is, as Schuchard, relying upon Lieu, has argued, that Johannine imagery is not so rigidly connected to a single concept that one should expect its application in one work of the corpus to apply to the same referent in another.[465]

In response, however, it will be argued (1) that the second through fourth of these premises are readily addressed on their own terms; (2) that a closer look at the activity of the third-person actor betrays it to be more devilish than divine; and, as such, (3) that the first of the four criticisms against this hypothesis – that it departs from Isaiah's original meaning – begs the question, that is, that departing from Isaiah's original meaning was, in fact, the evangelist's intent.

[1] The criticisms point by point
With regard to the second through fourth criticisms, though it is correct (b) that in a modified dualism, such as one finds at Qumran and in the Fourth Gospel,

---

464. Cited for this premise by Menken are John 6:64-65; 9:39; 10:26.
465. The first three premises are issued by Menken, "'He Has Blinded Their Eyes ... ' (John 12:40)", 109-11, 20 (quotation p. 111), on the second following Becker, *Das Evangelium nach Johannes*, 477-78. For the last premise, Schuchard, *Scripture within Scripture*, 100n34; cf. Lieu, 'Blindness in the Johannine Tradition', 90-92.

demonic forces ultimately function as agents of the divine,[466] the third-person actor at John 12:40 is not required to be the ultimate 'cause of obduracy'. That role need only depict its immediate cause; and inasmuch as 'the ruler of this world' does affect people for ill in the Fourth Gospel – by God's behest or no[467] – he (no less than God) can fulfil it. It is also without question (c) that in cognate Jewish and Christian literature God is sometimes conceived as making 'a negative determination to unbelief', that is, that he is depicted not only as enabling faith but also as causing disbelief – 'election' and 'reprobation', respectively, to use systematic theological terms. Apart from John 12:40, however – which, if considered as evidence, would beg the question – it is straining the text to see such a depiction in the Fourth Gospel. The divide between those who 'are' and 'are not' Jesus's sheep is by and large determined by (1) the Father's 'drawing', 'teaching' and 'giving' of some to the Son and (2) the Son's own choice.[468] And the passage which Menken cites for the Father's 'negative determination', John 9:39, does not press as far as he supposes, since Jesus's assertion there that he came into the world 'that those who see may become blind (τυφλοί)' says nothing of how such blindness was wrought. That process must be determined by reading the verse in a larger, plausible context within the Fourth Gospel; and inasmuch as no such context exists for ascribing it to a divine 'negative determination' (other than John 12:40 itself), it cannot, in itself, stand as evidence for such a view.

Finally, (d) it is correct that, without textual warrant, the 'blinding' by darkness at 1 John 2:11 should not be read into 'blinding' by 'the ruler of this world' in the Fourth Gospel. Such licence, however, may follow from two factors. The first is part of the point on 1 John 2:11 made by Painter: that in the only other *locus* where τυφλοῦν is used in the New Testament it similarly describes the activity of an apocalyptically evil figure, one with an epithet similar to that in John: 'the god of this age' (ὁ θεὸς τοῦ αἰῶνος) at 2 Corinthians 4:3-4. And further (as noted above for another issue), in that passage, as in John 12:40, τυφλοῦν appears in close proximity with the verb πωροῦν to describe the impaired perception of Israelites and unbelievers:

> Having, then, such hope, we act with much boldness; not as Moses used to put a veil upon his face, that the sons of Israel not gaze into the close of something

---

466. For Qumran Menken doubtless has in mind 1QS iii 21-24, where 'the aberration of all the sons of righteousness' occurs 'by the angel of darkness' but nonetheless happens 'according to the mysteries of God'. For the Fourth Gospel, Menken cites John 6:70-71; 8:43-44; and 13:2 for the devil's activity and asserts that these verses 'say nothing on the determining force behind him'; '"He Has Blinded Their Eyes ... " (John 12:40)', 109. In fact, however, such a force is evident in John 13, where, after entering Judas with the morsel, 'Satan' is bidden by Jesus to 'do what you do quickly' (John 13:27).

467. Besides stirring Judas to betray Jesus (John 13:2, 27), the devil drives people to murder and lie (John 8:44) and, as is noted below, metaphorically 'deafens' the Jews from hearing the import of Jesus's words (John 8:43, 47).

468. See notes 333 and 455.

being brought to naught. But their minds were hardened (ἐπωρώθη τὰ νοήματα αὐτῶν); for to this very day the same veil remains upon the reading of the old covenant, not being lifted because (only) in Christ is it is brought to naught … And even if our gospel is veiled, it is veiled to those who are perishing, in whose case the god of this age blinded the minds (ἐτύφλωσεν τὰ νοήματα) of the unbelievers so as not to see the light of the gospel of the glory of Christ, who is the image of God.[469]

The second factor is that in the Fourth Gospel the activity of 'the ruler of this world' (ὁ ἄρχων τοῦ κόσμου τούτου) coincides with the imagery of 'darkness'. As recounted above, Painter has noted that these quotations at John 12:37-41 (a) are preceded by the gospel's first mention of 'the ruler of this world',[470] then (b) sandwiched within imagery of 'darkness' and 'light' before and after.[471] And this association can be pressed further, inasmuch as the imagery of 'darkness' (including 'night'[472]) throughout the Johannine narrative is so intertwined with 'the ruler of this world' that the presence of one amounts to the presence of the other: in particular, the 'night' which 'comes, when no one can work' is the period in which 'the ruler of this world' also 'comes, and has nothing in (Jesus)'.[473] And when 'Satan entered' Judas and was commanded by Jesus to do what he was about to do 'quickly', 'he immediately went out and (likewise) it was night'.[474] This concurrence, coupled with the usage of τυφλοῦν for 'the god of this age' in Paul, may suggest that the 'blinding' by 'darkness' at 1 John 2:11 operates as 'blinding' by 'the ruler of this world' at John 12:40.[475]

[2] Diabolical activity
More revealing for this hypothesis, however, is a comparison of the activities described for 'the cause of obduracy' with those ascribed to the devil in John 8. In a

---

469. 2 Cor 3:12-14; 4:3-4. Both of these points were partly broached above in this chapter, under *[c] 'The ruler of this world'* and *(a) 'He hardened' or 'he maimed'?*
470. John 12:31.
471. John 12:35-36a, 44-46; Painter, 'The Quotation of Scripture and Unbelief in John 12.36b-43', 442–43, 450–51.
472. John 9:4-5; 11:9-10.
473. John 9:4; 14:30.
474. John 13:27, 30.
475. Further, the verb τυφλοῦν in John's rendering of Isa 6:10 weakens the otherwise striking correspondence that would exist between that reference and *4QDibHam*[a](4Q504) 18 4. Both texts conceive Isaiah's ocular impairment to have already occurred; both reconfigure the operative verb in that verse to express as much; and both juxtapose that image to Israelite/Jewish unresponsiveness in the face of 'signs', be it by text (*4QDibre Ha-Me'orot*[a]) or by typology (John). But by reading 'blind' (τυφλοῦν) as the Greek counterpart to Hebrew 'smear over' (שעע), the Johannine rendering distances itself from the Qumran fragment and betrays more affinity with texts connoting cosmic evil: τυφλοῦν is not used as a gloss for HB שעע in the LXX, yet it depicts the activity of 'darkness' and 'the god of this age' at 1 John 2:11 and 2 Cor 4:3-4.

word, the same type of metaphorical impairment done by the third-person actor at John 12:40 is attributed to the devil at John 8:42-47. The passage in question at John 8 is primarily known for tracing the Jews' lineage to that figure: 'You are of your father, the devil', retorts Jesus in his debate with the crowd.[476] At two places, however, it also depicts the Jews as figuratively unable to hear (and, therefore, believe) Jesus's message; and perhaps significantly, the second of these is framed with the same syntactical construct that introduces Isaiah 6:10 at John 12:39, διὰ τοῦτο ... ὅτι:

> Jesus said to them, 'If God were your Father, you would love me, for I came forth and come from God. For I have not come of myself; but he sent me. Why do you not know my discourse? Because *you are not able to hear my word* (οὐ δύνασθε ἀκούειν τὸν λόγον τὸν ἐμόν). You are of your father, the devil, and you wish to do the desires of your father. He was a murderer from the beginning and did not stand firm in the truth, for there is no truth in him. When he speaks a lie, he speaks from his own nature, for he is a liar and the father of such. But because I speak the truth, *you do not believe me* (οὐ πιστεύετέ μοι). Who among you exposes me concerning sin? If I speak truth, *why do you not believe me* (διὰ τί ὑμεῖς οὐ πιστεύετέ μοι)? The one who is of God hears my words. *For this reason you do not hear* (διὰ τοῦτο ὑμεῖς οὐκ ἀκούετε), *that/because* (ὅτι) *you are not of God'*.

That the Jews cannot 'hear' the import of Jesus's 'word' in this passage is an auditory counterpart to them not being able to 'see' the salvific significance of his 'signs' at John 12:39-40. That is, if the Jews are rendered metaphorically 'blind' in the quotation of Isaiah 6:10, they have been rendered metaphorically 'deaf' in the scenario of John 8. Since this 'deafness' in John 8 has apparently come upon them because they are in thrall to the 'the ruler of this world' – that is, because they 'are not of God' but 'of ... the devil' – should not the same be inferred for John 12? Or put differently, if the metaphorical impairment to the ears of the Jews is done by 'their father, the devil', does it not stand to reason that the metaphorical impairment of their eyes will have come from the same – and all the more so, given that the only other usage of τυφλοῦν in earliest Christian (at least New Testament) literature associates its activity with 'the god of this age' (in Paul) and 'darkness' (in 1 John)?[477]

---

476. John 8:44a.

477. Ostensibly 'the ruler of this world' as third-person actor also finds support from 1QH^a xv 5-6 (Suk vii 2-3), introduced above in this chapter (under *(a) 'He hardened'* or *'he maimed'?*), a Qumran text deemed by Reim to be cognate to this quotation; see *Jochanan*, 39n72. The passage lexically dovetails HB Isa 6:10 on six terms; and it articulates the idea that the hymnist's perception was obstructed by evil rather than by the Lord: his eyes are smeared over 'from seeing evil'; his ears are the same 'from (hearing of) bloodshed'; and his heart is destroyed 'from evil design'. Such phenomena are not precisely the same as an animate 'devil'; but by their (im)moral association with such a figure they could lend support to the prospect that 'the cause of obduracy' at John 12:40 is 'the ruler of this world'.

[3] 'That those who see may become blind', John 9:39

In this light Jesus's stated purpose regarding 'the blind' at John 9:39 can be revisited and seen as exposé rather than cause: 'For judgment I came into this world, that (ἵνα) those who do not see may see and those who see may become blind (τυφλοί)'. It was posited above that, in itself, the benign predicate 'may become blind' offers no clue to the cause of that blindness; such a source must be plausibly inferred from the larger Johannine context.[478] With 'the cause of obduracy' as 'the ruler of this world' (as now discussed), that cause readily fits the devil; and for John 9:39 this, accordingly, means that 'becoming blind' with the advent of Jesus into the world is, in fact, having the effects of the devil's impairment exposed to view. That is, 'becoming blind' in an encounter with Jesus is not to be rendered such by Jesus or the Father; it is rather to have a previous, devil-wrought condition now laid bare.

Schuchard argues along a similar line in his case for Jesus's message as 'the cause of obduracy': reading John 9:39 in the context of John 3:16-21, he contends that Jesus did not judge but simply exposed conditions that merited such a fate:

> Jesus has indeed come for judgment, 'that those who see may become blind' (9:39). But the judgment that Jesus brings is not something he either desires (3:17) or personally executes. Instead, it is a judgment he provokes: 'this is the judgment, that the light has come into the world and men loved darkness rather than light' (3:20). Provoked by Jesus' self-revelation, Jesus' protagonists show themselves to be 'condemned already' (3:18). In other words, those who 'see'

A closer look, however, shows the scenario described by these lines to be foreign to the Fourth Gospel. If applied to the quotation, it suggests that the Jews were 'blinded' and 'hardened' to the salvific significance of Jesus's signs by evil befalling them from the devil. But no such dynamic occurs in the Book of Signs. There are several junctures which describe characters who encounter Jesus's signs (by sight or report) and do not (immediately) appreciate their soteric import: Nicodemus, after Jesus's signs in Jerusalem during Passover (John 3:1-2); the Jews at the unnamed festival in John 5 (as well as at Tabernacles in John 7), after seeing the man ill for thirty-eight years had been cured (John 5:10-18; 7:21-24, 32, 45-49); the Jews at the second Passover, after being fed from five loaves and two fish and deducing Jesus's miraculous crossing over the Sea of Tiberias (John 6:25-29); the Jews (including Pharisees) at Tabernacles, after encountering the cured man born blind (John 9:13-41); and some of the Jews, as well as the Pharisees and Sanhedrin, after seeing (or hearing) that Jesus raised Lazarus (John 11:46-53). In none of these passages, however, are the characters depicted as responding this way because they were afflicted with calamity by 'the ruler of this world'. Those at the second Passover are described as doing so 'because (they) ate of the loaves and were satisfied' (John 6:26). And the misfortune of being born blind, which had befallen the man in John 9, is ascribed not to the devil (or to the man's own sin) but to the divine plan: 'that the works of God might be manifested in him' (John 9:3).

478. Above in this chapter, under *[1] The criticisms point by point*.

(i.e., those who presume that they are able to see) show themselves to be actually blind and thereby 'become blind'. (9:39)[479]

The same can be argued instead for the prospect proposed here; that is, if at John 3:18 unbelievers 'show themselves to be "condemned already"', at John 9:39 they show themselves to have been 'blinded' already – and this, by 'the ruler of this world' as the third-person actor at John 12:40/Isaiah 6:10.

c. Summary

To summarize, the quotation of Isaiah 6:10 at John 12:40 is a dramatically reworked reference to the LXX, which casts the pre-incarnate Christ as answering Isaiah's lament over the Jews' unbelief at John 12:38/Isaiah 53:1. Alongside myriad changes serving the evangelist's style and *Tendenz*, it has assimilated Mark 8:17-18 (or a tradition akin to it), as well as a term (τυφλοῦν) associated with (fallen) angelology in Johannine and Pauline literature; and with such adaptations it attributes the Jews' unbelief in Jesus to a perception impaired by 'the ruler of this world'. By being explicitly ascribed to Isaiah (as was Isaiah 53:1 at John 12:38), the quotation is connected with two other *loci* in the broader narrative: the allusion to Isaiah's throne room vision at John 12:41 and (by *inclusio*) the quotation of Isaiah 40:3 at John 1:23. As such, it depicts the 'glory' encountered by Isaiah to be the pre-incarnate Jesus and traces the obstruction of John's 'make straight the way of the Lord' to Satan.

D. Conclusion: *The Isaianic* inclusio

It was noted above that the dynamic operative in an *inclusio* is not standard and fixed. In any given text it depends on factors such as authorial intent and context[480]; and, that being so, its effect in this instance would arguably be to bring closure to the Book of Signs. Through the mouth of Isaiah it unfolds as (1) a call to believe in Jesus, (2) a lament that no one had and (3) a disclosure that the acuity needed to do so had been cosmically impaired by 'the ruler of this world'. The call to believe (that is, 'our report') was issued by Isaiah, John, Moses, the Father (through signs) and Jesus himself – all, through the course of Jesus's public ministry. The lament that no one had done so was uttered by Isaiah to the pre-incarnate Christ amid the throne room vision of Isaiah 6. And the disclosure that the insight needed for such faith had been obstructed by 'the ruler of this world' was given by that pre-incarnate Christ to Isaiah in response to his despair. As such, the role of this device is to look back on the failure of Jesus's public ministry and bring the cause of its disappointing result into relief.

---

479. *Scripture within Scripture*, 100–01.
480. Above in this chapter, *2. Ascriptions to Isaiah in the Book of Signs*.

Part II

THE DISCIPLES, THE SPIRIT AND THE SCRIPTURES

Chapter 3

PSALM 69:10, THE PROMISE OF A NEW TEMPLE

A. Quotations with 'remembrance' formulae

The second cluster of quotations is marked by 'remembrance' formulae. These are the only three whose fulfilment is explicitly said to have been 'remembered' by Jesus's disciples. The first is the quotation of Psalm 69:10 at John 2:17, where, after Jesus disrupts the vendors and moneychangers in the temple,[481] it is said that 'his disciples *remembered* (ἐμνήσθησαν) that it is written, "Zeal for your house will consume me"'. The second and third are the quotations of Psalm 118:25-26 at John 12:13 and Zechariah 9:9 at John 12:15. After Jesus is greeted outside Jerusalem with a recitation of Psalm 118:25-26, then rides into the city in fulfilment of Zechariah 9:9,[482] the commentary at John 12:16 reads, 'His disciples did not know these things at first; but when Jesus was glorified, then they *remembered* (ἐμνήσθησαν) that these things were written about him and that they did these things to him.' The compound object 'that these things were written about him' and 'that they did these things to him' (arguably[483]) refers to the biblical passages just recited and fulfilled in the preceding verses; and, as such, it links these two quotations to Psalm 69:10 at John 2:17 as the only three in John which are said to have been 'remembered' (μιμνήσκεσθαι) by Jesus's disciples.

Tied to these quotations is the pericope which follows the temple cleansing, at John 2:18-22. Immediately after his action in the temple, Jesus is asked by the Jews to give a justifying sign for his conduct. He responds that if they destroy 'this sanctuary', he will raise it in three days; and the following commentary explains (a) that he was referring to his body and (b) that after his resurrection his disciples remembered (μιμνήσκεσθαι) and believed both his reply at this juncture and 'the scripture':

The Jews therefore answered and said to him (Jesus),
'What sign do you show us, that you do these things'?
Jesus answered and said to them,

---

481. John 2:13-16.
482. John 12:12-15.
483. A case for this is made in Chapter 4, under *Excursus: Is this a quotation?*

'Destroy this sanctuary and in three days I will raise it' …
But he was speaking about the sanctuary of his body.
When, therefore, he was raised from the dead,
his disciples remembered (ἐμνήσθησαν) that he was saying this,
and they believed the scripture (τῇ γραφῇ) and the word (τῷ λόγῳ)
which Jesus spoke.[484]

The 'remembrance' here does not concern a quotation of scripture per se but a *logion* of Jesus: 'his disciples remembered (ἐμνήσθησαν) that he was saying this.' It should nonetheless be taken with the 'remembrance' formulae at John 2:17 and John 12:16, however, on two bases. First, it represents the only other *locus* in the Fourth Gospel where such language appears. And second, the mention of 'scripture' at John 2:22c may specifically refer to the quotation at John 2:17. That clause places Jesus's *logion* and 'scripture' side by side as tandem objects of the disciples' faith: 'and they believed the scripture (τῇ γραφῇ) and the word (τῷ λόγῳ) which Jesus spoke'[485]; and while the term γραφή in this sentence could denote the whole of scripture in general[486] or an individual but unspecified verse within it,[487] it may also refer precisely to Psalm 69:10 at John 2:17[488] and, as such, should be considered along with it (and John 12:16) when interpreting the quotations 'remembered' by the disciples.

---

484. John 2:18-22.
485. On a related (but different) question, this juxtaposition invests Jesus's *logion* with a status equal to that of scripture; Clark-Soles, *Scripture Cannot Be Broken*, 294-95; and cf. Obermann, *Die christologische Erfüllung der Schrift im Johannesevangelium*, 41.
486. A 'close parallel' in such a case may be John 20:9, 'For they did not yet know the scripture (τὴν γραφήν) that he must rise from the dead'; see, for instance, Hoskyns, *The Fourth Gospel*, 196; Bultmann, *Gospel of John*, 128n3; and Barrett, *Gospel according to St. John*, 201 (from whom the quotation comes).
487. Regularly suggested is Ps 16:10, 'For you will not forsake my life to Sheol, nor deliver your faithful one to see the pit'; e.g. B.F. Westcott, *The Gospel according to St. John: The Authorized Version with Introduction and Notes* (1882; repr., Grand Rapids, MI: William B. Eerdmans, 1981), 43; Bernard, *Critical and Exegetical Commentary on the Gospel according to St. John*, 1:97; Brown, *Gospel according to John*, 1:116. Also suggested are Exod 3:6, cited by Jesus to defend resurrection against the Sadducees at Mark 12:26-27, or Isa 53:12: for the first, R.H. Lightfoot, *St. John's Gospel: A Commentary*, ed. C.F. Evans (Oxford: Clarendon Press, 1956), 130; for the second, Leon Morris, *The Gospel according to John: The English Text with Introduction, Exposition and Notes*, rev. ed., NICNT (Grand Rapids, MI: William. B. Eerdmans, 1995), 204.
488. Barrett does not equate 'the scripture' in this verse with Ps 69:10a at John 2:17, because in his judgement it would require an untenable reading of the anomaly 'will consume' (καταφάγεται) in that quotation. Assuming that the link between John 2:17/ Ps 69:10a and John 2:22c would be Jesus's prediction of his destroyed body at John 2:19 ('destroy this sanctuary'), he concludes that such a connection would require Ps 69:10a to mean that Jesus's zeal for the temple in John 2 would effect a reprisal that led to his demise; and for him such a rendering represents 'a very strained interpretation' of that verse; *Gospel*

3. Ps 69:10, The Promise of a New Temple

1. An earlier arrangement: 'Remembrance' quotations as a piece

Before examining these quotations, two factors about them implied by their 'remembrance' formulae. The first concerns their arrangement. In the narrative as it stands they form an *inclusio* bracketing the Book of Signs. The first two formulae appear at John 2:17 and John 2:22; the last, at John 12:16; and so, the motifs in their quotations can be expected to resonate with one another across chapters 2–12, similar to the way the Isaianic quotations do across chapters 1–12. From two features in the text, however, it is conceivable that in an earlier stage of their tradition- or composition history, they lay contiguous with one another – that is, more precisely, that prior to their current placement, John 2:13-22 followed directly on John 12:12-16, unfolding in a sequence of three pericopes: Jesus's entry into Jerusalem (John 12:12-16), his cleansing of the temple (John 2:13-17) and his defence of his authority (John 2:18-22).[489]

One of these features is their mutual allusions to the eschatological vision of Zechariah 14; that is, both John 2:13-22 and John 12:12-16 appear to allude to Zechariah 14 in a way that suggests they were once of a piece. In the first passage this likely occurs in Jesus's admonition to the dove sellers at John 2:16, 'Do not make my Father's house a house of merchandise (οἶκον ἐμπορίου).' If the term כנעני in HB Zechariah 14:21 is taken to be 'merchant' rather than 'Canaanite', that verse reads, 'And on that day there will no longer be a merchant (כנעני) in the house of

---

according to St. John, 201. Barrett's critique of consensus opinion on Ps 69:10a at John 2:17 is supported below (in this chapter, under *a. 'Consume' as 'reprisal'?*); but, contrary to his inference from that judgement, it is argued that a connection between the quotation at John 2:17 and 'the scripture' of John 2:22c nevertheless does occur: the bridge between the two, it is maintained, is not the prediction of Jesus's death ('destroy this sanctuary') but the prophecy of his resurrection ('and in three days I will raise it').

489. This prospect has been seriously entertained by Johannine scholars. Noting the recurrence of the 'remembrance' formula at John 12:12-16 (after those at John 2:13-22), for instance, Raymond Brown asked, 'Is this repetition an echo of the fact that these two scenes were once joined in John even as they are in the Synoptics'?; *Gospel according to John*, 1:463. And somewhat more forcefully, Lindars asserted that 'it certainly looks as if (the temple cleansing) came to John in company with the triumphal entry (12.12-19), and that he used it in that chapter in the first instance'; *Gospel of John*, 136 (parenthetical clarification added). More explicit is Reim, who goes so far as to speculate that John 2:13 now picks up the temporal marker for the temple cleansing originally furnished at John 11:55; *Jochanan*, 11–12. The likelihood of such juxtaposition was earlier entertained in an unpublished paper delivered by G.P. Lewis at the Birmingham New Testament Seminar, 23 April 1929; reported by W.F. Howard in *The Fourth Gospel in Recent Criticism and Interpretation*, ed. C.K. Barrett, 4th ed. (London: Epworth, 1955), 126–27, 303 (Appendix D).

The discussion here develops observations made earlier in Michael A. Daise, 'Jesus and the Historical Implications of John's Temple Cleansing', in *Jesus Research: The Gospel of John in Historical Inquiry*, ed. James H. Charlesworth and Jolyon G.R. Pruszinski, Jewish and Christian Texts (London: T&T Clark Ltd, 2019), 217–19.

the Lord of hosts'; and this, in turn, has suggested to many that it furnishes the source behind Jesus's reprimand – that is, that at John 2:16 Jesus alludes to Zechariah 14:21.[490] As for the second passage, John 12:12-16, the allusion to Zechariah 14 may be embedded in the 'branches of palm trees' carried by the pilgrims to greet Jesus at John 12:12-13. Where Matthew has the people hail Jesus by cutting generic 'branches from the trees' (κλάδους ἀπὸ τῶν δένδρων)[491] and Mark has them do so by cutting 'rushes ... from the fields' (στιβάδας ... ἐκ τῶν ἀγρῶν),[492] John specifically has them taking 'branches of palm trees' as they go out to receive him: 'The next day a great crowd which had come to the feast, having heard that Jesus was coming to Jerusalem, took branches of palm trees (τὰ βαΐα τῶν φοινίκων) and went out to meet him ...'[493] Part of the vision in Zechariah 14 requires the annual observance of Tabernacles among the nations[494]; and inasmuch as 'branches of palm trees' are one of the 'four kinds' of ritual flora prescribed for observance of that festival,[495] this detail, too, may represent a reference to that chapter. That both John 2:13-22 and John 12:12-16 make reference to Zechariah 14 carries implications for the *inclusio* that operates between them (as is developed below).[496] It also, however, supports the prospect that at one point in their tradition- or composition history these passages were of a piece.

More striking, however, is the second feature – that when John 2:13-22 and John 12:12-16 are adjoined, they create a triptych of 'remembered' scriptural fulfilments which implies literary design. At John 12:16 the disciples 'remember' (ἐμνήσθησαν) Jesus's fulfilment of Psalm 118:25-26 and Zechariah 9:9 at his entrance into Jerusalem; at John 2:17 (which would immediately follow) they 'remember' (ἐμνήσθησαν) his fulfilment of Psalm 69:10a at his cleansing of the temple; and at John 2:22 they 'remember' (ἐμνήσθησαν) his fulfilment of 'scripture' (perhaps Psalm 69:10a) and his own self-predicted resurrection – all after his glorification (Table 25).[497]

---

490. For doubts, see Bultmann, *Gospel of John*, 124n1; and Keener, *Gospel of John*, 1:527.
491. Matt 21:8.
492. Mark 11:8.
493. John 12:12-13.
494. Zech 14:16-19.
495. 'And on the first day you shall take the ripened fruit from the tree, and palm sprays (κάλλυνθρα φοινίκων), thick shoots of a willow tree and branches of the agnus tree from a channel, to rejoice before the Lord your God seven days of the year' (LXX Lev 23:40).
496. Zechariah 14 would readily integrate into the two royal motifs to be argued for the 'remembrance' quotations below: the dynastic anticipation of John 2:17/Ps 69:10 and the *Nordreichs-* and *Südreichschristologie* of John 12:13/Ps 118:25-26 and John 12:15/Zech 9:9. The purge it forecasts is conducted by the Lord as king: 'And it shall be that the Lord will become king upon the whole earth; on that day the Lord will be one, and his name one' (Zech 14:9).
497. Further supporting such a putative arrangement is that by bringing Jesus's reference to the 'sign' of his resurrection (John 2:18-22) to chapter 12, it would introduce this ultimate σημεῖον after (rather than before) the penultimate one of raising Lazarus (John 11:1-44).

Table 25 Jesus's entry into Jerusalem and temple cleansing in John (John 12:12-16/John 2:13-22)

Episode	Synthesis	Quotations
Entry into Jerusalem, John 12:12-16	The next day a great crowd which had come to the festival, having heard that Jesus was coming to Jerusalem, took branches of palm trees and went out to meet him and were crying out, 'Hosanna! Blessed is the one who comes in the name of the Lord, the king of Israel.' And having found a young donkey, Jesus sat upon it, as it is written, 'Fear not, daughter (of) Zion; behold your king comes, sitting upon a foal of a donkey.' His disciples did not know these things at first; but when Jesus was glorified, then they *remembered* (ἐμνήσθησαν) that these things were written about him and that they did these things to him.	Ps 118:25-26 Zech 9:9
Cleansing of the temple, John 2:14-17	And in the temple he found those who were selling oxen, sheep and doves, and the money-changers sitting. And having made a whip of cords, he cast all out of the temple, the sheep and oxen; and he poured out the coinage and overturned the tables of the money-changers. And to those selling the doves he said, 'Take these things from here; do not make my Father's house a house of merchandise'! His disciples *remembered* (ἐμνήσθησαν) that it is written, 'Zeal for your house will consume me.'	Ps 69:10
Legitimation of Jesus's actions, John 2:18-22	The Jews therefore answered and said to him, 'What sign do you show us, that you do these things'? Jesus answered and said to them, 'Destroy this sanctuary and in three days I will raise it.' The Jews therefore said, 'This sanctuary was built over forty-six years, and will you raise it in three days'? But he was speaking about the sanctuary of his body. When, therefore, he was raised from the dead, his disciples remembered (ἐμνήσθησαν) that he was saying this, and they believed the scripture (τῇ γραφῇ) and the word (τῷ λόγῳ) which Jesus spoke.	Scripture

The full scenario that would have been portrayed is fleshed out below, after all three quotations have been interpreted.[498] In its broad contours, however, it would turn on Jesus realizing the eschatological vision of Zechariah 14 by entering Jerusalem amid hints of Tabernacles (palm branches) and purging its temple of merchants and merchandise.

---

498. Chapter 4, in the section *1. The putative tradition*.

2. A 'geistgewirkte Erinnern'

The second factor implied by the 'remembrance' formulae is their link with the Fourth Gospel's pneumatology. They are tethered to the Johannine conception of the Spirit in such a way as to cast their quotations as a post-resurrection illumination of the events to which they are attached.[499] Fundamental here is John 14:25-26, where in the Farewell Discourse Jesus promises his disciples a Spirit-wrought recollection after his resurrection, what Martin Hengel has called '*das geistgewirkte Erinnern*'[500]:

> These things I have spoken to you while abiding with you.
> But the Paraklete, the Holy Spirit, whom the Father will send in my name,
> he will teach you all things and will remind you (ὑπομνήσει ὑμᾶς) of all that I said to you.

The item to be remembered in this passage is not 'scripture' per se but Jesus's teaching: 'he will ... remind you of all that I said to you', says Jesus to the disciples. Two considerations, however, suggest both are in view – and therefore that the 'reminding' (ὑπομιμνήσκειν) of which this passage speaks is one and the same with the 'remembering' (μιμνήσκεσθαι) done in these quotations. The first has just been noted, namely, that at John 2:22 Jesus's teaching and scripture are intertwined. The datum which the disciples are said to have 'remembered' in this verse is Jesus's *logion* on the dismantling and raising of the sanctuary at John 2:19: 'When, therefore, he was raised from the dead, his disciples remembered (μιμνήσκεσθαι) that he was saying this.' In the next clause, however, that *logion* is paired with 'scripture', both as tandem objects of the disciples' post-resurrection faith; and, as also just noted,[501] the 'scripture' in question may, in fact, be the ('remembered') quotation of Psalm 69:10 at John 2:17 – 'and they believed the scripture (τῇ γραφῇ) and the word (τῷ λόγῳ) which Jesus spoke'.

The second consideration is that two (if not all three) of the recollections in these quotations are dated to the same time at which the Spirit was to remind the disciples of these matters according to John 14:25-26, that is, after the resurrection. This is without question at John 2:22 and John 12:16, where the disciples are

---

499. Earlier reflections on this matter appear in Daise, 'Quotations with "Remembrance" Formulae in the Fourth Gospel', 86–88; and Daise, 'Jesus and the Historical Implications of John's Temple Cleansing', 209–11.

500. 'Die Schriftauslegung des 4. Evangeliums auf dem Hintergrund der urchristlichen Exegese', in '*Gesetz*' *als Thema biblischer Theologie*, ed. I. Baldermann et al., Jahrbuch für Biblische Theologie 4 (Neukirchen-Vluyn: Neukirchener Verlag, 1989), 271–75; and in the abbreviated English version of this article, Martin Hengel, 'The Old Testament in the Fourth Gospel', *HBT* 12 (1990): 29–30; cf. Obermann, *Die christologische Erfüllung der Schrift im Johannesevangelium*, 25n135.

501. Above in this chapter, under A. *Quotations with 'remembrance' formulae*.

said to have remembered 'when ... (Jesus) was raised from the dead' and 'when Jesus was glorified', respectively. As for John 2:17, no such marker appears, and this has been taken by some to indicate a 'remembrance' that occurred 'in the actual situation' rather than after the resurrection.[502] Three features of the context, however, suggest otherwise: (1) this 'remembrance' formula is lexically and thematically tied to the other two, which do date their 'recollections' after the resurrection; (2) this formula lies in close proximity to the formula at John 2:22 – and thereby, might be expected to carry the same import; and as just noted, (3) the quotation of this 'remembrance' formula (at John 2:17) may be one and the same with the 'scripture' mentioned at John 2:22c. Such considerations suggest that the absence of a chronological marker at John 2:17 may rather reflect an ellipsis, a deliberate omission of information that is expected to be supplied from elsewhere. That is, the disciples' 'remembrance' at John 2:17 may lack post-resurrection language simply because the evangelist expected it to be inferred from John 2:22 (and perhaps from John 12:16).[503] As such, the 'remembrances' ascribed to the disciples at John 2:17, 22 and John 12:12-16 are quite likely part of the 'recollection' they were promised to receive from the Spirit at John 14:25-26[504]; and for the matter at hand, this means that the quotations they recall are meant to represent a post-resurrection, Spirit-wrought insight into the events with which they are associated.[505]

B. *The Johannine rendering of Psalm 69:10*

Like the Isaianic quotations treated in the last two chapters, these 'remembrance' quotations carry unsettled exegetical issues and, as already noted, also form an *inclusio* which theologically resonates across the Book of Signs. This being so, they will be examined in this chapter and the next in a sequence parallel to that in Chapters 1 and 2: John 2:17/Psalm 69:10 in this chapter; John 12:13/Psalm 118:25-26 and John 12:15/Zechariah 9:9 in Chapter 4.

---

502. Schnackenburg, *Gospel according to St John*, 1:347.

503. Among commentators supporting such a reading are Bultmann, *Gospel of John*, 124 (cf. also p. 418); and Brown, *Gospel according to John*, 1:123. An inference of post-resurrection language from John 12:16 would be even more likely in the putative scenario argued above, namely, that at one point in the Fourth Gospel's tradition- or composition history John 2:13-22 immediately followed John 12:12-16; see above in this chapter, under *1. An earlier arrangement: 'Remembrance' quotations as a piece*.

504. See further Gary M. Burge, *The Anointed Community: The Holy Spirit in the Johannine Tradition* (Grand Rapids, MI: William B. Eerdmans, 1987), 212; and Allison A. Trites, *The New Testament Concept of Witness*, SNTSMS 31 (Cambridge: Cambridge University Press, 1977), 120. Cf. Daise, 'Quotations with "Remembrance" Formulae in the Fourth Gospel', 88n38.

505. On this, see also Schnackenburg, *Gospel according to St John*, 2:377; and Keener, *Gospel of John*, 1:530-31.

1. The texture of the quotation

To begin, then, Psalm 69:10a at John 2:17.[506] This quotation is recalled by Jesus's disciples in the wake of his protest in the temple.[507] When Jesus enters the temple during the Passover that inaugurates his ministry, he sees livestock and dove vendors along with currency traders conducting business on its precincts. Making a 'whip of cords', he routs the livestock (possibly with their vendors and the currency traders[508]), upends the exchange stands and commands the dove sellers to 'take these things from here' and not make '(his) Father's house a house of merchandise'; and these actions, in turn, are said to have been interpreted by his disciples through a recollection of Psalm 69:10a: 'His disciples remembered that it is written, "Zeal for your house will consume me"'.

The HB, LXX and Johannine renderings of the verse are as follows (Table 26).

Table 26 Psalm 69:10 in the HB, LXX and John

HB Psalm 69:10[509]	LXX Psalm 69:10	John 2:17
כי קנאת ביתך אכלתני וחרפות חורפיך נפלו עלי	ὅτι ὁ ζῆλος τοῦ οἴκου σου κατέφαγέν με, καὶ οἱ ὀνειδισμοὶ τῶν ὀνειδιζόντων σε ἐπέπεσαν ἐπ' ἐμέ.	ὁ ζῆλος τοῦ οἴκου σου καταφάγεταί με.
For zeal for your house has consumed me; and the reproaches of those who reproach you have fallen upon me.	For zeal for your house consumed me; and the reproaches of those who reproach you fell upon me.	Zeal for your house will consume me.

a. The version cited

Save for the future καταφάγεται (for κατέφαγεν) John's quotation follows the LXX verbatim. The LXX, itself, does more or less the same with the HB, diverging only by accounting for the perfect tense of the verb (אכלתני) with the aorist (κατέφαγεν);

---

506. Freed has suggested this quotation might also be traced to LXX Ps 119:139a, which in Sinaiticus, Verona and a correction to Alexandrinus (not Vaticanus, as he asserts) reads, 'Zeal for your house melted me (ἐξέτηξέν με)'; *Old Testament Quotations in the Gospel of John*, 8. As noted by Obermann, however, the greater correspondence between John 2:17 and Ps 69:10 (over against the lexical incongruence that occurs between John's rendering and the verb ἐκτήκειν in this alternate proposal) renders the suggestion unnecessary; *Die christologische Erfüllung der Schrift im Johannesevangelium*, 114n1.

507. John 2:13-17.

508. The ambiguity turns on the possibilities for reading the construct πάντας ... τε ... καί in John 2:15, that is, whether the clause 'he cast all out of the temple' is restricted to the object 'the sheep and oxen', which immediately follows, or whether it includes the sellers and money changers noted in John 2:14. See Harold K. Moulton, '*Pantas* in John 2:15', *BT* 18 (1967): 126-27.

509. Besides the MT, Ps 69:10 is attested in 4QPs[a].

and this allows for the quotation to have been drawn from a Hebrew rather than Greek *Vorlage*. As noted in the Introduction,[510] however, John's concurrence with the LXX in such a scenario favours that version as his *Vorlage* unless compelling evidence militates against it; and since no such evidence occurs here, Psalm 69:10 is best traced to the Greek.

Two further premises have been offered in support of the LXX, but both are open to question. One, argued by Menken (and also noted in the Introduction), appeals to vocabulary: had John translated from the Hebrew, (a) he would more likely have translated 'house' (בית) with οἰκία than with οἶκος and (b) he would have chosen from options other than κατεσθίειν to translate 'consume' (לאכל): ἐσθίειν, as in the LXX and other Christian writings; or καταναλίσκειν ('to consume'), as in Symmachus.[511] This contention, however, is at best suggestive, since (as already observed) the vocabulary preserved in Johannine literature is not sizable enough to signal which terms among synonyms would have been preferred.

The other premise, argued by Obermann, appeals to quotations from Psalm 69 elsewhere in the Fourth Gospel. Psalm 69 is possibly cited at two other junctures in the narrative: John 15:25 (Psalm 69:5) and John 19:28-29 (Psalm 69:22). For Obermann these references are drawn from the LXX; and on that basis he supports a LXX *Vorlage* for Psalm 69:10 at John 2:17, reasoning that the same text is likely drawn upon there.[512] This may be so, but bidding caution are two further observations. First, that at John 19:28-29 the *locus* traceable to Psalm 69:22 (John 19:29) may not be the reference designated by the introductory formula[513]; and even were it so, it is an allusion (not a quotation) and cannot be traced to the LXX over against the HB with any certainty (Table 27).

Table 27 Psalm 69:22 and John 19:28

HB/LXX Psalm 69:22	John 19:28-29
They gave venom for my food; and for my thirst (ולצמאי/ εἰς τὴν δίψαν μου) they gave me vinegar (חמץ/ὄξος) to drink.	After this, Jesus, having known that all had now been accomplished, that the scripture might be completed, said, 'I thirst (διψῶ)'. A jar was lying there, full of vinegar (ὄξους). Therefore, wrapping a sponge full of the vinegar (τοῦ ὄξους) around hyssop, they brought (it) to his mouth.

510. For this point and the following paragraph on Menken, see the Introduction, under *a. Confirming the Septuagint*.
511. '"Zeal for Your House Will Consume Me" (John 2:17)', 38–40.
512. *Die christologische Erfüllung der Schrift im Johannesevangelium*, 114.
513. The *locus* designated by the introductory formula may instead be Jesus's cry 'I thirst' (διψῶ), which immediately follows it (still within John 19:28); as such, it would rather be traceable to either LXX Ps 42:3 or LXX Ps 63:2 – see the synopsis of the discussion in Johannes Beutler, 'Psalm 42/43 im Johannesevangelium', *NTS* 25 (1978–79): 56. Moreover, the introductory formula itself, 'that the scripture might be completed', may simply function as an adverbial modifier, referring generally to the whole of scripture, not to a specific verse quoted in John 19:28-29.

Second, the quotation at John 15:25 may, in fact, have two other passages in view (rather than Psalm 69:5): Psalm 35:19 or *Psalms of Solomon* 7:1 (Table 28).

Table 28 Psalm 69:5 and John 15:25

John 15:25		
But that the word might be fulfilled which is written in their law, 'They hated me without cause (ἐμίσησάν με δωρεάν)'.		
HB/LXX Psalm 69:5	**HB/LXX Psalm 35:19**	***Psalms of Solomon* 7:1**
Those who hate me without cause (שנאי חנם/ οἱ μισοῦντές με δωρεάν) have increased beyond the hairs of my head; those who destroy me have become numerous, those wrongfully hostile to me …	May those who hate me wrongfully not rejoice over me; those who hate me without cause (שנאי חנם/ οἱ μισοῦντές με δωρεάν) pinch the eye.	Dwell not apart from us, O God, lest those who hated us without cause (οἳ ἐμίσησαν ἡμᾶς δωρεάν) set themselves upon us.

In sum, the likely *Vorlage* for Psalm 69:10a at John 2:17 is, indeed, the LXX. Its determination, however, best rests on the concurrence of John's rendering with that version, not on the vocabulary of the quotation relative to Johannine parlance or possible references to Psalm 69 elsewhere in the narrative.

In this light it can be noted that, with the exception of its initial καί, LXX Psalm 69:10b is cited verbatim at Romans 15:3; and, as such, this verse may in some way have been brokered to John through Paul:

For, indeed, Christ did not please himself; but as it is written, the reproaches of those who reproach you fell upon me (οἱ ὀνειδισμοὶ τῶν ὀνειδιζόντων σε ἐπέπεσαν ἐπ' ἐμέ).

Inasmuch, however, as Paul only cites the second colon of the verse (while John only cites the first), that mediation – if it occurred – might best be understood as a catalyst for John's thought (rather than the direct source of his text). That is, Paul's usage of LXX Psalm 69:10b would have moved John to consult the biblical text himself, then draw LXX Psalm 69:10a directly from that (original) context.

b. Anomalies and hypotheses

The language of this quotation has been modified in two ways: the conjunction ὅτι has been removed and the aorist κατέφαγεν ('consumed') has been rendered future καταφάγεται ('will consume'). Alternate readings resolve these differences, on the side of either the LXX (reading the future καταφάγεται[514]) or the Fourth Gospel (adding ὅτι[515] or reading the aorist κατέφαγεν[516]); and the LXX alternates have

---

514. So, Vaticanus and Sinaiticus.
515. P[66] P[75] W (from a later supplement) 050.
516. Family[13]; see Barrett, *Gospel according to St. John*, 198.

been entertained seriously by several exegetes.[517] C.K. Barrett, however, suggests the attestations for the aorist κατέφαγεν at John 2:17 are a reflex of the later textual retroversion into Syriac, 'where naturally the Semitic perfect was resumed'.[518] And, as has been widely surmised, all of these variants more likely reflect scribal attempts to harmonize the two *loci*.[519] As such, the quotation has doubtless been reshaped in both respects just recounted: the removal of its initial conjunction and the change of its verbal tense.

As is the case with John's quotations of Isaiah 40:3 and Isaiah 6:10, so here: these departures from the quotation's *Vorlage* raise two interlaced questions. How can they be explained textually? And what do they mean theologically? For the first question, exegetical attention has focused on καταφάγεται and has yielded two overarching hypotheses. One is that it reflects an effort by the evangelist to cast Jesus's action more explicitly as fulfilling prophecy, either by an apt rendering of the Hebrew perfect[520] or by deliberate alteration of the Greek aorist.[521] The other is that it forecasts the reprisal Jesus would eventually receive from the Jews; and this now has two lines of argument.[522] The long-standing, conventional line maintains that the verb was made future to fit (what is deemed to be) the Fourth Gospel's depiction of Jesus's temple cleansing as the ultimate cause of his demise. In this reading the verb 'consume' is not understood to mean 'possess', as if Jesus's zeal for the temple took control of his emotions at that moment. Rather, it means 'to effect consequences that end in reprisal'; and, so, the import of the assertion 'zeal for your house will consume me' is taken to mean that Jesus's action at the temple in this instance provoked hostility that would later culminate in his crucifixion (that is, that would later 'consume' him).

The premises for this view – particularly, as offered by Menken – are two, the second depending upon the first. The first is that this understanding of 'consume' represents the sense of the verb in Psalm 69 itself. The second colon of the verse, Psalm 69:10b (not cited by John), articulates the repercussions experienced by the psalmist for his actions: 'the reproaches of those who reproach you (God) have fallen upon me'. This is taken to lie in synonymous parallelism with the first

---

517. Braun, *Les grandes traditions d'Israël et l'accord des Écritures selon le Quatrième Évangile*, 14; Burney, *Aramaic Origin of the Fourth Gospel*, 114–15; Bultmann, *Gospel of John*, 124n3 (apparently); Humann 'The Function and Form of the Explicit Old Testament Quotations in the Gospel of John', 42. For a review of this position, see the discussion by Schuchard, *Scripture within Scripture*, 20–21.

518. *Gospel according to St. John*, 198–99.

519. See, for instance, Rahlfs, *Septuaginta*, ad loc. (apparatus); as well as Barrett, *Gospel according to St. John*, 198–99; Menken, '"Zeal for Your House Will Consume Me" (John 2:17)', 38–39; and Obermann, *Die christologische Erfüllung der Schrift im Johannesevangelium*, 114.

520. Barrett, *Gospel according to St. John*, 28.

521. Bultmann, *Gospel of John*, 124n3; followed by Freed, *Old Testament Quotations in the Gospel of John*, 10, 117; Reim, *Jochanan*, 10–11; and von Wahlde, *Gospel and Letters of John*, 3:297.

522. A further variation, suggested by Bernard, holds the quotation to mean that Jesus's zeal will ultimately fatigue him; *Critical and Exegetical Commentary on the Gospel according to St. John*, 1:92.

colon (which is quoted by John), and so that line, too, is read to express the same sentiment. 'The parallelism between vv. 10a and 10b', writes Menken,

> makes it likely that the same thought has been expressed in v. 10a:
> the option in favour of God, now called zeal for God's house,
> has brought him the misery he describes. (cf. vv. 2-3, 15-16)[523]

The second premise is that such a reading of the verse matches the broader early Christian use of Psalm 69, wherein either the second colon (Psalm 69:10b) or other verses from the psalm (Psalm 69:5, 22) are cited to interpret Jesus's Passion (Table 29).[524]

Table 29 Psalm 69 in John and cognate literature[525]

The verse referenced	The quotation or allusion
• Psalm 69:10 For zeal for your house has consumed me; and the reproaches (οἱ ὀνειδισμοί) of those who reproach you have fallen upon me.	• Romans 15:3 (Psalm 69:10b) For, indeed, Christ did not please himself; but as it is written, 'the reproaches of those who reproach you fell upon me'. • Hebrews 11:26 (Psalm 69:10b) having considered the reproach (τὸν ὀνειδισμόν) of Christ greater wealth than the treasures of Egypt, for he looked toward the reward.
• Psalm 69:5 Those who hate me without cause (οἱ μισοῦντές με δωρεάν) have increased beyond the hairs of my head; those who destroy me have become numerous, those wrongfully hostile to me …	• John 15:25 But that the word might be fulfilled which is written in their law, 'They hated me without cause (ἐμίσησάν με δωρεάν)'.[526]
• Psalm 69:22 They gave venom for my food; and for my thirst (εἰς τὴν δίψαν μου) they gave me vinegar (ὄξος) to drink.	• John 19:28-29 After this, Jesus, having known that all had now been accomplished, that the scripture might be completed, said, 'I thirst (διψῶ)'. A jar was lying there, full of vinegar (ὄξους). Therefore, wrapping a sponge full of the vinegar (τοῦ ὄξους) around hyssop, they brought (it) to his mouth.[527]

523. Menken, '"Zeal for Your House Will Consume Me" (John 2:17)', 41.
524. Menken, '"Zeal for Your House Will Consume Me" (John 2:17)', 40–41.
525. Where references are allusions, key words associating them with Psalm 69 are given in Greek.
526. As noted in Table 28, Ps 69:5 is but one of several passages which may inform this quotation, the others being Ps 35:19; *Pss. Sol. 7:1*.
527. As with the quotation at John 15:25 – and as observed in note 513 – the verse being referenced here is traceable to other psalms (Pss 42:3; 63:2); and further, any allusion to Ps 69:22 may extend beyond John 19:28 (identified by Menken) into the description of soldiers offering Jesus vinegar at John 19:29 (as represented here). For both of the above premises, see Menken, '"Zeal for Your House Will Consume Me" (John 2:17)', 40–41; and cf. before him (on one and/or the other) Bultmann, *Gospel of John*, 124n5; Schnackenburg, *Gospel according to St John*, 1:347.

3. Ps 69:10, The Promise of a New Temple

The second line of argument for this hypothesis has been proposed independently by Steven Bryan and Benjamin Lappenga.[528] It, too, contends that the future 'will consume' anticipates Jesus's demise at the hands of the Jews. But it interprets the 'zeal' of the quotation to be describing not (only) the state of Jesus but (also) that of the Jews who would kill him in the end; that is, 'zeal for your house will consume me' does not (just) mean that Jesus's ardour for the temple in John 2 will provoke reprisal from the Jews. It rather (or also) means that the Jews' 'zeal' for the temple will be the impetus behind his execution. For Bryan, this 'zeal' is epitomized in the fear expressed by the chief priests and Pharisees at John 11:48, namely, that if Jesus was allowed to continue, 'the Romans will come and will take both our place (ἡμῶν ... τὸν τόπον) and our nation'.[529] For Lappenga, that 'zeal' is, indeed, reflected at John 11:48, but it also embraces the entire crescendo of hostility which the Jews cultivate towards Jesus throughout his public ministry and trial.[530]

The cases made by Bryan and Lappenga differ in detail: most significantly, perhaps, by Lappenga's contention that through *double entendre* the quotation's 'zeal' also applies to Jesus. By and large, however, each argument dovetails with the other to form three overall premises for the position. The first is similar to the second premise in the other line of argument for this hypothesis: that reading 'zeal' as the Jews' 'zeal' for the temple aligns with John's use of Psalm 69 elsewhere in the narrative – that is, the quotation of Psalm 69:5 at John 15:25 and the allusion to Psalm 69:22 at John 19:28-29. Specifically, it is argued (1) that Jesus's introduction to the quotation at John 15:25 as 'their law' implies the Jews' (zealous) hatred of him proceeded from a self-perceived 'fidelity to the law' (and, therefore, ardour for the temple); (2) that the allusion to Psalm 69:22 at John 19:28-29 reflects an association of the whole psalm with Jesus's death; (3) that the context of Psalm 69, itself, invites the ascription of its 'zeal' to the Jews[531]; (4) that, like Psalm 69:10 at

---

528. Steven M. Bryan, 'Consumed by Zeal: John's Use of Psalm 69:9 and the Action in the Temple', *BBR* 21 (2011): 479-89; Benjamin J. Lappenga, 'Whose Zeal Is It Anyway? The Citation of Psalm 69:9 in John 2:17', in *Abiding Words: The Use of Scripture in the Gospel of John*, 141-58.

529. 'Consumed by Zeal: John's Use of Psalm 69:9 and the Action in the Temple', 485-86.

530. 'Whose Zeal Is It Anyway? The Citation of Psalm 69:9 in John 2:17', 145-47. The parenthetical comments in this description of the position are meant to delineate the nuance (about to be noted) by which the positions of Bryan and Lappenga differ: while Bryan does not allow for Jesus's own 'zeal' to have provoked reprisal against him, Lappenga does. See Bryan, 'Consumed by Zeal: John's Use of Psalm 69:9 and the Action in the Temple', 480-81, 485; Lappenga, op. cit., 141-42, 148-50, 158.

531. Specifically, contends Bryan, (a) if the verse cited (Ps 69:10a) is read in synonymous parallelism with the next colon (Ps 69:10b), its verb 'consume' is analogous to bearing 'reproach'; (b) the bulk of the piece bewails an experience of unjust suffering (Ps 69:4, 9-12, 19, 21); (c) the devaluation of sacrifice at Ps 69:30-31 implies the psalmist's enemies controlled the cult (and, therefore, that he harboured a 'zeal' for the temple over against them); and (d) the similar language in Sinaiticus, Verona and Alexandrinus LXX Ps

John 2:17, Psalm 69:5 at John 15:25 contains a verb describing antagonism ('consume' [κατεσθίειν]/'hate' [μισεῖν]) followed by the enclitic pronoun με ('those who hate me [οἱ μισοῦντές με] without cause') – since the antagonists there are Jesus's opponents, so must it be at John 2:17; and (5) that the verb 'destroy' (HB) or 'banish' (LXX) in the verse's next colon, Psalm 69:5b ('those who destroy/banish me [מצמיתי/οἱ ἐκδιώκοντές με]'), informs Jesus's *logion* at John 2:19 ('destroy [λύσατε] this sanctuary ...').[532]

The second premise is that the quotation represents a post-resurrection retrospective on the whole of Jesus's ministry and, as such, the 'zeal' of which it speaks can reflect that of the Jews later in the narrative – not (just) that of Jesus at the time of the temple cleansing.[533] By virtue of its association with the 'remembrance' formulae at John 2:22 and John 12:16 (which place the recollections after the resurrection) the import of Psalm 69:10 at John 2:17 was not fully understood until after Jesus was glorified. It should not, therefore, be taken as 'an immediate response to Jesus's emotional state during the temple action'[534] but as 'Spirit-guided' hindsight into the full scope of Jesus's ministry (which includes the Jews' 'zeal' against him later in the narrative). The formula was placed at the close of the temple cleansing, claims Bryan, to show the disciples' initial misinterpretation of the event and to entice readers 'to share initially in the misunderstanding of the disciples'.[535] The 'zeal' of which the quotation speaks, however, was that of the Jews (not Jesus) and was yet to emerge in Jesus's public ministry.

Finally, the third premise, argued by Bryan, is that the christological import of the quotation aligns with the first half of Jesus's *logion* at John 2:19 and, as such, implies the destruction of Jesus's body (presumably driven by the 'zeal' of the Jews). The quotation is linked to the *logion*, argues Bryan, by two means: the commentary at John 2:22, where (for him) Psalm 69:10 is 'the scripture' which is believed alongside Jesus's 'word' by the disciples; and the imperative 'destroy' (λύσατε) in the opening of the *logion*, which (again for him) functions as a future indicative and so semantically aligns with the future 'will consume' at John 2:17 –

119:139a ('zeal for your house melted me [ἐξέτηξέν με ὁ ζῆλος τοῦ οἴκου σου]') suggests the writer of Psalm 69 is victim to malice; 'Consumed by Zeal: John's Use of Psalm 69:9 and the Action in the Temple', 483–85.

532. Numbers (1) to (3) for this premise are posited by Bryan, 'Consumed by Zeal: John's Use of Psalm 69:9 and the Action in the Temple', 482–85 (quotation for [1], p. 482); numbers (4) and (5), by Lappenga, 'Whose Zeal Is It Anyway? The Citation of Psalm 69:9 in John 2:17', 154–58.

533. Bryan, 'Consumed by Zeal: John's Use of Psalm 69:9 and the Action in the Temple', 486–89; Lappenga, 'Whose Zeal Is It Anyway? The Citation of Psalm 69:9 in John 2:17', 149–52.

534. Bryan, 'Consumed by Zeal: John's Use of Psalm 69:9 and the Action in the Temple', 489.

535. 'Consumed by Zeal: John's Use of Psalm 69:9 and the Action in the Temple', 486–87 (quotation p. 487). Here Bryan is somewhat anticipated by Schuchard, *Scripture within Scripture*, 32.

'Destroy this sanctuary' is tantamount to saying 'You will destroy this sanctuary'. This being so, reasons Bryan, the *logion* at John 2:19 serves as a hermeneutical guide of sorts to the quotation at John 2:17; and since the former forecasts the destruction of Jesus's body, so must the latter.[536]

2. *The import of the quotation*[537]

a. *'Consume' as 'reprisal'?*

To address these hypotheses, it should first be said that the removal of the initial conjunction (ὅτι) was likely done to facilitate the quotation's new context. In LXX Psalm 69, itself, verse 10a is grammatically subordinate to verse 9, articulating the reason for the psalmist's alienation from his family: 'I became estranged from my brothers, a stranger to my mother's sons; for (ὅτι) zeal for your house consumed me.' By removing the conjunction the evangelist transforms the line from a causal to an independent clause; this syntactically frees it from any 'effect' stated earlier in the pericope and allows it simply to define Jesus's conduct as 'zeal'.

As for the second anomaly, καταφάγεται, it is, in fact, not done justice by the two hypotheses stated above. The suggestion that it casts Jesus's action more explicitly as fulfilled prophecy cannot be sustained since, as Menken has pointed out, preterites in similar Johannine quotations are not so altered.[538] And the proposal that it forecasts the reprisal Jesus would receive from the Jews falters along both lines by which it is argued: that Jesus's action in the temple, itself, provokes the enmity that will end in his demise; and that the 'zeal' in question is that of the Jews against Jesus (not that of Jesus for the temple). The first labours under three difficulties: (1) the sense it gives to the verb 'consume'; (2) the relevance it sees in cognate references to Psalm 69:10b (as well as in other references to Psalm 69 in John); and (3) the trajectory it alleges between Jesus's temple cleansing and death in the gospel narrative.

On the first difficulty (1), this hypothesis invests the verb 'consume' with a(n elaborate) meaning it does not normally carry: 'to catalyze a dynamic that will bring reprisal' rather than 'to possess the emotions'. But more importantly, its inference for doing so from Psalm 69:10 does not necessarily follow. It assumes that the two cola in that verse relate in synonymous parallelism, so that the 'zeal consuming' the psalmist in Psalm 69:10a is one and the same with 'reproaches falling upon him' in Psalm 69:10b. In fact, however, the two lines can be read in

---

536. 'Consumed by Zeal: John's Use of Psalm 69:9 and the Action in the Temple', 486, 489.

537. The critique of these hypotheses, as well as the proposal of a new one (below), develops points made in Michael A. Daise, 'Ritual Transference and Johannine Identity', *Annali di storia dell'esegesi* 27 (2010): 46–49; and Daise, 'Jesus and the Historical Implications of John's Temple Cleansing', 211–15.

538. Citing John 12:38/Isa 53:1; John 12:40/Isa 6:10; John 13:18/Ps 41:10; John 15:25/Ps 35:19 or Ps 69:5; John 19:24/Ps 22:19; Menken, '"Zeal for Your House Will Consume Me" (John 2:17)', 40.

synthetic (rather than synonymous) parallelism, as cause-to-effect rather than articulation and repetition:

> For zeal for your house consumed me,
> and (therefore) the reproaches of those who reproach you fell upon me.

In such a reading, the 'reproaches' that fall upon the psalmist in Psalm 69:10b are not one and the same with the 'consuming' he experiences in Psalm 69:10a. Rather, they are repercussions of it; and this, accordingly, allows the verb ἐσθίειν to carry the metaphorical sense it normally connotes: for 'zeal' to 'consume' the psalmist or Jesus is for ardour to seize their state of mind.[539]

This first point leads to the second: (2) the bearing of references to Psalm 69:10b (or other Johannine references to Psalm 69) on John 2:17/Psalm 69:10a. If Psalm 69:10 is read as just described (in synthetic rather than synonymous parallelism), early Christian references that apply Psalm 69:10b to Jesus's Passion do not require the same import for Psalm 69:10a at John 2:17. Put otherwise, if Paul and the author of Hebrews apply the one (Psalm 69:10b) to Jesus's suffering and death,[540] it does not mean that John could not have applied the other (Psalm 69:10a) to Jesus's disposition during the temple cleansing. Further, there is little warrant for applying the meaning given to other verses from Psalm 69 in the Fourth Gospel to Psalm 69:10a at John 2:17. Much of the psalm does, indeed, articulate the unjust suffering endured by the psalmist.[541] At points, however, that motif is offset by verses which rehearse the virtue for which the psalmist faced such suffering. Psalm 69:8a offers a hint: 'For it is *on your behalf* (כי־עליך/ὅτι ἕνεκα σοῦ) that I have borne reproach.' In the two verses following Psalm 69:10, however – as is being argued here of Psalm 69:10, itself – the repercussions endured by the psalmist are articulated in the second colon, while the conduct for which he endured them is recited in the first. In the following, the repercussions appear in normal font; the virtues in question are italicized:

> *For zeal for your house has consumed me*;
> and the reproaches of those who reproach you have fallen upon me.
> *I grieved my soul with fasting*,
> and it turned into reproaches against me.
> *I exchanged my clothing for sackcloth*,
> and I became a byword to them.[542]

This being so, references to other verses in Psalm 69 elsewhere in John's narrative ought not determine the meaning of Psalm 69:10 at John 2:17. 'Those who hate me without cause' (John 15:25/Psalm 69:5) and 'they gave me vinegar to drink'

---

539. Similar here is Freed, *Old Testament Quotations in the Gospel of John*, 9.
540. Rom 15:3; Heb 11:26.
541. Also Ps 69:2-5, 9, 16, 20-22.
542. Ps 69:10-12.

(John 19:28-29/Psalm 69:22) may tell the aftermath of the psalmist's (and Jesus's) integrity; 'zeal for your house will consume me', however, identifies the integrity itself.[543]

And with regard to (3) – the relevance of Jesus's temple cleansing to his death in the Fourth Gospel – in John Jesus's action in the temple does not, in fact, provoke a reprisal that leads to his death. The immediate response to it at John 2:18-22 contains nothing of the sort; and the wish to kill him expressed elsewhere in the gospel is evoked by other factors: his healing on the Sabbath, his professed parity with God, his potential provocation of Rome and his claim to royalty.[544] As such (and taking into account the previous two points), this second premise for reading καταφάγεται as 'forthcoming reprisal' proves as problematic as the first. The future 'will consume' at John 2:17 is no more a harbinger of the crucifixion than it is an explicit indicator of fulfilled prophecy. As Barrett has put it, reading the quotation this way is 'a very strained interpretation … [t]here seems … to be no good reason why the Psalmist and John should not both have spoken of consuming zeal'.[545]

As for the second line of argument for this position – that the quotation speaks of the Jews' zeal for the temple (against Jesus) – it carries at least two difficulties: (1) the interpretive import it gives other references to Psalm 69 in John; and (2) its account of the quotation's placement in the narrative. Regarding (1), since the first premise of this line coincides with the second premise of the other line of argument for this position, it labours under the same difficulties. It claims that such a reading aligns with the uses of Psalm 69 elsewhere in the gospel; but in the psalm, itself, it fails to delineate between passages which speak of the suffering endured by the psalmist and those that articulate the faithfulness which gave rise to it.

As for (2), its claim that the quotation speaks of the Jews' later animosity against Jesus does not adequately explain its placement directly after the temple cleansing. It is agreed (and argued above) that the reference is a retrospect, given to the disciples after the resurrection: its 'remembrance' formula (ἐμνήσθησαν) carries affinities to the Spirit-wrought recollection (ὑπομνήσει ὑμᾶς) promised to the disciples during the Farewell Discourse; and its dating to that event is likely to be

---

543. Further on this point, see Freed, *Old Testament Quotations in the Gospel of John*, 9.

544. John 5:16-18; 7:1, 19-25; 8:57-59; 10:31-33; 11:45-53; 18:33-38; 19:1-22. The temple cleansing is inferred into these other factors by Paul Anderson, who contends that it tacitly carries over into the Jews' wish to kill him for healing on the Sabbath and calling God his Father at John 5:16-18; *The Riddles of the Fourth Gospel: An Introduction to John* (Minneapolis, MN: Fortress, 2011), 200; cf. Paul N. Anderson, *The Fourth Gospel and the Quest for Jesus: Modern Foundations Reconsidered*, LNTS 321/Library of Historical Jesus Studies (London: T&T Clark, 2006), 158. Without discernible basis in the text, however, this begs the question. Schnackenburg, himself an advocate of the theory under discussion, admits that in the Fourth Gospel 'Jesus's action (in the temple) has no recognizable after-effects' and that the incident 'which gives the final impulse to the decision on Jesus's death' is rather 'the raising of Lazarus'; *Gospel according to St John*, 1:355 (parenthetical clarification added).

545. *Gospel according to St. John*, 199, 201.

inferred from the explicit language to that effect at John 2:22 and John 12:16.[546] But if the 'zeal' of which it speaks is that of the Jews later in the narrative, why is it placed after such a display of fervour by Jesus? Why not, instead, for instance, at John 11:48, immediately after the concern for 'our place' expressed by the chief priests and Pharisees? Lappenga answers that the 'zeal' is meant to describe both the Jews and Jesus; and Bryan presses further to suggest that its placement directly after the temple incident is designed to reflect the disciples' initial misunderstanding of its application (and evoke the same from readers).[547] But (contra Bryan), as a post-resurrection, Spirit-wrought insight into scripture, Psalm 69:10a carries no more riddles[548]; and (contra Lappenga), given the antecedent to the 'remembrance' formula at John 12:16, one is hard-pressed to explain why the 'remembered' quotation at John 2:17 must refer to the zeal of both Jesus (then) and the Jews (later). If the disciples' 'remembrance' at John 12:16 is simply taken to illuminate the events which immediately precede it at John 12:12-15, why must the same type of 'remembrance' at John 2:17 cover the gamut of Jesus's public ministry with complex ambiguity?[549]

b. Prolepsis of a new sanctuary
Excursus: Wrath against idolatry (Deuteronomy 32:19-22)
A more promising way forward might be forged along either of two other lines: one, suggesting (once again) a conflation of the quotation with another passage; the other, appealing to a highly engaged feature of the Fourth Gospel's narrative – the Johannine 'temple' motif. The first, offered but not endorsed here, is that the future καταφάγεται reflects a conflation of Psalm 69:10 with Deuteronomy 32:19-22. This passage recounts the Lord becoming jealous over idolatry; and, like Psalm 69:10, it places verbal cognates of the noun 'zeal' (ζῆλος) in close proximity to the future tense of the verb 'to consume' (לאכל/κατεσθίειν): in the Hebrew, לקנא ('to be [piel][550] or make [hiphil] jealous/zealous'); in the Greek, ζηλοῦν ('to be[come] jealous/zealous') and παραζηλοῦν ('to make jealous/zealous'). For Psalm 69:10 at John 2:17 the LXX would be favoured, given the criterion set out for anomalies

---

546. Above in this chapter, under 2. A 'geistgewirkte Erinnern'.
547. Above in this chapter, under *b. Anomalies and hypotheses*.
548. John 16:25-28.
549. Arguably problematic also for this line of argumentation is its third premise: that due to its connection with Jesus's *logion* at John 2:19 (partly through the reference to 'scripture' at John 2:22), the quotation at John 2:17 is to be understood in connection with Jesus's words, 'Destroy this sanctuary'. It is not clear that the context of these two verses requires such a close-knit hermeneutical relationship between them. And, even if it does, that relationship could be expanded to include both parts of the *logion*: (a) that the 'destruction' of the 'sanctuary' of Jesus's body corresponds to the 'destruction' being invoked upon the Jerusalem edifice by the vendors and money changers on its precincts; and, accordingly, (b) that Jesus's purge of that edifice in his temple act corresponds to the 'raising' he will do to the 'sanctuary' of his new body.
550. For reading the piel קנאוני at Deut 32:21 as causative (הקנאוני), see BDB, 888.

through conflation, namely, that hypotheses will be preferred which align (rather than mix) the versions of the base and assimilated passages (Table 30).[551]

Table 30 Deuteronomy 32:19-22, Psalm 69:10a and John 2:17

John 2:17
His disciples remembered that it is written, 'Zeal (ὁ ζῆλος) for your house will consume me (καταφάγεταί με).'

HB/LXX Deuteronomy 32:19-22	HB/LXX Psalm 69:10a
The Lord saw and disdained/was zealous (– /ἐζήλωσεν[552]) out of anger toward his sons and daughters. And he said …, 'They made me jealous (קנאוני/παρεζήλωσάν με) with what is no god, they angered me with their vanities; but I will make them jealous (אקניאם/ παραζηλώσω αὐτούς) with what is not a people; with a senseless nation I will anger them. For a fire has been kindled by my anger, and it burns to lowest Sheol; it will consume (ותאכל/καταφάγεται) the earth and its produce, and will enflame the foundations of the mountains.'	For zeal (קנאת/ὁ ζῆλος) for your house (has) consumed me (אכלתני/κατέφαγέν με).

The passage declares that having been provoked to 'jealousy' (or 'zeal') by his people's idolatry, the Lord will reciprocate by 'consuming' the earth with his wrath; and, merged with Psalm 69:10 in the context of the Johannine temple cleansing, it might depict Jesus's action in the temple as being similarly provoked – in this case by the commerce being conducted on its precincts.

(1) 'The Father's house' rebuilt
The second line forward, endorsed here, is that the future tense 'will consume' depicts Jesus's action in the temple as proleptic of a metaphorized temple act to occur later in the narrative. That is, as zeal for his Father's house 'consumes' Jesus at the onset of his ministry, so will it do once more at the culmination of that ministry; and this, in turn, follows two temple motifs through the rest of the gospel – both of them tied to Jesus's resurrection.

(a) The risen body of Jesus (John 2:19-22)
[1] The 'sanctuary' of Jesus's body
The first is close by: the 'sanctuary' of Jesus's resurrected body, articulated at John 2:18-22. When Jesus is pressed by the Jews in these verses to substantiate his action

---

551. Introduction, under *b. Expecting the Hebrew Bible*.
552. The Hebrew verb here is not לקנא, but לנאץ.

in the temple, he answers, 'Destroy this sanctuary (λύσατε τὸν ναὸν τοῦτον)[553] and in three days I will raise it'; and when he is then misunderstood to be referencing the Herodian edifice, the evangelist interjects that he had been speaking of his body and in so doing identifies Jesus's resurrection metaphorically with the building of a new 'sanctuary':

> 'What sign do you show us, that you do these things'?
> Jesus answered and said to them,
> 'Destroy this sanctuary and in three days I will raise it'.
> The Jews therefore said,
> 'This sanctuary was built over forty-six years, and will you raise it in three days'?
> But he was speaking about the sanctuary of his body.[554]

[2] *'Dismantling', 'raising' and enthronement*

The second temple motif is the indwelling of the Father and Son in the believer through the Spirit, developed in John 14. Before examining it, however, a further word on the 'destruction' and 'raising' of Jesus's body, in anticipation of the royal connotations which emerge at John 12:12-16. In a word, Jesus's *logion* at John 2:19,

---

553. The shift in terminology from ἱερόν in the temple cleansing (John 2:14) to ναός in the following dialogue (John 2:19, 21) may signal a narrowing of interest in these pericopes from the temple precincts at large (John 2:13-17) to the holy place within the court of priests (John 2:18-22); and to accommodate that possibility, the latter is translated 'sanctuary' rather than 'temple'. A case can be made, however, that in this context the two terms function as synonyms. Elsewhere ναός designates the temple precincts as well as the inner sanctuary (*J.W.* 6.293; *Ag. Ap.* 2.119; see BAGD 533). And, if the temporal phrase 'forty-six years' (τεσσεράκοντα καὶ ἓξ ἔτεσιν) at John 2:20 is taken to log the duration of building activity on the edifice (Smyth, *Greek Grammar*, 358), it may suggest that Jesus's interlocutors had the larger area in mind, since (a) Herod completed the holy place by 18 BCE (*Ant.* 15.380, 421; cf. *J.W.* 1.401) but (b) work apparently continued on the rest until the procuratorship of Albinus in 62–64 CE (*Ant.* 20.215-221; see *Josephus* vol. 10, p. 462n[a] in Marcus and Wikgren, LCL, as well as the more extensive review of the chronological possibilities and implications of this phrase in R. Alan Culpepper, 'John 2:20, "Forty-Six Years": Revisiting J.A.T. Robinson's Chronology of Jesus' Ministry', in *Jesus Research: The Gospel of John in Historical Inquiry*, 142–54). It is possible that Jesus's interlocutors nonetheless have the holy place alone in view, inasmuch as Herod's renovation of that structure suffered foundation problems into the reign of Nero that presumably needed later attention (*Ant.* 15.391). From the usage of ναός in the Synoptic tradition of this *logion*, however (see Table 31), it is more likely that the term originally designated the holy place (in that tradition), then came to embrace the entire temple precincts by proximity to ἱερόν in its new Johannine context.

554. John 2:18-21. This connection is somewhat buttressed by the prospect, noted above, that the 'scripture' (τῇ γραφῇ) in the next verse (John 2:22) may be Ps 69:10 at John 2:17 and that both that 'scripture' and the *logion* in question here (at John 2:19) are paired as objects of the disciples' faith; see above in this chapter, under A. *Quotations with 'remembrance' formulae.*

itself, carries royal resonance – particularly, through the ancient Near Eastern idea that a new dynasty is marked by a new shrine. To appreciate this, the other extant instances of this saying are here revisited in light of Herod's rebuilding of the sanctuary, as recounted by Josephus.[555]

In various forms this *logion* appears in six other places: twice (once each in Matthew and Mark) where it is falsely ascribed to Jesus during his trial before the Sanhedrin; twice (once each in Matthew and Mark) where it is a vilification levelled at Jesus during the crucifixion; and twice (once each in the Acts of the Apostles and the *Gospel of Thomas*) where it speaks of the sanctuary's destruction but not (necessarily) its rebuilding – in Acts, where the destruction is assigned to Jesus in a false charge against Stephen; in *Thomas*, where (as in John) it is spoken by Jesus (Table 31).[556]

Table 31 'Destroying' and 'building' the sanctuary in early Christian literature

Jesus's trial before the Sanhedrin (Matthew and Mark)	Jesus's crucifixion (Matthew and Mark)
And the chief priests and the whole Sanhedrin were seeking false testimony against Jesus, that they might put him to death; and they were not finding any, though many false witnesses had come forward. But at last, two, coming forward, said, 'This one said, "I am able to destroy the sanctuary of God (καταλῦσαι τὸν ναὸν τοῦ θεοῦ) and in three days build (οἰκοδομῆσαι) (it)"'. (Matthew 26:59-61)	And those passing by were vilifying him, wagging their heads and saying, 'You who destroys the sanctuary (ὁ καταλύων τὸν ναόν) and builds (οἰκοδομῶν) (it) in three days, save yourself! If you are the Son of God, come down from the cross'! (Matthew 27:39-40)
And some, having risen, were bearing false witness against him, saying, 'We heard him saying, "I will destroy this sanctuary (ἐγὼ καταλύσω τὸν ναὸν τοῦτον) made with hands and in three days will build (οἰκοδομήσω) another not made with hands"'. (Mark 14:57-58)	And those passing by were vilifying him, wagging their heads and saying, 'So, you who destroys the sanctuary (ὁ καταλύων τὸν ναόν) and builds (οἰκοδομῶν) (it) in three days, save yourself by coming down from the cross'! (Mark 15:29-30)

(Continued)

555. Much of this section draws upon preliminary reflections presented in Michael A. Daise, 'Destroying and Rebuilding the Temple: Light from Flavius Josephus' (paper presented to the Historical Jesus section of the 3rd Annual Meeting on Christian Origins, Centro Italiano di Studi Superiori sulle Religioni, Centro Residenziale Universitario di Bertinoro, 29 September–1 October 2016).

556. The passages on Jesus's posture towards the temple are conveniently assembled by Chrystian Boyer in *Jésus contre le temple? Analyse historico-critique des textes*, Héritage et Projet 68 (Saint-Laurent, QC: Éditions Fides, 2005), 19–22. Boyer also infers Jesus predicting the temple's destruction from a passage in which Jesus speaks of destroying the sacrificial system maintained by the temple: *Gos. Eb.* fragment 7 (which he lists as fragment 6): 'I came to destroy (καταλῦσαι) sacrifices; and if you do not cease sacrificing, wrath will not cease from you' (= Epiphanius, *Pan.* 30.16.4-5). Text: Bart D. Ehrman and Zlatko Pleše, *The Apocryphal Gospels: Texts and Translations* (Oxford: Oxford University Press, 2011).

Stephen's trial before the Sanhedrin (Luke-Acts)	Jesus's teaching (*Gospel of Thomas*)
And they stirred up the people, the elders and the scribes; and having come up, they seized him and led (him) to the Sanhedrin. And they set up false witnesses who were saying, 'This man does not cease speaking words against this holy place and the law. For we have heard him saying that this Jesus of Nazareth will destroy (καταλύσει) this place and change the customs which Moses delivered to us.' (Acts 6:12-14)	Jesus said, 'I shall destroy [thi]s house (ϯⲛⲁϣⲟⲣ[ϣⲣ̄ ⲙ̄ⲡⲉⲉ]ⲓⲏⲉⲓ), and no one will be able to build it (ⲙⲛ̄ ⲗⲁⲁⲩ ⲛⲁϣⲕⲟⲧϥ̄).[... ... ...]' (*Gospel of Thomas* §71)[557]

This saying is often categorized with two others, in which Jesus speaks of the temple's demise: his prediction to the disciples that not one of its stones will be left upon another[558] and the *Quoties volui* (Matthew and Luke, or Q), in which he tells Jerusalem that its house is being left to it desolate.[559] But, while this grouping may be appropriate for the versions of the *logion* that only speak of the sanctuary's destruction – Acts 6:12-14 and the *Gospel of Thomas* §71 – those that also speak of its rebuilding seem to convey a different idea; and this is confirmed when it is noted that their language dovetails that used by Josephus for Herod's renovation of the Second Temple sanctuary.[560] Over an eighteen-month period (*c*. 20–18 BCE) Herod dismantled the sanctuary he had inherited and rebuilt a new one; and at the beginning and end of Josephus's account of it the vocabulary used to describe that task overlaps the vocabulary in this *logion* of Jesus 'destroying' and 'building' (or 'raising') a sanctuary in three days.

The first instance is Herod's initial attempt to assuage the Jews' fear that he might begin but not finish the task. Suspecting at the start that the populace would be

---

557. Text: Ehrman and Pleše, *The Apocryphal Gospels*. Among Thomasine specialists the text's final lacuna at this *logion* has been reconstructed to allow rebuilding by Jesus – that is, 'I shall destroy [thi]s house, and no one will be able to build it [except me]'; see the review by Andrea Annese, 'The Temple in the *Gospel of Thomas*: An Interpretive Perspective on Some Words Attributed to Jesus', in *Texts, Practices, and Groups: Multidisciplinary Approaches to the History of Jesus' Followers in the First Two Centuries. First Annual Meeting of Bertinoro (2-5 October 2014)*, ed. Adriana Destro and Mauro Pesce, Judaïsme ancien et origines du christianisme (Turnhout, Belgium: Brepols, 2017), 229–31; citing Mark Goodacre, *Thomas and the Gospels: The Case for Thomas's Familiarity with the Synoptics* (Grand Rapids, MI: William B. Eerdmans, 2012), 167–68.

558. Matt 24:1-2; Mark 13:1-2; Luke 21:5-6. Boyer notes that Luke also applies the expression 'stone upon stone' to the destruction of Jerusalem, itself, at Luke 19:43-44; *Jésus contre le temple?*, 20.

559. Matt 23:37-39; Luke 13:34-35. On these further texts, Boyer, *Jésus contre le temple?*, 19–20.

560. *Ant.* 15.380-423.

apprehensive about such an undertaking, Herod endeavours to prepare them for it by addressing them on its need.⁵⁶¹ When that address is complete, Josephus describes the people's response in its aftermath; and in that description he employs ναός for the 'sanctuary' (as one might expect), but also καταλύειν (used in Matthew and Mark) for its 'dismantling' and ἐγείρειν (used in John) for the 'raising' of a new edifice⁵⁶²:

> These things Herod spoke, but the word frightened most, falling out as fancy. While on the one hand doubt over his aspiration did not provoke them, on the other they were apprehensive that, having first dismantled (μὴ φθάσας καταλῦσαι) the entire work, he might not have sufficient to bring the plan to an end. The risk appeared greater to them (than the prospect), and the magnitude of the endeavor seemed difficult to take in hand. As they were so disposed, the king assured them, saying he would not first pull down the sanctuary (οὐ πρότερον καθαιρήσειν ... τὸν ναόν) before all things had been prepared for its completion ...
>
> And having taken up the old foundations and laid others, he raised the sanctuary (τὸν ναὸν ἤγειρε) upon them ...⁵⁶³

The second instance occurs after Josephus recounts the work of renovation: as he begins his report on its completion, he uses the term ναός again, but also a fourth term found in Jesus's *logion* – οἰκοδομεῖν, 'to build' (used also in Matthew and Mark):

> As the sanctuary had been built (τοῦ δὲ ναοῦ ... οἰκοδομηθέντος) in a year and six months, the people were now filled with joy and were observing thanksgivings to God – first, for the swiftness (of the effort), then for the good will of the king – celebrating and extolling the renovation.⁵⁶⁴

This correspondence need not signal literary dependence, especially given the complication arising from Josephus's use of scribal assistants for his Greek texts.⁵⁶⁵ It more likely indicates a common way of speaking about such endeavours, shared by Josephus and Jesus tradition. Moreover, it carries a number of implications for the use of this language in gospel circles.⁵⁶⁶ Its import for the issue at hand,

---

561. *Ant.* 15.380-87.
562. Compare with Table 31.
563. *Ant.* 15.388-391. The text (though not the translation) for *Jewish Antiquities* is Marcus and Wikgren, LCL.
564. *Ant.* 15.421.
565. Cf. *J.W.* 1.3.
566. Among these, (1) that when coupled with verbs for rebuilding, καταλύειν (or its cognate λύειν in John) connotes a 'dismantling' more than a 'destruction' of the sanctuary; (2) that where the *logion* includes the idea of rebuilding, it does not issue a woe against

however – Jesus's risen body as a metaphorical new temple at John 2:13-22 – comes sharply into view in the rest of Josephus's account of the task's completion, that is, in the remainder of the second segment quoted. Citing it here in full:

> As the sanctuary had been built (τοῦ δὲ ναοῦ ... οἰκοδομηθέντος) in a year and six months, the people were now filled with joy and were observing thanksgivings to God – first, for the swiftness (of the effort), then for the good will of the king – celebrating and extolling the renovation. And the king sacrificed three hundred oxen to God, and each of the others (celebrating) according to their ability ... For it had fallen to the time scheduled for the work of the sanctuary to coincide with the day of accession for the king, which they would regularly celebrate; and from the two, the festival became most distinguished.[567]

Inasmuch as the culmination of the work coincided 'with the day of accession for the king',[568] it appears that Herod had synchronized the two for his own political purposes. He had long been struggling to establish his royal line in Judaea over against the (memory of the) Hasmonean dynasty; and ancient Near Eastern custom had even longer associated the enthronement of a new dynasty with the building of a new shrine. Herod seems to have brought this custom to bear on his dilemma by having the 'dismantling' and 'raising' of the Jewish sanctuary climax on the festal celebration of his royal appointment; and the language shared between his project and the *logion* at John 2:19 suggests the same connotations apply to the 'sanctuary' of Jesus's body. That is, its 'dismantling' and 'raising' through his death and resurrection do not merely speak of the temple's demise. They signal the establishment of a new dynasty; and, as such, the metaphorical sanctuary for which Jesus's 'zeal' will yet 'consume' him carries royal overtones.[569]

the temple (and, therefore, should not be categorized with other sayings that do); (3) that in the Johannine context of the *logion* (John 2:18-22) the Jews' reference to the Herodian sanctuary in response to it is not entirely *Mißverständis*; (4) that the description of rebuilding as 'raising' (ἐγείρειν) in John does not necessarily represent a theological replacement for 'building' (οἰκοδομεῖν) in Matthew and Mark (so as to underscore Jesus's resurrection as the erection of a new temple); and (5) that the Johannine version of the *logion* (with Jesus's resurrected body as the new temple) does not necessarily betray a post-70 CE date. The reference point for the language is not the destruction of the temple in 70 CE but Herod's renovation of it in 20 BCE.

567. *Ant.* 15.421-423.
568. *Ant.* 15.423.
569. In this light it might also be noted that the time required for Herod to complete his work may be echoed in the claim of the *logion* that Jesus would 'dismantle' and 'raise' the sanctuary 'in three days'. Herod accomplished his renovation in 'a year and six months' and was lauded by the people 'for the swiftness' with which he did so; *Ant.* 15. 421. How much greater the king who could do the same in a fraction of that time.
  Further, though more work must be done on it, this reading of the *logion* lends a coherence to the Sanhedrin trial scenes in Matthew and Mark that might otherwise be lacking. In both accounts the trial begins with the Council hearing false testimony that

(b) The indwelling of the Godhead by the Spirit (John 14:1-2)
The second temple motif to which John 2:17 may point is the indwelling of the Father and Son in the believer through the Spirit, developed in John 14. This emerges more subtly than the first motif, turning on the interplay that occurs between the phrase 'Father's house' at John 2:16 and John 14:1-2. In the first passage, Jesus employs it amid his protest in the temple to refer to the Jerusalem edifice itself; in the second, he uses it during his Farewell Discourse to depict the place he is about to prepare for his disciples:

> Take these things from here; do not make my Father's house (τὸν οἶκον τοῦ πατρός μου) a house of merchandise.[570]

> Do not let your heart be troubled;
> you believe in God, believe also in me.
> In my Father's house (ἐν τῇ οἰκίᾳ τοῦ πατρός μου) are many rooms (μοναὶ πολλαί).
> If not, I would have told you,
> for I go to prepare a place for you.[571]

The phrase 'Father's house' at John 2:16 rolls over into the quotation of Psalm 69:10 in the next verse, suggesting a further referent for the future tense verb in that rendering; that is, the 'house' for which zeal 'will (yet) consume' Jesus is the 'Father's house' which he will prepare for his disciples through his death and resurrection.

The term for 'house' at John 14:1-2 (οἰκία) is cognate to the term used for it at John 2:16-17 (οἶκος); and, though it may, like οἶκος, refer to an 'edifice' (and, thus, a 'temple'),[572] its usage elsewhere in Johannine literature allows it also to mean 'household'[573] or (perhaps) both 'edifice' and 'household'.[574] Were this the case, the metaphor in John 14 would not align precisely with the referent in John 2 and, therefore, would not (necessarily) represent a further temple motif. Several factors,

Jesus said such a thing, then culminates with the high priest demanding Jesus confess messiahship and the Council conveying Jesus to Pilate on the charge he claimed to be 'king of the Jews' (Matt 26:57-66; 27:1-2, 11; Mark 14:53-64; 15:1-2). If the saying at issue here simply meant that Jesus had been speaking ill of the temple, it makes little sense in this scenario, because even a false accusation of such an act could not lead to the charge of messianic kingship the Council was seeking. Were it an idiom connoting the establishment of a new dynasty, however, it fits hand-in-glove with the presumed agenda of the Council and brings a consistent rationale to its litigation.

570. John 2:16.
571. John 14:1-2.
572. John 11:31; 12:3.
573. John 4:53.
574. John 8:35; 2 John 10. Οἶκος, for its part, is only used in Johannine literature for 'edifice'; John 11:20 (cf. John 7:53).

however, indicate this is not the case. One, proposed by Mary Coloe, concedes a difference in meaning between the two terms, but contends it nonetheless reflects a development of the temple theme (not two different metaphors). By John 14, she argues, the Johannine idea of temple has mutated from 'edifice' (οἶκος) into a set of relationships between Father, Son, Spirit and believer; and the term οἰκία at John 14:1-2, she contends, was chosen to signal such a change without departing from the initial motif: the temple now may be a 'building' turned 'family', but it is still a temple.[575]

Two further factors, however, suggest there need be no such metaphorical difference between the two words – that is, that οἰκία at John 14:1-2 no less than οἶκος at John 2:16-17 means 'temple edifice'. One comes into relief once the imagery of these verses is defined (and so will be recounted below), namely, that the 'Father's οἰκία' of John 14:1-2 coincides with the worship 'in spirit and truth' which, according to John 4:21-24, is to replace the cultic centres of Jerusalem and Gerizim. The other, more pointed, is that the language of John 14:1-2, itself, suggests a building rather than a family. Jesus says 'in my Father's house are many *rooms*', not 'many wives, children or servants'; and this implies his metaphor draws an analogy from a building rather than (merely) a domestic network.[576]

This being so, the theological referent to this temple imagery at John 14:1-2 is the Spirit-wrought indwelling of the Godhead in the believer. Pivotal for that determination are two components of these verses and their context: the word μονή, translated at John 14:1-2 in the plural as 'many rooms' (μοναὶ πολλαί); and Jesus's promise of the Spirit at John 14:15-18. The referent of 'many rooms' in this imagery becomes clear in the only other place where μονή is used in Johannine literature: John 14:23. There 'room' is defined as the Father and Son 'coming' to inhabit the obedient believer:

> Jesus answered and said to him (Judas, not Iscariot),
> 'If any one loves me he will keep my word,
> and my Father will love him and we will come (ἐλευσόμεθα) to him
> and will make a room with him (καὶ μονὴν παρ' αὐτῷ ποιησόμεθα)'.

And that 'coming', for its part, is explained more concretely at John 14:15-18, where Jesus's return to his disciples is made one and the same with the advent of the Spirit after his resurrection:

---

575. *God Dwells with Us: Temple Symbolism in the Fourth Gospel* (Collegeville, MN: Liturgical Press, 2001), 161–62; here citing Robert H. Gundry, "'In My Father's House Are Many Μοναί" (John 14:2)', *ZNW* 58 (1967): 70; and James McCaffrey, *The House with Many Rooms: The Temple Theme of John 14, 2–3*, AnBib 114 (Roma: Editrice Pontificio Istituto Biblico, 1987), 31; see Daise, 'Ritual Transference and Johannine Identity', 49n18.

576. On this matter, see Daise, 'Ritual Transference and Johannine Identity', 48–49.

> If you love me, you will keep my commandments.
> And I will ask the Father, and he will give you another Paraklete,
> that he may be with you forever – the Spirit of truth,
> whom the world cannot receive, for it neither beholds nor knows him.
> You know him, for he abides with you and will be in you.
> I will not leave you as orphans; I am coming (ἔρχομαι) to you.

Putting these elements together, this motif identifies 'the Father's house' with a second theological phenomenon: the post-resurrection presence of the Father and Jesus in the believer, mediated through the Holy Spirit. Such a connection has also been noticed, on slightly different grounds, by Coloe. Aware of the cognate relationship between μονή and μένειν, she observes how each is used in John 14 and 15 'to describe a variety of interpersonal relationships between the Father, Jesus, Paraklete, and believers', expressed in the Johannine language of 'room' and 'abiding'. 'These various relationships', she writes, 'are appropriately introduced by the phrase "many dwellings" (μοναὶ πολλαί)'; and among them is 'the Father and Jesus who will make their dwelling (μονήν) with the believer' in John 14:23.[577]

This construct, in turn, coincides readily with the new *locus* of worship predicted by Jesus to the Samaritan woman at John 4:21-24 (and so furnishes a further premise that οἰκία at John 14:1-2 speaks of a temple):

> Believe me, woman, an hour is coming when neither in this mountain nor in Jerusalem shall you worship the Father ... But an hour is coming and now is, when the true worshippers will worship the Father in spirit and truth; for, indeed, the Father seeks such as worshippers of him. God is spirit; and those who worship him must worship in spirit and truth.[578]

As true worshippers would be worshipping the Father 'neither in this mountain nor in Jerusalem' but 'in spirit and truth', so Jesus's 'Father's house' is no longer the brick-and-mortar 'edifice' of the Jerusalem temple but the habitation of God in the obedient believer.

With respect to the future tense 'will consume' at John 2:17, this theological phenomenon represents a second metaphorized temple to which that verb points. As with Jesus's resurrected body at John 2:19-21, so with this Spirit-wrought indwelling of Father and Son in the believer at John 14:1-2: it is a figurative shrine yet to come in the narrative, and the future καταφάγεται at John 2:17 signals that the 'zeal' which 'consumed' Jesus when he purged the Herodian structure will do so again as he 'prepares' this metaphysical one – indeed, as with the first temple metaphor, through his death and resurrection.

---

577. *God Dwells with Us*, 162; and on this hypothesis as argued here, see also Daise, 'Ritual Transference and Johannine Identity', 47–48.
578. John 4:21, 23-24.

(c) Coalescing metaphors and 'the ruler of this world'

Two final notes on the import of this anomaly. First, these two temple metaphors are not incompatible and, in fact, may be reconciled by developing a remark made by Barrett. Deliberating on Jesus's body as a temple (at John 2:19-21), he suggests it is bound up with the mutual indwelling of Father and Son, articulated at John 14:10 and elsewhere: 'Do you not believe that I am in the Father and the Father is in me'? As the Jerusalem temple was the *locus* in which God once dwelt, he reasons, so Jesus's body becomes the *locus* in which the Father dwells. 'John's thought', he writes,

> rests not upon general observations or speculations about the relation of the human soul to God but upon the unique mutual indwelling of the Father and the Son (14.10 and often); the human body of Jesus was the place where a unique manifestation of God took place and consequently became the only true Temple, the only centre of true worship; cf. 4.20-4.[579]

If this mutual indwelling of Father and Son makes Jesus's body a new temple, it can be noted that with Jesus's death and resurrection that indwelling expands to include believers and, as such, coincides with the new temple depicted at John 14:1-2. 'In that day', Jesus tells his disciples, 'you will know that I am in my Father and you in me and I in you'[580]; 'keep them in your name', he asks the Father, 'that they may be one, as we'[581]; 'for those who believe in me through their word', he continues, 'I ask ... that all may be one: as you, Father, are in me and I in you, that they also may be in us'[582]; and so also at John 14:23 (the passage tied to John 14:1-2 by the term μονή) – 'If any one loves me he will keep my word, and my Father will love him and we will come to him and will make a room with him.'[583] That is to say, if Jesus's body was a temple (John 2:19-21) because the twofold indwelling of Father and Son made it 'the place where a unique manifestation of God took place' (as Barrett has it), then the threefold indwelling of Father, Son and believer allows the same for the Spirit-wrought habitation of Father and Son in the believer (John 14:1-2). And inasmuch as that threefold indwelling occurs through the very acts that create Jesus's body as a new temple (his death and resurrection), the two ostensibly discrete metaphors fuse into one. To quote Barrett again, as he concludes, 'It was his own body, killed on the cross, that Christ raised up, but in doing so he brought the church into being.'[584]

579. *Gospel according to St. John*, 201.
580. John 14:20.
581. John 17:11.
582. John 17:20-21.
583. John 14:23.
584. *Gospel according to St. John*, 201. In his reflections on the new temple envisioned in John, Schnackenburg does not include John 14:1-2, but likewise combines the two ideas under discussion by suggesting that the communal image (the new temple as the eschatological Johannine 'worshipping community') is made possible by the christological image (the new temple as Jesus's resurrected body): John's 'ecclesiology', he asserts, 'is based entirely on Christology'; *Gospel according to St John*: 1:352, 356–57 (quotations pp. 356 and 352, respectively).

3. Ps 69:10, The Promise of a New Temple

Second, suggestive for the *chiasmus* created by these Isaianic and 'remembrance' quotations is that the same verb used for Jesus 'casting out' all from the temple at John 2 (ἐκβάλλειν) is used for him 'casting out' the 'ruler of this world' during his passion and glorification. The opening of the temple cleansing episode reads, 'And in the temple he found those who were selling oxen, sheep and doves, and the money-changers sitting. And having made a whip of cords, he cast all out of the temple (ἐξέβαλεν ἐκ τοῦ ἱεροῦ), the sheep and oxen ...'[585] And, as Jesus arrives in Jerusalem for his final Passover and is about to embark on his Passion, he declares, 'Now is the judgment of this world; now the ruler of this world will be cast out (ἐκβληθήσεται ἔξω).'[586] If, as has been argued, the first 'casting out' was done to purge the Jerusalem temple while Jesus was 'consumed' with 'zeal' for his 'Father's house', the future tense 'will consume' in the quotation suggests the same is anticipated for a second 'casting out' – this time, a purge of 'the ruler of this world' to 'prepare' a new 'Father's house', the indwelling of the Godhead in the believer. Thus, the inner *inclusio* picks up where the outer left off: an anticipation of Jesus ridding himself of the figure who prevented him from 'healing' during his public ministry.

(2) Summary

The quotation of Psalm 69:10 at John 2:17, then, is drawn from the LXX and has been edited in two ways for as many reasons: its initial conjunction has been removed, likely to allow it simply to depict Jesus's state of mind during the temple incident; and its aorist verb 'consumed' has been made future, to portray Jesus's 'zeal' in that incident as proleptic of the ardour he will have for establishing a twofold, metaphorized temple through his death and resurrection: the 'sanctuary of his body' and the 'Father's house' of the indwelling Godhead.

---

585. John 2:14-15.
586. John 12:31.

Chapter 4

PSALM 118:25-26 AND ZECHARIAH 9:9, THE RESTORATION OF THE UNITED MONARCHY

A. A 'remembrance' inclusio

The quotations of Psalm 118:25-26 and Zechariah 9:9 at John 12:12-16 conclude with the only other 'remembrance' formula to be found in John: 'His disciples did not recognize these things at first; but when Jesus was glorified, then they *remembered* (ἐμνήσθησαν) that these things were written of him and that they did these things to him.'[587] As such, like the quotations of Isaiah at John 12:37-41, these form an *inclusio* with the references linked to the earlier 'remembrance' formulae: the quotation of Psalm 69:10 at John 2:17 and the mention of 'scripture' at John 2:22. But where the Isaianic *inclusio* brought closure to the Book of Signs (by disclosing the angelic hindrance behind Jesus's public ministry), this one (it will be argued) brings anticipation of the Book of Glory (by forecasting the new dynasty to be established with Jesus's death and resurrection).

B. The Johannine renderings

1. The texture of the quotations

a. Psalm 118:25-26 (John 12:13)
The quotation of Psalm 118:25-26 is recited by pilgrims receiving Jesus into Jerusalem for his final Passover. A day earlier (six days before Passover) Jesus had arrived at Bethany, was anointed by Mary and was greeted by a multitude which learned he was there.[588] Now (the next day) he travels to Jerusalem and is similarly greeted – this time, however, by a 'great crowd' of pilgrims, who take up palm branches and recite an adaptation of these verses:

> The next day a great crowd which had come to the festival,
> having heard that Jesus was coming to Jerusalem,

---

587. John 12:16.
588. John 12:1-9.

took branches of palm trees and went out to meet him and were crying out,
'Hosanna!
Blessed is the one who comes in the name of the Lord,
the king of Israel.'[589]

Excursus: Is this a quotation?

Before this reference is examined, a more fundamental question must be asked of it. Is it a quotation at all? Or at least, should it be treated in a study focused on formal citations of Jewish scripture? The answer among several exegetes has been 'no', for one of two reasons: primarily, because it is not accompanied by an introductory formula,[590] but also because it represents 'not a reference to the Old Testament *per se*, but simply a rendering of a popular Jewish festal greeting derived from Ps 118(117)'.[591] Consequently, an *apologia* of sorts is in order before proceeding.[592]

For such a defence, it should first be noted that, quotation or not, John 12:13/Psalm 118:25-26 and John 12:15/Zechariah 9:9 are so interwoven that any treatment of the one (John 12:15) requires consideration of the other (John 12:13). As much is implied by the evangelist himself in the commentary that follows both references at John 12:16: 'His disciples did not know these things at first; but when Jesus was glorified, then they remembered that these things were written about him and that they did these things to him.' The clause 'that these things were written about him' speaks of Jesus fulfilling Zechariah 9:9 by riding into Jerusalem at John 12:14-15; and the clause 'that they did these things to him' doubtless refers to the crowd

---

589. John 12:12-13. From the mandate for priests to bless 'in the name of the Lord' at Deut 21:5, as well as the description of David doing the same at 2 Sam 6:18, that phrase in Ps 118:26a (בשם יהוה/ἐν ὀνόματι κυρίου) is often taken with the opening participle ברוך/εὐλογημένος ('blessed') rather than with the substantive participle הבא/ὁ ἐρχόμενος ('the one who comes') which immediately precedes it: 'Blessed in the name of the Lord is the one who comes'; see Bernard, *Critical and Exegetical Commentary on the Gospel according to St. John*, 2:424; and Brown, *Gospel according to John*, 1:457. Following Bultmann and Brown, however, this discussion takes the latter option and reads the colon as the grammar unfolds; Bultmann, *Gospel of John*, 418n1 (and Brown, loc. cit.).

590. Humann, 'The Function and Form of the Explicit Old Testament Quotations in the Gospel of John', 31; Menken, *Old Testament Quotations in the Fourth Gospel*, 11-13; followed by Sheridan, *Retelling Scripture*, 105-06. Franke, Braun and Freed, too, refrain from identifying John 12:13/Ps 118:25-26 as a quotation, but treat the reference nonetheless in their discussions – Freed, because he takes the absence of introductory formula to be compensated by the fulfilment language at John 12:16; Franke, *Das alte Testament bei Johannes*, 256-57, 271, 273, 288-89; Braun, *Les grandes traditions d'Israël et l'accord des Écritures selon le Quatrième Évangile*, 8; Freed *Old Testament Quotations in the Gospel of John*, xii, 67.

591. Schuchard, *Scripture within Scripture*, xiv, 76n31 (quotation p. xiv). Like Braun and Freed, however, Schuchard does, in fact, engage aspects of John 12:13/Ps 118:25-26 in his discussion of John 12:15/Zech 9:9 (pp. 76-78).

592. The core of this defense is also set out in Daise, 'Quotations with "Remembrance" Formulae in the Fourth Gospel', 80-83.

greeting Jesus with Psalm 118:25-26 at John 12:13.[593] Grammatically, the pronoun of this second clause may refer instead to Jesus's disciples; but inasmuch as those disciples have done nothing at this juncture to which it might refer, its antecedent is likely the crowd.[594] Since, then, the acts associated with both these references are coupled in this commentary as having been 'remembered' by the disciples, it seems the evangelist viewed them somehow as a piece; and this, in turn, suggests that the latter (John 12:15/Zechariah 9:9) ought not be engaged apart from the former (John 12:13/Psalm 118:25-26).

But further on this point, understanding John 12:13/Psalm 118:25-26 is pivotal to the interpretation of John 12:15/Zechariah 9:9. At John 12:14-15, as at Matthew 21:4-7, Jesus sits on a colt in fulfilment of Zechariah 9:9. But unlike the case in Matthew, in John Jesus does this after – not before – the crowd hails him as 'the one who comes in the name of the Lord'[595]; and this sequence (with other features in the text) raises a question for the Johannine entry into Jerusalem that does not emerge in the Matthean account. By sitting upon the colt was Jesus accepting the crowd's recitation of Psalm 118 at John 12:13? Or was he correcting it? If he was accepting it, then John 12:13/Psalm 118:25-26, like John 12:15/Zechariah 9:9, reflects the royal christology being endorsed in this pericope. If he was correcting it, then John 12:13/Psalm 118:25-26 serves as a foil to that royal christology – now over against John 12:15/Zechariah 9:9.[596] Whichever is the case, the issue requires as much attention be given to John 12:13/Psalm 118:25-26 as to John 12:15/Zechariah 9:9; and, for the point at issue here, this means that the former (John 12:13/Psalm 118:25-26) is omitted from consideration at one's exegetical peril.

593. So also von Wahlde, *Gospel and Letters of John*, 3:304-305, 304n29.

594. Inclined towards the antecedent as the crowd is Bultmann, *Gospel of John*, 418n5. In Synoptic parallels the disciples do, in fact, act at this juncture by procuring the donkey for Jesus: Matt 21:6-7; Mark 11:4-7; Luke 19:32-35. In John, however, it is Jesus who does this (John 12:14). Some have nonetheless insisted that the clause 'that they did these things to him' at John 12:16 betrays a Johannine 'awareness' (Barrett) or presupposition of Synoptic tradition; Bernard, *Critical and Exegetical Commentary on the Gospel according to St. John*, 2:427; Morris, *Gospel according to John*, 587n49; Barrett, *Gospel according to St. John*, 419; Hengel, 'Die Schriftauslegung des 4. Evangeliums auf dem Hintergrund der urchristlichen Exegese', 273, 273n88; Hengel, 'The Old Testament in the Fourth Gospel', 30, 40n40. Their position, however, is unnecessary, since the Johannine context (John 12:12-13) portrays the pilgrims as acting in such a way as the clause describes – taking branches of palm trees, going out to meet him and crying out 'Hosanna ...'.

595. Cf. John 12:12-16 relative to Matt 21:1-9.

596. A defence of Jesus as correcting the crowd's greeting is offered by Brown, *Gospel according to John*, 1:461-63; who was anticipated by Hoskyns (*The Fourth Gospel*, 420–21); a sentiment advocating (or at least willing to consider) the opposite is articulated by Barrett (*Gospel according to St. John*, 416–19); and a *via media* has come from Alfred Loisy, who suggested that, though mistaken, the crowd contributed 'unconsciously (*inconsciemment*) to the fulfillment of the prophecy' (*Le Quatrième Évangile, Les Épitres dites de Jean*, 2nd ed. [Paris: Émile Nourry, 1921], 365–68 [quotation p. 367]).

But to press further, John 12:13/Psalm 118:25-26 is, indeed, a quotation, on two grounds: (1) its base text relative to its source, and (2) its anomalies relative to other Johannine quotations. With regard to (1), the language of the base text at John 12:13 meets (what should be regarded as) the single determinative criterion for defining a quotation: it matches the passage from which it is drawn. If 'allusions' and 'echoes' are distinguished from 'quotations' by the degree to which their language departs from their *Vorlagen*, a reference that follows its source verbatim should not be disqualified as a 'quotation' simply because it lacks an introductory formula, and (as is set out with more detail below) this is precisely the case with John 12:13. 'Blessed is the one who comes in the name of the Lord' at John 12:13c follows LXX Psalm 118:26a word-for-word; and, allowing the *Qerê* אדני for יהוה, it does the same with its HB counterpart.[597]

As for (2) – the anomalies in John 12:13/Psalm 118:25-26 relative to other Johannine quotations – the departures of John's rendering from Psalm 118:25-26 betray the same type of treatment one finds in other Johannine quotations, namely, the assimilation of outside passages into its base text. As has been demonstrated above for some quotations[598] (and can also be shown for others[599]), anomalies in the base texts of John's quotations often suggest they have been conflated with other passages; and the same is arguable for Psalm 118:25-26 at John 12:13. To anticipate discussion below, the opening 'Hosanna' may reflect a merger with any of four verses: Psalms 8:3; 20:7, 10; or Jeremiah 31:7. And the apposition '[even] the king of Israel' may do the same with Genesis 49:10; Isaiah 44:6; Zephaniah 3:15; or Zechariah 9:9.

In sum, John 12:13/Psalm 118:25-26 meets key criteria for a quotation and is required by its context to be treated alongside John 12:15/Zechariah 9:9. Its lack of introductory formula is likely an exigency, needed because it is recited by a crowd rather than the evangelist or (as in the case of John at John 1:23/Isaiah 40:3) a single character.[600] That absence should not, however, remove it from discussion of explicit quotations.

---

597. Along a different line, Obermann identifies one of the key features of quotations to be their ability to be recognized as coming from an earlier context while maintaining their own character in the new one, what he calls 'an alien assertion' (*eine fremde Aussage*). As such, he perceives the evangelist to display their presence in the text not only with introductory formulae but also by having characters (such as this crowd) recite them in direct speech; *Die christologische Erfüllung der Schrift im Johannesevangelium*, 73.

598. Thus far, the possibility of this dynamic has been seen in all quotations treated except John 12:38/Isa 53:1.

599. Alongside the quotation of Zech 9:9 at John 12:15 (treated below) – and among references whose sources are somewhat discernible – see the possibly conflated texts for quotations at John 6:31; 15:25; and 19:36 in Appendix 2.

600. Schnackenburg, *Gospel according to St John*, 2:375.

4. Ps 118:25-26 and Zech 9:9, The Restoration of the Monarchy

(1) The version cited and its anomalies

As with the quotation of Isaiah 6:10 at John 12:40, the question of version for this quotation is indissolubly linked to the issues raised by its anomalies; and further, the issues raised by those anomalies are, themselves, inextricably woven into those of the anomalies in the quotation of Zechariah 9:9 at John 12:15. In this light, conclusions on Psalm 118:25-26 will not be made immediately but will be suspended until Zechariah 9:9 has also been reviewed. At that juncture a proposal will be made for both quotations as a whole.

The HB, LXX and Johannine renderings of the verse are as follows (Table 32).

Table 32 Psalm 118:25-26 in the HB, LXX and John

HB Psalm 118:25-26[601]	LXX Psalm 118:25-26	John 12:13
אנא יהוה הושיעה נא	ὦ κύριε, σῶσον δή,	ὡσαννά·
אנא יהוה הצליחה נא	ὦ κύριε, εὐόδωσον δή.	εὐλογημένος
ברוך הבא בשם יהוה	εὐλογημένος ὁ ἐρχόμενος	ὁ ἐρχόμενος
ברכנוכם מבית יהוה	ἐν ὀνόματι κυρίου·	ἐν ὀνόματι κυρίου,
	εὐλογήκαμεν ὑμᾶς ἐξ οἴκου κυρίου.	[καὶ] ὁ βασιλεὺς τοῦ Ἰσραήλ.
We implore you, Lord, save us!	O Lord, save now!	Hosanna!
We implore you, Lord, prosper us!	O Lord, prosper now!	
Blessed is the one who comes in the name of the Lord; we have blessed you from the house of the Lord.	Blessed is the one who comes in the name of the Lord; we have blessed you from the house of the Lord.	Blessed is the one who comes in the name of the Lord, [even] the king of Israel.

The core text cited at John 12:13 follows LXX Psalm 118:26a verbatim: 'Blessed is the one who comes in the name of the Lord.' Inasmuch as the LXX of this line largely follows the HB – and on the prospect that ὡσαννά may reflect a direct translation of Hebrew הושיעה נא – it is argued by Reim that the ultimate source of the reference is the HB.[602] The LXX, however, does diverge from the HB by rendering the tetragrammaton (יהוה) as 'Lord' (κύριος); and because the Johannine rendering follows suit – and otherwise matches the LXX word-for-word (following the criterion set out in the Introduction[603]) – it more likely reflects a re-presentation of the Greek than a translation of the Hebrew.

Anomalies number two. Where one expects Psalm 118:25, the quotation reads 'Hosanna' (ὡσαννά); and where one expects Psalm 118:26b, it reads (in some manner) 'king of Israel' ([καὶ ὁ] βασιλεὺς τοῦ Ἰσραήλ) – articular[604] or anarthrous,[605]

---

601. Besides the MT, Ps 118:25-26 is attested in 4QPs[b] and 11QPs[a].
602. *Jochanan*, 26. Reim still allows, however, that this ultimate source was mediated to the fourth evangelist through a tradition shared with the Synoptics (pp. 27-28).
603. Under *a. Confirming the Septuagint*.
604. P[66] ℵ (second correctors) D K Θ family[1] 565.
605. A Γ Δ family[13] 700 892 [from a later supplement] 1241 1424 Sinai lectionary 844 and the majority of manuscripts.

the articular in some witnesses preceded by καί[606] as either a copulative ('and') or epexegetical ('even')[607] conjunction.

(2) Hypotheses

(a) 'Hosanna'

The first anomaly, 'Hosanna' (ὡσαννά), is fundamentally identified as a transliteration of a Semitic original, and this has been proposed along two lines. One is that the term transliterated is drawn from a different text, which John (or a putative tradent) merged with Psalm 118:25-26. In three of the passages proposed the verb thought to have been assimilated is the same as that in Psalm 118:25, the hiphil להושיע: HB Psalm 20:7 and HB Psalm 20:10,[608] where the psalmist bids the Lord to 'save' (הושיע[ה]) the king; and HB Jeremiah 31:7,[609] where the people are summoned to bid the Lord to 'save' (הושע) Israel's remnant (Table 33).

Table 33 Assimilated passages for 'Hosanna'

HB Psalm 20:7, 10	HB Jeremiah 31:7
Now I know that the Lord has saved (הושיע יהוה) his anointed; he will answer him from his holy heaven with mighty acts of deliverance by his right hand ...	For thus says the Lord, 'Cry with joy for Jacob, and raise a shout over the head of the nations; proclaim, praise and say, "Save, O Lord (הושע יהוה), your people, the remnant of Israel"'!
Lord, save (יהוה הושיעה) the king. Answer us on the day of our calling!	

In a fourth passage, proposed by T.K. Cheyne, the operative word differs: Aramaic עושנא for Hebrew עז at Psalm 8:3. The thesis is an attempt to resolve a grammatical and semantic problem attending the Matthean and Markan accounts of the quotation. There, ὡσαννά is modified with dative phrases that (at least ostensibly) conflict with a cry to 'save': specifically, the phrase 'to the son of David' (τῷ υἱῷ Δαυίδ) and the phrase 'in the highest' (ἐν τοῖς ὑψίστοις) (Table 34).

606. א (original and second correctors) B L Q W Ψ 579.
607. So, Menken, '"Do Not Fear, Daughter Zion ..." (John 12:15)', in *Old Testament Quotations in the Fourth Gospel*, 89n38; first publ. in *ZNW* 80 (1989).
608. Noted as 'reminiscent' by Charles Cutler Torrey, *Our Translated Gospels: Some of the Evidence* (London/New York: Harper & Brothers, 1936), 21-22 (quotation p. 22); Charles Cutler Torrey, *Documents of the Primitive Church* (New York/London: Harper & Brothers, 1941), 77-78; Charles Cutler Torrey, *The Four Gospels: A New Translation*, 2nd ed. (New York: Harper, 1947), 295; and followed to some degree by Freed, *Old Testament Quotations in the Gospel of John*, 69-71. Cf. Eric Werner, 'Hosanna in the Gospels', *JBL* 65 (1946): 104-05.
609. Franke, *Das alte Testament bei Johannes*, 271.

4. Ps 118:25-26 and Zech 9:9, The Restoration of the Monarchy

Table 34 'Hosanna' (ὡσαννά) in Matthew and Mark

Matthew 21:9b-d	Mark 11:9b-10
ὡσαννὰ <u>τῷ υἱῷ Δαυίδ</u>·	ὡσαννά·
εὐλογημένος ὁ ἐρχόμενος	εὐλογημένος ὁ ἐρχόμενος
ἐν ὀνόματι κυρίου·	ἐν ὀνόματι κυρίου·
ὡσαννὰ <u>ἐν τοῖς ὑψίστοις</u>.	εὐλογημένη ἡ ἐρχομένη βασιλεία
	τοῦ πατρὸς ἡμῶν Δαυίδ.
	ὡσαννὰ <u>ἐν τοῖς ὑψίστοις</u>.
Hosanna <u>to the son of David</u>!	Hosanna!
Blessed is the one who comes	Blessed is the one who comes
in the name of the Lord.	in the name of the Lord.
Hosanna <u>in the highest</u>!	Blessed is the coming kingdom
	of our father David.
	Hosanna <u>in the highest</u>!

Discussion of the matter has turned on whether these modifications could be reconciled with the idea of 'saving' or whether the cry, itself, has changed from plea to praise[610]; and Cheyne argues for a *via media* by proposing that ὡσαννά reflects a targumic assimilation of the verse which Jesus quotes directly after entering Jerusalem at Matthew 21:16, Psalm 8:3 – 'From the mouth of children and infants you have established strength (עז) …'. The targumic counterpart to the Hebrew 'strength' (עז) is Aramaic עושנא; and according to Cheyne this is the term that lies behind ὡσαννά.[611]

The other line for identifying ὡσαννά traces it in some way to הושיעה נא at Psalm 118:25a – if not as a direct transliteration of that term,[612] then as the rendering of a source mediating or related to that verse: an Aramaic gospel *Vorlage*[613]; Hellenized popular usage[614]; or the Aramaic term designating the *lûlāb*, הושענא. On this last

---

610. See the reviews of the debate in Werner, 'Hosanna in the Gospels', 97–112; Eduard Lohse, 'Hosanna', *NovT* 6 (1963): 113–19; and Marvin H. Pope, 'Hosanna', *ABD* 3: 290-91.

611. 'Hosanna', in *Encyclopaedia Biblica: A Critical Dictionary of the Literary, Political and Religious History, the Archaeology, Geography and Natural History of the Bible*, ed. T.K. Cheyne and J. Sutherland Black, 4 vols. (New York: Macmillan, 1899–1903), 2:2118; cf. Werner, 'Hosanna in the Gospels', 101. *Tg. Ket.* Ps 8:3, 'From the mouth of youth and children you have established strength (עושנא) …'; text: Paulus de Lagarde, ed., *Hagiographa Chaldaice* (Leipzig: B.G. Teubner, 1873).

612. Marvin H. Pope, 'Hosanna', 3:290; cf. Noack, *Zur johanneischen Tradition*, 87; and Obermann, *Die christologische Erfüllung der Schrift im Johannesevangelium*, 186. The Hebrew *Vorlage* is traced by Lindars to a putative tradition behind Mark 11:10 that was allegedly based solely on Ps 118:26; *Gospel of John*, 422–23.

613. See the references to Torrey in note 608; and cf. Freed, *Old Testament Quotations in the Gospel of John*, 70–71.

614. Schuchard, *Scripture within Scripture*, 76n31.

proposal, it is argued by F.C. Burkitt that ὡσαννά may reflect הושענא as the actual syllables recited by Jews arriving at the temple for pilgrimage festivals. The Aramaic term, he notes, is used in *Targum to Esther* 3:8 to describe the ritual flora (*lûlabîn*) used by Jews to celebrate Tabernacles[615]; and from this he suspects that the palm branch came to be called such because phonetically this was the actual cry issued by Jews when they shook those *lûlabîn* in festal observance.[616] Inasmuch as Psalm 118, he believes, was written for Hanukkah – and because, according to 2 Maccabees 10:6-7, Hanukkah was observed using the same ritual flora as were employed during Tabernacles – he concludes that הושיעה נא at Psalm 118:25 is a Hebrew equivalent of the original Aramaic הושענא and that in place of that Hebrew term John substitutes a transliteration of the Aramaic exemplar.[617]

(b) 'The king of Israel'
The second anomaly, '(and/even) the king of Israel', in fact, creates another *inclusio* within the Book of Signs – in this case, with the confession made by Nathanael at John 1:45-49. When Nathanael is first informed about Jesus in that passage, he doubts that 'anything good' can 'be from Nazareth'; and, as his scepticism is dispelled by Jesus's awareness of his earlier movements, he declares him to be a messiah, using the very same title: 'Rabbi, you are the Son of God; you are king of Israel (σὺ βασιλεὺς εἶ τοῦ Ἰσραήλ).'[618] This declaration and John 12:13 are the only two *loci* in which that title appears in John; and so, its presence in this quotation serves as the second component of another *epanalepsis*, again spanning Jesus's public ministry.

This anomaly, too, has been explained along two lines – once again, neither exclusive of the other. One assumes John's dependence on the Synoptics and suggests it was catalysed by the rendering in Luke: 'Blessed is the one who comes, the king (ὁ βασιλεύς), in the name of the Lord.'[619] The other is that it reflects a

---

615. 'And making the *lûlāb* (הושענא) for themselves ...'; text: Alexander Sperber, ed., *The Hagiographa*, vol. 4A of *The Bible in Aramaic Based on Old Manuscripts and Printed Texts* (Leiden: E.J. Brill, 1968). Sperber's text does not distinguish between *Targum Rishon* and *Targum Sheni* to Esther (see p. vii).

616. For the waving of *lûlabîn*, m. *Sukkah* 3:9.

617. 'W and Θ: Studies in the Western Text of St Mark', *JTS* 17 (1916): 140–42; cf. Michael A. Daise, 'Jesus and the Jewish Festivals: Methodological Reflections', in *Jesus Research: New Methodologies and Perceptions. The Second Princeton-Prague Symposium on Jesus Research, Princeton 2007*, ed. James H. Charlesworth with Brian Rhea, Princeton-Prague Symposia Series on the Historical Jesus 2 (Grand Rapids, MI: William B. Eerdmans, 2014), 288n16. Similar to Burkitt is Lohse, 'Hosianna', 114–15.

618. John 1:49.

619. Luke 19:38bc; so Freed, *Old Testament Quotations in the Gospel of John*, 74. In W and 579 the title does not appear; in א (original reading) and perhaps 69 it is not cast as 'coming' (ἐρχόμενος); in Bezae it is relocated to a (created) colon following the one in question – 'Blessed is the one who comes in the name of the Lord; blessed is the king (εὐλογημένος ὁ βασιλεύς)'; and in an array of witnesses it is anarthrous – 'Blessed is the one who comes, a king (βασιλεύς), in the name of the Lord' (א [second corrector] A K L N Γ Δ Θ Ψ family[1] family[13] 565 700 892 1241 1424 2542 Sinai lectionary 844 and the majority of manuscripts).

4. Ps 118:25-26 and Zech 9:9, The Restoration of the Monarchy

conflation of Psalm 118:25-26 with any of four passages: Genesis 49:10; Isaiah 44:6 (particularly in the LXX); Zephaniah 3:15; or Zechariah 9:9.

The case for Genesis 49:10, made by Joseph Blenkinsopp, traces the phrase to a messianized, targumic paraphrase of Jacob's oracle on Judah:

> The scepter shall not depart from Judah,
> nor the staff from between his feet,
> until Shiloh (he whose it is) comes,
> to whom belongs the obedience of the peoples.[620]

In extant *targumim* on the passage the HB 'until Shiloh comes' (עד כי-יבא שילה) has been rendered messianically as 'until the time at which King Messiah comes' (עד זמן ד[י]ייתי מלכא משיחא)[621] or 'until the Messiah comes' (עד דייתי משיחא)[622]; and according to Blenkinsopp, such a rephrasing (if not in these, then in a putative *targum*) would fit aptly into John's account of Jesus's entry into Jerusalem: it shares the verb 'to come' with both Psalm 118:25-26 and the quotation of Zechariah 9:9 at John 12:15[623]; it aligns with the royal christology attached to that verb throughout the Fourth Gospel[624]; and it resonates with the royal character of Psalm 118 itself.[625] As such, Blenkinsopp concludes, 'king of Israel' is drawn from that (type of) *locus*.[626]

---

620. Gen 49:10; the full oracle spans Gen 49:8-12.

621. *Tg. Ps.-J.* Gen 49:10; *Frg. Tg.* Gen 49:10. Texts: E.G. Clarke, *Targum Pseudo-Jonathan of the Pentateuch: Text and Concordance* (Hoboken, NJ: Ktav Pub. House, 1984); Michael L. Klein, *The Fragment-Targums of the Pentateuch: According to their Extant Sources*, 2 vols., AnBib 76 (Rome: Biblical Institute Press, 1980). Brackets reflect a minor difference between the readings.

622. *Tg. Onq.* Gen 49:10. Text: Alexander Sperber, ed., *The Pentateuch according to Targum Onkelos*, vol. 1 of *The Bible in Aramaic Based on Old Manuscripts and Printed Texts* (Leiden: E.J. Brill, 1959).

623. 'Blessed is the one who comes (ὁ ἐρχόμενος) in the name of the Lord' (John 12:13/ Ps 118:25-26); 'Behold, your king comes (ἔρχεται), sitting upon a foal of a donkey' (John 12:15/Zech 9:9).

624. Specifically, that the miraculously fed multitude deems Jesus 'the prophet who is coming (ὁ ἐρχόμενος) into the world', then attempts to make him king (John 6:14-15); that Martha synonymously confesses him to be Christ, Son of God, and 'the one who is coming (ὁ … ἐρχόμενος) into the world' (John 11:27); and that Jesus, himself, affirms Pilate's interrogation about his kingship saying, 'To this end I have been born and to this end I have come (ἐλήλυθα) into the world, that I may testify to the truth' (John 18:37); 'The Oracle of Judah and the Messianic Entry', *JBL* 80 (1961): 59.

625. Here Blenkinsopp points to the psalm's call to 'open … the gates of righteousness', in order that its author (the king?) may 'enter by them' (Ps 118:19); 'The Oracle of Judah and the Messianic Entry', 59.

626. 'The Oracle of Judah and the Messianic Entry', 56–59.

As for Isaiah 44:6, Zephaniah 3:15 and Zechariah 9:9, the first two attest the title in language that matches or closely aligns with the attestations in the textual traditions behind John 12:13 – for the LXX, in particular, Isaiah 44:6 reading the articular ὁ βασιλεὺς τοῦ Ισραηλ[627]; Zephaniah 3:15 reading the anarthrous βασιλεὺς Ισραηλ. And all three carry features in their contexts that would make them apt for assimilation into Psalm 118:25-26. Zephaniah 3:15 and Zechariah 9:9 share the verbs 'to save' (להושיע/σῴζειν) and (in the Hebrew) 'to rejoice' (לגיל). And HB Zephaniah 3:15, as well as HB/LXX Isaiah 44:6, lie in proximity to the exhortation 'fear not', which could explain that anomaly in Zechariah 9:9 at John 12:15: this appears in Isaiah 44:2 for Isaiah 44:6; in Zephaniah 3:16 for Zephaniah 3:15 (Table 35).[628]

Table 35 Assimilated texts for 'king of Israel' (John 12:13/Psalm 118:25-26)

John 12:13b-d/Psalm 118:25-26
Hosanna! Blessed is the one who comes in the name of the Lord, [even] the king of Israel ([καὶ] ὁ βασιλεὺς τοῦ Ἰσραήλ).

HB/LXX Isaiah 44:2, 6	HB/LXX Zephaniah 3:15-17[629]	HB/LXX Zechariah 9:9
Thus says the Lord who attends you, and fashions you from the womb; he will help you. 'Fear not (אל-תירא/μὴ φοβοῦ), my servant Jacob, Jeshurun, whom I have chosen …' Thus says the Lord, the king of Israel, (מלך-ישראל/ ὁ βασιλεὺς τοῦ Ισραηλ), even the one who redeems him, the Lord of hosts, 'I am first and I am the last; apart from me there is no god …'	The Lord has removed your judgments; he has turned away your foes. The king of Israel (מלך ישראל/βασιλεὺς Ισραηλ), the Lord, is in your midst; you will not fear evil again. On that day it will be said to Jerusalem, 'Fear not/take courage (אל-תירא/θάρσει), Zion; let your hands not sink. The Lord, your God, is in your midst; a mighty one who (will) save(s) (יושיע/σώσει). He will exult over you with joy; he will renew you with his love; he will rejoice (יגיל/ –) over you with a ringing cry.'	Rejoice (גילי/) greatly, daughter (of) Zion; shout, daughter (of) Jerusalem. Behold your king (מלכך/ ὁ βασιλεὺς σου) comes to you, righteous and saved/saving (ונושע/σῴζων) is he, humble and riding upon an ass, even upon a foal of jennies.

627. This, notwithstanding the omission of ὁ βασιλεύς in Sinaiticus, as well as the presence of the article before Ισραηλ only in Sinaiticus, Alexandrinus and 965; see Menken's critique of Schuchard's argument for this passage; '"Do Not Fear, Daughter Zion …" (John 12:15)', 84n21; cf. Schuchard, *Scripture within Scripture*, 76–78.

628. See Brown, *Gospel according to John*, 1:458; Boismard and Lamouille, *L'Évangile de Jean*, 308–09; and (particularly on LXX Isa 44:6) Schuchard, *Scripture within Scripture*, 77–78, 78n34.

629. LXX Zeph 3:16 attests 'take courage' (θάρσει) rather than 'fear not' (μὴ φοβοῦ), but for reasons of synonymity set out below in this chapter (under *(a) 'Fear not'*) that verb is represented here.

b. Zechariah 9:9 (John 12:15)

The quotation at John 12:15, for its part, is cited by the evangelist as commentary on what Jesus does after the greeting at John 12:13. As the pilgrims recite Psalm 118, Jesus finds a colt and sits upon it; and, as he does, the evangelist declares (a) that in so doing he fulfilled Zechariah 9:9 and (b) that after his glorification his disciples remembered that such things were written about and done to him:

> And having found a young donkey, Jesus sat upon it, as it is written,
> 'Fear not, daughter (of) Zion;
> behold your king comes,
> sitting upon a foal of a donkey.'
> His disciples did not know these things at first;
> but when Jesus was glorified, then they *remembered* (ἐμνήσθησαν)
> that these things were written about him and that they did these things to him.[630]

(1) The version cited and its anomalies

The HB, LXX and Johannine renderings of the verses are as follows (Table 36).

Table 36 Zechariah 9:9 in the HB, LXX and John

HB Zechariah 9:9	LXX Zechariah 9:9	John 12:15
גילי מאד בת-ציון הריעי בת ירושלם הנה מלכך יבוא לך צדיק ונושע הוא עני ורכב על-חמור ועל-עיר בן-אתנות	χαῖρε σφόδρα, θύγατερ Σιων· κήρυσσε, θύγατερ Ιερουσαλημ· ἰδοὺ ὁ βασιλεύς σου ἔρχεταί σοι, δίκαιος καὶ σῴζων αὐτός, πραῢς καὶ ἐπιβεβηκὼς ἐπὶ ὑποζύγιον καὶ πῶλον νέον.	μὴ φοβοῦ, θυγάτηρ Σιών· ἰδοὺ ὁ βασιλεύς σου ἔρχεται, καθήμενος ἐπὶ πῶλον ὄνου.

Rejoice greatly,
   daughter (of) Zion;
shout,
   daughter (of) Jerusalem.
Behold, your king comes
   to you,
righteous and saved is he,
humble and riding
   upon a donkey,
even upon an ass,
   the foal of jennies.
	Rejoice greatly, daughter (of) Zion,
	proclaim, daughter (of) Jerusalem.
	Behold your king comes to you,
	righteous and saving is he,
	meek and mounted upon an ass,
	   even a young foal.
		Fear not,
		   daughter (of) Zion;
		behold your king comes,
		sitting upon a foal
		   of a donkey.

Regarding the version, as with Isaiah 6:10 at John 12:40, so here: the LXX diverges from the HB and John's rendering has both affinities to and deviations from each. The differences between the LXX and HB number between three and four: (1) for the passive participle 'saved' (נושע) at HB Zechariah 9:9d, the LXX has the present participle 'saving' (σῴζων); (2) for the present participle 'riding' (רכב) at Zechariah 9:9e, the LXX has the perfect participle 'mounted' (ἐπιβεβηκώς);

---

630. John 12:14-16.

(3) where the HB modifies its second term for the donkey with an apposition at Zechariah 9:9f ('even upon an ass, a foal of jennies'), the LXX does so with an adjective ('even a young foal'); and, (4) depending on how the indeclinable proper nouns Σιων and Ιερουσαλημ at Zechariah 9:9ab modify the prior θύγατερ which precedes them – that is, as appositions ('daughter Zion' and 'daughter Jerusalem') or as genitive constructs ('daughter of Zion' and 'daughter of Jerusalem') – the Greek may depart from the Hebrew of those epithets.[631]

As for the Johannine rendering, (a) it overlaps both versions in one, possibly two, of its components; (b) it departs from both in five of its components; and (c) it follows one over against the other in four of its components – two for each version. For (a) – its correspondence with HB and LXX Zechariah 9:9 – it coincides with the exhortation 'behold your king comes' at Zechariah 9:9c; and, if one reads either the nominative θυγάτηρ in LXX Sinaiticus (with John's rendering of the same[632]) or the vocative θύγατερ in certain textual witnesses to John 12:15[633] (with the LXX rendering of the same), it also coincides with the address to 'daughter (of) Zion' at Zechariah 9:9a.[634] For (b) – its divergence from HB and LXX Zechariah 9:9 – John's rendering reads 'fear not' for 'rejoice greatly' at John 12:15a/Zechariah 9:9a; it omits Zechariah 9:9bd and the first two words of Zechariah 9:9e ('humble/meek and'); it similarly omits the dative 'to you' (which appears at Zechariah 9:9c in all HB/LXX manuscripts except LXX 534); it reduces the compound objects of the prepositional phrases for the animal being ridden into a single word modified by a genitive – 'a foal of a donkey' (πῶλον ὄνου); and it replaces the HB and LXX verbs for Jesus's posture on that animal with the verb καθῆσθαι – for לרכב, if working from the HB[635]; for ἐπιβαίνειν, if working from the LXX.

Finally, for (c) – its alignment with one version over against the other – it follows the LXX over against the HB by rendering 'king' as articular rather than anarthrous (ὁ βασιλεύς σου) and by similarly reading πῶλος for the animal ridden

---

631. Advocating the constructs as appositional genitives ('daughter Zion', 'daughter Jerusalem') has been W.F. Stinespring, 'No Daughter of Zion: A Study of the Appositional Genitive in Hebrew Grammar', *Enc* 26 (1965): 133–41; defending the prospect that they are possessive genitives ('daughter of Zion', 'daughter of Jerusalem') now is Michael H. Floyd, 'Welcome Back, Daughter of Zion!', *CBQ* 70 (2008): 487–92. Cf. Kubiś, *Book of Zechariah in the Gospel of John*, 76n219.

632. P⁶⁶ A B D K L Q W Δ 0218 565 579; and with the articular, P⁷⁵ (apparently) B (second corrector).

633. ℵ Γ Θ Ψ family¹ family¹³ 700 892 (a later supplement) 1241 1424 Sinai lectionary 844 and the majority of manuscripts.

634. On these variations Menken, followed by Schuchard, suspects the textual tradition has been too fluid to yield a definitive conclusion for one against the other; Menken, '"Do Not Fear, Daughter Zion …" (John 12:15)', 79n1; Schuchard, *Scripture within Scripture*, 75n21. A further factor here would be point (4) in the previous paragraph: the grammatical options created by the indeclinable Σιων in both John and the LXX.

635. It is judged here that were the evangelist working from the HB, καθῆσθαι would be better identified as a 'replacement' than a 'translation' of לרכב: it is only used once to translate that verb in the LXX (at LXX Isa 19:1) and, thereby, does not appear to describe an action routinely equivalent to 'riding'.

by Jesus (notwithstanding that πῶλος is a common LXX gloss for Hebrew עיר)[636]: in the LXX, 'even a young foal' (καὶ πῶλον νέον); at John 12:15, 'upon a foal of a donkey' (ἐπὶ πῶλον ὄνου). Conversely, it follows the HB over against the LXX by casting the verb describing Jesus's posture on the donkey as a present (רכב/καθήμενος) rather than perfect (ἐπιβεβηκώς) participle and by employing the term ὄνος for 'donkey': ὄνος is used elsewhere in the LXX to translate all three terms found at HB Zechariah 9:9ef: חמור seventy-three times; עיר twice; אתון thirty times; it does not occur, however, in LXX Zechariah 9:9.

(2) Hypotheses

As was done for the quotation of Isaiah 6:10 at John 12:40, hypotheses on the version and anomalies of this quotation will be organized around the latter and rehearsed as they unfold, in this case from John 12:15a-c: in order, views on (1) the exhortation 'fear not' at John 12:15a, (2) the omission of Zechariah 9:9b, (3) the omission of the dative pronoun 'to you' from Zechariah 9:9c at John 12:15b, (4) the omission of Zechariah 9:9d and the first two words of Zechariah 9:9e (hereafter referenced as the 'attributes of the king'[637]), (5) the verb 'sitting' at John 12:15c and (6) the prepositional phrase 'upon a foal of a donkey' in that same line.[638]

(a) 'Fear not'

The exhortation 'fear not' (μὴ φοβοῦ) for 'rejoice greatly' (גילי מאד/χαῖρε σφόδρα) has been ascribed to either the evangelist directly, a conflation with another passage or both.[639] For the evangelist, himself, it has been assigned, on one hand, to a defective memory[640] and, on the other, to his sense of semantics: specifically (for the latter) to the prospect that he viewed 'fear not' as roughly equivalent to the verb it supplants – 'rejoice greatly'. Support is drawn from Joel 2 and Zephaniah 3. In Joel 2:21, 23, as well as in LXX Zephaniah 3:14, 16, the Hebrew 'fear not' (אל-תיראי) or its LXX counterpart 'take courage' (θάρσει) occurs in parallelism with 'rejoice' (גיל) and גילו/χαῖρε and χαίρετε)[641]; LXX Zephaniah 3:14a may, in fact, follow LXX Zechariah 9:9a verbatim – χαῖρε σφόδρα, θύγατερ Σιων.[642] Consequently, it is surmised, the

---

636. In the LXX πῶλος is used five out of seven times to translate עיר.

637. So, Kubiś, *Book of Zechariah in the Gospel of John*, 80–81.

638. An extensive treatment of these anomalies can be found in Kubiś, *Book of Zechariah in the Gospel of John*, 76–100.

639. Barrett, for instance, is persuaded that the evangelist imported Isa 40:9 into Zech 9:9 by citing from memory; *Gospel according to St. John*, 418–19.

640. See Barrett, note 639.

641. 'Fear not/take courage (אל-תיראי/θάρσει), O earth; rejoice (גילי/χαῖρε) and be glad ... And children of Zion, rejoice (גילו/χαίρετε) and be glad in the Lord your God' (Joel 2:21, 23); 'Cry out/rejoice greatly (– /χαῖρε σφόδρα), daughter (of) Zion! Shout, O Israel! Be glad and exult with whole heart, daughter (of) Jerusalem! ... On that day it will be said to Jerusalem, "Fear not/take courage (אל-תיראי/θάρσει), O Zion ..."' (Zeph 3:14, 16). Since HB Zeph 3:14 reads a verb other than 'rejoice' – 'cry out' (רני) – the Hebrew term for it is not represented alongside its Greek counterpart.

642. The exhortation χαῖρε σφόδρα at LXX Zeph 3:14a is well attested (W 36 46 49 68 87 130 147 233 [corrected] 239 311 407 449 534 613 711 764 770); σφόδρα, however, is absent in Sinaiticus, Vaticanus, Alexandrinus and Marchalianus.

evangelist could have read the two verbs as synonyms and for his quotation replaced the one with the other, perhaps thinking (theologically) that the more sober 'fear not' was better suited to the imminence of Jesus's death in the narrative.[643]

As for a conflation with another passage, 'fear not' has also been thought to reflect a merger of Zechariah 9:9 with any one or more of some fifteen passages, HB or LXX, a number of which share other vocabulary with it (Table 37).[644]

Table 37 Assimilated texts for 'fear not'[645]

John 12:15
Fear not (μὴ φοβοῦ), daughter (of) Zion (θυγάτηρ Σιών);
behold (ἰδού) your king comes (ὁ βασιλεύς σου ἔρχεται),
sitting upon a foal of a donkey.

HB/LXX Zechariah 9:9
Rejoice greatly (גילי מאד/χαῖρε σφόδρα), daughter (of) Zion (בת- ציון/θύγατερ Σιων);
shout/proclaim (הריעי/κήρυσσε), daughter (of) Jerusalem (בת ירושלם/θύγατερ Ιερουσαλημ).
Behold (הנה/ἰδού), your king comes (מלכך יבוא/ὁ βασιλεύς σου ἔρχεται) to you,
righteous and saved/saving (ונושע/σῴζων) is he,
humble and riding upon an ass,
even upon a donkey, the foal of jennies.

HB/LXX Isaiah 10:24-34	HB/LXX Isaiah 35:4
Therefore, thus says the Lord, Yahweh of hosts, 'My people who dwell in Zion, fear not (אל-תירא/μὴ φοβοῦ) Asshur, which smites you with the rod and lifts its staff upon you in the way of Egypt …'	Say to those anxious of heart, 'Hold strong; fear not (אל-תיראו/μὴ φοβεῖσθε). Behold (הנה/ἰδού) your God, vengeance will come (יבוא/ –); the recompense of God;
[HB] Yet today, standing at Nob, he (Asshur) will wield his hand at the mount of the daughter (of) Zion (בית-ציון),[646] the hill of Jerusalem.[647]	he will come (יבוא/ –) and he will save you (ויושעכם/σώσει).'

643. Freed, *Old Testament Quotations in the Gospel of John*, 79; and Humann, 'The Function and Form of the Explicit Old Testament Quotations in the Gospel of John', 45–46 (especially 45nn51, 53) – the latter of which (for the context of Jesus's death) follows Robert H. Strachan, *The Fourth Gospel: Its Significance and Environment*, 3rd ed. (London: S.C.M., 1941), 252.

644. Most of the passages are listed by Schuchard, *Scripture within Scripture*, 75n22. To them are added Isa 41:14-16 and Zech 8:13-15 from Kubiś, *Book of Zechariah in the Gospel of John*, 84–86.

645. With the exception of Isa 10:24-34, the translations are drawn from the HB, with the operative LXX terms inserted next to the Hebrew: for Isa 10:32 the versions differ dramatically and are represented separately. Further, with the exception of LXX 'take courage' (θαρσεῖν) for Hebrew 'fear not' (אל-תירא/ו), HB and LXX terms which do not match those used at HB/LXX Zech 9:9 or John 12:15 are left blank: occurrences of θαρσεῖν are retained, given the hypothesis (just articulated) on its equivalence with μὴ φοβεῖσθαι.

646. Here apparently reading the *Qerê* -בת for -בית, as also in 1QIsa^a; 4QIsa^c.

647. The only other word in this passage shared with Zech 9:9 is Hebrew 'to come' (לבוא) at HB Isa 10:28, 'He comes (בא) to Aiath'; the Greek reads ἥκειν.

HB/LXX Isaiah 10:24-34 (cont.)	

[LXX]
Summon the daughter (of) Zion
  (τὴν θυγατέρα Σιων) today
  to remain in the way;
summon with the hand, O mountain,
and you hills which are in Jerusalem.	

HB/LXX Isaiah 40:9-10[648]	**HB/LXX Isaiah 41:8-10**

Ascend a high mountain,
  herald of Zion (ציון/Σιων);
raise your voice with power,
  herald of Jerusalem.
Raise it; fear not (אל-תיראי/μὴ φοβεῖσθε);
say to the cities of Judah,
'Behold (הנה/ἰδού) your God.
Behold (הנה/ἰδού), the Lord Yahweh
  comes (יבוא/ἔρχεται) as a mighty one;
and his arm is ruling for him.
Behold (הנה/ἰδού), his reward is with him,
his recompense before him.'
	But you, Israel, my servant;
	Jacob, whom I have chosen;
	seed of Abraham, my friend ...
	Fear not (אל-תירא/μὴ φοβοῦ),
	  for I am with you;
	be not anxious, for I am your God;
	I have strengthened you;
	yea, I have helped you.
	Indeed, I have upheld you with the right hand
	of my righteousness.

HB/LXX Isaiah 41:11-13	**HB/LXX Isaiah 41:14-16**

Indeed, all who are incensed against you
shall be shamed and humiliated ...
For I am the Lord your God,
  upholding your right hand;
the one who says to you,
  'Fear not (אל-תירא/μὴ φοβοῦ),
  I have helped you.'
	Fear not (אל-תיראי/ –), worm of Jacob,
	men of Israel!
	'I have helped you', says the Lord.
	Redeeming you is the Holy One of Israel.
	Behold (הנה/ἰδού), I have set you
	  as a sharpened threshing sledge,
	  new, double-edged.
	You shall thresh and crush the mountains;
	and the hills you shall set as chaff ...
	And you shall rejoice (ואתה תגיל/ –)
	  in the Lord;
	in the Holy One of Israel you shall boast.

HB/LXX Isaiah 43:1	**HB/LXX Isaiah 43:5-7**

But now thus says the Lord,
the one who created you, Jacob,
the one who formed you, O Israel!
'Fear not (אל-תירא/μὴ φοβοῦ),
  for I have redeemed you;
I have called your name,
  you who are mine.'
	Fear not (אל-תירא/μὴ φοβοῦ),
	  for I am with you.
	From the east I will bring (אביא/ –) your seed;
	and from the west I will gather you.
	I will say '... bring (הביאי/ –) my sons
	  from afar ...
	everyone who is called by my name,
	  whom for my glory I created, formed,
	  indeed, made'.

(Continued)

648. Reim sees the connection of Isa 40:9-10 to Zech 9:9 mediated through Isa 62:10-11 (presumably in the HB, where the lexical correspondence is more precise). Both Isa 62:10-11 and Isa 40:9-10 (in its broader context) speak of 'preparing the way' (פנו דרך, Isa 40:3b/ Isa 62:10b) and of the Lord coming with recompense (הנה שכרו אתו ופעלתו לפניו, Isa 40:10cd/ Isa 62:11ef); and both Isa 62:10-11 and Zech 9:9 address the 'daughter of Zion' (ל[בת-ציון], Zech 9:9a/Isa 62:11b); *Jochanan*, 30.

HB/LXX Isaiah 44:1-2	HB/LXX Isaiah 44:6-8
Hear now, Jacob my servant, And Israel, whom I have chosen. Thus says the Lord who attends you, and fashions you from the womb; he will help you. 'Fear not (אל-תירא/μὴ φοβοῦ), my servant Jacob, Jeshurun, whom I have chosen.'	Thus says the Lord, the king of Israel, (מלך-ישראל/ὁ βασιλεὺς τοῦ Ισραηλ),[649] even the one who redeems him, the Lord of hosts, 'I am first and I am the last; apart from me there is no god. Who is like me? … Let them announce to them what is coming (before it comes) (תבאנה/ τὰ ἐπερχόμενα πρὸ τοῦ ἐλθεῖν). Be not in dread; and fear not (ואל-תיראו /–).[650] Have I not from of old proclaimed to you? Have I not declared? You are my witnesses. Is there a god besides me? There is no (such) rock; I have not known (one).'
HB/LXX Isaiah 51:7	**HB/LXX Isaiah 54:4**
Hear me, you who know righteousness, a people with my law in their heart; fear not (אל-תיראו/μὴ φοβεῖσθε) the reproach of man; and be not dismayed from their invectives.	Fear not (אל-תירא/μὴ φοβοῦ), for you will not be ashamed; be not cast down, for you will not show dishonor. For the shame of your youth you will forget; and the reproach of your widowhood you will no longer remember.
HB Jeremiah 46(LXX 26):27-28	**HB/LXX Zephaniah 3:14-17**
'But you, fear not (אל-תירא/μὴ φοβηθῇς), my servant Jacob, and be not dismayed, O Israel. For behold, I am saving you (הנני מושעך/ἰδοὺ ἐγὼ σῴζω σε) from afar; your seed from the land of their captivity … And you, fear not (אל-תירא/μὴ φοβοῦ), my servant, Jacob', says the Lord, 'for I am with you …'	Cry out/rejoice greatly (– /χαῖρε σφόδρα), daughter (of) Zion (בת-ציון/θύγατερ Σιων)! Shout (הריעי/κήρυσσε), O Israel/ daughter (of) Jerusalem (– /θύγατερ Ιερουσαλημ)! Be glad and exult with whole heart, daughter (of) Jerusalem (בת ירושלם/ θύγατερ Ιερουσαλημ)! The Lord has removed your judgments; he has turned away your foes. The king (מלך/βασιλεὺς) of Israel, the Lord, is in your midst; you will not fear evil again. On that day it will be said to Jerusalem, 'Fear not/take courage (אל-תיראי/μὴ θάρσει), O Zion (ציון/Σιων); let your hands not sink. The Lord, your God, is in your midst; a mighty one who (will) save(s) (יושיע/σώσει). He will exult over you with joy; he will renew you with his love; he will rejoice (יגיל/ –) over you with a ringing cry.'

649. For the LXX attestation of this title, see note 627.
650. Here drawing from 1QIsa[a] rather than MT ואל-תרהו.

HB/LXX Zechariah 8:13-15

And it will be that just as you have been
   a curse among the nations,
   house of Judah and house of Israel,
so will I save you (אושיע אתכם/διασώσω ὑμᾶς)
   and you shall be a blessing.
Fear not/take courage (אל-תיראו/θαρσεῖτε);
let your hands be strong.
For thus says the Lord of hosts,
'Just as I intended to bring evil upon you
   when your fathers provoked me to wrath',
   says the Lord of hosts,
'and I was not satisfied,
so I have turned; I have intended in these days
   to deal kindly with Jerusalem
   and the house of Judah.
Fear not/take courage (אל- תיראו/θαρσεῖτε)'.

(b) The omission of Zechariah 9:9b
With a few exceptions little attention has been given to the two major omissions in the quotation: Zechariah 9:9b and the 'attributes of the king'. Reim simply assigns their removal to prior oral tradition.[651] And, though Menken assumes they were done to adapt the verse to its Johannine context, he offers no detail and goes so far as to say that 'theological reasons' for omitting the latter (the 'attributes of the king') 'can hardly be found within John's gospel'.[652]

For the absence of Zechariah 9:9b, however – 'shout/proclaim, daughter (of) Jerusalem' – three possible motives for the omission are now offered by Kubiś: that the LXX spelling of 'Jerusalem' (Ιερουσαλημ) differs from the convention used by John (Ιεροσολυμα in one of its inflections)[653]; that its address to 'Jerusalem' restricts Jesus's destination to the city (while 'Zion' in the previous colon can speak of all Israel)[654]; and that its exhortation to 'shout/proclaim' is unsuited to John's admonition 'fear not'.[655]

(c) 'Your king comes'
Assuming that the absence of σοι ('to you') from Zechariah 9:9c in LXX 534 does not reflect an alternate textual tradition,[656] its omission from John 12:15b has been ascribed to any one or combination of five factors: (1) meter, (2) style, (3) the

---

651. *Jochanan*, 30–32.
652. "'Do Not Fear, Daughter Zion ...' (John 12:15)", 80–81 (quotation p. 81n5).
653. John 1:19; 2:13, 23; 4:20-21, 45; 5:1-2; 10:22; 11:18, 55; 12:12.
654. Kubiś contemplates this from the observation of Jon Levenson that, by metonymy, 'Zion' in some instances came to designate Israel at large; 'Zion Traditions', *ABD* 6: 1098–99.
655. *Book of Zechariah in the Gospel of John*, 76–78.
656. It may, in fact, have been removed from this manuscript to harmonize the verse with John 12:15; see Menken, "'Do Not Fear, Daughter Zion ...' (John 12:15)", 79n2; Schuchard, *Scripture within Scripture*, 73n11.

quotation of Psalm 118:25-26 at John 12:13, (4) a merger with (or reflection on) an analogous text and/or (5) the evangelist's soteriology. Regarding (1) meter, it is argued that the absence of the pronoun balances the quotation's cadence.[657] Concerning (2) style, it is observed that for Jesus coming to 'people' the evangelist rather uses ἔρχεσθαι with πρός plus the accusative.[658] For (3) Psalm 118:25-26 at John 12:13, it is proposed that the evangelist rendered ἔρχεσθαι as absolute in Zechariah 9:9 to align it with the absolute use of the same verb in that prior quotation; that is, 'behold your king comes' at John 12:15, it is alleged, now seems more clearly of a piece with 'the one who comes in the name of the Lord' at John 12:13.[659] And regarding (4) – the influence of other texts on the quotation – it is

Table 38 Assimilated texts for 'your king comes'

John 12:15
Fear not, daughter (of) Zion;   behold <u>your king comes</u> (ὁ βασιλεύς σου ἔρχεται),   sitting upon a foal of a donkey.

HB/LXX Zechariah 9:9
Rejoice greatly, daughter (of) Zion (בת-ציון/θύγατερ Σιων);   shout, daughter (of) Jerusalem.   Behold, your <u>king comes</u> (מלכך יבוא/ὁ βασιλεύς σου ἔρχεται) to you,   righteous and saved/saving is he,   humble and riding upon an ass,   even upon a donkey, the foal of jennies.

HB/LXX Genesis 49:10-11	HB/LXX Isaiah 40:9-10	HB/LXX Zechariah 2:14
The scepter shall not depart from Judah, nor the staff from between his feet, until Shiloh/that which is kept for him comes (יבא/ἔλθῃ), to whom belongs the obedience of the peoples. Binding to the vine his donkey, even the foal of his jenny to the choice vine, he washes his raiment in wine, and his clothes in the blood of grapes.	Ascend a high mountain, herald of <u>Zion</u> (ציון/Σιων); raise your voice with power, herald of Jerusalem. Raise it; fear not; say to the cities of Judah, 'Behold your God. Behold, <u>the Lord Yahweh comes</u> (יבוא/ἔρχεται) as a mighty one; and his arm is ruling for him. Behold, his reward is with him, his recompense before him.'	'Cry out and be glad, daughter of Zion (בת-ציון/θύγατερ Σιων)! For, behold, I come (הנני-בא/ἰδοὺ ἐγὼ ἔρχομαι) and I will settle in your midst', says the Lord.

657. Freed, *Old Testament Quotations in the Gospel of John*, 79; followed by Schuchard, *Scripture within Scripture*, 80n47. Freed left this unexplained, but Menken has since noticed that the removal of the pronoun results in John 12:15bc (= Zech 9:9cef) carrying ten syllables each; "'Do Not Fear, Daughter Zion …" (John 12:15)', 89.

658. John 1:29; 13:6; 14:18, 23, 28; 16:7 (here, of the Spirit 'coming to'); Schuchard, *Scripture within Scripture*, 80n47.

659. Menken, "'Do Not Fear, Daughter Zion …" (John 12:15)', 89. Along a similar line it is suggested by Nozomi Miura that Zech 9:9 has been conflated with another passage that

maintained that the evangelist cited Zechariah 9:9 by merging it with (or reflecting on) Genesis 49:10-11; Isaiah 40:9-10; and/or Zechariah 2:14. Inasmuch as in these passages ἔρχεσθαι occurs alone, it is surmised that in his rendering of Zechariah 9:9 the evangelist followed suit (see Table 38).[660]

Finally, with respect to (5) – the evangelist's universalism – it has been argued by Menken that the removal of the pronoun accommodates the global scope of the evangelist's soteriology. Though Jesus began his ministry by 'coming to his own',[661] Menken maintains, he had since been rejected by most and is now being cast by the evangelist as coming for 'the world'. Part of this portrayal lay with the Johannine use of ἔρχεσθαι throughout the narrative to designate a 'coming' to 'all'.[662] It is also framed, however, by cues at the end of the Book of Signs,[663] as well as by the context and texture of the reference to Zechariah 9:9 itself.[664] And so with σοι in Zechariah 9:9c at John 12:15 – as a *dativus commodi*, contends Menken, it limited the destination and purpose of the quotation to Israel; and so, the evangelist removed it 'to put forward the universal significance of Jesus' coming as king'.[665]

(d) The omission of the 'attributes of the king'
The removal of the three traits describing the king – that he is 'righteous', 'saved'/ 'saving' and 'humble'/'meek' – has been attributed to (what may be counted as) three motives: meter (as with the absence of σοι),[666] economy and theology. By economy and theology, more specifically, is meant the inference of Kubiś that the evangelist removed these modifiers to avoid redundancy and contradiction, respectively, in

---

uses the verb 'come' in the absolute, Zech 14:5d: 'The Lord my God will come (יבוא/ἥξει), and all the holy ones with him'; 'The Temple Motifs in the Fourth Gospel: Intertextuality and Intratextuality of the Temple Motifs', *AJBI* 37 (2011): 51. Weakening the proposal, however, is the LXX use of ἥκειν (rather than ἔρχεσθαι) for 'come' in this verse.

660. Menken, 'The Quotations from Zech 9,9 in Mt 21,5 and in Jn 12,15', 575; Menken, '"Do Not Fear, Daughter Zion …" (John 12:15)', 88–89; Kubiś, *Book of Zechariah in the Gospel of John*, 79.

661. John 1:11.

662. Cited here are John 1:9; 3:19; 6:14; 9:39; 11:27; 12:46; 16:28; 18:37.

663. Listed are John 11:52, where Caiaphas's prophecy is interpreted to mean that Jesus 'would gather into one the dispersed children of God'; John 12:19, where the Pharisees lament that 'the world has departed after him'; John 12:20-26, where Jesus is sought by the Greeks; John 12:32, where Jesus declares that he 'will draw all' to himself when 'lifted up'; and, beyond the Book of Signs, John 18:37, where to Pilate Jesus confesses he is king but qualifies it by declaring, 'Everyone who is of the truth hears my voice.'

664. In view here are two considerations: the worldwide rule ('well being for the nations') foretold at Zech 9:10; and, assuming the assimilation of Gen 49:10 into Zech 9:9ef at John 12:15c, the 'ruler' from Judah as the one 'to whom belongs the obedience of the peoples'.

665. 'The Quotations from Zech 9,9 in Mt 21,5 and in Jn 12,15', 575–76; Menken, '"Do Not Fear, Daughter Zion …" (John 12:15)', 90-91 (quotation p. 91); Menken, 'The Minor Prophets in John's Gospel', 84–85; followed by Kubiś, *Book of Zechariah in the Gospel of John*, 78–80, 80n232.

666. Freed, *Old Testament Quotations in the Gospel of John*, 80.

his depiction of Jesus: redundancy, because Jesus had already been established as 'righteous' and 'saving'[667]; contradiction, because, on the assumption that the temple cleansing at John 2:13-22 originally followed immediately upon Jesus's entry into Jerusalem at John 12:12-16, 'humble'/'meek' would have been incompatible with the 'zeal' Jesus was about to display against the vendors and money changers.[668]

(e) 'Sitting'

On Jesus 'sitting' (καθήμενος) rather than 'riding' (ורכב) or 'mounted' (ἐπιβεβηκώς), hypotheses have ascribed it to three factors: (1) style, (2) translation (of the HB) or (3) synonymity (with its LXX counterpart).

For (1) style, it is argued by Freed that in the service of variety the evangelist chose καθῆσθαι as a complement to καθίζειν at John 12:14. Freed reasons that since Jesus in the Fourth Gospel does not process into Jerusalem (as he does in the Synoptics[669]), he had to be described in the quotation at John 12:15 as doing nothing more than the activity with which he began his entrance at John 12:14. Inasmuch as that activity was simply 'sitting' (ἐκάθισεν), the evangelist chose καθῆσθαι as a synonym to that verb, reiterating the action while endowing the account with 'sufficient variation of style and balance'.[670]

As for (2) translation, it is maintained by Menken that καθῆσθαι is a translation choice for HB לרכב. In part this turns on the single instance in which such a rendering occurs in the LXX.[671] Primarily, however, it appeals to LXX translations of לרכב which employ cognates to καθῆσθαι. At various *loci* the LXX renders that verb with terms grammatically kindred to καθῆσθαι – καθίζειν itself,[672] ἐπικαθίζειν,[673] ἐπικαθῆσθαι[674]; and that grammatical kinship, contends Menken, would have given leave for the evangelist to do the same with καθῆσθαι in his quotation of Zechariah 9:9.[675] Particularly important for Menken is the network of cognates which appears in 1 Kings/3 Kingdoms 1, a chapter which on other grounds has been viewed as typologically anticipatory to John 12:12-19.[676] Here

---

667. Cited for Jesus as 'righteous' are John 5:30; 10:30; 17:25; for Jesus as 'saving', John 4:42.
668. Kubiś, *Book of Zechariah in the Gospel of John*, 80-81. For Kubiś on the temple incident relative to Jesus's entry into Jerusalem, see pp. 398-407.
669. Matt 21:8-9; Mark 11:8-10; Luke 19:36-38.
670. Freed, 'The Entry into Jerusalem in the Gospel of John', *JBL* 80 (1961): 337-38; Freed, *Old Testament Quotations in the Gospel of John*, 80 (quotation pp. 338 and 80, respectively). This chapter in Freed's monograph is a similar version of the earlier article.
671. Isa 19:1.
672. LXX Lev 15:9 (in Alexandrinus); 2 Kgdms 22:11 (in Alexandrinus).
673. 2 Kgdms 13:29; 22:11 (except for Alexandrinus); 3 Kgdms 1:38, 44; 4 Kgdms 10:16.
674. 2 Kgdms 16:2.
675. '"Do Not Fear, Daughter Zion …" (John 12:15)', 92-94. Menken's case is entertained, though not necessarily (or altogether) endorsed, by Schuchard, *Scripture within Scripture*, 80-81; and Kubiś, *Book of Zechariah in the Gospel of John*, 92-94.
676. See Marie de Mérode, 'L'accueil triomphal de Jésus selon Jean, 11-12', *RTL* 13 (1982): 56; Harald Sahlin, *Zur Typologie des Johannesevangelium* (Uppsala: Lundequistska bokhandeln, 1950), 47-48; and cf. Menken, '"Do Not Fear, Daughter Zion …" (John 12:15)', 93n53.

Solomon accedes to the throne over the usurper Adonijah, in part by 'riding' to Gihon 'upon the mule (פרד/ἡμίονος) of king David'; and in its telling, by both the HB and LXX, (a) the Hebrew term for Solomon's 'riding' is לרכב (albeit in the hiphil)[677]; (b) the glosses for that term in the LXX are ἐπιβιβάζειν (the causal of ἐπιβαίνειν)[678] and ἐπικαθίζειν[679]; and (c) *passim* throughout the LXX version appear the two verbs for 'sitting' in John 12:14-15 – καθίζειν[680] and καθῆσθαι, itself.[681] From this amalgam, in particular, Menken is persuaded that καθῆσθαι becomes semantically interchangeable with the other Greek verbs and that on such a basis the evangelist used it for Zechariah 9:9.[682]

This last factor, in turn, leads to the last hypothesis – on (3) synonymity, held by Schuchard (and followed somewhat by Obermann). Schuchard agrees with Menken on the semantic cross-pollination that occurs with καθῆσθαι in 3 Kingdoms 1: but, where Menken sees it as allowing the evangelist to translate לרכב from a HB *Vorlage*, Schuchard sees it leading him to replace ἐπιβαίνειν in the LXX rendering.[683]

(f) 'Upon a foal of a donkey'
Finally, John's reading 'upon a foal of a donkey'. Along one line, this, too, has been laid directly at the door of the evangelist, as due either to carelessness or to his wish to condense the prolix biblical renderings – this last, perhaps, to avoid (or correct) the confusion in Matthew's quotation of the verse, where the attempt to account for the complete biblical vocabulary of the king's mount appears to depict Jesus sitting astride two animals: 'mounted upon a donkey and upon a foal, the offspring of an ass' (ἐπιβεβηκὼς ἐπὶ ὄνον καὶ ἐπὶ πῶλον υἱὸν ὑποζυγίου).[684] The phrase has also, however, been contemplated as either a trimmed translation of the Hebrew or a merger of Zechariah 9:9 with Genesis 49:11. A translation of the Hebrew, inasmuch as in the LXX πῶλος translates עיר five times and ὄνος translates אתון thirty times.[685] A merger with Genesis 49:11 on two bases: that the verse is part of the Jacob oracle on Judah (Genesis 49:8-12), from which (it is maintained) John draws elsewhere in

677. 1 Kgs 1:33, 38, 44.
678. 3 Kgdms 1:33.
679. 3 Kgdms 1:38, 44.
680. 3 Kgdms 1:13, 46.
681. 3 Kgdms 1:17, 20, 24, 27, 30, 35, 48.
682. Menken, "'Do Not Fear, Daughter Zion ...' (John 12:15)", 91-94.
683. Schuchard, *Scripture within Scripture*, 81–82; Obermann, *Die christologische Erfüllung der Schrift im Johannesevangelium*, 204–05. Obermann leans towards the Greek, particularly because he also traces the language for Jesus's mount (which immediately follows) to LXX Gen 49:11.
684. Matt 21:5. For these first two suggestions on this phrase in John, Barrett, *Gospel according to St. John*, 419; followed by Freed, *Old Testament Quotations in the Gospel of John*, 79–80; and cf. Bernard, *Critical and Exegetical Commentary on the Gospel according to St. John*, 2:426.
685. See the detailed discussion by Kubiś, *Book of Zechariah in the Gospel of John*, 95–96.

the narrative[686]; and that both HB and LXX versions of it read 'the foal of his jenny/ donkey'. The LXX nouns are articular rather than anarthrous, but are the same Greek words used by John and occur in the same order (Table 39).[687]

Table 39 'A foal of his donkey' and Genesis 49:11

HB/LXX Zechariah 9:9	HB/LXX Genesis 49:11	John 12:15
Rejoice greatly, daughter (of) Zion; shout, daughter (of) Jerusalem. Behold, your king comes to you, righteous and saved is he, humble and riding upon a donkey/ass (על-חמור/ἐπὶ ὑποζύγιον), even upon an ass, the foal of jennies (ועל-עיר בן-אתנות)/even a young foal (καὶ πῶλον νέον).	Binding to the vine his donkey/ foal (עירה/τὸν πῶλον αὐτοῦ), even the foal of his jenny (בני אתנו)/the foal of his donkey (τὸν πῶλον τῆς ὄνου αὐτοῦ) to the choice vine, he washes his raiment in wine, and his clothes in the blood of grapes.	Fear not, daughter (of) Zion; behold your king comes, sitting upon a foal of a donkey (ἐπὶ πῶλον ὄνου).

2. Version, anomalies and import of the quotations

The two questions raised by anomalous quotations previously in these studies must now be addressed for the quotations at issue here. What sources (or editorial activity) are reflected in their forms? And what theological implications do they carry? To proceed, two starting points can be established without complex discussion at the outset: the version of the base texts and the Johannine choice to have Jesus 'sitting' on his mount. Moving beyond these, however, requires fusing these two questions and toggling between their version, anomalies and import. The linchpin is the designation 'king of Israel' at John 12:13/Psalm 118:25-26. Clarity on this, then (it is argued), opens vistas on 'Hosanna', 'fear not', 'upon a foal of a donkey' and finally the omissions in the quotation of Zechariah 9:9 – that is, Zechariah 9:9b, σοι and 'the attributes of the king'.

a. Starting points

(1) The base texts

The base texts of both these quotations are almost certainly drawn from the LXX. Notwithstanding the absence of σοι in the quotation of Zechariah 9:9, the second lines of each citation follow their LXX counterparts verbatim[688]; and though the

---

686. See Reim, *Jochanan*, 127–28; Reim 'Joh 9 – Tradition und zeitgenössische messianische Diskussion', in *Jochanan*, 328–29; first publ. in *BZ* 22 (1978); Reim, 'Targum und Johannesevangelium', 334–35, 337, 340.

687. Menken, '"Do Not Fear, Daughter Zion …" (John 12:15)', 94–95; Schuchard, *Scripture within Scripture*, 83n62; followed by Kubiś, *Book of Zechariah in the Gospel of John*, 97–98.

688. 'Blessed is the one who comes in the name of the Lord' (John 12:13/Ps 118:25-26); 'behold your king comes' (John 12:15/Zech 9:9).

LXX, itself, does the same with the HB (albeit rendering the tetragrammaton by the *Qerê* אדני [κύριος] for Psalm 118:25-26), the absence of compelling evidence to favour the Hebrew over John's congruence with Greek suggests that both lines (and, therefore, both base texts) re-present the LXX rather than translate the HB.

Both of these quotations are similarly cited with LXX base texts in the Synoptic gospels; and this lends itself to the prospect that they were brokered to the fourth evangelist through Matthew, Mark and/or Luke. LXX Psalm 118:25-26 is referenced with ὡσαννά in Matthew and Mark[689]; without it in Luke, as well as in the *Quoties volui* of Matthew and Luke (or Q) (Table 40).[690]

Table 40 'Hosanna' (ὡσαννά) in the Synoptic gospels

Matthew 21:9b-d	Mark 11:9b-10
ὡσαννὰ τῷ υἱῷ Δαυίδ· εὐλογημένος ὁ ἐρχόμενος ἐν ὀνόματι κυρίου· ὡσαννὰ ἐν τοῖς ὑψίστοις.	ὡσαννά· εὐλογημένος ὁ ἐρχόμενος ἐν ὀνόματι κυρίου· εὐλογημένη ἡ ἐρχομένη βασιλεία τοῦ πατρὸς ἡμῶν Δαυίδ· ὡσαννὰ ἐν τοῖς ὑψίστοις.

Hosanna to the son of David!
 Blessed is the one who comes
    in the name of the Lord.
 Hosanna in the highest!
	Hosanna!
	 Blessed is the one who comes
	    in the name of the Lord.
	 Blessed is the coming kingdom
	    of our father David.
	 Hosanna in the highest!

Luke 19:38	**Matthew 23:39/Luke 13:35**
εὐλογημένος ὁ ἐρχόμενος, ὁ βασιλεὺς ἐν ὀνόματι κυρίου· ἐν οὐρανῷ εἰρήνη καὶ δόξα ἐν ὑψίστοις.	εὐλογημένος ὁ ἐρχόμενος ἐν ὀνόματι κυρίου.

Blessed is the one who comes,
    the king, in the name of the Lord.
 Peace in heaven
    and glory in the highest!
	Blessed is the one who comes
	    in the name of the Lord.

The core of LXX Zechariah 9:9, for its part, is conflated with LXX Isaiah 62:11b and cited in Matthew 21:5 (see Table 41).

Debate over Synoptic mediation in these instances has been complex.[691] For this discussion, however, it may suffice to note that in a response to Frans Neirynck, Menken makes a point about the quotations of Zechariah 9:9 in John 12:15 and

689. Matt 21:9; Mark 11:9-10.

690. Luke 19:38, as well as Matt 23:39/Luke 13:35. The more complex issue of Synoptic brokerage and ὡσαννά is treated below in this chapter, under *[1] The source*.

691. Among exegetes specifically working on quotations in John, for instance, see Franke, *Das alte Testament bei Johannes*, 286; Freed, *Old Testament Quotations in the Gospel of John*, 73–75; Reim, *Jochanan*, 27–28, 31–32; Kubiś, *Book of Zechariah in the Gospel of John*, 99–100. And particularly on John's description of Jesus's mount, see Walter Bauer, 'The "Colt" of Palm Sunday', *JBL* 72 (1953): 220–29.

Table 41 Zechariah 9:9 in Matthew and John

Matthew 21:5	John 12:15
εἴπατε τῇ θυγατρὶ Σιών· (Isaiah 62:11b) ἰδοὺ ὁ βασιλεύς σου ἔρχεταί σοι, πραῢς καὶ ἐπιβεβηκὼς ἐπὶ ὄνον καὶ ἐπὶ πῶλον υἱὸν ὑποζυγίου.	μὴ φοβοῦ, θυγάτηρ Σιών· ἰδοὺ ὁ βασιλεύς σου ἔρχεται, καθήμενος ἐπὶ πῶλον ὄνου.
Say to (the) daughter (of) Zion, 'Behold your king comes to you, meek and mounted upon a donkey and upon a foal, the offspring of an ass.'	Fear not, daughter (of) Zion; behold your king comes, sitting upon a foal of a donkey.

Matthew 21:5 that concurs with the position taken here.[692] He argues that even if John were apprised of Matthew in this instance, the text form of his reference is better ascribed to Zechariah directly[693]; and given the likelihood that the rare ὡσαννά has come to John through Synoptic tradition,[694] this may furnish the explanation for both Zechariah 9:9 at John 12:15 and Psalm 118:25-26 at John 12:13. That is, if these quotations were known to John in the forms they took in Synoptic tradition, parts of those forms (ὡσαννά) he seems to have retained, while others (LXX Isaiah 62:11b at Matthew 21:5) he apparently dismissed in favour of his own direct engagement with the original text.

(2) 'Sitting'
Regarding the verb 'sit' (καθῆσθαι) for HB 'ride' (לרכב) or (especially now) LXX 'mount' (ἐπιβαίνειν), Menken is doubtless correct that it 'could very well serve to emphasize Jesus' royal dignity'.[695] If so, however, the mechanism by which it gained synonymity with its HB and LXX counterparts might better be traced to two passages not sufficiently considered by Menken, Schuchard or Kubiś: Jeremiah 17:24-25; 22:3-4. In both *loci* the two verbs are coupled within a similar context of 'kings' and 'rulers' entering the gates of Jerusalem; and in the Hebrew *Vorlage* to the LXX, the verb behind ἐπιβαίνειν is לרכב. Respectively, they are as follows:

> 'And it shall be, if you indeed listen to me', says the Lord, 'so as not to bring a burden through the gates of this city on the Sabbath day, and to consecrate the Sabbath day, so as not to do any business on it, then shall come through the gates of this city kings (מלכים/βασιλεῖς) and princes, sitting (ישבים/καθήμενοι) upon the throne of David, riding/mounted (רכבים/ἐπιβεβηκότες) on chariot and

---

692. See the Introduction, under 3. *Mediating sources*.
693. Menken, "'Do Not Fear, Daughter Zion …'" (John 12:15)', 82n13; cf. Frans Neirynck, 'John and the Synoptics: 1975-1990', in *John and the Synoptics*, ed. Adelbert Denaux, BETL 101 (Leuven: Leuven University Press, 1992), 26–28.
694. See the discussion below in this chapter, under *[1] The source*.
695. Menken, "'Do Not Fear, Daughter Zion …'" (John 12:15)', 93. Menken documents the royal usage of καθῆσθαι on p. 92nn46-48.

horses – they and their princes, each a man of Judah and residents of Jerusalem. And this city shall remain forever'.

Thus says the Lord,
'Do justice and righteousness, and snatch one who has been seized from the hand of the oppressor. Neither oppress nor wrong the sojourner, orphan or widow; and shed not innocent blood in this place. For if you indeed do this thing, through the gates of this house shall come kings (מלכים/βασιλεῖς) sitting (ישבים/καθήμενοι) as David upon his throne, riding/mounted (רכבים/ἐπιβεβηκότες) on chariot and horses – each, his servant and his people.'

Better, however, is Freed's appeal to style, that is, that the evangelist simply wished to reiterate the 'sitting' (καθίζειν) Jesus began in John 12:14 and employed καθῆσθαι as a synonym to that verb: 'and having found a young donkey, Jesus sat (ἐκάθισεν) upon it'; 'behold your king comes, sitting (καθήμενος) upon a foal of a donkey'. This explanation is rejected by Menken on the grounds (as he perceives it) that the evangelist would have done the same with the terms for the donkey[696], but there may be a misunderstanding. Menken pits the diminutive ὀνάριον in John 12:14 over against the full term πῶλος ὄνου in John 12:15 (and presumably sees no synonymity between ὀνάριον and πῶλος in that comparison). The resemblance as Freed saw it, however, is solely between ὀνάριον and ὄνος; 'κάθημαι following after καθίζω', he writes, 'gave (the evangelist) sufficient variation of style and balance as with ὄνος following after ὀνάριον'.[697] On Freed's terms, then, ἐκάθισεν/καθήμενος is consistent with ὀνάριον/ὄνου.

More to the point, however, there is ample precedent in the LXX for the coupling of καθῆσθαι and καθίζειν. They are often placed in close proximity to each other[698]; and in no less than fifteen of these places they serve (as they do in John 12:14-15) as synonyms to describe the same activity being done by a single person[699]:

And having gone out, she (Hagar) sat (ἐκάθητο) far off opposite him (Ishmael), about the shot of a bow, for she said, 'I will not watch the death of my child.' And she sat (ἐκάθισεν) opposite him; and crying aloud, the child wept.[700]

---

696. '"Do Not Fear, Daughter Zion ..." (John 12:15)', 91; followed by Obermann, *Die christologische Erfüllung der Schrift im Johannesevangelium*, 204n6; and Kubiś, *Book of Zechariah in the Gospel of John*, 94–95.
697. *Old Testament Quotations in the Gospel of John*, 80 (parenthetical remark added for clarity).
698. LXX Gen 21:16; LXX Lev 15:6; LXX Judg 6:10-11 (Vaticanus); 1 Kgdms 1:23; 20:5; 22:5; 23:14; 27:5 (Alexandrinus); 2 Kgdms 19:9; 3 Kgdms 2:36, 38; 20:9-13 (Alexandrinus); 4 Kgdms 7:3-4; 1 Esd 8:68-69; LXX Job 2:7-9 (Alexandrinus); LXX Jonah 4:5; LXX Isa 47:8; LXX Jer 15:17; 31:18; LXX/Theodotion Dan 7:9-10.
699. For the purpose of illustration, both of these verbs are translated 'sit' in all the examples below, even where context might suggest more nuanced glosses.
700. LXX Gen 21:16.

And Elkana, her (Hanna's) husband, said to her, 'Do that which is good in your eyes. Sit (κάθου) until you wean him (Samuel); but may the Lord effect that which proceeds from your mouth.' And the woman sat (ἐκάθισεν) and nursed her son until she weaned him.[701]

And David said to Jonathan, 'Behold, the new moon (is) already tomorrow; and when I sit (καθίσας), I will not sit (οὐ καθήσομαι) with the king to eat. And you will send me off, and I will hide myself in the plain until evening.'[702]

And the prophet Gad said to David, 'Do not sit (μὴ κάθου) in the compound; go, and you shall come into the land of Judah.' And David went, and came and sat (ἐκάθισεν) in the city Sarich.[703]

And David sat (ἐκάθισεν) in the wilderness in Maserem, in the narrows; and he sat (ἐκάθητο) in the wilderness in Mount Ziph, in the dry land; and Saul was seeking him all the days, but the Lord did not deliver him into his hands.[704]

And David said to Anchous, 'If indeed your servant has found favor in your eyes, let them grant me a place in one of the rural towns and sit me (κάθισόν με) there. Why does your servant sit (κάθηται) in a royal city with you'?[705]

And the king arose and sat (ἐκάθισεν) in the gate. And all the people proclaimed, saying, 'Behold, the king sits (κάθηται) in the gate.' And all the people entered before the face of the king.[706]

And the king summoned Semei and said to him,
'Build yourself a house in Jerusalem and sit (κάθου) there;
and you shall in no way go out from there …'
And Semei said to the king, 'The word which you have spoken is good, my lord, king; thus will your servant do.' And Semei sat (ἐκάθισεν) in Jerusalem three years.[707]

And four men, leprous, were near the entrance to the city, and one said to another, 'Why do we sit (καθήμεθα) here until we die? If we say, "Let us enter into the city", and famine is in the city, we shall die there; and if we sit (καθίσωμεν) here, we shall also die. And now come, let us fall upon the ranks of Syria; if they preserve us alive, we shall live; and if they kill us, we shall die.'[708]

701. 1 Kgdms 1:23.
702. 1 Kgdms 20:5.
703. 1 Kgdms 22:5.
704. 1 Kgdms 23:14.
705. 1 Kgdms 27:5 (Alexandrinus).
706. 2 Kgdms 19:9.
707. 3 Kgdms 2:36, 38.
708. 4 Kgdms 7:3-4.

4. Ps 118:25-26 and Zech 9:9, The Restoration of the Monarchy

And it came about that at the moment I heard these things I rent my garments and the sacred vestment, and I pulled the hair of (my) head and beard to pieces, and sat (ἐκάθισα) pondering and grief-stricken. And as many as were ever stirred by the word of the Lord of Israel were gathered to me, as I lamented this lawlessness; and I sat (ἐκαθήμην) grief-stricken until the evening sacrifice.[709]

And the devil went out from the Lord,
and he struck Job with a foul abscess from feet to head.
And he (Job) took a shard of earthenware, that he might scrape off the discharge;
and he sat (ἐκάθητο) on the dunghill outside the city.
And after much time had gone by, his wife said to him,
'How long will you endure, saying
"Behold, I will wait yet a little while, expecting the hope of my salvation"? …
You, yourself, passing the night in the open air to sit (καθίσαι)
in the rot of worms …'[710]

And Jonah went out of the city and sat (ἐκάθισεν) opposite the city.
And he made a tent for himself there, and sat (ἐκάθητο) beneath it in the shade until such time as he would have a view of what would occur in the city.[711]

And now hear these things, exacting woman,
who sits (καθημένη) having prevailed,
who says in her heart, 'I am, and there is no other;
I shall not sit (οὐ καθιῶ) widowed,
nor shall I know bereavement.'[712]

I did not sit (οὐκ ἐκάθισα) in their council when they were jesting,
but I was circumspect before your hand.
I sat (ἐκαθήμην) alone, because I was full of bitterness.[713]

Descend from glory and sit (κάθισον) in dampness;
sitting (καθημένη) it/she is destroyed,
because Moab has perished;
he who disgraces your stronghold rose against you.[714]

---

709. 1 Esd 8:68-69.
710. LXX Job 2:7-9 (Alexandrinus and 157).
711. LXX Jonah 4:5.
712. LXX Isa 47:8.
713. LXX Jer 15:17.
714. LXX Jer 31:18.

b. The major anomalies

(1) John 12:13/Psalm 118:25-26

(a) 'King of Israel'

Given that the phrase 'upon a foal of a donkey' at John 12:15/Zechariah 9:9 may be reworked in light of Genesis 49:11, it is tempting to follow Blenkinsopp and ascribe 'the king of Israel' at John 12:13/Psalm 118:25-26 to a messianized *targum* of Genesis 49:10 – something akin to 'King Messiah' (מלכא משיחא) or 'Messiah' (משיחא) in *Targum Pseudo-Jonathan*, the *Fragmentary Targum* or *Targum Onqelos*. Jacob's oracle on Judah, then, would serve as a 'brace' of sorts, into which both quotations have been fastened.

Three factors, however, give preference to LXX Zephaniah 3:15 as the source behind this title. The first two can also apply to LXX Isaiah 44:6, namely, their wording and contexts. Both verses enjoy a more precise lexical affinity to the title than would a targumic paraphrase of Genesis 49:10: in Isaiah, it is articular (ὁ βασιλεὺς τοῦ Ισραηλ)[715]; in Zephaniah, anarthrous (βασιλεὺς Ισραηλ)[716] – and either of these coincide with textual traditions attesting '[the] king of Israel' at John 12:13.[717] Moreover, terms from the contexts surrounding each of these verses resonate with both John 12:13/Psalm 118:25-26 and John 12:15/Zechariah 9:9 – 'fear not' (μὴ φοβοῦ) at LXX Isaiah 44:2 could arguably account for that anomaly at John 12:15/Zechariah 9:9; and though LXX Zephaniah 3:16 reads 'take courage' (θάρσει) for 'fear not', LXX Zephaniah 3:14-17 shares some six other terms with LXX Zechariah 9:9 (besides the title) that could attract it to that same quotation (that is, to John 12:15/Zechariah 9:9): 'rejoice greatly' (χαῖρε σφόδρα), 'daughter (of) Zion' (θύγατερ Σιων), 'shout' (κήρυσσε), 'daughter (of) Jerusalem' (θύγατερ Ιερουσαλημ [twice]), 'Zion' (Σιων [again]) and 'save' (σώσει) – this last, thematically coinciding also with the force of ὡσαννά ('save us'!) at John 12:13/Psalm 118:25-26.[718]

Favouring LXX Zephaniah 3:15 even further, however, is a factor drawn from an observation made above: the assertion of this title by Nathanael at John

---

715. Though, again see the variants listed in note 627.

716. So also Obermann, *Die christologische Erfüllung der Schrift im Johannesevangelium*, 186n4.

717. See the listing of variants above in this chapter under *(1) The version cited and its anomalies*–specifically, this subheading as listed beneath *a. Psalm 118:25-26 (John 12:13)*.

718. The first of these shared terms, 'rejoice greatly', notwithstanding the absence of σφόδρα from Zeph 3:14 in some key LXX manuscripts; see note 642.

1:49.⁷¹⁹ It was noted (a) that when Nathanael's scepticism about Jesus is dispelled, he declares him 'the Son of God' and 'king of Israel' (σὺ βασιλεὺς εἶ τοῦ Ἰσραήλ); and (b) that this declaration, in turn, forms an *inclusio* with the crowd's recitation of that title at John 12:13/Psalm 118:25-26. More specifically, however, Nathanael's doubts are expelled because Jesus hails him as 'an Israelite in whom is no deceit' (ἐν ᾧ δόλος οὐκ ἔστιν); and these words are likely an allusion to Zephaniah 3:13, two verses prior to Zephaniah 3:15, which speaks of the faithful remnant who will be protected from enemies by that 'king of Israel'. To cite both verses in their full context:

> On that day you shall not be shamed for all your wanton deeds
> by which you have transgressed against me.
> For at that time I will remove from your midst those who exult
>   in your haughtiness;
> and you shall no longer continue to be lofty on my holy mountain.
> But I will leave in your midst a people humble and lowly;
> and the remnant of Israel will seek refuge in the name of the Lord.
> They will do no unrighteousness; they shall not speak falsehood;
> nor shall there be found in their mouth <u>a deceitful tongue</u>
>   (לשון תרמית/γλῶσσα δολία) ...
> Cry out, daughter (of) Zion! Shout, O Israel!
> Be glad and exult with whole heart, daughter (of) Jerusalem!
> The Lord has removed your judgments; he has turned away your foes.
> <u>The king of Israel</u> (מלך ישראל/βασιλεὺς Ισραηλ), the Lord, is in your midst;
> you will not fear evil again.⁷²⁰

It appears, then, that Nathanael's encounter with Jesus in John 1 is framed on this portion of Zephaniah 3; and insofar as this first component of the *inclusio* (John 1:49) alludes to that passage, it becomes all the more likely that its second component (John 12:13/Psalm 118:25-26) does the same. Taken with the precise match operating between the titles at LXX Zephaniah 3:15 and John 12:13 – as well as the lexical correspondence enjoyed between LXX Zephaniah 3:14-17 and John 12:15/Zechariah 9:9 – a strong case emerges that 'king of Israel' at John 12:13/Psalm 118:25-26 is assimilated from LXX Zephaniah 3:15.⁷²¹

---

719. Above in this chapter, under *(b) 'The king of Israel'*–not to be confused with the subheading of this segment, *(a) 'King of Israel'*; and further on this connection, see Morris, *Gospel according to John*, 585.

720. Zeph 3:11-15.

721. In turn, this would lend weight to the anarthrous reading of the title in the Johannine textual tradition: 'king of Israel' (βασιλεὺς τοῦ Ἰσραήλ).

(b) 'Hosanna'

[1] The source

The cry ὡσαννά, for its part, can be addressed in two respects: its source and its ramifications for the rest of the quotation (that is, for Psalm 118:26a and the designation 'king of Israel'). For the first – its source – on phonetic grounds it is best understood as a transliteration of either the Hebrew הושיעה נא ('save us') at HB Psalm 118:25a or the Aramaic הושענא (*lûlāb*), argued by Burkitt (as being associated with הושיעה נא). When compared with the other candidates, (a) it is too phonetically (and morphologically) removed from LXX σῶσον δή to have been drawn from that version; (b) its final syllable -να implies an enclitic precative particle not found in the forms of other Hebrew texts alleged to have been assimilated – הושיעה at HB Psalm 20:7, 10 or הושע at HB Jeremiah 31:7; and (c) the rough breathing with which it begins (ὡ-) makes doubtful the Aramaic עושנא for Hebrew עז in HB Psalm 8:3, argued by Cheyne. Indeed, the syllables in ὡσαννά do not even account for the *hireq yod* in הושיעה נא at HB Psalm 118:25a (as well as in HB Psalm 20:7, 10), making its closest phonetic match the Aramaic הושענא.

Whichever is behind it – הושיעה נא or הושענא – ὡσαννά likely carries the force of the former in Psalm 118:25a: a plea to 'save'. It appears in John's rendering just where one expects to find that verse (that is, immediately prior to Psalm 118:26); if it is traced back to *lûlabîn*, those flora would still have been shaken at the moment that verse (that is, its call to 'save') was recited in festal observance, as Burkitt has noted; and since in John ὡσαννά is unencumbered by dative modifiers which could transpose its force into adoration (as may occur in the Synoptics), it doubtless conveys the same force there as הושיעה נא does in HB Psalm 118:25a – 'Save us'! 'If we ... consider the phonetic proximity of the absolute ὡσαννά to the Hebrew הושיעה נא in its primary force as a cry for help (*Hilferufes*)', writes Obermann, 'ὡσαννά in our passage is best understood as a cry for help (*Hilferuf*), which bellows amidst the entrance of festal pilgrims into Jerusalem for Passover'.[722]

At this juncture the issue of source meshes with that of Synoptic brokerage. If this term is, indeed, traceable to a Semitic source, it reflects mixed versions in the quotation, since (as has been observed) the next line in the quotation is a verbatim rendering of LXX Psalm 118:26a.[723] This, in turn, would run against the expectation here that assimilated texts are cited from the same versions as their base texts.[724] The quotations of this passage in the Synoptics, however, allow the prospect that ὡσαννά was mediated to John through one or more of them (or

---

722. *Die christologische Erfüllung der Schrift im Johannesevangelium*, 195.

723. See above in this chapter, under *(1) The version cited and its anomalies* – specifically, this subheading as listed beneath *a. Psalm 118:25-26 (John 12:13)*.

724. Introduction, under *b. Expecting the Hebrew Bible*. Advocating such a mix, however, is Obermann, *Die christologische Erfüllung der Schrift im Johannesevangelium*, 185–86.

through a tradition common to them[725]); and, were such the case, that term, no less than LXX Psalm 118:26a in the next colon, would have been assimilated (at least most immediately) from a Greek source.

[2] 'Hosanna' and 'king of Israel'
With respect to ὡσαννά and the rest of the quotation at John 12:13, the removal of all other language from Psalm 118:25 – that is, between 'Hosanna!' and 'Blessed is the one …' – effectively shifts the addressee of this 'call to save' from God (as it is in the intact psalm) to Jesus. In its full form Psalm 118:25-26 begins with a plea to the Lord to save (verse 25), then follows with a benediction upon the one who comes in his name (verse 26). It is surmised that during pilgrimage festivals the first (verse 25) would have been recited by pilgrims as they approached the temple and the second (verse 26) would have been antiphonally rehearsed by priests in response[726]:

Pilgrims	We implore you, Lord, save us!
	We implore you, Lord, prosper us!
Priests	Blessed is the one who comes in the name of the Lord;
	we have blessed you from the house of the Lord.

By reading ὡσαννά alone for Psalm 118:25 (with no vocative 'Lord') – and by putting the following blessing, as well, in the mouth of the festal pilgrims – John, by contrast, has those pilgrims directing this plea to Jesus, as 'the one who comes in the name of the Lord'. Putting this anomaly together with the other in this quotation ('king of Israel'), both combine to depict Passover pilgrims beseeching Jesus to 'save' as 'king of Israel'.[727]

(2) John 12:15/Zechariah 9:9

(a) Nordreichschristologie *and 'fear not'*
At this juncture the precise source behind the exhortation 'fear not' at John 12:15/Zechariah 9:9 remains elusive. Candidates can be narrowed but not reduced to one. Proposals that assign it to the evangelist's poor memory or his wish to temper the

---

725. Reim, *Jochanan*, 27–28; followed by von Wahlde, *Gospel and Letters of John*, 3:304-305.

726. Cf. Westcott, *Gospel according to St. John*, 179; Hoskyns, *The Fourth Gospel*, 421. The Synoptics, for their part, cast the verses as being shouted by the crowds (Matt 21:8-9; Mark 11:8-10) – or disciples among them (Luke 19:36-38) – entering into the city with Jesus.

727. On John's restriction of the priestly blessing to Jesus alone, see Lightfoot, *St. John's Gospel*, 250.

quotation in light of Jesus's imminent death carry little force.[728] And among the passages suggested for assimilation (Table 37), seven diverge enough from LXX Zechariah 9:9 to make them less likely than their peers,[729] leaving eight: LXX Isaiah 10:24-34; 41:8-10, 11-13; 43:1, 5-7; 44:1-2; 54:4: LXX Jeremiah 26:27-28.

Within grasp, however, is the force of this exhortation. That is, why does John have Zechariah crying 'fear not' instead of 'rejoice greatly' (regardless of the source from which that anomaly may have been drawn)? A plausible answer emerges from looking more closely at two other components of these quotations: the epithet 'daughter (of) Zion' which immediately follows that exhortation; and (again) the title 'king of Israel' which precedes it in John 12:13.

[1] 'Daughter (of) Zion'

Here it must be noticed that the people exhorted to 'fear not' in this quotation are not the same as those who are pleading with Jesus to 'save' as 'king of Israel'. The latter, as noted, are Passover pilgrims: 'a' or 'the great crowd that had come to the festival'.[730] Those addressed in the quotation of Zechariah 9:9, however, are 'the

---

728. To take them in reverse order (as set out above in this chapter, under *(a) 'Fear not'*), the unbelieving inhabitants of Jerusalem (that is, the 'daughter [of] Zion' to whom Zech 9:9 is addressed) would hardly require sensitivity to the prospect of Jesus's demise. And as for the evangelist citing from memory, this has been addressed by Schuchard and recounted above: quotations from memory, no less than quotations from a written text, would have been drawn from discernible *loci* (see the Introduction, under *a. The criticisms point by point*); and in the case of a biblically literate evangelist such as John, forgetting part of one passage (Zech 9:9) may simply have led to importing part of another – in this case, the candidates for assimilation in Table 37.

729. Two (Isa 41:14-16; 44:6-8), because in the LXX (the base text for the quotation) they attest no (argued) Greek equivalent for 'fear not'; two (Zeph 3:14-17; Zech 8:13-15), because notwithstanding the lexical affinity operating between LXX Zeph 3:14-17 and Zech 9:9 – see above in this chapter, under *(a) 'King of Israel'* – their LXX forms read 'take courage' (θάρσει/θαρσεῖτε) rather than 'fear not' (μὴ φοβοῦ); and three (Isa 35:4; 40:9-10; 51:7), because in the LXX they employ the second-person plural (rather than singular) imperative (μὴ φοβεῖσθε). LXX Jer 26:27-28 also attests an alternate form of the verb – the second-person singular aorist passive subjunctive (μὴ φοβηθῇς); along with it, however, it reads μὴ φοβοῦ: 'And you, fear not (μὴ φοβοῦ), my servant, Jacob ...'.

730. John 12:12a. Important for the provenance of this crowd (to be treated below, note 743) is that the term is attested as both articular and anarthrous: ὁ ὄχλος πολύς P[66] B L family[13]; ὁ ὄχλος ὁ πολύς P[66] (corrected) Θ; ὄχλος πολύς P[2] ℵ A D K Q W Γ Δ Ψ family[1] 33 565 579 700 892 (a later supplement) 1241 1424 Sinai lectionary 844 and the majority of manuscripts. Metzger does not treat it in the second edition of his textual commentary; in the first edition, however, he references the similar alternatives at John 12:9 and notes the committee's struggle to choose between the articular *lectio difficilior* (ὁ ὄχλος πολύς) – a predicate construct functioning as an attributive – and the grammatically sound anarthrous (ὄχλος πολύς); *A Textual Commentary on the Greek New Testament* (Stuttgart: United Bible Societies, 1971), 237.

daughter (of) Zion', a sobriquet that specifically designates the inhabitants of Jerusalem (not pilgrims visiting it for Passover): 'Fear not, daughter (of) Zion; behold your king comes.' The term 'daughter (of)' (בת-) in this appellation has elicited a wide range of hypotheses on its connotations for 'the female personification of cities'[731]; and, as Kubiś has pointed out, the name 'Zion' (employed alone) in some instances came to designate the Israelite people at large (not just the inhabitants of Jerusalem).[732] Discussion on the full phrase 'daughter (of) Zion', however, assumes that, like 'daughter (of) Jerusalem', it designates the residents of that city[733]; and the Johannine context here of Jesus 'coming to Jerusalem'[734] suggests nothing other. The people urged to 'fear not' are not the festal pilgrims who have just come out to greet Jesus as 'king of Israel'. They are Jerusalemites, still inside the city.

[2] The festal pilgrims and Nordreichstheologie
This identification becomes significant when, pressing further on the *inclusio* between Nathanael's confession at John 1 and John 12:13/Psalm 118:25-26, it is seen that the title 'king of Israel' reflects what Reim has called a *Nordreichstheologie*, a northern conception of royal christology.[735] As recounted above, 'king of Israel' at John 12:13 answers to Nathanael's confession of that same title at John 1:49; and that confession, in turn, is embedded in a broader allusion to Zephaniah 3 in John 1:45-49: the title is drawn from Zephaniah 3:15; and Jesus's prior comment that Nathanael was 'an Israelite in whom is no deceit (ἐν ᾧ δόλος οὐκ ἔστιν)' alludes to the remnant whom that king will restore at Zephaniah 3:13 (see Table 42).[736]

As Reim notes, however, this episode also resonates with a motif dear to northern, Israelite sensibilities: Jacob tradition.[737] Northern moorings are immediately evident from two features of the pericope: Philip's identification of Jesus as 'Jesus, son of Joseph, from Nazareth'; and Jesus's identification of Nathanael as 'an Israelite (not a Ἰουδαῖος) in whom is no deceit'.[738] Reim, for his part, detects such northern motifs throughout the gospel[739]; and to the two features of this story noted here he adds two more from John 1: that the depiction of Nathanael as having

---

731. Floyd, 'Welcome Back, Daughter of Zion!', 494–502.
732. See above in this chapter, under *(b) The omission of Zechariah 9:9b*.
733. *Passim*, for instance, in Floyd, 'Welcome Back, Daughter of Zion!' and Stinespring, 'No Daughter of Zion: A Study of the Appositional Genitive in Hebrew Grammar'.
734. John 12:12.
735. This, in his essay 'Nordreich – Südreich: Der vierte Evangelist als Vertreter christlicher Nordreichstheologie', in *Jochanan*, 360–67; first publ. in BZ^{NF} 36 (1992).
736. These observations were made above in this chapter under two similarly titled subheadings: *(b) 'The king of Israel'* and *(a) 'King of Israel'*.
737. 'Nordreich – Südreich: Der vierte Evangelist als Vertreter christlicher Nordreichstheologie', 360–61.
738. John 1:45, 47.
739. Besides this episode, Jesus's sojourn in Sychar, the prophetic Mosaic christology and allusions to Jesus as Elijah.

Table 42 Zephaniah 3 and the call of Nathanael

HB/LXX Zephaniah 3:11-15	John 1:45-49
On that day you shall not be shamed for all your wanton deeds by which you have transgressed against me. For at that time I will remove from your midst those who exult in your haughtiness; and you shall no longer continue to be lofty on my holy mountain. But I will leave in your midst a people humble and lowly; and the remnant of Israel will seek refuge in the name of the Lord. They will do no unrighteousness; they shall not speak falsehood; nor shall there be found in their mouth <u>a deceitful tongue</u> (לשון תרמית/γλῶσσα δολία) … Cry out, daughter (of) Zion! Shout, O Israel! Be glad and exult with whole heart, daughter (of) Jerusalem! The Lord has removed your judgments; he has turned away your foes. <u>The king of Israel</u> (מלך ישראל/βασιλεὺς Ισραηλ), the Lord, is in your midst; you will not fear evil again.	Philip found Nathanael and said to him, 'We have found him of whom Moses in the law and the prophets wrote, Jesus, son of Joseph, from Nazareth.' Nathanael said to him, 'Can anything good be from Nazareth'? Philip said to him, 'Come and see'. Jesus saw Nathanael coming to him and said of him, 'Behold, truly an Israelite <u>in whom is no deceit</u> (ἐν ᾧ δόλος οὐκ ἔστιν)'. Nathanael said to him, 'From where do you know me'? Jesus answered and said him, 'Before Philip called you, while you were under the fig tree, I saw you.' Nathanael answered him, 'Rabbi, you are the Son of God! You are <u>king of Israel</u> (βασιλεὺς … τοῦ Ἰσραήλ)'!

'no deceit' is a deliberate counterpoint to Jacob, who did[740]; and, further, that upon Nathanael's confession, he and the other disciples are promised a new version of the *Jakobserlebnisse* at Bethel (the *locus* of a key northern shrine). As Jacob had seen heaven opened above Bethel to reveal angels ascending and descending upon a ladder, so the disciples will see it opened above Jesus to reveal angels doing the same upon the Son of Man.[741] Given Nathanael's initial doubt about Jesus – that is, whether 'anything good' could 'be from Nazareth' – the episode seems to portray him as being christologically converted in his views of the north, from expecting nothing messianic to come from it to seeing its typology realized in 'Jesus, son of Joseph, from Nazareth'; and this, in turn, suggests that the title he utters from Zephaniah carries that same force: 'king of Israel' speaks of a returned king of the northern monarchy.[742] Inasmuch, then, as that title is now repeated in an

---

740. For this point Reim cites three passages, none of which make explicit mention of Jacob's 'deceit': Gen 27:36; 32:28(29); Hos 12:4(5); 'Nordreich – Südreich: Der vierte Evangelist als Vertreter christlicher Nordreichstheologie', 361n1. Perhaps better is LXX Gen 27:35 – 'But (Isaac) said to (Esau), "Your brother, coming with deceit (μετὰ δόλου), took your blessing"'.

741. Gen 28:10-22; John 1:50-51.

742. Perhaps pressing too far, Reim suggests Nathanael initially hoped for a messiah from Judah according to Jacob's oracle (Gen 49:8-12); 'Nordreich – Südreich: Der vierte Evangelist als Vertreter christlicher Nordreichstheologie', 361n1.

inclusio by the pilgrims greeting Jesus at John 12:13, it appears that the import of Psalm 118:25-26 is to identify Jesus as fulfilling northern monarchical hopes: the 'king of Israel' who 'comes in the name of the Lord' resonates with a northern royal christology.[743]

It is for this reason that John switches out Zechariah's 'rejoice greatly' for 'fear not'. At this moment residents of Jerusalem would have every reason to be afraid. In part, this was due to the way they had treated Jesus up to this point in the narrative. The figure who, since John 5, had been so opposed by the city that his very presence put him at risk of arrest and death[744] was now entering as a monarch besought for salvation by a 'great crowd' of pilgrims. But stoking this fear all the more was the kind of king he was being proclaimed to be by those pilgrims, embodied in the title 'king of Israel'. Whereas Jerusalemites inhabited the seat of southern kingdom messianic hopes, what might be dubbed a *Südreichschristologie*, Jesus was being hailed as a northern kingdom monarch, a *Nordreichschristologie*.

(b) Südreichschristologie and 'upon a foal of a donkey'
Such a scenario, in turn, explains the last two major anomalies at John 12:15/ Zechariah 9:9 – the description of Jesus's mount and the omissions of Zechariah 9:9b, σοι and 'the attributes of the king'.

---

743. This, contra Schuchard (following Peter J. Tomson) that 'king of Israel' and 'king of the Jews' were different ways in which Jews designated the same figure: ὁ βασιλεὺς τοῦ Ἰσραήλ when discoursing among themselves; ὁ βασιλεὺς τῶν Ἰουδαίων when doing so with Gentiles; Schuchard, *Scripture within Scripture*, 79n44; Tomson, 'The Names Israel and Jew in Ancient Judaism and in the New Testament', *Bijdr* 47 (1986): 120-40. Jesus is about to take on the second title ('king of the Jews'), as well (John 18:33, 39; 19:3, 14-15, 19, 21), but (to anticipate the point being argued here) this will be to assuage Jerusalemite fears over his northern provenance and restore the divided kingdoms in himself.

Perhaps supporting this *Nordreichschristologie* further is the possibility that the pilgrims at John 12:12-13 had come from the city named 'Ephraim' at John 11:54. If the phrase by which they are designated is articular – that is, 'the great crowd' (ὁ ὄχλος πολύς) rather than 'a great crowd' (ὄχλος πολύς), see note 730–the definite article would imply they had already been introduced into the narrative. This would point back to 'the many' who 'before Passover went up to Jerusalem from the country (ἐκ τῆς χώρας) to purify themselves' at John 11:55; and that 'country', in turn, was likely 'the country (τὴν χώραν) near the wilderness' where Jesus had made retreat to 'a city called Ephraim' after his anointing at Bethany (John 11:54). Ephraim, also known as Aphairema, Ophrah or Ephron, was located within the region designated for Benjamin (Josh 18:23) – and, so, southern. During the split between northern and southern kingdoms, however, it initially lay within the north (2 Chron 13:19); and prior to the accession of Jonathan Hasmoneus it was situated in Samaria (1 Macc 11:34). Even if its provenance was Judahite, however, its name connotes northern interests and may be meant to do so here. See Herbert G. May, *Oxford Bible Atlas*, 2nd ed. (London: Oxford University Press, 1974), 122, 128, 136; Adrian Curtis, *Oxford Bible Atlas*, 4th ed. (Oxford: Oxford University Press, 2007), 103.

744. John 5:16-18; 7:2-9, 13, 19, 25, 30, 32, 44; 8:20, 59; 9:22; 10:31, 39; 11:8, 16, 47-53.

The first of these – the anomalies in Jesus's mount ('upon a foal of a donkey') – meshes with the question attending John 12:14, rehearsed above: that is, in responding to the pilgrims' chants by 'finding a young donkey' and 'sitting upon it', was Jesus correcting their recitation of Psalm 118:25-26? Or was he endorsing it?[745] The issue turns on the sequence of events in the Johannine account. Where in Matthew Jesus makes this gesture before the crowd recites the quotation,[746] in John it is the other way round; and this allows for Jesus's action in John to be a refutation of the crowd's sentiment (rather than an affirmation or inducement of it).

[1] The case for Jesus correcting the pilgrims
The case for Jesus correcting the crowd argues that he was hailed by that crowd as a conventional king and that by sitting on the donkey he aimed to show them otherwise. It rests on four premises[747]:

(1) that the crowd greets Jesus with standard protocol for receiving kings: specifically, the language describing the crowd's reception is typical for greeting Hellenistic royalty[748]; the 'branches of palm trees' (τὰ βαΐα τῶν φοινίκων) carried by the crowd connote nationalist royal triumph[749]; and the Hebrew equivalent of 'Hosanna' is used in the HB to address kings.[750]

---

745. See above in this chapter, under *Excursus: Is this a quotation?*
746. Matt 21:1-9.
747. Drawn from Hoskyns, *The Fourth Gospel*, 420–21; and Brown, *Gospel according to John*, 1:461-63.
748. They 'took branches of palm trees and went out to meet him (εἰς ὑπάντησιν αὐτῷ)' (John 12:13); 'And the citizens of Antioch, when they learned that Titus was near ... hastened to meet (him) (ἐπὶ τὴν ὑπάντησιν) ...' (Josephus, *J.W.* 7.100). On this point Brown draws from André Feuillet, *Johannine Studies*, trans. Thomas E. Crane (Staten Island, NY: Alba House, 1965), 142–43.
749. 'On the twenty-third day of the second month of the one hundred and seventy-first year, they entered (the citadel) with praise and palm branches (βαΐων) ... because a great enemy of Israel was crushed' (1 Macc 13:51); 'Therefore, having wands wreathed in ivy and ripened shoots, as well as palms (φοίνικας), they raised up hymns to him who had enabled the place (temple) to be purified' (2 Macc 10:7); 'for again an innumerable multitude are revealed, clothed in white and illustrious with palms of victory (*palmis victoriae*) – indeed, triumphing over Antichrist' (Tertullian, *Scorp.* 12); 'And when Levi became as a sun, behold, a certain young man gave him twelve branches of palm trees (βαΐα φοινίκων δώδεκα, *T. Naph.* 5:4)'; and Bar Kosiba coinage. Here Brown relies on W.R. Farmer, 'The Palm Branches in John 12,13', *JTS*[NS] 3 (1952): 62–66. The text for Tertullian is A. Reifferscheid and G. Wissowa, eds., '*Scorpiace*', in *Tertullianus, Opera II: Opera Montanistica*, ed. A. Gerlo et al., CCSL 2 (Turnhout, Belgium: Brepols, 1954); for the *Testament of Naphtali*, R.H. Charles, *The Greek Versions of the Testaments of the Twelve Patriarchs* (Oxford: Clarendon Press, 1908).
750. 2 Sam 14:4; 2 Kgs 6:26.

(2) that the tandem use of the terms 'king' (βασιλεύς) and 'come' (ἔρχεσθαι) at Psalm 118:25-26 is also applied to Jesus by the miraculously fed crowd at John 6:14-15, but there Jesus rebuffs their attempt to make him king.[751]
(3) that the removal of warrior language from the quotation of Zechariah 9:9 (at John 12:15) indicates that Jesus's 'regal advent is not for war, but in peace and in humility'[752]; and further, that Jesus's discourse in John 12:23-36 (on his impending death) clarifies the distinction between the messiah expected by the multitude and the messiah he came to be.
(4) and that the recollection of this event ascribed to the disciples in John 12:16 indicates that the real nature of Jesus's kingship would not be grasped until after the resurrection.

[2] Missed factors

[a] Problems with the dominant view
In two respects this view of Jesus's gesture at John 12:14 proves wanting. The first is its own inferential structure: its premises carry flaws. To begin with (2), the terms 'king' (βασιλεύς) and 'come' (ἔρχεσθαι) also occur in the quotation of Zechariah 9:9 at John 12:15, which indisputably represents the type of royalty endorsed by Jesus: 'behold your king comes (ἰδοὺ ὁ βασιλεύς σου ἔρχεται) ...' On (3), John's rendering of Zechariah 9:9, in fact, omits the very language that would underscore Jesus as a king coming 'in peace and in humility' rather than 'for war', as Hoskyns would have it[753]: absent are 'the attributes of the king', 'righteous and saving is he, meek ...' (δίκαιος καὶ σῴζων αὐτός, πραῢς ...). With regard to (4), the new perspective gained by the disciples after Jesus's glorification according to John 12:16 does not correct the crowd's recitation of Psalm 118:25-26. It rather recalls it, as a Spirit-wrought vantage point for understanding Jesus's actions at that point, alongside (and as peer to) the clearly endorsed quotation of Zechariah 9:9 at John 12:15 – 'then they remembered that these things were written about him (Zechariah 9:9 and Psalm 118:25-26) and that they did these things to him (recited Psalm 118:25-26)'.

And as for (1) – that the crowd greets Jesus with standard protocol for receiving kings – the pilgrims in question were doubtless unaware of the otherworldly kingdom Jesus was coming to establish; but given the Johannine use of irony, it does not follow that the psalm they recite (with its anomalies) would not still apply. In the previous chapter Caiaphas galvanized the Sanhedrin against Jesus by declaring it was 'expedient that one man die for the people and that the whole nation not perish', and

---

751. 'The people ... were saying, "This is truly the prophet who is coming (ὁ ἐρχόμενος) into the world" ... Jesus, therefore, knowing that they were about to come and seize him to make (him) king (βασιλέα), withdrew again to the mountain, he alone.'
752. Hoskyns, *The Fourth Gospel*, 420.
753. See note 752.

this is endorsed by the evangelist as prophecy, despite the *Mißverständis* in which it was said.[754] Why would Jesus not be 'king of Israel' who 'comes' to 'save ... in the name of the Lord', even if those who proclaimed him such were naïve to the sense in which it was true? In fact (as noted above), Jesus had already accepted the title 'king of Israel' in John 1. When he is confessed as such by Nathanael, he does not correct him: he simply tells him that the divine manifestation which induced him to make that confession would be exceeded by another, that is, that Nathanael (and his fellow disciples) would see 'the heaven open, and the angels of God ascending and descending upon the Son of Man'.[755]

[b] The Jacob oracle and Südreichstheologie

The second respect in which the dominant view of Jesus's gesture at John 12:14 falls short concerns two missed factors in the broader passage; and these, in turn, offer an alternate model for the dynamic at work in these quotations. The first follows from the observation made above on the sobriquet 'daughter (of) Zion',[756] namely, that Jesus's gesture of 'finding a young donkey' at John 12:14 was not directed at the pilgrims greeting him (and so, could not have been intended to 'correct' their sentiment). Like the exhortation 'fear not' in John 12:15/Zechariah 9:9, Jesus's act at John 12:14 was pitched to the residents of Jerusalem: as 'daughter (of) Zion', they were the ones for whom Zechariah's king was to come 'upon a foal of a donkey'; consequently, Jesus's gesture in the wake of the pilgrim's recitation of Psalm 118:25-26 could not have been designed to censor it.

The second factor missed by the dominant view is the source of the phrase 'upon a foal of a donkey', itself, in John's rendering of Zechariah 9:9. As Menken has observed, its language likely reflects a tailored assimilation of the articular phrase in LXX Genesis 49:11. Where the LXX of that verse reads 'the foal of his donkey' (τὸν πῶλον τῆς ὄνου αὐτοῦ), John has 'a foal of a donkey' (ἐπὶ πῶλον ὄνου)[757]: the evangelist would have simply removed the definite articles, along

---

754. John 11:49-52.

755. John 1:47-51 (quotation John 1:51). Jesus, in fact, implicitly confirms Nathanael's confession to be correct when in his next question he assumes that it reflects faith: 'Jesus answered and said to him, "Because I said to you that I saw you beneath the fig tree *do you believe*"'? (John 1:50).

Also problematic in the case for Jesus correcting the crowd is its assumption that 'palms' in 2 Macc 10:7 reflect nationalist triumphalism. As noted above 'branches of palm trees' also served as ritual objects for the observance of Tabernacles (Chapter 3, under *1. An earlier arrangement: 'Remembrance' quotations as a piece*), and the celebration of Hanukkah depicted in 2 Macc 10:1-8 is cast as emulating that festival (2 Macc 10:6): 'With cheer they celebrated for eight days after the manner of Tabernacles ...'

756. See above in this chapter, under *[1] 'Daughter (of) Zion'*.

757. See above in this chapter, under *(f) 'Upon a foal of a donkey'*.

4. Ps 118:25-26 and Zech 9:9, The Restoration of the Monarchy

with the final genitive pronoun 'his' (αὐτοῦ) which modifies the second of the two nouns.

Significant here is that, as noted above, Genesis 49:11 is, itself, part of the Jacob oracle on Judah, spanning Genesis 49:8-12:

> The scepter shall not depart from Judah,
> nor the staff from between his feet,
> until Shiloh (he whose it is) comes,
> to whom belongs the obedience of the peoples.
> Binding to the vine his foal (τὸν πῶλον αὐτοῦ),
> even the foal of his donkey (τὸν πῶλον τῆς ὄνου αὐτοῦ) to the choice vine,
> he washes his raiment in wine,
> and his clothes in the blood of grapes.[758]

This passage is a key *locus* for southern monarchical hopes; and, as such, the allusion to it in John's description of Jesus's mount serves as a deliberate counterpoint to the northern monarchical hope embodied in the title 'king of Israel' at John 12:13. The contrast has been noticed by Boismard and Lamouille, who assign each to a different recension in their diachronic hypothesis on the gospel's composition history: 'king of Israel' to their (earlier) Document C; the allusion to Genesis 49:11, to (the later) Jean II-A.[759] For the synchronic approach taken here, it offers an alternative rationale for the several exegetical issues under discussion – particularly, Jesus finding a donkey after the pilgrims recite Psalm 118:25-26 at John 12:13; the anomaly 'fear not' for 'rejoice greatly' at John 12:15/Zechariah 9:9; and the description of Jesus's mount in that same quotation. When the pilgrims' acclamation of Jesus as a northern king ('king of Israel') instils dread in the hearts of Jerusalemites who had remained in the city, Jesus assuages their distress ('fear not') by 'finding a young donkey' after the Jacob oracle on Judah and simultaneously entering the city as a southern king ('upon a foal of a donkey').

(c) The omissions

Further explained by this scenario are John's omissions of the dative 'to you' (σοι) and 'the attributes of the king' ('righteous and saving is he, meek ...'). Before treating them, it should be noted that the absence of Zechariah 9:9b (prior to these omissions) is best assigned to either or both of two motives: to preclude redundancy and/or, as Kubiś implies, to avoid the task of replacing its exhortation 'proclaim' with a verb equivalent to the (otherwise incompatible) anomaly 'fear not' in John's rendering of the colon before it – '*Fear not*, daughter (of) Zion; *proclaim*, daughter (of) Jerusalem.'[760]

---

758. Cited here is Gen 49:10-11.
759. *L'Évangile de Jean*, 309; cf. Kubiś, *Book of Zechariah in the Gospel of John*, 98.
760. See above in this chapter, under *(b) The omission of Zechariah 9:9b*.

As for the absence of 'to you' and 'the attributes of the king', some hypotheses can be challenged on their own terms. Was John, in fact, interested in metrical adjustments to the quotations he cited (a question raised by Kubiś[761])? Would he have wished to align ἔρχεσθαι in Zechariah 9:9c with its absolute use in Psalm 118:25-26 when Matthew (who also quotes both) did not (again, a critique issued by Kubiś[762])? Does the removal of σοι, in itself, give Zechariah 9:9 universalist implications (Schuchard against Menken[763])? Or (against Kubiś[764]) would John have been averse to reiterating Jesus's character as 'righteous and saving' given his repetition of the christological title 'king of Israel' at John 12:13 (relative to John 1:49)?

In light of the monarchical dynamics at play in these quotations, however, it is more likely that these words were simply removed because they are irrelevant to the operative element in the quotation: the description of Jesus's mount. If the quotation of Zechariah 9:9 is meant to offset Jesus's acclaim as 'king of Israel' with a gesture showing him also to be 'king of Judah', the issue at stake in its wording is not the people 'to whom' Jesus is coming (σοι), nor is it the character and disposition by which he was doing so ('righteous and saving is he, meek'). It is rather the way in which he was making this entry – 'upon a foal of a donkey' from Jacob's oracle on southern monarchical hopes; and, as such, all other distractions to that datum had to be removed.

(3) Summary

In sum, the language in the quotations of Psalm 118:25-26 and Zechariah 9:9 at John 12:13-15 reflects base texts from the LXX modified in four ways: (a) in place of Psalm 118:25 stands a transliteration (ὡσαννά) of either the Hebrew plea 'save us' from the first colon of that verse (הוֹשִׁיעָה נָּא) or the Aramaic *lûlāb* associated with that plea (הוֹשַׁעְנָא); (b) in place of 'rejoice greatly' from LXX Zechariah 9:9a stands the exhortation 'fear not' (μὴ φοβοῦ) – drawn from any one or more of eight possible passages which attest that precise construct; (c) in place of the participle 'mounted' (ἐπιβεβηκώς) in LXX Zechariah 9:9e stands a synonym (καθήμενος) to the evangelist's description of Jesus's movements at John 12:14; and (d) in place of the compound phrase 'upon an ass, even a young foal' (ἐπὶ ὑποζύγιον καὶ πῶλον νέον) in LXX Zechariah 9:9ef stands an anarthrous assimilation of LXX Genesis 49:11 (ἐπὶ πῶλον ὄνου).

c. The import of the quotations

Thematically, then, these two quotations depict Jesus coming to Jerusalem as a king who fulfils both northern and southern kingdom conceptions of monarchy: northern, by the acclamation he receives from pilgrims as 'king of Israel'; southern, by the gesture towards Jacob's oracle on Judah which he makes to Jerusalemites in

---

761. *Book of Zechariah in the Gospel of John*, 80-81.
762. *Book of Zechariah in the Gospel of John*, 79.
763. *Scripture within Scripture*, 80n47.
764. *Book of Zechariah in the Gospel of John*, 80-81.

4. Ps 118:25-26 and Zech 9:9, The Restoration of the Monarchy

response. Understood this way, these quotations, in fact, dramatize an allusion to Ezekiel 37 which Jesus had made earlier in the narrative, at John 10:16. There he predicted uniting all Israel under himself as its single shepherd by referencing Ezekiel's prophecy of David one day doing the same; and at John 12:12-16 that prediction is realized as Jesus enters Jerusalem:

> And I have other sheep that are not from this fold;
> I must bring them also, and they will hear my voice.
> And there shall be one flock, one shepherd.[765]

> Then say to them,
> 'Thus says the Lord Yahweh,
> "Behold, I am taking the children of Israel from the nations
>   in which they have walked;
> and I will gather them from every corner and bring them to their land.
> I will make them one nation in the land on the mountains of Israel;
> and one king shall be over all of them as king.
> And they shall no longer be as two nations;
> they shall no longer still be divided as two kingdoms.
> They shall no longer defile themselves with their idols,
> with their abhorrent things and all their transgressions.
> And I shall save them from all their apostacies by which they have sinned;
> and I shall cleanse them.
> And they shall be to me as a people, and I will be to them as God.
> My servant David shall be king over them;
> and all of them shall have one shepherd ..."'[766]

The conclusion to which Reim comes for this dynamic through the whole of the gospel applies just as aptly to these 'remembrance' quotations in John 12: 'Nordreich und Südreich – zwei Reiche – zwei Theologien – zwei Christologien'![767]

---

765. John 10:16.
766. Ezek 37:21-24.
767. 'Nordreich – Südreich: Der vierte Evangelist als Vertreter christlicher Nordreichstheologie', 364. On this basis one of the eight candidates for the anomaly 'fear not' in John's rendering of Zech 9:9 (above in this chapter, under *(a)* Nordreichschristologie *and 'fear not'*) may stand out from the rest as its source: LXX Isa 43:5-7, by virtue of its link to the gathering of Israel from east and west:

> Fear not (μὴ φοβοῦ), for I am with you.
> From the east I will bring your seed;
> and from the west I will gather you ...
> everyone who is called by my name,
> whom for my glory I created, formed, indeed, made.

C. Conclusions

1. The putative tradition

Before teasing out the *inclusio* which these quotations form with Psalm 69:10 at John 2:17, it bears considering the drama that would have unfolded if John 2:13-22 had once followed immediately upon John 12:12-16, as suggested above.[768] In such a scenario Jesus would be entering Jerusalem as monarch over the northern and southern kingdoms, then prefiguring the new sanctuary he will build as he establishes that dynasty. He is greeted as 'king of Israel' by pilgrims whose 'branches of palm trees' hint at the eschatological observance of Tabernacles in Zechariah's 'day ... of the Lord'[769]; and against the 'fear' this could incite among Jerusalemites, he takes pains to show himself their king, as well, by entering the city on the 'foal' of Jacob's oracle on Judah. When he finds the temple to be the 'house of merchandise' disparaged by Zechariah, he 'casts out' (ἐξέβαλεν) its merchants[770] as a harbinger of the way he will 'cast out' (ἐκβληθήσεται) 'the ruler of this world'[771] when he later accedes to the throne; and the 'zeal' he displays in doing so signals the 'zeal' by which he will 'raise' the 'dismantled sanctuary' of his crucified 'body' to establish this new dynasty, whose sacred mountain is 'in spirit and truth'.[772] The picture is not far removed from Herod's renovation of the sanctuary in 20 BCE (and may, in fact, have it in view as a foil for its christology). As Herod ruled a realm roughly the scope of the northern and southern kingdoms, and as he established his dynasty by 'dismantling' and 'raising' the 'sanctuary' which preceded him, so Jesus, in this piece. But where Herod's renovation took some eighteen months to complete, Jesus's death and resurrection would span only three days. How much greater the king!

2. The 'remembrance' inclusio

Whether or not such a putative arrangement existed, the current placement of these passages at the beginning and end of Jesus's public ministry splits their royal imagery and (as with the Isaianic quotations) creates an *inclusio* between their 'remembrance' formulae. But, if the Isaianic *inclusio* brought 'closure' to what came before (in the Book of Signs), this 'remembrance' inclusio might be said to bring 'anticipation' for what lies ahead (in the Book of Glory). By setting the temple cleansing first the evangelist inverts the sequence one expects from such imagery: where a would-be king would identify himself as such first, then establish his line by erecting a new shrine, Jesus (in the current text of John) proceeds the other way

---

768. Chapter 3, *1. An earlier arrangement: 'Remembrance' quotations as a piece.*
769. Zech 14:1.
770. John 2:15.
771. John 12:31.
772. John 4:23.

round: he first forecasts the building of the shrine (in chapter 2), then only later (in chapter 12) shows himself to have the royal legitimacy to do so. As the narrative unfolds, then, Jesus's public identification as 'king of Israel and Judah' in John 12 signals that he is poised to establish the sanctuary he had earlier promised in John 2. And so, where the Isaianic quotations look back (with closure) to Jesus's public ministry in the Book of Signs, the 'remembrance' quotations look ahead (with anticipation) to the erection of that sanctuary: Jesus's death and resurrection in the Book of Glory.

Part III

CHIASMUS AND THEOLOGY

Chapter 5

CONCLUSIONS

As noted in the Introduction, the two *inclusios* formed by these quotation clusters arrange themselves into a *chiasmus* within the Book of Signs. The Isaianic quotations are the first and last two to appear in John 1–12; the 'remembrance' quotations are the second and second-to-last to do the same in John 2–12. As such, they together unfold in an A-B-B′-A′ pattern, with the 'remembrance' *inclusio* tucked immediately within the Isaianic one. Since in such a device the outer *inclusio* serves as a foil to the inner, one expects the themes of the Isaianic quotations to bring those of the 'remembrance' quotations into relief; and this dynamic can serve as a springboard for reflecting theologically on them all.

Such reflection is now taken up here in two steps. First, the motifs attending each cluster will be synthesized into the overarching narrative created by the full *chiasmus*. Then that narrative will be canvassed for the theological implications that lay latent in it. Such canvassing cannot be done exhaustively. Nor can any theological issue distilled be brought into full conversation with the massive scholarly discussion of which it is part – the ousting of 'the ruler of this world' and the Johannine *theologia crucis*, for example; or the emblematic restoration of northern and southern kingdoms with the Fourth Gospel's ecclesiology. Such an exercise can, however, create points of contact with that broader discussion which can be explored with more depth in another context; and such is offered in this last chapter under five theological categories: christology, soteriology, eschatology, ecclesiology and pneumatology.

A. *The* chiasmus

To begin, then, with the *inclusios* and the *chiasmus* – taking John the Baptist's 'make straight the way of the Lord' at John 1:23 as a call to believe, the Isaianic quotations unfold as a threefold sketch of Jesus's public ministry to the Jews: (1) an invitation embodied in John for them to believe Jesus; (2) a lament anticipated by Isaiah that they had not done so; and (3) a disclosure made by the pre-incarnate Jesus that they had been disabled from doing so by the devil. Similarly, taking the future tense 'will consume' at John 2:17 as anticipating the 'zeal' by which Jesus will erect a new sanctuary, the 'remembrance' quotations proceed in a twofold forecast of Jesus's regal destiny, (1) casting his protest in the temple as the harbinger of a new dynasty and (2) and framing his entry into Jerusalem as the reunification of Israel and Judah under his single monarchy. By its testimony backed with signs the outer *inclusio* implicitly depicts Jesus as Moses, entreating the Jews to believe he has been sent by God (the Father) to deliver; and by its *Nordreichs-* and *Südreichschristologie*, the inner *inclusio* portrays Jesus as David *redivivus*, uniting the divided kingdoms of Israel and Judah as promised by Ezekiel.[773]

The bridge facilitating the synthesis of the two *inclusio*s (and the hinge on which they turn) is 'the ruler of this world'. In the first *inclusio* he is 'the cause of obduracy', thwarting the testimony and signs attesting Jesus as the one sent from the Father; in the second, he is the one who is to be 'cast out', being banished with the establishment of a new mode of worship through Jesus's death and resurrection. And herein may also be factored the tie between the 'remembrance' formulae and the '*geistgewirkte Erinnern*' given to Jesus's disciples after the resurrection[774]: as counterpoint to 'the ruler of this world' impairing the Jews from perceiving the salvific import of testimony and signs, the 'remembrance' quotations represent the Spirit of God illuminating the disciples to perceive the christological import of the Jewish scriptures.

In this light the two *inclusio*s fuse, so as to frame a theological storyline that runs through the whole of the gospel: the outer *inclusio*, by analepsis (to the Book of Signs), under a Mosaic typology; the inner, by prolepsis (towards the Book of Glory), under a Davidic one. During Jesus's public ministry he is presented (and presents himself) as the prophet 'of whom Moses … wrote',[775] 'sent' by the Father to deliver the Jews and attested by a 'report' which, for those still doubtful, is reinforced with 'signs' given him from that Father. By the end of this ministry not even the signs have sufficed to persuade the Jews of his commission; and through a reimagined contemplation of Isaiah's throne room vision in Isaiah 6, this is lamented by the prophet to the pre-incarnate Jesus and explained by Jesus as having been caused by a factor yet to be addressed in the narrative: the devil. As current sovereign of 'this world', he still has power to impair the Jews' perception of Jesus's testimony and deeds.

And so, the inner *inclusio*. Here, through select passages of scripture, the Spirit reveals to the disciples that if Jesus was Moses during his public ministry – thwarted by 'the ruler of this world' – he will be David over a united Israel and Judah through his death and resurrection – removing that obstruction and establishing a new order, 'not of this world',[776] in its place. Jesus's routing of the temple market serves as a 'type' of the expulsion he will perform on that figure; his entrance into Jerusalem discloses the royal right by which he will do so; and the 'Father's house' which heralds this new dynasty consists no longer in the brick-and-mortar edifice of the Jerusalem temple but in the 'spirit and truth'[777] of the Father and Son

---

773. John 10:16; Ezek 37:21-24.
774. John 14:25-26.
775. John 1:45; Deut 18:18-19.
776. John 18:36.
777. John 4:21-24.

indwelling each believer through the Spirit. Therein, in metaphorical fulfilment of Ezekiel's prophecy, the kingdoms of Israel and Judah will be reunited as 'one flock' under 'one shepherd':

> Then say to them,
> 'Thus says the Lord Yahweh,
> "Behold, I am taking the children of Israel from the nations
> in which they have walked;
> and I will gather them from every corner and bring them to their land.
> I will make them one nation in the land on the mountains of Israel;
> and one king shall be over all of them as king.
> And they shall no longer be as two nations;
> they shall no longer still be divided as two kingdoms.
> They shall no longer defile themselves with their idols,
> with their abhorrent things and all their transgressions.
> And I shall save them from all their apostacies by which they have sinned;
> and I shall cleanse them.
> And they shall be to me as a people, and I will be to them as God.
> My servant David shall be king over them;
> and all of them shall have one shepherd ... "'[778]

B. *The theology*

1. *John's debt to apocalypticism*

In his work *Understanding the Fourth Gospel* John Ashton argues that though the Fourth Gospel is 'decidedly *not* an apocalypse', it is 'profoundly indebted to apocalyptic in all sorts of ways'. To make his case Ashton selects four of those 'ways' for focused examination, each one twofold: John's division of time into this age and an age to come; his mode of disclosure as revelation followed by elucidation; his demarcation of recipients as either enlightened or unaware; and his partition of reality into 'this' and 'other worldly'.[779] Certainly to be included in this list is the Johannine 'ruler of this world'; and, when that figure is read as 'the cause of obduracy' at John 12:40, it creates no less than seven theological corollaries from the story latent in the *chiasmus*.

Categorizing those corollaries is somewhat arbitrary, since the elements of theological taxonomy are inextricably interwoven: a datum on the 'christology' of Jesus's death, for instance, carries inevitable repercussions for the 'soteriology' of his mission; and if it has bearing on the status of the devil – as is the case here – both that 'christology' and its concomitant 'soteriology' could readily be subsumed

---

778. Ezek 37:21-24.
779. *Understanding the Fourth Gospel*, 2nd ed. (Oxford: Oxford University Press, 2007), 307–29 (quotations p. 310, italics original).

under the 'eschatology' of Jesus's new age. With that caveat in view, these seven corollaries are treated under the five theological headings noted above: christology, soteriology, eschatology, ecclesiology and pneumatology.

2. Theological corollaries

a. Christology

The first corollary falls within the Johannine *theologia crucis* – specifically, the degree to which Jesus's death in John is required to effect something salvific. In discussion on the matter some have concluded that Jesus's purpose in the narrative rests solely on his incarnate manifestation of divine glory and that, as such, his cross serves no soteric end: it is either the mere means for returning to the Father (once such revelation had been given in his public ministry) or revelation in itself (with no salvific aspect attached).[780]

With 'the cause of obduracy' as 'the ruler of this world', the Isaianic *inclusio* supports the array of views which (by contrast) do detect something intrinsically soteric in Jesus's death. It exposes the inability of Jesus's incarnate public ministry, in itself, to save under the lingering hegemony of the devil; and it brings into relief the soteric necessity for that figure (the devil) to be 'cast out' by Jesus's passion and resurrection if salvation is to occur. As such, its conception of the soteric economy requires the events recounted in the Book of Signs to be followed by those depicted in the Book of Glory. Jesus can not merely 'reveal'. He must 'triumph'.

b. Soteriology

Exegetes who do see the soteric necessity of Jesus's death understand such an effect to be manifold. 'John offers no single reigning theory of atonement', writes Paul Rainbow in his thoroughgoing treatment of the subject, 'but rather a body

---

780. A review of discussion is covered in Andreas J. Köstenberger, *A Theology of John's Gospel and Letters*, Biblical Theology of the New Testament (Grand Rapids, MI: Zondervan, 2009), 534–47. For the first of these views, Köstenberger notes Rudolf Bultmann, *Theology of the New Testament*, trans. Kendrick Grobel (New York: Charles Scribner's Sons, 1951/1955), 2:54; trans. of *Theologie des Neuen Testaments*, Neue theologische Grundrisse (Tübingen: J.C.B. Mohr [Paul Siebeck], 1951/1955). More to the point here, perhaps, is 2:52-53, 'John has subsumed the death of Jesus under his idea of Revelation – in his death Jesus himself is acting as the Revealer and is not the passive object of a divine process of salvation.' Pressing yet further (in his case for the Fourth Gospel as 'naïvely docetic') is Ernst Käsemann: 'While Paul and the Synoptics also know the majesty of the earthly Jesus, in John the glory of Jesus determines his whole presentation so thoroughly from the very outset that the incorporation and position of the passion narrative of necessity becomes problematical'; *The Testament of Jesus: A Study of the Gospel of John in Light of Chapter 17*, trans. Gerhard Krodel (Philadelphia: Fortress Press, 1968), 7; trans. of *Jesu letzter Wille nach Johannes 17*, 2nd ed. (Tübingen: Mohr [Siebeck], 1966).

of metaphors, each a facet of a many-sided truth'.[781] By framing Jesus's ejection of the temple vendors as proleptic of him doing the same to 'the ruler of this world', the 'remembrance' *inclusio* coincides with (and enhances) two dimensions of this 'many-sided truth': its cosmic and its apotropaic effects – cosmic, inasmuch as it targets angelic malice (rather than human sin); apotropaic, inasmuch as it wards off evil (rather than propitiates or expiates transgression).

These aspects of the Johannine cross (particularly, the apotropaic), in fact, emerge in other christological motifs throughout the narrative: the pastoral (Good Shepherd) christology, where Jesus lays down his life to protect from the wolf[782]; the paschal (Passover) christology, where (presumably) Jesus's blood allows the Father's judgement to 'pass over' his own[783]; the political ('one-for-the-nation') christology (if you will), where Jesus's single demise as an individual preserves the nation from Roman reprisal[784]; and the 'friendship' christology, wherein the 'safety' of Jesus's disciples 'is assured by the personal sacrifice of one of their number'.[785] With Jesus's death also 'casting out' the angelic sovereign 'of this world', there comes another facet to this list that merits further reflection: a royal christology, where, in the 'dismantling' of 'the sanctuary of his body', Jesus removes the cosmic agent obstructing the reception of his message.

c. Eschatology
The removal of this cosmic agent is an eschatological act, reconceived from occurring in a remote future (as would be expected in a conventional eschatology) to happening at the cross of Christ (in what is deemed a 'realized' eschatology). If such an event occurs at this juncture, it suggests that the conditions for 'believing' change in the wake of the resurrection; and, though such a shift is not articulated explicitly in the gospel narrative, its ramifications might be inferred along three lines: the apologetic use of signs; the Jews as 'children of the devil'; and the role of divine determinism in the Johannine *ordo salutis*.

(1) The medium for encountering signs
The first of these does, in fact, show evidence of change in the text, in the so-called 'doubting Thomas' pericopes.[786] When Thomas misses Jesus's first resurrection appearance, he demands to see such a 'sign', himself, before believing.[787] But where

---

781. *Johannine Theology*, 207.
782. John 10:11-13.
783. Here (a) the declaration of Jesus as 'lamb of God' (John 1:29, 35-36); (b) the indicators that Jesus is conceived to have died on 14 Nisan (John 13:1, 29; 18:28, 38-40; 19:14, 31, 42); and (c) the application of paschal rubrics to the crucifixion pericopes (John 19:29/Exod 12:22; John 19:36/Exod 12:10, 46; Num 9:12).
784. John 11:49-52.
785. John 15:13-15. On the third and fourth of these motifs, particularly, see Rainbow, *Johannine Theology*, 207–08 (quotation p. 208).
786. John 20:24-29.
787. John 20:25.

Jesus before the crucifixion would have welcomed such a need to 'see' – as he did with the Jews at the Dedication and with Philip during the Farewell Discourse[788] – on this occasion he places a higher premium on believing testimony alone. He concedes to Thomas. But he also expresses disappointment that Thomas had not simply had faith in the word of his peers; and his rebuke is followed by the evangelist's commentary that this and Jesus's other signs in the gospel are now to be known through 'this book':

> Jesus said to him, 'Because you have seen me have you believed?
> Blessed are those *who have not seen and have believed*'.
> And indeed, Jesus did many other signs in the presence of his disciples,
> which are not written in this book;
> but these have been written that you may believe that Jesus is the Christ, the Son of God, and that believing you might have life in his name.[789]

To be clear, the shift being made does not preclude the further need for signs to accompany the message. They are now, however, folded into the testimony which conveys that message (with a connotation that no new signs will accompany it), so that – to put it in terms of Isaiah 53:1 – the 'arm of the Lord' is now part of 'our report'.[790]

A change is occurring, nonetheless, at this juncture, however; and though nothing in the narrative explicitly traces it to the ousting of 'the ruler of this world', might this not be inferred from the eschatological and soteriological logic of that event? That is to say, could it not be that with 'the cause of obduracy' now removed – so that 'eyes' are no longer 'blinded' and 'ears' no longer 'deafened' – signs could accompany John's christological message as part of it (to be heard and read) rather than alongside it (to be seen)?

(2) The Jews and the devil

The second ramification of the devil's ouster concerns his relationship to the Jews. In John 8:44 the Jews are cast by Jesus as having the devil as their father. It was noted above, however, (a) that in the immediately preceding clause this status is described as one and the same with having been metaphorically 'deafened' by the devil and (b) that such an act is an auditory counterpart to the metaphorical 'blinding' ascribed to that figure at John 12:40/Isaiah 6:10. The Jews are 'children' of the devil by virtue of being 'deafened' by him (to Jesus's words) and 'blinded' by him (to Jesus's signs):

---

788. John 10:37-38; 14:10-11.
789. John 20:29-31.
790. See further on this point, Richard Bauckham, *Gospel of Glory: Major Themes in Johannine Theology* (Grand Rapids, MI: Baker Academic, 2015), 70.

> Why do you not know my discourse?
> Because *you are not able to hear my word.*
> You are of your father, the devil ...[791]

> He has blinded their eyes ...
> *lest they see with the eyes ...*[792]

Taking this dynamic together with the removal of the devil upon Jesus's death, might it be that, like the medium for encountering signs, the status of the Jews relative to that figure has changed by the end of the gospel narrative? That is, if the Jews had the devil as their father in chapter 8 because as 'the ruler of this world', he had metaphorically deafened their ears and blinded their eyes during Jesus's public ministry, do they still stand in such filial relationship to him once he has been 'cast out' from doing so by Jesus's crucifixion? Perhaps John 8:44 is not the final Johannine word on the matter.

(3) Determinism and faith

The last ramification of Jesus 'casting out' the 'ruler of this world' concerns the necessity of divine election for salvation. It was noted above that the disciples' allegiance to Jesus ultimately depended on being selected for such by both the Father and the Son: no one comes to Jesus unless they have been 'drawn', 'taught' and 'given' to him by God[793]; and those who do have also been chosen by Jesus himself.[794] Given (once again) the disruptive power wielded by 'the ruler of this world' at the time these assertions were made, could it be that this 'determinism' (no less than 'signs') was but a temporary expedient, necessary to garner an 'apostolate' when it was impossible for humans to believe?

Instructive here is a point in one of the dialogues between Jesus and his disciples during the Farewell Discourse. When the disciples insist to Jesus that 'now' they 'believe' (πιστεύομεν) that he 'came from God' (the core claim Jesus had been making to the world), Jesus retorts with a rhetorical question that asserts otherwise – 'Do you now believe (ἄρτι πιστεύετε)'? – and then foretells that they will yet abandon him.[795] This suggests that even at this late hour in Jesus's ministry the differential between Jesus's disciples and the Jews did not lay in the faith of the one and the unbelief of the other but only in the disciples' election by the Father and the Son. And given that the hindrance to their faith was an angelic figure who would soon be deposed, one might ask whether that process of divine choice, too, was not conceived as a temporary measure, to muster disciples during a *heilsgeschichtlich* phase in which no human could come to Jesus by believing. Put

---

791. John 8:43-44 (cf. 8:47).
792. John 12:40/Isa 6:10; and see the section *[2] Diabolical activity* in Chapter 2.
793. See note 333.
794. See note 455.
795. John 16:29-33 (quotations vv. 30-31).

another way, is it possible that the Father's 'drawing' and the Son's 'choosing' were not envisioned by the evangelist as part of a timeless *ordo salutis*, but that they instead represent a stopgap measure, necessary to inaugurate a 'church' when 'the ruler of this world' marred human capacity to believe?

d. Ecclesiology and pneumatology
The final two corollaries from this *chiasmus* lie within ecclesiology and pneumatology – respectively, the royal identity and illumined perception of those who believe. The first, royal identity, follows from the regal aspects of the inner, 'remembrance' *inclusio*. More precisely, its connotation of Jesus entering Jerusalem as 'king of Israel' and 'king of Judah', as well as its forecast of Jesus 'making rooms' for his disciples in the 'Father's house' of a new (dynastic) sanctuary 'in spirit and truth', suggests that the collective of those who believe are at once (a) the subjects of a reunited monarchy and (b) the emblem of the new imperial era launched by that monarchy. Moreover, Jesus's entrance into Jerusalem is immediately followed by the request for an audience by the Greeks[796]; and, if the symbolism of the entry continues, this may intimate that with his death and resurrection, Jesus's restoration of *Nordreich* and *Südreich* is to be augmented with the prophetic fulfilment of the nations joining this re-established kingdom in worshipping the Lord.[797] This, in turn, would signify the identity of Gentiles among Johannine believers, once the Jewish core of that group had expanded to embrace them.

The last corollary (on pneumatology) emerges when the royal ecclesial identity of the inner *inclusio* is blended with the '*geistgewirkte Erinnern*' of its 'remembrance' formulae; and it casts post-resurrection Johannine believers as the diametric converse to the Jews at large in the Book of Signs. Where the latter were 'blinded' and 'deafened' by 'the ruler of this world' to the message and signs of Jesus's public ministry, the former are 'taught' and 'reminded' by the Holy Spirit of the regal dynamic tacitly at work in that ministry.[798]

In sum, the theology embedded within the *chiasmus* of these quotations suggests that in John (a) Jesus's death is as crucial to his purpose as is his incarnation (christology); that (b) this death removes the perceptual impairment to humanity caused by the devil (soteriology); that (c) this removal, in turn, changes the soteriological landscape so as to reconfigure the medium for conveying signs, free the Jews/world from the devil's thrall and shed the need for election (eschatology); and that the collective of believers created by this changed landscape is (d) part and emblem of a modulated form of the united monarchy (ecclesiology), as well as (e) privy to the deeper import of Jesus's public ministry (pneumatology).

---

796. John 12:20-26.
797. E.g., Zech 14:16-19.
798. John 14:25-26.

C. Epilogue

The study of biblical quotations in John was launched in the third section of Franke's *Das alte Testament bei Johannes*, where he completed his project with 'an examination of the significance which the Old Testament text has for the Johannine account'.[799] In the near century-and-a-half that has passed since, Franke's task has been taken up repeatedly with exegetical and theological rigour, and alongside the writing of this book it is being given new life yet again from other approaches abounding with fresh vantage points. It is hoped that this work might have gleaned some vestiges of insight still available through (what are now considered) more traditional methods, and it is anticipated that much more remains to be harvested from colleagues working with newly minted sets of questions.

---

799. *Das alte Testament bei Johannes*, 255.

APPENDICES

Appendix I References regarded as quotations in the Fourth Gospel[800]

Reference	Franke (1885)	Braun (1964)	Freed (1965)	Reim (1974/95)	Schuchard (1992)	Menken (1996)	Obermann (1996)	Clark-Soles (2003)	Sheridan (2012)*
John 1:23	√	√	√	√	√	√	√	√	√
John 1:45		√							
John 2:17	√	√	√	√	√	√	√	√	√
John 6:31	√	√	√	√	√	√	√	√	√
John 6:45	√	√	√	√	√	√	√	√	√
John 7:38	√	√	√	√		√		√	√
John 7:42	√	√	√	√		√			
John 8:17	√	√		√		√		√	
John 10:34	√	√	√	√	√	√	√	√	√
John 12:13		√	√				√	√	
John 12:15	√	√	√	√	√	√	√	√	√
John 12:34	√			√		√			
John 12:38	√	√	√	√	√	√	√	√	
John 12:40	√	√	√	√	√	√	√	√	
John 12:41								√	
John 13:18	√	√	√	√	√	√	√	√	
John 15:25	√	√	√	√	√	√	√	√	
John 17:12	√	√	√	√				√	
John 19:24	√	√	√	√	√	√	√	√	
John 19:28	√	√	√	√				√	
John 19:36	√	√	√	√	√	√	√	√	
John 19:37	√	√	√	√	√	√	√	√	
John 20:9	√								

* Only John 1:23–12:15
Notes:
Total proposed quotations: 23
Total accepted by all specialists (allowing that Sheridan only treats quotations up to John 12:15): 13 (56.5 per cent)

800. The exegetes surveyed for this chart are those listed in footnotes 2 and 3, omitting Kubiś (whose interest is restricted to quotations of Zechariah) and adding Braun, *Les grandes traditions d'Israël et l'accord des Écritures selon le Quatrième Évangile*, 3–21. Braun's work is not regarded here as one of the major treatments of the issue but is included, nevertheless, because it is cited by Kubiś on the matter of the precise number and *loci* of citations in the Fourth Gospel; *Book of Zechariah in the Gospel of John*, 14n8.

Appendix II Quotations and sacred books[801]

	Torah	Prophets	Writings	Apocrypha/Pseudepigrapha
John 1:23		Isa 40:3		
John 1:45	All messianic passages in the Law & Prophets	All messianic passages in the Law & Prophets		
John 2:17			Ps 69:10	
John 6:31	Exod 16:4 (?), 15 (?)		Ps 78:24 (?); Neh 9:15/ 2 Esd 19:15 (?)	
John 6:45		Isa 54:13		
John 7:38	???	???	???	???
John 7:42		Micah 5:1 (?)		
John 8:17	Deut 17:6 (?); 19:15			
John 10:34			Ps 82:6	
John 12:13			Ps 118:25-26	
John 12:15		Zech 9:9		
John 12:34		2 Sam 7:16 (?); Ezek 37:25 (?)	Ps 89:37 (?)	
John 12:38		Isa 53:1		
John 12:40		Isa 6:10		
John 12:41		Isa 6:1-13		
John 13:18			Ps 41:10	
John 15:25			Pss 35:19 (?); 69:5 (?)	Pss. Sol. 7:1 (?)
John 17:12		LXX Isa 57:4 (?)	Ps 41:10 at John 13:18 (?); LXX Prov 24:22a (?)	
John 19:24			Ps 22:19	
John 19:28			Pss 42:3 (?); 63:2 (?); 69:22 (?)	
John 19:36	Exod 12:10 (?), 46 (?); Num 9:12 (?)		Ps 34:21 (?)	
John 19:37		Zech 12:10		
John 20:9	???	???	???	???

801. This allocation more or less aligns with that of Martin Hengel, who adds John 1:1/Gen 1:1; John 1:51/Gen 28:12; John 3:14/Num 21:8; and John 4:5/Gen 48:22 (cf. also Gen 33:19; Josh 24:32) and remarks that 'their distribution corresponds to the demonstrated preference in early Christianity'; 'The Old Testament in the Fourth Gospel', 31–32, 40nn42-45 (quotation p. 32); Hengel, 'Die Schriftauslegung des 4. Evangeliums auf dem Hintergrund der urchristlichen Exegese', 275–76.

This second appendix primarily gives the single base text cited for each *locus*, even if that text may have been merged with other passages in the Johannine rendering. When a base text is elusive, however, and the plausible options are circumscribed to a few, those options are given, followed by a question mark in parentheses (?). Also followed by that mark is Micah 5:1 (?) for John 7:42, since, among the myriad passages in which that reference may consist,[802] this verse is quite likely one of them.

---

802. See note 19.

BIBLIOGRAPHY

I. Commentaries

Barrett, C.K. *The Gospel according to St. John*. 2nd ed. Philadelphia: Westminster Press, 1978.
Becker, Jürgen. *Das Evangelium nach Johannes*. 2 vols. 3rd ed. ÖTK 4/1-2 = Gütersloher Taschenbücher Siebenstern 505–506. Gütersloh: Gerd Mohn, 1991.
Bernard, J.H. *A Critical and Exegetical Commentary on the Gospel according to St. John*. 2 vols. ICC. Edinburgh: T&T Clark, 1928.
Boismard, Marie-Émile and Arnaud Lamouille. *L'Évangile de Jean*. Vol. 3 of *Synopse des quatre évangiles en français*. Paris: Éditions du Cerf, 1977.
Brown, Raymond E. *The Gospel according to John*. 2 vols. AB 29-29A. Garden City, NY: Doubleday, 1966/1970.
Bruce, F.F. *The Gospel of John: Introduction, Exposition, and Notes*. Grand Rapids, MI: William B. Eerdmans, 1983.
Bultmann, Rudolf. *The Gospel of John: A Commentary*. Translated by G.R. Beasley-Murray, R.W.N. Hoare and J.K. Riches. Philadelphia: Westminster, 1971. Translation of *Das Evangelium des Johannes: Ergänzungsheft*. KEK 2. Göttingen: Vandenhoeck & Ruprecht, 1964.
Haenchen, Ernst. *John 1-2*. Edited and translated by Robert W. Funk. 2 vols. Hermeneia. Philadelphia: Fortress, 1984.
Hoskyns, Edwyn Clement. *The Fourth Gospel*. Edited by Francis Noel Davey. 2nd ed. London: Faber & Faber, Ltd, 1947.
Keener, Craig S. *The Gospel of John: A Commentary*. 2 vols. Peabody, MA: Hendrickson, 2003.
Kysar, Robert. *John*. ACNT. Minneapolis, MN: Augsburg, 1986.
Lightfoot, R.H. *St. John's Gospel: A Commentary*. Edited by C.F. Evans. Oxford: Clarendon Press, 1956.
Lindars, Barnabas. *The Gospel of John*. NCB. Greenwood, SC: Attic Press, Inc., 1972.
Loisy, Alfred Firmin. *Le Quatrième Évangile, Les Épitres dites de Jean*. 2nd ed. Paris: Émile Nourry, 1921.
Morris, Leon. *The Gospel according to John: The English Text with Introduction, Exposition and Notes*. Rev. ed. NICNT. Grand Rapids, MI: William. B. Eerdmans, 1995.
Schnackenburg, Rudolf. *The Gospel according to St John*. Translated by Kevin Smyth, Cecily Hastings, Francis McDonagh, David Smith, Richard Foley, s.j. and G.A. Kon. 3 vols. New York: Crossroad, 1990. Translation of *Das Johannesevangelium*. HThKNT 4. Freiburg: Herder, 1965–75.
von Wahlde, Urban C. *The Gospel and Letters of John*. 3 vols. ECC. Grand Rapids, MI: William B. Eerdmans, 2010.
Wellhausen, Julius. *Das Evangelium Johannis*. Berlin: G. Reimer, 1908.
Westcott, B.F. *The Gospel according to St. John: The Authorized Version with Introduction and Notes*. 1882. Repr., Grand Rapids, MI: William. B. Eerdmans, 1981.

II. Monographs and articles

Abbott, Edwin A. *Johannine Grammar*. London: Adam and Charles Black, 1906.
Abegg, Martin G., Jr., ed. *The Dead Sea Scrolls Concordance. Volume One: The Non-Biblical Texts from Qumran*. 2 vols. Leiden/Boston: E.J. Brill, 2003.
Abegg, Martin G., Jr., ed. *The Dead Sea Scrolls Concordance. Volume Three: The Biblical Texts from the Judaean Desert*. 2 vols. Leiden/Boston: E.J. Brill, 2010.
Achtemeier, Paul J. 'Omne Verbum Sonat: The New Testament and the Oral Environment of Late Western Antiquity'. *JBL* 109 (1990): 3–27.
Aland, Barbara, Kurt Aland, Johannes Karavidopoulos, Carlo M. Martini and Bruce M. Metzger, eds. *Novum Testamentum Graece*. 28th rev. ed. Stuttgart: Deutsche Bibelgesellschaft, 2012.
Albl, Martin C. *And Scripture Cannot Be Broken: The Form and Function of the Early Christian Testimonia Collections*. NovTSup 96. Leiden: E.J. Brill, 1999.
Alexander, Philip S. and Geza Vermes, eds. '4Q256. 4QSerekh ha-Yaḥad^b'. Pages 39–64 in *Qumran Cave 4. XIX: Serekh Ha-Yahad and Two Related Texts*. DJD 26. Oxford: Clarendon Press, 1998.
Alexander, Philip S. and Geza Vermes, eds. '4Q258. 4QSerekh ha-Yaḥad^d'. Pages 83–128 in *Qumran Cave 4. XIX: Serekh Ha-Yahad and Two Related Texts*. DJD 26. Oxford: Clarendon Press, 1998.
Alexander, Philip S. and Geza Vermes, eds. '4Q259. 4QSerekh ha-Yaḥad^e'. Pages 129–52 in *Qumran Cave 4. XIX: Serekh Ha-Yahad and Two Related Texts*. DJD 26. Oxford: Clarendon Press, 1998.
Allegro, John M., ed. '176. Tanḥûmîm'. Pages 60–67 in *Qumrân Cave 4. I (4Q158–4Q186)*. DJD 5. Oxford: Clarendon Press, 1968.
Anderson, Paul N. *The Fourth Gospel and the Quest for Jesus: Modern Foundations Reconsidered*. LNTS 321/Library of Historical Jesus Studies. London: T&T Clark, 2006.
Anderson, Paul N. *The Riddles of the Fourth Gospel: An Introduction to John*. Minneapolis, MN: Fortress, 2011.
Annese, Andrea. 'The Temple in the *Gospel of Thomas*: An Interpretive Perspective on Some Words Attributed to Jesus'. Pages 227–45 in *Texts, Practices, and Groups: Multidisciplinary Approaches to the History of Jesus' Followers in the First Two Centuries. First Annual Meeting of Bertinoro (2–5 October 2014)*. Edited by Adriana Destro and Mauro Pesce. Judaïsme ancien et origines du christianisme. Turnhout, Belgium: Brepols, 2017.
Ashton, John. *Understanding the Fourth Gospel*. 2nd ed. Oxford: Oxford University Press, 2007.
Baillet, Maurice, ed. '4Q504 Paroles des Luminaires (i) (Pl. XLIX-LIII)'. Pages 137–68 in *Qumrân Grotte 4: III (4Q482–4Q520)*. DJD 7. Oxford: Clarendon Press, 1982.
Barrett, C.K. 'The Old Testament in the Fourth Gospel'. *JTS* 48 (1947): 155–69.
Barthélemy, Dominique. 'Le grand rouleau d'Isaïe trouvé près de la Mer Morte'. *RB* 57 (1950): 530–49.
Barthélemy, Dominique. *Les devanciers d'Aquila: première publication intégrale du texte des fragments du Dodécaprophéton trouvés dans le désert de Juda, précédée d'une étude sur les traductions et recensions grecques de la Bible réalisées au premier siècle de notre ère sous l'influence du rabbinat palestinien*. VTSup 10. Leiden: E.J. Brill, 1963.
Bauckham, Richard. *Gospel of Glory: Major Themes in Johannine Theology*. Grand Rapids, MI: Baker Academic, 2015.

Bauer, Walter. 'The "Colt" of Palm Sunday'. *JBL* 72 (1953): 220–29.
Bauer, Walter, William F. Arndt, F. Wilbur Gingrich and Frederick W. Danker, eds. *A Greek-English Lexicon of the New Testament and Other Early Christian Literature*. 2nd ed. Chicago: University of Chicago Press, 1979.
Beutler, Johannes. 'Psalm 42/43 im Johannesevangelium'. *NTS* 25 (1978–79): 33–57.
Blank, Josef. *Krisis: Untersuchungen zur johanneischen Christologie und Eschatologie*. Freiburg im Breisgau : Lambertus-Verlag, 1964.
Blenkinsopp, Joseph. 'The Oracle of Judah and the Messianic Entry'. *JBL* 80 (1961): 55–64.
Böhl, Eduard. *Die alttestamentlichen Citate im Neuen Testament*. Wien: W. Braumüller, 1878.
Boismard, Marie-Émile. *Moses or Jesus: An Essay in Johannine Christology*. Translated by B.T. Viviano. Minneapolis, MN: Fortress Press/Leuven: Peeters Press, 1993. Translation of *Moïse ou Jésus: Essai de christologie johannique*. BETL 84. Leuven: Uitgeverij Peeters and Leuven University Press, 1988.
Boyer, Chrystian. *Jésus contre le temple? Analyse historico-critique des textes*. Héritage et Projet 68. Saint-Laurent, Québec: Éditions Fides, 2005.
Braun, François-Marie. *Les grandes traditions d'Israël et l'accord des Écritures selon le Quatrième Évangile*. Vol. 2 of *Jean le théologien*. EBib. Paris: J. Gabalda et Cie, 1964.
Brooke, George J. 'Isaiah 40:3 and the Wilderness Community'. Pages 117–32 in *New Qumran Texts and Studies: Proceedings of the First Meeting of the International Organization for Qumran Studies, Paris 1992*. Edited by George J. Brooke and Florentino García Martínez. STDJ 15. Leiden: E.J. Brill, 1994.
Brooke, George J. 'The Place of Prophecy in Coming Out of Exile: The Case of the Dead Sea Scrolls'. Pages 535–50 in *Scripture in Transition: Essays on Septuagint, Hebrew Bible, and Dead Sea Scrolls in Honour of Raija Sollamo*. Edited by Anssi Voitila and Jutta Jokiranta. Supplements to the Journal for the Study of Judaism 126. Leiden: E.J. Brill, 2008.
Brown, Francis, S.R. Driver and Charles A. Briggs, eds. *Brown-Driver-Briggs Hebrew and English Lexicon*. N.p.: Snowball Publishing, 2010.
Bryan, Steven M. 'Consumed by Zeal: John's Use of Psalm 69:9 and the Action in the Temple'. *BBR* 21 (2011): 479–94.
Bullinger, E.W. *Figures of Speech Used in the Bible Explained and Illustrated*. 1898. Repr., Grand Rapids, MI: Baker Book House, 1968.
Bultmann, Rudolf. *Theology of the New Testament*. Translated by Kendrick Grobel. New York: Charles Scribner's Sons, 1951/1955. Translation of *Theologie des Neuen Testaments*. Neue theologische Grundrisse. Tübingen: J.C.B. Mohr (Paul Siebeck), 1951/1955.
Burge, Gary M. *The Anointed Community: The Holy Spirit in the Johannine Tradition*. Grand Rapids, MI: William B. Eerdmans, 1987.
Burkitt, F.C. 'W and Θ: Studies in the Western Text of St Mark'. *JTS* 17 (1916): 139–52.
Burney, C.F. *The Aramaic Origin of the Fourth Gospel*. Oxford: Clarendon Press, 1922.
Burrows, Millar, ed., with John C. Trevor and William H. Brownlee. *The Dead Sea Scrolls of St. Mark's Monastery*. 2 vols. New Haven, CT: American Schools of Oriental Research, 1950–51.
Bynum, William Randolph. *The Fourth Gospel and the Scriptures: Illuminating the Form and Meaning of Scriptural Citation in John 19:37*. NovTSup 144. Leiden: E.J. Brill, 2012.
Charles, R.H. *The Greek Versions of the Testaments of the Twelve Patriarchs*. Oxford: Clarendon Press, 1908.

Charlesworth, James H. 'Intertextuality: Isaiah 40:3 and the Serek Ha-Yaḥad'. Pages 197–224 in *The Quest for Context and Meaning: Studies in Biblical Intertextuality in Honor of James A. Sanders*. Edited by Craig A. Evans and Shemaryahu Talmon. BibInt 28. Leiden: E.J. Brill, 1997.

Charlesworth, James H. with Henry W.L. Rietz, eds., *The Rule of the Community and Related Documents*. Vol. 1 of *The Dead Sea Scrolls: Hebrew, Aramaic, and Greek Texts with the English Translations*. PTSDSSP 1. Tübingen: J.C.B. Mohr (Paul Siebeck)/Louisville: Westminster John Knox, 1994.

Chazon, Esther G. 'Is *Divrei ha-Me'orot* a Sectarian Prayer'? Pages 3–17 in *The Dead Sea Scrolls: Forty Years of Research*. Edited by Devorah Dimant and Uriel Rappaport. STJD 10. Leiden: E.J. Brill/Jerusalem: Magnes Press/Hebrew University: Yad Izhak Ben-Zvi, 1992.

Cheyne, T.K. 'Hosanna'. Vol. 2 pages 2117–19 in *Encyclopaedia Biblica: A Critical Dictionary of the Literary, Political and Religious History, the Archaeology, Geography and Natural History of the Bible*. Edited by T.K. Cheyne and J. Sutherland Black. 4 vols. New York: Macmillan, 1899–1903.

Clark-Soles, Jaime. *Scripture Cannot Be Broken: The Social Function of the Use of Scripture in the Fourth Gospel*. Leiden: E.J. Brill, 2003.

Clarke, E.G. *Targum Pseudo-Jonathan of the Pentateuch: Text and Concordance*. Hoboken, NJ: Ktav Pub. House, 1984.

Coloe, Mary L. *God Dwells with Us: Temple Symbolism in the Fourth Gospel*. Collegeville, MN: Liturgical Press, 2001.

Colwell, Ernest. *The Greek of the Fourth Gospel: A Study of its Aramaisms in the Light of Hellenistic Greek*. Chicago: Chicago University Press, 1931.

Culpepper, R. Alan. 'John 2:20, "Forty-Six Years": Revisiting J.A.T. Robinson's Chronology of Jesus' Ministry'. Pages 142–54, 293–96 in *Jesus Research: The Gospel of John in Historical Inquiry*. Edited by James H. Charlesworth and Jolyon G.R. Pruszinski. Jewish and Christian Texts. London: T&T Clark Ltd, 2019.

Curtis, Adrian. *Oxford Bible Atlas*. 4th ed. Oxford: Oxford University Press, 2007.

Daise, Michael A. 'Destroying and Rebuilding the Temple: Light from Flavius Josephus'. Paper presented to the Historical Jesus section of the 3rd Annual Meeting on Christian Origins, Centro Italiano di Studi Superiori sulle Religioni. Centro Residenziale Universitario di Bertinoro, 29 September–1 October 2016.

Daise, Michael A. 'Jesus and the Historical Implications of John's Temple Cleansing'. Pages 203–22, 311–19 in *Jesus Research: The Gospel of John in Historical Inquiry*. Edited by James H. Charlesworth and Jolyon G.R. Pruszinski. Jewish and Christian Texts. London: T&T Clark Ltd, 2019.

Daise, Michael A. 'Jesus and the Jewish Festivals: Methodological Reflections'. Pages 283–304 in *Jesus Research: New Methodologies and Perceptions. The Second Princeton-Prague Symposium on Jesus Research, Princeton 2007*. Edited by James H. Charlesworth with Brian Rhea. Princeton-Prague Symposia Series on the Historical Jesus 2. Grand Rapids, MI: William B. Eerdmans, 2014.

Daise, Michael A. 'Quotations in John and the Judaean Desert Texts'. Paper presented to the Johannine Literature section of the Society of Biblical Literature, International Meeting, University of St. Andrews. St. Andrews, Scotland, 7–11 July 2013.

Daise, Michael A. 'Quotations with "Remembrance" Formulae in the Fourth Gospel'. Pages 75–91 in *Abiding Words: The Use of Scripture in the Gospel of John*. Edited by Alicia D. Myers and Bruce G. Schuchard. RBS 81. Atlanta, GA: SBL Press, 2015.

Daise, Michael A. 'Ritual Transference and Johannine Identity'. *Annali di storia dell'esegesi* 27 (2010): 45–52.

de Lagarde, Paulus, ed. *Hagiographa Chaldaice*. Leipzig: B.G. Teubner, 1873.
de Mérode, Marie. 'L'accueil triomphal de Jésus selon Jean, 11-12'. *RTL* 13 (1982): 49-62.
de Waard, Jan. *A Comparative Study of the Old Testament in the Dead Sea Scrolls and in the New Testament*. STDJ 4. Leiden: E.J. Brill, 1965.
Dimant, Devorah. 'Non pas l'exil au désert mais l'exil spirituel: l'interprétation d'Isaïe 40,3 dans la *Règle de la Communauté*'. Pages 21-36 in *Qoumrân et le Judaïsme du tournant de notre ère: Actes de la Table ronde, Collège de France, 16 novembre, 2004*. Edited by André Lemaire and Simon C. Mimouni. Collection de la REJ 39. Paris: Peeters, 2006. First publ. in *Meghillot: Studies in the Dead Sea Scrolls* 2 (2004): 21-36.
Dimant, Devorah. 'The Qumran Manuscripts: Contents and Significance'. Pages 37-58 in *Time to Prepare the Way in the Wilderness: Papers on the Qumran Scrolls*. Edited by Devorah Dimant and Lawrence H. Schiffman. STDJ 16. Leiden: E.J. Brill, 1995.
Dodd, C.H. *Historical Tradition in the Fourth Gospel*. Cambridge: Cambridge University Press, 1963.
Dodd, C.H. *The Interpretation of the Fourth Gospel*. Cambridge: Cambridge University Press, 1953.
Ehrman, Bart D. and Zlatko Pleše. *The Apocryphal Gospels: Texts and Translations*. Oxford: Oxford University Press, 2011.
Elliger, Karl and Wilhelm Rudolph, eds. *Torah, Nevi'im uKethuvim: Biblia Hebraica Stuttgartensia*. Stuttgart: Deutsche Bibelgesellschaft, 1977.
Elliger, Karl and Wilhelm Rudolph, eds. *Torah, Nevi'im uKethuvim: Biblia Hebraica Stuttgartensia*. 2nd rev. ed. Stuttgart: Deutsche Bibelgesellschaft, 1983.
Evans, Craig A. 'From Prophecy to Testament: An Introduction'. Pages 1-22 in *From Prophecy to Testament: The Function of the Old Testament in the New*. Edited by Craig A. Evans. Peabody, MA: Hendrickson, 2004.
Evans, Craig A. 'The Function of Isaiah 6:9-10 in Mark and John'. *NovT* 24 (1982): 124-38.
Evans, Craig A. ''On the Quotation Formulas in the Fourth Gospel'. *BZ* 26 (1982): 79-83.
Evans, Craig A. *To See and Not Perceive: Isaiah 6.9-10 in Early Jewish and Christian Interpretation*. JSOTSup 64. Sheffield: Sheffield Academic, 1989.
Farmer, W.R. 'The Palm Branches in John 12,13'. *JTS*^{NS} 3 (1952): 62-66.
Feuillet, André. *Johannine Studies*. Translated by Thomas E. Crane. Staten Island, NY: Alba House, 1965.
Floyd, Michael H. 'Welcome Back, Daughter of Zion!'. *CBQ* 70 (2008): 484-504.
Fortna, Robert T. *The Fourth Gospel and Its Predecessor: From Narrative Source to Present Gospel*. Philadelphia: Fortress, 1988.
Fortna, Robert T. *The Gospel of Signs: A Reconstruction of the Narrative Source Underlying the Fourth Gospel*. SNTSMS 11. Cambridge: Cambridge University Press, 1970.
Franke, August H. *Das alte Testament bei Johannes: Ein Beitrag zur Erklärung und Beurtheilung der johanneischen Schriften*. Göttingen: Vandenhoeck & Ruprecht's Verlag, 1885.
Freed, Edwin D. 'Jn 1,19-27 in Light of Related Passages in John, the Synoptics, and Acts'. Vol. 3 pages 1943-61 in *The Four Gospels 1992. Festschrift Frans Neirynck*. Edited by F. van Segbroek. 3 vols. BETL 100. Leuven: Leuven University-Peeters, 1992.
Freed, Edwin D. 'The Entry into Jerusalem in the Gospel of John'. *JBL* 80 (1961): 329-38.
Freed, Edwin D. *Old Testament Quotations in the Gospel of John*. NovTSup 11. Leiden: E.J. Brill, 1965.
Fuller, Russell E. '4QXIIe (Pl. XLVII)'. Pages 257-65 in *Qumran Cave 4: X, The Prophets*. DJD 15. Oxford: Clarendon Press, 1997.

Goodacre, Mark. *Thomas and the Gospels: The Case for Thomas's Familiarity with the Synoptics*. Grand Rapids, MI: William B. Eerdmans, 2012.

Goodwin, Charles. 'How Did John Treat His Sources?' *JBL* 73 (1954): 61–75.

Gundry, Robert H. '"In My Father's House Are Many Μοναί" (John 14:2)'. *ZNW* 58 (1967): 68–72.

Hanhart, Robert. Introduction to *The Septuagint as Christian Scripture: Its Prehistory and the Problem of Its Canon*, by Martin Hengel. Translated by Mark E. Biddle. OTS. Edinburgh: T&T Clark, 2002.

Harris, J. Rendel. *Testimonies*. 2 vols. Cambridge: Cambridge University Press, 1916–1920.

Heekerens, Hans-Peter. *Die Zeichen-Quelle der johanneischen Redaktion: Ein Beitrag zur Entstehungsgeschichte des vierten Evangeliums*. SBS 113. Stuttgart: Katholisches Bibelwerk, 1984.

Hengel, Martin. 'Die Schriftauslegung des 4. Evangeliums auf dem Hintergrund der urchristlichen Exegese'. Pages 249–88 in *'Gesetz' als Thema biblischer Theologie*. Edited by I. Baldermann, E. Dassmann, O. Fuchs, B. Hamm, O. Hofius, B. Janowski, N. Lohfink, H. Merklein, W.H. Schmidt, G. Stemberger, P. Stuhlmacher, M. Welker and R. Weth. Jahrbuch für Biblische Theologie 4. Neukirchen-Vluyn: Neukirchener Verlag, 1989.

Hengel, Martin. 'The Old Testament in the Fourth Gospel'. *HBT* 12 (1990): 19–41.

Hollenbach, Bruce, 'Lest They Should Turn and Be Forgiven: Irony'. *BT* 34 (1983): 312–21.

Holmes, Michael W., ed. and trans. *The Apostolic Fathers: Greek Texts and English Translations*. 3rd ed. Grand Rapids, MI: Baker Academic, 2007.

Howard, W.F. *The Fourth Gospel in Recent Criticism and Interpretation*. Edited by C.K. Barrett. 4th ed. London: Epworth, 1955.

Humann, Roger J. 'The Function and Form of the Explicit Old Testament Quotations in the Gospel of John'. *Lutheran Theological Review* 1 (1988–89): 31–54.

Jauhiainen, Marko. *The Use of Zechariah in Revelation*. WUNT 2/199. Tübingen: Mohr Siebeck, 2005.

Josephus. Translated by Henry St. John Thackeray, Ralph Marcus, Allen Wikgren and Louis H. Feldman. 13 vols. LCL. London: W. Heinemann/New York: Putnam, 1926–65.

Käsemann, Ernst. *The Testament of Jesus: A Study of the Gospel of John in Light of Chapter 17*. Translated by Gerhard Krodel. Philadelphia: Fortress Press, 1968. Translation of *Jesu letzter Wille nach Johannes 17*. 2nd ed. Tübingen: Mohr (Siebeck), 1966.

Klein, Michael L. *The Fragment-Targums of the Pentateuch: According to Their Extant Sources*. 2 vols. AnBib 76. Rome: Biblical Institute Press, 1980.

Köstenberger, Andreas J. *A Theology of John's Gospel and Letters*. Biblical Theology of the New Testament. Grand Rapids, MI: Zondervan, 2009.

Kubiś, Adam. *The Book of Zechariah in the Gospel of John*. EBib, New series 64. Pendé, France: J. Gabalda et Cie, 2012.

Kühschelm, Roman. *Verstockung, Gericht und Heil: Exegetische und bibeltheologische Untersuchung zum sogenannten 'Dualismus' und 'Determinismus' in Joh 12, 35-50*. BBB 76/Athenäum Monographien: Theologie. Frankfurt am Main: Anton Hain, 1990.

Lake, Kirsopp. *Codex 1 of the Gospels and Its Allies*. Vol. 7/3 of *Texts and Studies: Contributions to Biblical and Patristic Literature*. Edited by J. Armitage Robinson. Cambridge: Cambridge University Press, 1902.

Lappenga, Benjamin J. 'Whose Zeal Is It Anyway? The Citation of Psalm 69:9 in John 2:17'. Pages 141–59 in *Abiding Words: The Use of Scripture in the Gospel of John*. Edited by Alicia D. Myers and Bruce G. Schuchard. RBS 81. Atlanta, GA: SBL Press, 2015.

Levenson, Jon D. 'Zion Traditions'. *ABD* 6: 1098–1102.
Lieu, Judith M. 'Blindness in the Johannine Tradition'. *NTS* 34 (1988): 83–95.
Lim, Timothy H. *The Formation of the Jewish Canon*. Anchor Yale Bible Reference Library. New Haven: Yale University Press, 2013.
Lohse, Eduard. 'Hosianna'. *NovT* 6 (1963): 113–19.
Martone, Corrado. 'Creative Reception: The Bible and Its Interpretations at Qumran'. Paper presented at 'The Reception of Jewish Scripture in Early Judaism and Christianity'. Università degli Studi di Napoli 'L'Orientale', Naples, 12–15 June 2017.
Martone, Corrado. 'Sectarian Variant Readings and Sectarian Texts in the Qumran Corpus and Beyond: Reflections on an Elusive Concept'. Pages 393–400 in *Ricercare la sapienza di tutti gli antichi (Sir. 39,1): Miscellanea in onore di Gian Luigi Prato*. Edited by Marcello Milani and Marco Zappella. Supplementi alla Rivista biblica 56. Bologna: Edizioni Dehoniane Bologna, 2013.
May, Herbert G. *Oxford Bible Atlas*. 2nd ed. London: Oxford University Press, 1974.
Mayoral, José Antonio. 'Chiasmus'. Page 89 in *Encyclopedia of Rhetoric*. Edited by Thomas O. Sloane. Oxford: Oxford University Press, 2001.
McCaffrey, James. *The House with Many Rooms: The Temple Theme of John 14, 2–3*. AnBib 114. Roma: Editrice Pontificio Istituto Biblico, 1988.
Menken, Maarten J.J. '"And They Shall All Be Taught by God" (John 6:45)'. Pages 67–77 in *Old Testament Quotations in the Fourth Gospel: Studies in Textual Form*. Edited by Maarten J.J. Menken. CBET 15. Kampen: Kok Pharos Publishing House, 1996. First publ. in *ETL* 64 (1988): 164–72.
Menken, Maarten J.J. '"Do Not Fear, Daughter Zion…" (John 12:15)'. Pages 79–97 in *Old Testament Quotations in the Fourth Gospel: Studies in Textual Form*. Edited by Maarten J.J. Menken. CBET 15. Kampen: Kok Pharos Publishing House, 1996. First publ. in *ZNW* 80 (1989): 193–209.
Menken, Maarten J.J. '"He Has Blinded Their Eyes…" (John 12:40)'. Pages 99–122 in *Old Testament Quotations in the Fourth Gospel: Studies in Textual Form*. Edited by Maarten J.J. Menken. CBET 15. Kampen: Kok Pharos Publishing House, 1996. First publ. in *JSNT* 40 (1990): 61–79.
Menken, Maarten J.J. '"He Who Eats My Bread, Has Raised His Heel against Me" (John 13:18)'. Pages 123–38 in *Old Testament Quotations in the Fourth Gospel: Studies in Textual Form*. Edited by Maarten J.J. Menken. CBET 15. Kampen: Kok Pharos Publishing House, 1996. First publ. in *JSNT* 40 (1990): 61–79.
Menken, Maarten J.J. '"I Am the Voice of One Crying in the Wilderness…" (John 1:23)'. Pages 21–35 in *Old Testament Quotations in the Fourth Gospel: Studies in Textual Form*. Edited by Maarten J.J. Menken. CBET 15. Kampen: Kok Pharos Publishing House, 1996. First publ. in *Bib* 66 (1985): 190–205.
Menken, Maarten J.J. 'Interpretation of the Old Testament and the Resurrection of Jesus in John's Gospel'. Pages 189–205 in *Resurrection in the New Testament: Festschrift J. Lambrecht*. Edited by R. Bieringer, V. Koperski and B. Lataire. BETL 165. Dudley, MA: Peeters, 2002.
Menken, Maarten J.J. 'Jezus tegenover de Farizeeën in het vierde evangelie: Joh. 8,12-20'. Pages 103–17 in *Jodendom en vroeg christendom: continuïteit en discontinuïteit. Opstellen van leden van de Studiosorum Novi Testamenti Conventus*. Edited by Tjitze Baarda, Henk Jan de Jonge and Maarten J.J. Menken. Kampen: Kok Pharos Publishing House, 1991.
Menken, Maarten J.J. 'The Minor Prophets in John's Gospel'. Pages 79–96 in *The Minor Prophets in the New Testament*. Edited by Steve Moyise and Maarten J.J. Menken. LNTS 377. London: T&T Clark, 2009.

Menken, Maarten J.J. 'Observations on the Significance of the Old Testament in the Fourth Gospel'. *Neot* 33 (1999): 125–43.
Menken, Maarten J.J. *Old Testament Quotations in the Fourth Gospel: Studies in Textual Form*. Edited by Maarten J.J. Menken. CBET 15. Kampen: Kok Pharos Publishing House, 1996.
Menken, Maarten J.J. 'The Quotations from Zech 9,9 in Mt 21,5 and in Jn 12,15'. Pages 571–78 in *John and the Synoptics*. Edited by Adelbert Denaux. BETL 101. Leuven: Leuven University Press, 1992.
Menken, Maarten J.J. '"They Hated Me without Reason" (John 15:25)'. Pages 139–45 in *Old Testament Quotations in the Fourth Gospel: Studies in Textual Form*. Edited by Maarten J.J. Menken. CBET 15. Kampen: Kok Pharos Publishing House, 1996.
Menken, Maarten J.J. '"They Shall Look on Him Whom They Have Pierced" (John 19:37)'. Pages 167–85 in *Old Testament Quotations in the Fourth Gospel: Studies in Textual Form*. Edited by Maarten J.J. Menken. CBET 15. Kampen: Kok Pharos Publishing House, 1996. First publ. in *CBQ* 55 (1993): 494–511.
Menken, Maarten J.J. 'The Use of the Septuagint in Three Quotations in John: Jn 10,34; 12,38; 19,24'. Pages 367–93 in *The Scriptures in the Gospels*. Edited by C.M. Tuckett. BETL 131. Louvain: Leuven University, 1997.
Menken, Maarten J.J. 'Vertaling als interpretatie: Twee citaten uit Jesaja in het vierde evangelie (Joh 12,38,40)'. Pages 35–43 in *Exegeten aan het werk: Vertalen en interpreteren van de bijbel. Opstellen van leden van het Bijbels Werkgenootschap St. Hiëronymus*. Edited by P.H.M. Welzen. Brugge/'s Hertogenbosch/Tabor: Katholieke Bijbelstichting, 1998.
Menken, Maarten J.J. '"Zeal for Your House Will Consume Me" (John 2:17)'. Pages 37–45 in *Old Testament Quotations in the Fourth Gospel: Studies in Textual Form*. Edited by Maarten J.J. Menken. CBET 15. Kampen: Kok Pharos Publishing House, 1996. First publ. pages 157–64 in *Broeder Jehosjoea, opstellen voor Ben Hemelsoet: biij zijn afscheid als hoogleraar in de exegese van het Nieuwe Testament van de Katholieke Theologische Universiteit te Utrecht*. Edited by Dick Akerboom, Jan Engelen, Monique Leygraaf and Dirk Monshouwer. Kampen: Kok Pharos Publishing House, 1994.
Metso, Sarianna. 'The Use of Old Testament Quotations in the Qumran Community Rule'. Pages 217–31 in *Qumran between the Old and New Testaments*. Edited by Frederick H. Cryer and Thomas L. Thompson. JSOTSup 290/Copenhagen International Seminar 6. Sheffield: Sheffield Academic Press, 1998.
Metzger, Bruce M. *A Textual Commentary on the Greek New Testament*. Stuttgart: United Bible Societies, 1971.
Metzger, Bruce M. *A Textual Commentary on the Greek New Testament*. 2nd ed. Stuttgart: Deutsche Bibelgesellschaft/United Bible Societies, 1994.
Miura, Nozomi. 'The Temple Motifs in the Fourth Gospel: Intertextuality and Intratextuality of the Temple Motifs'. *AJBI* 37 (2011):19–59.
Morgan, Richard. 'Fulfillment in the Fourth Gospel: The Old Testament Foundations'. *Int* 11 (1957): 155–65.
Moulton, Harold K. '*Pantas* in John 2:15'. *BT* 18 (1967): 126–27.
Moulton, James H. *Prolegomena*. Vol. 1 of *A Grammar of New Testament Greek*. 3rd ed. Edinburgh: T&T Clark, 1908.
Myers, Alicia D. 'A Voice in the Wilderness: Classical Rhetoric and the Testimony of John (the Baptist) in John 1:19-34'. Pages 119–39 in *Abiding Words: The Use of Scripture in the Gospel of John*. Edited by Alicia D. Myers and Bruce G. Schuchard. RBS 81. Atlanta, GA: SBL Press, 2015.

Myers, Alicia D. 'Abiding Words: An Introduction to Perspectives on John's Use of Scripture'. Pages 1–20 in *Abiding Words: The Use of Scripture in the Gospel of John*. Edited by Alicia D. Myers and Bruce G. Schuchard. RBS 81. Atlanta, GA: SBL Press, 2015.

Neirynck, Frans. 'John and the Synoptics: 1975–1990'. Pages 3–62 in *John and the Synoptics*. Edited by Adelbert Denaux. BETL 101. Leuven: Leuven University Press, 1992.

Noack, Bent. *Zur johanneischen Tradition: Beiträge zur Kritik an der literarkritischen Analyse des vierten Evangeliums*. Det Laerde selskabs skrifter: Teologiske Skrifter 3. København: Rosenkilde Og Bagger, 1954.

Obermann, Andreas. *Die christologische Erfüllung der Schrift im Johannesevangelium: Eine Untersuchung zur johanneischen Hermeneutik anhand der Schriftzitate*. WUNT 2/83. Tübingen: J.C.B. Mohr (Paul Siebeck), 1996.

O'Rourke, John J. 'John's Fulfillment Texts'. *ScEccl* 19 (1967): 433–43.

Painter, John. 'The Quotation of Scripture and Unbelief in John 12.36b-43'. Pages 429–58 in *The Gospels and the Scriptures of Israel*. Edited by Craig A. Evans and W. Richard Stegner. JSNTSup 104/SSEJC 3. Sheffield: Sheffield Academic Press, 1994.

Patrologia graeca. Edited by J.-P. Migne. 162 vols. Paris, 1857–1886.

Peters, Heiner. 'Epanalēpsis'. Pages 250–51 in *Encyclopedia of Rhetoric*. Edited by Thomas O. Sloane. Oxford: Oxford University Press, 2001.

Plett, Heinrich F. 'Figures of Speech'. Pages 309–14 in *Encyclopedia of Rhetoric*. Edited by Thomas O. Sloane. Oxford: Oxford University Press, 2001.

Pope, Marvin H. 'Hosanna'. *ABD* 3: 290–91.

Preuschen, Erwin. *Der Johanneskommentar*. Vol. 4 of *Origenes Werke*. GCS 2. Leipzig. J.C. Hinrichs'sche Buchhandlung, 1903.

Quinn, Arthur and Lyon Rathbun. 'Epanalepsis'. Page 228 in *Encyclopedia of Rhetoric and Composition: Communication from Ancient Times to the Information Age*. Edited by Theresa Enos. New York/London: Garland Publishing, 1996.

Quinn, Arthur and Lyon Rathbun. 'Figures of Speech'. Pages 269–71 in *Encyclopedia of Rhetoric and Composition: Communication from Ancient Times to the Information Age*. Edited by Theresa Enos. New York/London: Garland Publishing, 1996.

Quinn, Arthur, and Lyon Rathbun. 'Inclusio'. Page 346 in *Encyclopedia of Rhetoric and Composition: Communication from Ancient Times to the Information Age*. Edited by Theresa Enos. New York/London: Garland Publishing, 1996.

Rahlfs, Alfred, ed. *Septuaginta: Id est Vetus Testamentum graece iuxta LXX interpretes*. 2nd ed. 2 vols. Stuttgart: Deutsche Bibelgesellschaft, 1979.

Rainbow, Paul A. *Johannine Theology: The Gospel, the Epistles and the Apocalypse*. Downers Grove, IL: IVP Academic, 2014.

Reifferscheid, A. and G. Wissowa, eds. 'Scorpiace'. In *Tertullianus, Opera II: Opera Montanistica*. Edited by A. Gerlo, A. Kroymann, R. Willems, J.H. Waszink, J.G.P. Borleffs, A. Reifferscheid, G. Wissowa, E. Dekkers, J.J. Thierry, E. Evans and A. Harnack. CCSL 2. Turnhout, Belgium: Brepols, 1954.

Reim, Günter. *Jochanan: Erweiterte Studien zum alttestamentlichen Hintergrund des Johannesevangeliums*. Hessdorf-Hannberg: Eigenverlag des Autors/Erlangen: Vertrieb durch den Verlag der Ev.-Luth. Mission, 1995. 1st part is repr. of *Studien zum alttestamentlichen Hintergrund des Johannesevangeliums*. SNTSMS 22. London/New York: Cambridge University Press, 1974.

Reim, Günter. 'Joh 9 – Tradition und zeitgenössische messianische Diskussion'. In *Jochanan: Erweiterte Studien zum alttestamentlichen Hintergrund des Johannesevangeliums*. Hessdorf-Hannberg: Eigenverlag des Autors/Erlangen: Vertrieb durch den Verlag der Ev.-Luth. Mission, 1995. First publ. in *BZ* 22 (1978): 245–53.

Reim, Günter. 'Nordreich-Südreich: Der vierte Evangelist als Vertreter christlicher Nordreichstheologie'. Pages 360–67 in *Jochanan: Erweiterte Studien zum alttestamentlichen Hintergrund des Johannesevangeliums*. Hessdorf-Hannberg: Eigenverlag des Autors/Erlangen: Vertrieb durch den Verlag der Ev.-Luth. Mission, 1995. First publ. in *BZ*^{NF} 36 (1992): 235–40.

Reim, Günter. 'Targum und Johannesevangelium'. Pages 334–47 in *Jochanan: Erweiterte Studien zum alttestamentlichen Hintergrund des Johannesevangeliums*. Hessdorf-Hannberg: Eigenverlag des Autors/Erlangen: Vertrieb durch den Verlag der Ev.-Luth. Mission, 1995. First publ. in *BZ*^{NF} 27 (1983): 1–13.

Rensberger, David. Review of *Scripture within Scripture: The Interrelationship of Form and Function in the Explicit Old Testament Citations in the Gospel of John*, by Bruce G. Schuchard. *JBL* 113 (1994): 344–46.

Richter, Georg. 'Die alttestamentlichen Zitate in der Rede vom Himmelsbrot Joh 6,26-51a'. Pages 199–265 in *Studien zum Johannesevangelium*. Edited by Josef Hainz. Biblische Untersuchungen 13. Regensburg: Verlag Friedrich Pustet, 1977. First publ. pages 193–279 in *Schriftauslegung: Beiträge zur Hermeneutik des Neuen Testamentes und im Neuen Testament*. Edited by Josef Ernst. Paderborn: Verlag Ferdinand Schöningh, 1972.

Ruckstuhl, Eugen. *Die literarische Einheit des Johannesevangeliums: Der gegenwärtige Stand der einschlägigen Forschungen*. NTOA 5. Freiburg, Schweiz: Universitätsverlag/Göttingen: Vandenhoeck & Ruprecht, 1987.

Rytel-Adrianik, Pawel. 'Use of Isaiah in the Fourth Gospel in Comparison to the Synoptics and Other Places in the New Testament'. Ph.D. diss., St. Cross College, University of Oxford, 2013.

Sahlin, Harald. *Zur Typologie des Johannesevangelium*. Uppsala: Lundequistska bokhandeln, 1950.

Schnackenburg, Rudolf. 'Joh 12,39-41. Zur christologischen Schriftauslegung des vierten Evangelisten'. Pages 143–52 in *Ergänzende Auslegungen und Exkurse*. Vol. 4 of *Das Johannesevangelium*. HThKNT 4/4. Freiburg: Herder, 1984. First publ. pages 167–77 in *Neues Testament und Geschichte: Historisches Geschehen und Deutung im Neuen Testament: Oscar Cullmann zum 70. Geburtstag*. Edited by Heinrich Baltensweiler and Bo Reicke. Zürich: Theologischer Verlag/Tübingen: Mohr, 1972.

Schnackenburg, Rudolf. 'Das Schriftzitat in Joh 19,37'. Pages 239–47 in *Ergänzende Auslegungen und Exkurse*. Vol. 4 of *Das Johannesevangelium*. HThKNT 4/4. Freiburg: Herder, 1984. First publ. pages 239–47 in *Wort, Lied und Gottesspruch: Beiträge zu Psalmen und Propheten. Festschrift für Joseph Ziegler*. Edited by Josef Schreiner. FB 2. Würzberg: Echter Verlag, 1972.

Schuchard, Bruce G. *Scripture within Scripture: The Interrelationship of Form and Function in the Explicit Old Testament Citations in the Gospel of John*. SBLDS 133. Atlanta, GA: Scholars Press, 1992.

Schweizer, Eduard. *Ego eimi…: Die religionsgeschichtliche Herkunft und theologische Bedeutung der johanneischen Bildreden, zugleich ein Beitrag zur Quellenfrage des vierten Evangeliums*. FRLANT 56/38^{NF}. Göttingen: Vandenhoeck & Ruprecht, 1939.

Septuaginta: Vetus Testamentum Graecum auctoritate Societatis Litterarum Gottingensis editum. Göttingen: Vandenhoeck & Ruprecht, 1931–(2006).

Sheridan, Ruth. *Retelling Scripture: 'The Jews' and the Scriptural Citations in John 1: 19-12:15*. BibInt 110. Leiden/Boston: E.J. Brill, 2012.

Silva, Moisés. *Biblical Words and Their Meaning: An Introduction to Lexical Semantics*. Rev. ed. Grand Rapids, MI: Zondervan, 1994.
Skehan, Patrick W. and Eugene Ulrich, eds. '4QIsa^f'. Pages 99–111 in *Qumran Cave 4. X: The Prophets*. Edited by Eugene Ulrich, Frank Moore Cross, Russell E. Fuller, Judith E. Sanderson, Patrick W. Skehan and Emanuel Tov. DJD 15. Oxford: Clarendon Press, 1997.
Smith, D. Moody. 'The Setting and Shape of a Johannine Narrative Source'. *JBL* 95 (1976): 231–41.
Smyth, Herbert Weir. *Greek Grammar*. Edited by Gordon M. Messing. Rev. ed. Cambridge, MA: Harvard University Press, 1956.
Sperber, Alexander, ed. *The Hagiographa*. Vol. 4A of *The Bible in Aramaic Based on Old Manuscripts and Printed Texts*. Leiden: E.J. Brill, 1968.
Sperber, Alexander, ed. *The Latter Prophets according to Targum Jonathan*. Vol. 3 of *The Bible in Aramaic Based on Old Manuscripts and Printed Texts*. Leiden: E.J. Brill, 1962.
Sperber, Alexander, ed. *The Pentateuch according to Targum Onkelos*. Vol. 1 of *The Bible in Aramaic Based on Old Manuscripts and Printed Texts*. Leiden: E.J. Brill, 1959.
Spitta, Friedrich. *Das Johannes-Evangelium als Quelle der Geschichte Jesus*. Göttingen: Vandenhoeck & Ruprecht, 1910.
Stegemann, Hartmut with Eileen Schuller, eds. *1QHodayot^a*. DJD 40. Oxford: Clarendon Press, 2009.
Stendahl, Krister. *The School of St. Matthew and Its Use of the Old Testament*. Uppsala universitet: Nytestamentliga seminar, Acta 20. Uppsala: C.W.K. Gleerup, Lund, 1954.
Stinespring, W.F. 'No Daughter of Zion: A Study of the Appositional Genitive in Hebrew Grammar'. *Enc* 26 (1965): 133–41.
Strachan, Robert H. *The Fourth Gospel: Its Significance and Environment*. 3rd ed. London: S.C.M., 1941.
Strack, Hermann L. and Günter Stemberger. *Introduction to the Talmud and Midrash*. Translated and edited by Markus Bockmuehl. 2nd ed. Minneapolis, MN: Fortress Press, 1991. Translation of *Einleitung in Talmud und Midrasch*. 7th ed. München: C.H. Beck'sche Verlagsbuchhandlung (Oscar Beck), 1982.
Strugnell, John. 'Notes en marge du volume V des "Discoveries in the Judaean Desert of Jordan"'. *RevQ* 7 (1970): 163–276.
Sukenik, Eleazar Lipa, ed. *The Dead Sea Scrolls of the Hebrew University*. Jerusalem: Magnes Press, 1955.
Tomson, Peter J. 'The Names Israel and Jew in Ancient Judaism and in the New Testament'. *Bijdr* 47 (1986): 120–40.
Torrey, Charles Cutler. *Documents of the Primitive Church*. New York/London: Harper & Brothers, 1941.
Torrey, Charles Cutler. *The Four Gospels: A New Translation*. 2nd ed. New York: Harper, 1947.
Torrey, Charles Cutler. *Our Translated Gospels: Some of the Evidence*. London/New York: Harper & Brothers, 1936.
Tov, Emanuel. 'Categorized List of the "Biblical Texts"'. Pages 165–83 in *The Texts from the Judaean Desert: Indices and an Introduction to the* Discoveries in the Judaean Desert *Series*. Edited by Emanuel Tov. DJD 39. Oxford: Clarendon Press, 2002.
Tov, Emanuel. 'The *Discoveries in the Judaean Desert* Series: History and System of Presentation'. Pages 1–25 in *The Texts from the Judaean Desert: Indices and an Introduction to the* Discoveries in the Judaean Desert *Series*. Edited by Emanuel Tov. DJD 39. Oxford: Clarendon Press, 2002.

Trites, Allison A. *The New Testament Concept of Witness*. SNTSMS 31. Cambridge: Cambridge University Press, 1977.

Ulrich, Eugene. 'Index of Passages in the "Biblical Texts"'. Pages 185–201 in *The Texts from the Judaean Desert: Indices and an Introduction to the Discoveries in the Judaean Desert Series*. Edited by Emanuel Tov. DJD 39. Oxford: Clarendon Press, 2002.

Ulrich, Eugene and Peter W. Flint, eds. *Qumran Cave 1. II: The Isaiah Scrolls*. 2 vols. DJD 32. Oxford: Clarendon Press, 2010.

van Belle, Gilbert. *Les parenthèses dans l'Évangile de Jean: Aperçu historique et classification. Texte grec de Jean*. SNTA 11. Leuven: Leuven University Press, 1985.

VanderKam, James and Peter Flint. *The Meaning of the Dead Sea Scrolls: Their Significance for Understanding the Bible, Judaism, Jesus, and Christianity*. New York: HarperSanFrancisco, 2002.

Wagner, J. Ross. *Heralds of the Good News: Isaiah and Paul 'in Concert' in the Letter to the Romans*. NovTSup 101. Leiden: E.J. Brill, 2002.

Werner, Eric. 'Hosanna in the Gospels'. *JBL* 65 (1946): 97–122.

Wiles, Maurice F. *The Spiritual Gospel: The Interpretation of the Fourth Gospel in the Early Church*. Cambridge: Cambridge University Press, 1960.

Williams, Catrin H. '"He Saw His Glory and Spoke of Him": The Testimony of Isaiah and Johannine Christology'. Pages 53–80 in *Honouring the Past and Shaping the Future: Religious and Biblical Studies in Wales. Essays in Honour of Gareth Lloyd Jones*. Edited by Robert Pope. Leominster: Gracewing, 2003.

Williams, Catrin H. 'Isaiah in John's Gospel'. Pages 101–16 in *Isaiah in the New Testament*. Edited by Steve Moyise and Maarten J.J. Menken. London: T&T Clark, 2005.

Williams, Catrin H. 'The Testimony of Isaiah and Johannine Christology'. Pages 107–24 in *'As Those Who Are Taught': The Interpretation of Isaiah from the LXX to the SBL*. Edited by Claire Matthews McGinnis and Patricia K. Tull. SymS 27. Atlanta, GA: Society of Biblical Literature, 2006.

Wright, Robert B., ed. *The Psalms of Solomon: A Critical Edition of the Greek Text*. Jewish and Christian Texts in Contexts and Related Studies 1. New York: T&T Clark, 2007.

Yadin, Yigael. *Masada VI. Yigael Yadin Excavations 1963–1965: Final Reports*. The Masada Reports. Jerusalem: Israel Exploration Society and The Hebrew University of Jerusalem, 1999.

Yadin, Yigael. *Tefillin from Qumran (X Q Phyl 1-4)*. Jerusalem: Israel Exploration Society and the Shrine of the Book, 1969.

Young, Franklin W. 'A Study of the Relation of Isaiah to the Fourth Gospel'. *ZNW* 46 (1955): 215–33.

ANCIENT SOURCES INDEX

Hebrew Bible/Septuagint

Genesis
- 1:1 — 213n. 801
- 21:16 LXX — 181n. 698, 181n. 700
- 24:60 — 17n. 57
- 27:15 — 17t. 2
- 27:36 — 190n. 740
- 28:10–22 — 190n. 741
- 28:12 — 213n. 801
- 32:28(29) — 190n. 740
- 33:19 — 213n. 801
- 46:27 — 17t. 2
- 48:22 — 213n. 801
- 49:8–12 — 177, 190n. 742, 195
- 49:10 — 160, 165, 165nn. 620–621, 175n. 664
- 49:10–11 — 174t. 38, 175
- 49:10–12 — 195n. 758
- 49:11 — 177, 177n. 683, 178t. 39, 184, 194, 195

Exodus — 7n. 22
- 3:6 — 128n. 487
- 3:12–14 — 104n. 401
- 4 — 104
- 4:1–9 — 101, 102, 103t. 21
- 4:8 — 104n. 403
- 4:17 — 103n. 393
- 4:28 — 103n. 393
- 4:30 — 103n. 393
- 7:3 — 104n. 398
- 7:9 LXX — 103n. 393
- 8:19 — 104n. 398
- 10:1–2 — 104n. 398
- 11:9–10 LXX — 104n. 398
- 12:10 — 9n. 30, 17t. 2, 23t. 3, 24t. 4, 207n. 783, 213
- 12:22 — 207n. 783
- 12:46 — 9n. 30, 17t. 2, 19n. 69, 22n. 80, 23t. 3, 24t. 4, 207n. 783, 213
- 14:21–22 — 45n. 171
- 16:4 — 13n. 48, 15t. 2, 19n. 69, 23t. 3, 24t. 4, 27n. 92, 213
- 16:15 — 13n. 48, 15t. 2, 23t. 3, 24t. 4, 27n. 92
- 23:5 — 17n. 56
- 23:20 — 36n. 120, 52, 60

Leviticus
- 15:6 LXX — 181n. 698
- 15:9 LXX — 176n. 672
- 23:40 LXX — 130n. 495

Numbers — 7n. 22
- 9:12 — 9n. 30, 17t. 2, 19n. 69, 23t. 3, 24t. 4, 207n. 783, 213
- 14:11 — 104n. 400
- 14:22 — 104n. 400
- 21:8 — 213n. 801
- 26:10 LXX — 104n. 400
- 35:30 — 19n. 67

Deuteronomy — 7n. 22
- 4:34 — 104n. 398
- 6:22 — 104n. 398
- 7:19 — 104n. 398
- 11:3 — 104n. 398
- 17:6 — 13n. 47, 15t. 2, 22n. 80, 23t. 3, 24t. 4, 213
- 18:18–19 — 102, 204n. 775
- 19:15 — 13n. 47, 15t. 2, 19n. 67, 22n. 80, 23t. 3, 24t. 4, 213
- 26:8 — 104n. 398
- 29:1–3 — 91, 104n. 398, 104n. 400, 114, 118nn. 461–462
- 29:3 — 117, 118, 118t. 24

32:19–22	8, 144, 145t. 30	2:33	6n. 19
32:21	144n. 550	2:36	181n. 698, 182n. 707
34:10–12	104n. 398	2:38	181n. 698, 182n. 707
		18:6	17t. 2
Joshua		20:9–13	181n. 698
18:23	191n. 743		
24:17	104n. 398	2 Kings/4 Kingdoms	
24:32	213n. 801	7:3–4	181n. 698, 182n. 708
		10:16	176n. 673
1 Samuel/1 Kingdoms 22n. 80			
1:23	181n. 698, 182n. 701	Isaiah	4, 7n. 22, 10, 36
1:33	177n. 677	6	32, 32n. 100, 68, 92,
1:38	177n. 677		124, 204
1:44	177n. 677	6:1 LXX	32n. 100
4:20	85t. 17	6:1–13	213
16:18	6n. 19	6:9	73, 78, 79t. 13, 84, 94,
17:12	6n. 19		96, 105n. 404
17:58	6n. 19	6:9a LXX	97n. 368
20:5	181n. 698, 182n. 702	6:9–10	68n. 256, 79, 79t. 14,
20:6	6n. 19		84t. 17, 85t. 18, 86, 89,
22:5	181n. 698, 182n. 703		92n. 350, 96, 96t. 20,
23:14	181n. 698, 182n. 704		97, 105n. 404
27:5	181n. 698, 182n. 705	6:10	9n. 28, 13n. 47, 16t. 2,
			19n. 69, 22n. 80, 23t. 3,
2 Samuel/2 Kingdoms 7n. 22, 22n. 80			24t. 4, 25n. 86, 31, 32,
6:18	158n. 589		67, 67–124, 68, 69, 72,
6:26	192n. 750		72n. 272, 72t. 12, 73,
7:12	6n. 19		77, 77n. 285, 78, 81n.
7:16	16t. 2, 213		298, 83t. 16, 84, 86, 87,
13:29	176n. 673		93, 94, 95, 95t. 19, 96,
14:4	192n. 750		97, 97n. 366, 98, 105n.
16:2	176n. 674		404, 108, 109, 110, 112,
19:9	181n. 698, 182n. 706		113, 113t. 22, 114, 117,
22:11	176nn. 672–273		118, 119, 121n. 475,
22:51	6n. 19		122, 122n. 477, 124,
			137, 141n. 538, 161,
1 Kings/3 Kingdoms			167, 169, 208, 209n.
1	176–177		792, 213
1:13	177n. 680	6:10a	72n. 272, 73, 74, 75,
1:17	177n. 681		76, 82, 83
1:20	177n. 681	6:10ac	74, 76, 82, 83, 94, 95n.
1:24	177n. 681		362, 98, 115
1:27	177n. 681	6:10acf LXX	75
1:30	177n. 681	6:10a-g	73n. 273
1:33	177n. 678	6:10b	73, 97n. 368
1:35	177n. 681	6:10b-cg	73
1:38	176n. 673, 177n. 679	6:10be	74, 76, 98, 105n. 404
1:44	176n. 673, 177n. 679	6:10c	73, 74, 74n. 275, 75
1:46	177n. 680	6:10cg	76
1:48	6n. 19, 177n. 681	6:10d	74, 75

6:10d-f	73		48, 48n. 186, 50, 53, 58, 61
6:10df	75, 83, 94		
6:10e LXX	74n. 274	40:3-5	36n. 120, 60
6:10f	73, 74, 75, 76	40:8	36n. 120
6:10g	20n. 71, 73, 74, 75, 76, 77n. 286, 115	41:8-10	171t. 37, 188
		40:9-10	171n. 648, 171t. 37, 174t. 38, 175
9:2 LXX	17t. 2		
10:17 LXX	15t. 2	40:10cd	171n. 648
10:24-34	170-1t. 37, 170n. 645, 188	41:9-10	171n. 648
		41:11-13	171t. 37, 188
10:32	170n. 645	41:14-16	170n. 644, 171t. 37, 188n. 729
11:16	45n. 171		
12:40	74n. 276	42	80n. 294
19:1	176n. 671	42:1	80n. 294
26:11	15t. 2	42:3	80n. 294
29:10 LXX	77	42:4	80n. 294
29:18 LXX	78, 79t. 13	42:6-7	80n. 294
30:27	15t. 2	42:8	80n. 294
32:6 LXX	85t. 17	42:9	80n. 294
35:4	170t. 37	42:13	80n. 294
40	35	42:16	80n. 294
40:1-5a	57n. 214	42:18-20 LXX	80t. 14, 95
40:2 LXX	35, 35n. 109	42:19 LXX	93n. 355
40:3	9n. 28, 11, 11n. 36, 13n. 48, 14t. 2, 18, 19n. 69, 21n. 75, 23t. 3, 24t. 4, 26, 27n. 91, 31-66, 31n. 98, 32, 33t. 5, 34, 34n. 107, 35, 36n. 119, 37t. 6, 39, 39n. 131, 39n. 135, 40t. 7, 42n. 143, 43, 44, 45, 46, 47, 48n. 186, 50, 51n. 194, 51t. 8, 52, 52n. 197, 53, 55, 56, 57, 57n. 214, 59, 59n. 220, 60, 61, 62, 64, 65, 66, 68, 69, 70, 71n. 270, 92, 97, 105, 108, 124, 137, 160, 213	43:1	171t. 37, 188
		43:5-7	171t. 37, 188, 197n. 767
		43:8 LXX	80t. 14
		43:14-21	45n. 171
		43:16	45n. 171
		44	86
		44:1-2	172t. 37, 188
		44:2	166, 166t. 35, 184
		44:2-3 LXX	86n. 313
		44:6	86n. 313, 160, 165, 166, 166t. 35, 184
		44:6-8	172t. 37, 188n. 729
		44:8 LXX	86n. 313
		44:18	85, 85t. 17, 86, 86t. 18, 95
40:3a	49	44:22-24 LXX	86n. 313
40:3ab	34, 36, 38, 41, 58, 60	44:28 LXX	86n. 313
40:3b	33n. 105, 35n. 108, 35n. 113, 36n. 120, 48, 48n. 186, 58, 59, 60, 61, 65, 171n. 648	45:13	34n. 107
		47:7 LXX	85t. 17
		47:8 LXX	181n. 698
		51:7	172t. 37
40:3bc	48, 57	51:10	45n. 171
40:3c	33n. 105, 34, 35, 35n. 108, 35n. 113, 36, 37, 38, 39n. 131, 41, 43,	53:1	6n. 19, 9n. 28, 9n. 31, 13n. 45, 15t. 2, 16t. 2, 19n. 69, 22n. 80, 23t.

	3, 24t. 4, 27n. 96, 32, 67, 67–124, 68, 69, 70, 70n. 264, 70t. 11, 71, 72, 88, 92, 94, 97, 97n. 366, 104, 105, 105n. 404, 105n. 410, 106n. 411, 107, 108, 109n. 427, 110, 112, 113, 113t. 22, 114, 124, 141n. 538, 208, 213	Joel 2 2:21 2:23	169 169, 169n. 641 169, 169n. 641
		Jonah 4:5 LXX	181n. 698, 183n. 711
		Micah 7n. 22 5:1	6n. 19, 213, 214
53:1a	68n. 256, 71n. 266, 105n. 404, 107, 107n. 418, 108	Zephaniah 3	169, 185, 189
53:1b	70, 70n. 264, 106, 107, 107n. 418, 108, 113	3:11–15 3:13	185n. 720, 190t. 42 189
53:12	128n. 487	3:14 LXX	169, 184n. 718
54:4	172t. 37, 188	3:14a LXX	169
54:13	13n. 47, 15t. 2, 18, 19n. 69, 20n. 71, 23t. 3, 24t. 4, 31n. 99, 36n. 118, 213	3:14–17 3:15 3:15–17 3:16 LXX	172t. 37, 188n. 729 160, 165, 166, 189 166t. 35, 184, 185 166n. 629, 169
56:9–10 LXX	80t. 14	9:9a LXX	169
57:4 LXX	213		
62:10b	171n. 648	Zechariah	7n. 22
62:10–11	171n. 648	2:14	174t. 38, 175
62:11b	171n. 648, 179, 180	8:13–15	170n. 644, 173t. 37, 188n. 729
62:11ef	171n. 648	9:9	2nn. 3–4, 9n. 29, 13n. 47, 16t. 2, 19n. 67, 19n. 68, 20n. 71, 22n. 80, 23t. 3, 24t. 4, 127, 130, 130n. 496, 131t. 25, 133, 157, 157–99, 158, 158n. 591, 159, 160, 160n. 599, 161, 165, 165n. 623, 166, 166t. 35, 167, 167t. 36, 168, 169, 170, 170n. 645, 170n. 647, 170t. 37, 171n. 648, 174, 174n. 659, 175, 176, 177, 178, 178n. 688, 178t. 39, 179, 180, 180t. 41, 184, 187, 188, 188n. 728, 191, 193, 194, 195, 196, 197n. 767, 213
Jeremiah 5:21 15:17 LXX 23:5 26:27–28 LXX 31:7 31:18 LXX 33:22 33:25–26 46(LXX 26):27–28	96 181n. 698, 183n. 713 6n. 19 188, 188n. 729 160, 162, 162t. 33, 186 181n. 698, 183n. 714 6n. 19 6n. 19 172t. 37		
Ezekiel 12:2 37 37:21–24 37:25	7n. 22 117n. 458 197 197n. 766, 204n. 773, 205n. 778 16t. 2, 213		
Hosea 12:4(5)	190n. 740	9:9a 9:9ab	168, 171n. 648 168

9:9b	173, 178	41:10	6n. 19, 13n. 46, 16t. 2, 19, 19n. 70, 20n. 71, 23t. 3, 24t. 4, 27, 141n. 538, 213
9:9bd	168		
9:9c	168, 175, 196		
9:9d	167		
9:9e	168, 169, 196	41:10b LXX	20n. 71
9:9ef	175n. 664, 196	42:3	9n. 30, 23t. 3, 24t. 4, 135n. 513, 138n. 527, 213
9:9f	168, 169		
9:10	175n. 664		
12:10	2n. 3, 3, 9n. 30, 13n. 46, 17t. 2, 19n. 70, 20n. 71, 22n. 80, 23t. 3, 24t. 4, 25, 25n. 84, 27, 27n. 91, 213	63:2	9n. 30, 23t. 3, 24t. 4, 135n. 513, 138n. 527, 213
		69	26, 115n. 448, 135, 137, 138, 138t. 29, 139, 140n. 531, 141, 142, 143
14	129, 130, 130n. 496, 131		
14:1	198n. 769	69:2–5	142n. 541
14:5d	175n. 659	69:4	139n. 531
14:8	2n. 3	69:5	13n. 48, 16t. 2, 17, 18, 18n. 60, 19n. 67, 23t. 3, 24t. 4, 36nn. 118–119, 71n. 270, 115n. 448, 135, 136, 136t. 28, 138, 138n. 526, 138t. 29, 139, 140, 141n. 538, 142, 213
14:16–19	130n. 494, 210n. 797		
14:21	129, 130		
Malachi			
3:1	36n. 120, 42n. 143, 42n. 148, 49n. 187, 50, 51t. 8, 52, 52n. 197, 60, 61, 62		
		69:5b	140
3:23	42n. 148, 50, 51t. 8, 52	69:8a	142
3:23–24	50	69:9	142n. 541
		69:9–12	139n. 531
Psalms 7n. 22		69:10	7–8, 8, 9n. 29, 13n. 48, 15t. 2, 17, 18n. 60, 19n. 69, 20n. 71, 23t. 3, 24t. 4, 26, 27n. 96, 115n. 448, 127, 127–55, 128, 130n. 496, 131t. 25, 132, 133, 134n. 506, 134t. 26, 135, 138t. 29, 140, 141, 142, 144, 145, 146n. 554, 151, 155, 157, 213
5:9	34n. 107		
8:3	160, 162, 163, 186		
16:10	128n. 487		
18:51	6n. 19		
20:7	160, 162, 162t. 33, 186		
20:10	160, 162, 162t. 33, 186		
22:19	6n. 19, 9n. 30, 13n. 45, 17t. 2, 18n. 60, 19n. 69, 22n. 80, 23t. 3, 24t. 4, 27n. 96, 141n. 538		
34:21	9n. 30, 17t. 2, 19n. 69, 23t. 3, 24t. 4, 213	69:10a	14, 14t. 1, 128n. 488, 129n. 488, 130, 134, 136, 138, 139n. 531, 141, 142, 144, 145t. 30
35:7 LXX	16t. 2		
35:19	13n. 48, 16t. 2, 17, 18, 18n. 60, 23t. 3, 24t. 4, 36nn. 118–119, 71n. 270, 136, 136t. 28, 138n. 526, 141n. 538, 213	69:10b	136, 137, 138, 138t. 29, 139n. 531, 141, 142
		69:10–12	142n. 542
		69:16	142n. 541
41:8	17n. 56	69:19	139n. 531

69:20–22	142n. 541	29:15 LXX	80t. 14
69:21	139n. 531	33:23 LXX	85t. 17
69:22	9n. 30, 23t. 3, 24t. 4, 115n. 448, 135, 135t. 27, 138, 138n. 527, 138t. 29, 139, 143, 213	38:25	43n. 154

Proverbs 7n. 22, 46, 65, 66

		1:11 LXX	16t. 2
69:24 LXX	115n. 448	4:24–27	54, 54t. 10
69:30–31	139n. 531	4:25–26	39, 40t. 7, 53, 53n. 198, 53n. 203, 55n. 206, 57
78:24	13n. 48, 15t. 2, 19n. 69, 23t. 3, 24t. 4, 27n. 92, 213	9:14–15 LXX	39, 40t. 7, 53n. 198, 55n. 206
78:42–43	104n. 398	9:14–16	54, 54t. 10
82:6	6n. 19, 13n. 45, 16t. 2, 19n. 69, 22n. 80, 23t. 3, 24t. 4, 27n. 96, 213	9:15	34n. 107
		12:7–8 LXX	86n. 318
		12:18 LXX	86n. 318
89:4–5	6n. 19	13:13a LXX	39, 40t. 7, 53n. 198, 55n. 206
89:30	6n. 19		
89:36–37	6n. 19	15:21	34n. 107, 39, 40t. 7, 55n. 206
89:37	16t. 2, 213		
105:26–27	104n. 398	16:23 LXX	85t. 17
115:5–6	117n. 458	20:24 LXX	39, 40t. 7, 53n. 198, 55
118	158, 159, 164, 165, 167	24:22a LXX	213
118:19	165n. 625	26:14 LXX	87n. 319
118:25	161, 162, 164, 187	26:18–19 LXX	87n. 319
118:25a	163, 186	29:27	39, 40t. 7, 54, 54t. 10, 55n. 206
118:25–26	6n. 19, 9, 9n. 29, 9n. 31, 13n. 45, 15t. 2, 16t. 2, 19n. 68, 23t. 3, 24t. 4, 127, 130, 131t. 25, 133, 157, 157–99, 158, 158n. 591, 159, 160, 161, 161n. 601, 161t. 32, 162, 165, 165n. 623, 166, 166t. 35, 174, 178, 178n. 688, 179, 180, 184, 185, 187, 189, 191, 192, 193, 195, 196, 213	30:23 LXX	18n. 59

Qoheleth

		1:8	117n. 458

Nehemiah 7n. 22

		9:15	13n. 48, 15t. 2, 23t. 3, 24t. 4, 27n. 92, 213

1 Chronicles

		17:11	6n. 19
118:26a	13n. 45, 160, 186, 187		
118:26b	161	2 Chronicles	
119:139a LXX	134n. 506	13:19	191n. 743
135:8–9	104n. 398	32:30	34n. 107
135:16–17	117n. 458		

Non-Septuagint Greek versions

Job

Aquila

2:3 LXX	16t. 2	Isaiah 40:3	34, 35n. 113
2:7–9 LXX	183n. 710	Psalm 35:19	16t. 2, 18
17:7 LXX	81, 81n. 298, 93n. 355, 95		

Symmachus

29:1–3 LXX	80t. 14	Psalm 22:19	17t. 2

Psalm 69:5	16t. 2, 18	7:1	13n. 48, 16t. 2, 17, 18, 18n. 60, 23t. 3, 24t. 4, 36nn. 118–119, 71n. 270, 136, 136t. 28, 213
Psalm 69:10	15t. 2, 135		
		18:5	103, 103n. 397

Deuterocanonical Books
Tobit
7:7 LXX	93n. 355

Testament of Naphtali
5:4	192n. 749

Wisdom of Solomon
2:21	80t. 14, 93n. 355
10:15–16	104n. 398

Judaean Desert Texts
1QExod 1 4–5
Exod 16:15	23t. 3, 24t. 4

Sirach 46, 65, 66
2:2 LXX	39, 40t. 7, 55n. 206
2:6	39, 39n. 131, 40t. 7, 53n. 198, 55n. 206
6:9 LXX	18n. 59
6:17 LXX	39, 40t. 7, 55n. 206
10:7 LXX	18n. 59
37:15	39, 39n. 131, 40t. 7, 53n. 198, 55n. 206
38:10 LXX	39, 40t. 7, 55n. 206
39:24 LXX	39, 40t. 7, 55n. 206
45:3	104n. 398
48:8–9 LXX	53n. 198, 55n. 206
49:8–9 LXX	39, 40t. 7
49:9	39n. 131

4QpaleoGen-Exod^l
Exod 12:10	23t. 3, 24t. 4
Exod 12:46	23t. 3, 24t. 4
Exod 16:4	23t. 3, 24t. 4

4QExod^c
Exod 12:46	23t. 3, 24t. 4

4QpaleoExod^m
Exod 16:4	23t. 3, 24t. 4

4QDeut^j
Exod 12:46	23t. 3, 24t. 4

1 Maccabees
4:7	15t. 2
11:34	191n. 743
13:51	192n. 749

4QDeut^{k2}
Deut 19:15	24t. 4

1QIsa^a 22n. 80
Isa 6:10	23t. 3, 24t. 4, 72n. 272, 73, 75, 81, 86, 86n. 316, 93
Isa 10:32	170n. 646
Isa 40:3	23t. 3, 24t. 4, 33n. 105
Isa 44:8	172n. 650
Isa 53:1	23t. 3, 70, 24t. 4, 70n. 264, 70n. 265
Isa 54:13	23t. 3, 24t. 4

2 Maccabees
10:6–7	164
10:7	192n. 749, 194n. 755

1 Esdras
8:68–69	181n. 698, 183n. 709

2 Esdras 7n. 22
19:15	13n. 48, 15t. 2, 23t. 3, 24t. 4, 27n. 92, 213

1QIsa^b 22n. 80
Isa 40:3	23t. 3, 24t. 4
Isa 53:1	70, 23t. 3, 24t. 4, 70n. 264, 70n. 265

4 Maccabees
18:21	93n. 355

Old Testament Pseudepigrapha
Psalms of Solomon

4QIsa^b
Isa 40:3	33n. 105

4QIsa^c
   Isa 10:32   170n. 646
   Isa 53:1   23t. 3, 70n. 264

4QIsa^f
   Isa 6:10   23t. 3, 24t. 4, 72n. 272, 73, 75, 86

4QXII^e
   Zech 12:10   25n. 83

4QPs^b 22n. 80
   Ps 69:10   134n. 509
   Ps 118:25–26   161n. 601

11Ps^a
   Ps 118:25–26   161n. 601

4QPhyl A
   Exod 12:46   23t. 3, 24t. 4

4QPhyl M
   Exod 12:46   23t. 3, 24t. 4

8QPhyl
   Exod 12:46   23t. 3, 24t. 4

XQPhyl
   Exod 12:46   23t. 3, 24t. 4

8HevXIIgr 25, 25n. 84

1QpHab 21n. 75

1QapGen (*Genesis Apocryphon*) 22n. 80

1QS (*Serekh ha-Yaḥad*) 53, 54, 54n. 204, 54n. 205, 60, 61, 62, 64
   iii 13-iv 1   119
   iii 13-iv 26   91
   iii 21–24   120n. 466
   iv 2   24t. 4
   iv 2–3   51n. 194, 53, 53n. 202, 55, 57
   iv 2–6   53n. 200
   iv 20–21   20n. 73
   viii,59   60
   viii 1–6   57n. 215
   viii 1–13   60
   viii 10–14   57n. 216
   viii 10–16   57, 59
   viii 13   60n. 222
   viii 13–14   24t. 4
   viii 14   11n. 41, 20n. 73, 21n. 75, 23t. 3, 33n. 105, 34n. 107, 53, 57
   viii 14–16   46–7, 46n. 176
   viii 15   58n. 217
   viii 15–16   58n. 218
   ix   60
   ix 12–15   59n. 219
   ix 12–21   59, 59n. 219
   ix 17–18   59n. 219
   ix 19–20   23t. 3, 24t. 4, 34n. 107
   ix 19–21   11n. 41, 46–7, 46n. 177, 53, 54n. 205, 54t. 10, 57, 59, 59n. 220
   ix 20   20n. 73
   ix 20–21   59n. 221

1QM (*Sefer ha-Milḥama*) 22n. 80

1QH^a (*1QHodayot^a*)
   iv 37–38   20n. 73
   x 41   23t. 3, 24t. 4
   xii 12   20n. 73, 23t. 3, 24t. 4
   xiii 25–26   20n. 73, 23t. 3, 24t. 4
   xv 5–6 (Suk vii 2–3)   117n. 458, 122n. 477
   xv 9–10   20n. 73
   xv 13   23t. 3, 24t. 4
   xv 17   23t. 3, 24t. 4
   xvi 17   20n. 73
   xvi 37   23t. 3, 24t. 4
   xx 14–16   20n. 73

CD (*Damascus Document*)
   i-viii   21n. 75
   ii 12   20n. 73
   xix-xx   21n. 75
   xx 3–4   23t. 3, 24t. 4

4QTanh (*4QTanḥûmîm*) 34n. 105
   1–2 i 4–9   57n. 214
   1–2 i 6–7   11n. 41, 23t. 3, 24t. 4, 33n. 105, 54n. 205, 57

4QS^b (*4QSerekh ha-Yahad^b*)	54, 54n. 204, 55n. 205	15.421–423	150n. 567
		15.423	150n. 568
xviii 1–4	59n. 219	20.215–221	146n. 553
xviii 3–4	11n. 41, 54n. 205		

Jewish War

4QS^d (*4QSerekh haYahad^d*)	54, 55n. 205	1.3	149n. 565
vi 1–8	57n. 215	1.401	146n. 553
vii 4–5	54n. 205	6.293	146n. 553
vii 13	59n. 219	7.100	192n. 748
viii 1–5	59n. 219		
viii 4	55n. 205	*New Testament*	
viii 4–5	11n. 41	Matthew	1n. 1, 2n. 5, 36, 41, 52, 60, 97
4QS^e (*4QSerekh haYahad^e*)	33n. 105, 54, 54n. 204, 55n. 205, 57n. 216	3:1	61n. 227
		3:1–2	42n. 144
		3:2	62n. 232
		3:3	11n. 41, 26n. 89, 36n. 121, 51t. 9, 60n. 223
ii 9–18	57n. 215		
ii 18-iii 5	57n. 216		
iii 1–6	57n. 215	3:4–12	42n. 144
iii 3	57n. 216	3:7–10	62n. 234
iii 4–5	11n. 41	3:11	63n. 242, 63nn. 237–238
iii 6	58n. 217		
iii 6-iv 2	59n. 219	3:11–12	41n. 139
iii 19	11n. 41	3:12	63n. 239
iii 19-iv 2	54n. 205	3:13–17	42n. 149
iv 1–2	11n. 41	4:12	42n. 149
		11:7	62n. 229
4QMMT (*Miqṣat Ma'ase Ha-Torah*)	21n. 75	11:10	42n. 143, 42n. 148, 49n. 187, 51t. 9
		11:13–14	42n. 148
4QDibHam^a (*4QDibre ha-Me'orot^a*)	117n. 457, 118, 119, 121n. 475, 165, 118n. 459	13:10–15	111n. 433
		13:13–15	97n. 367
18 2–3	118t. 24	13:14–15	68n. 256
18 2–4	116, 117t. 23, 118t. 24, 119	13:15b	97n. 368
		14:3–4	62n. 236
18 4	25n. 86, 118, 121n. 475	17:10–13	42n. 148
		21:1–9	159n. 595, 192n. 746
		21:4–7	159
Josephus		21:5	2n. 4, 19n. 68, 177n. 684, 179, 180, 180t. 41
Against Apion			
2.119	146n. 553	21:6–7	159n. 594
		21:8	130n. 491
Jewish Antiquities		21:8–9	176n. 669, 187n. 726
15.380	146n. 553	21:9	179n. 689
15.380–387	149n. 561	21:9b-d	163t. 34, 179t. 40
15.380–423	148n. 560	21:16	163
15.388–391	149n. 563	21:31–32	65
15.391	146n. 553	21:31c–32	63n. 240
15.421	149n. 564, 150n. 569	23:37–39	148n. 559

23:39	179n. 689, 179t. 40	1:80	61n. 228
24:1–2	148n. 558	3:1–3	42n. 144
26:57–66	151n. 569	3:3	62n. 231
26:59–61	147t. 31	3:4	37n. 123
27:1–2	151n. 569	3:4–6	11n. 41, 26n. 89, 36n. 121, 51t. 9, 60n. 223
27:11	151n. 569		
27:39–40	147t. 31	3:7–9	62n. 233
		3:7–18	42n. 145
Mark	1n. 1, 36, 36n. 120, 52, 60	3:15–16	41n. 139
		3:16	63nn. 237–238
1:2	42n. 143, 42n. 148	3:17	63n. 239
1:2–3	11n. 41, 26n. 89, 36n. 121, 49n. 187, 52n. 195, 60n. 223	3:19–20	62n. 236
		3:19–22	42n. 149
		3:23	61n. 228
1:3	37n. 123	5:1–11	102n. 390
1:4	61n. 226, 62n. 231	7:10–14	62n. 235
1:4–8	42n. 144	7:18	62n. 235
1:7	63n. 237, 63n. 242	7:24	62n. 229
1:8	63n. 238	7:27	42n. 143, 42n. 148, 49n. 187, 51t. 9
1:9–11	42n. 149		
1:14	42n. 149	8:9–10	111n. 433
3:5	80n. 296, 81t. 15	13:34–35	148n. 559
4, 92	92n. 350	13:35	179n. 690, 179t. 40
4:10–12	89, 111n. 433	19:32–35	159n. 594
4:11–12	92n. 350, 97n. 369	19:36–38	187n. 726
6:16–18	62n. 236	19:38	179n. 690, 179t. 40
6:51–52	81t. 15	19:43–44	148n. 558
6:52	80n. 296	21:5–6	148n. 558
8:17	80n. 296, 81t. 15	22:53	90n. 344
8:17–18	94, 96, 96t. 20, 97, 124		
9:11–13	42n. 148	John	1n. 1, 2n. 5, 41, 52, 60
11:4–7	159n. 594	1	10, 185, 189, 194
11:8	130n. 492	1:1	213n. 801
11:8–10	176n. 669, 187n. 726	1:6–8	47n. 179, 105n. 406
11:9	19n. 68	1:6–9	41n. 140
11:9–10	179n. 689	1:7	65n. 248, 90n. 335
11:9b–10	163t. 34, 179t. 40	1:9	175n. 662
12:26–27	128n. 487	1:11	175n. 661
13:1–2	148n. 558	1:11b	67
14:53–64	151n. 569	1:14	112, 112n. 438
14:57–58	147t. 31	1:15	14t. 2, 16t. 2, 36n. 114, 42n. 152, 44n. 161, 44n. 165, 47n. 179, 49n. 189, 105n. 406
15:1–2	151n. 569		
15:29–30	147t. 31		
		1:18	87n. 325
Luke	1n. 1, 36n. 120, 41, 52, 97	1:19	35n. 109, 35n. 112, 173n. 653
1:16–17	52n. 196		
1:76	11n. 41, 36n. 120, 42n. 143, 51t. 9, 60, 61	1:19–23	32n. 101
		1:19–27	41n. 141

1:19–12:50	10, 12, 68, 100n. 380, 105n. 406, 108, 124, 124n. 480, 133, 157, 164, 175, 175n. 663, 198–9, 203, 204, 206, 210	1:36	44n. 162, 49n. 189
		1:38	87n. 320
		1:45	6n. 18, 189n. 738, 204n. 775, 212, 213
		1:45–49	164, 190t. 42
1:21	42n. 151	1:47	189n. 738
1:23	5n. 18, 9n. 28, 10, 11, 11n. 36, 13n. 48, 14t. 2, 18, 19n. 63, 19n. 69, 23t. 3, 24t. 4, 26, 27n. 91, 31, 31n. 99, 32, 33n. 103, 33t. 5, 34, 35, 35n. 112, 36, 36n. 116, 36n. 119, 37, 38n. 129, 39, 39n. 131, 40t. 7, 41nn. 141–142, 42, 42nn. 146–149, 42n. 153, 42nn. 143–144, 43nn. 154–156, 44n. 159, 46, 47n. 180, 48nn. 183–184, 49, 53, 55, 56, 62n. 230, 63, 64, 65, 66, 68, 69, 71n. 270, 92, 97, 105, 108, 124, 203, 212, 213	1:47–51	194n. 755
		1:49	189, 196
		1:50	16t. 2, 194n. 755
		1:50–51	190n. 741
		1:51	194n. 755, 213n. 801
		1–2	113n. 441
		1–12	4, 32, 106n. 411, 203
		2	8, 10, 56, 128n. 488, 151, 155, 198, 199
		2:1–12	101n. 382
		2:11	16t. 2, 71n. 270, 91, 101, 102, 102n. 389, 103t. 21, 106n. 415
		2:12	102n. 388
		2:13	129n. 489, 130n. 496, 173n. 653
		2:13–16	127n. 481
		2:13–17	129, 134n. 507, 146n. 553
1:23–12:15	1n. 2	2:13–22	129, 129n. 489, 130, 131t. 25, 133n. 503, 150, 176, 198
1:24	35n. 109		
1:25–26	42n. 145		
1:26	42n. 150, 44n. 163, 47n. 179, 119n. 464	2:14	146n. 553
		2:14–15	155n. 585
1:26–27	49n. 189	2:14–17	131t. 25, 134n. 508
1:27	39n. 134, 42n. 152, 44n. 161	2:15	134n. 508, 160, 198n. 770
1:28	42n. 145, 64n. 243	2:16	15t. 2, 17n. 53, 129, 130, 140, 151, 151n. 570
1:29	44n. 160, 47n. 179, 174n. 658, 207n. 783		
1:29–33	49n. 189	2:16–17	151, 152
1:29–34	44n. 162, 49n. 189	2:17	5n. 18, 8, 8n. 26, 9n. 29, 10, 10n. 32, 13n. 48, 14, 14t. 1, 15t. 2, 17, 17n. 54, 18n. 60, 19n. 69, 20n. 71, 23t. 3, 24t. 4, 26, 27n. 96, 36n. 119, 71, 115n. 448, 127, 128, 128n. 488, 129, 129n. 488, 130, 130n. 496, 132, 133, 134, 134n. 506, 134t. 26, 135, 136, 137, 140,
1:29–37	42n. 150, 42n. 153		
1:30	16t. 2, 42n. 152, 44n. 161, 44n. 165		
1:31	16t. 2, 42n. 145, 44n. 163, 47n. 179, 71n. 270, 109n. 420		
1:32–34	105n. 406		
1:33	42n. 145, 44n. 163		
1:34	49n. 189		
1:35–36	47n. 179, 207n. 783		
1:35–37	65		

	141, 142, 143, 144, 144n. 549, 145t. 30, 146n. 554, 151, 153, 155, 157, 198, 203, 212, 213	4:23	198n. 772
		4:23–24	153n. 578
		4:34	104n. 402
		4:42	92n. 351, 176n. 667
		4:45	173n. 653
2:18–21	146n. 554	4:46–54	101n. 382, 111n. 431
2:18–22	128n. 484, 129, 130n. 497, 131t. 25, 143, 145, 146n. 553, 150n. 566	4:47	88, 110n. 430
		4:48	99n. 375, 100n. 377, 104n. 399
2:19,	128n. 488, 140, 141, 146n. 553, 146n. 554, 150	4:53	15t. 2, 17n. 53, 151n. 573
		4:53–54	99n. 375
2:19–21	153, 154	4:54	101, 103t. 21
2:19–22	8, 10, 10n. 32, 144n. 549, 145, 146	5,	123 191
		5:1–2	173n. 653
2:21	146n. 553	5:1–9	111n. 431
2:22	129, 132, 133, 140, 144, 144n. 549, 146n. 554, 157	5:10–18	123
		5:13	88, 110n. 430
		5:16	109n. 422
2:22c	128, 128n. 488, 129n. 488, 133	5:16–18	8n. 27, 143n. 544, 191n. 744
2:23	99n. 375, 173n. 653	5:17	106n. 415
2:23–25	56n. 209	5:18	109n. 423
2–12	129, 203	5:19	106n. 415
3:1–2	123	5:19–20	116n. 453
3:11	105n. 411	5:22	115, 115n. 447
3:14	213n. 801	5:23–24	104n. 402
3:16–17	90n. 335	5:24–25	92n. 351
3:16–21	123	5:26–27	115, 115n. 447
3:17–18	92n. 351, 123	5:30	104n. 402, 115n. 449, 116n. 453, 176n. 667
3:18	123, 124		
3:19	175n. 662	5:31–32	105n. 408, 113n. 442
3:19–21	41n. 140	5:33	47n. 179
3:20	92n. 351, 123	5:33–35	105n. 406
3:21	71n. 270	5:35	47n. 179
3:22–24	42n. 153	5:36–37	113n. 442
3:23	64nn. 244–245, 106n. 415	5:36–38	105n. 408
		5:37	87n. 325, 104n. 402
3:26	64n. 243, 105n. 406	5:39–40	105n. 409
3:27–30	42n. 150, 42n. 153	5:45–47	105n. 409
3:28	42n. 152, 49n. 189	6	27n. 92, 56, 65
3:29–30	47n. 179	6:2	99n. 375
3:32	78n. 288	6:5	83n. 307
3:32–33	105n. 405	6:5–13	107n. 418
4:5	213n. 801	6:6	56n. 210
4:14	39n. 134	6:11	17t. 2
4:20–21	173n. 653	6:14	99n. 375, 175n. 662
4:21	153	6:14–15	165n. 624, 193
4:21–24	153, 204n. 777	6:22	107n. 418

6:25–29	123	7:37	14t. 2, 36n. 114
6:26	99n. 375, 107n. 418, 110, 123	7:38	2n. 3, 6n. 19, 15t. 2, 19n. 67, 212, 213
6:26–51a	7n. 23	7:42	6n. 19, 15t. 2, 19n. 67, 212, 213, 214
6:28–29	65n. 249		
6:29	56	7:44	83n. 307, 191n. 744
6:30	98n. 372, 99n. 375	7:45–49	123
6:31	5n. 18, 13n. 48, 15t. 2, 19n. 69, 23t. 3, 24t. 4, 27, 160n. 599, 212, 213	7–8	56
		8	121, 122
		8:12	41n. 140
6:31–32	78n. 288	8:13–18	105n. 405
6:37	89n. 333	8:16	104n. 402, 115n. 450
6:38	90n. 335	8:17	13n. 47, 15t. 2, 19n. 67, 22n. 80, 23t. 3, 24t. 4, 212, 213
6:38–39	104n. 402		
6:39	6n. 19, 89n. 333		
6:44	104n. 402	8:17–18	105n. 408
6:44–45	31n. 99	8:18	104n. 402
6:45	5n. 18, 13n. 47, 15t. 2, 18, 19n. 69, 20n. 71, 23t. 3, 24t. 4, 36n. 118, 92n. 351, 212, 213	8:20	191n. 744
		8:26	104n. 402
		8:29	104n. 402
		8:35	15t. 2, 17n. 53, 151n. 574
6:46	87n. 325		
6:54	19n. 64	8:38	78n. 288
6:60	92n. 351	8:42	78n. 288
6:63–65	109n. 420	8:42–47	122
6:64–65	119n. 464	8:43	92n. 351
6:65	89n. 333, 109n. 420	8:43–44	120n. 466, 120n. 467, 209n. 791
6:70ab	116n. 455		
6:70–71	120n. 466	8:44	120n. 467, 208, 209
7	123	8:44a	122n. 476
7:1	143n. 544	8:47	89n. 332, 92n. 351, 109n. 424, 120n. 467, 209n. 791
7:2–9	191n. 744		
7:3–4	102, 106n. 415		
7:4	71n. 270	8:50b	115
7:12	8n. 27	8:57–59	8n. 27, 143n. 544
7:13	191n. 744	8:59	56n. 211, 191n. 744
7:16	104n. 402	9	78, 82n. 302
7:19	191n. 744	9:1–2	78n. 291
7:19–25	8n. 27, 143n. 544	9:1–7	111n. 431
7:21–22	109n. 420	9:3	71n. 270, 106n. 415, 123
7:21–24	123		
7:25	191n. 744	9:3–4	98n. 372, 99n. 375
7:28	14t. 2, 36n. 114, 104n. 402	9:4	104n. 402, 106n. 415, 121n. 473
7:30	83n. 307, 191n. 744	9:4–5	121n. 472
7:31	99n. 375	9:13	78n. 291
7:32	90n. 335, 123, 191n. 744	9:13–41	123
		9:16	98n. 372
7:33	104n. 402	9:17–20	78n. 291

9:22	191n. 744	11:37	78n. 290
9:22–23	109n. 420	11:41	83n. 307
9:24–25	78n. 291	11:43	14t. 2, 36n. 115
9:30	18n. 61, 18n. 62	11:44	83n. 307
9:32	78n. 290, 78n. 291	11:45–53	8n. 27, 143n. 544
9:38	99n. 375	11:46–53	123
9:39	78, 79t. 13, 89, 92n. 351, 119n. 464, 120, 123, 124, 175n. 662	11:47–48	99n. 375
		11:47–53	191n. 744
		11:48	139, 144
9:39–41	78n. 291	11:49–52	194n. 754, 207n. 784
10:3–4	92n. 351	11:50	82n. 303
10:4	89n. 333	11:52	175n. 663
10:11–13	207n. 782	11:54	191n. 743
10:12–13	18n. 62	11:55	129n. 489, 173n. 653, 191n. 743
10:16	92n. 351, 197n. 765, 204n. 773		
		12	10, 122, 130n. 497, 199
10:17	109n. 425	12:1–9	157n. 588
10:21	78n. 290	12:3	15t. 2, 17n. 53, 151n. 572
10:22	173n. 653, 208		
10:25	105n. 408	12:12a	188n. 730
10:25c-30	116n. 456	12:12–13	130, 130n. 493, 158n. 589, 159n. 594, 191n. 743
10:27	89n. 333, 92n. 351		
10:29	89n. 333		
10:30	176n. 667	12:12–15	127n. 482, 144
10:31–33	8n. 27, 143n. 544, 191n. 744	12:12–16	10, 10n. 32, 129, 129n. 489, 130, 131t. 25, 133, 133n. 503, 146, 157, 159n. 595, 173n. 653, 176, 197
10:32	106n. 415		
10:34	2n. 4, 5n. 18, 6n. 19, 9n. 31, 13n. 45, 16t. 2, 19n. 69, 22n. 80, 23t. 3, 24t. 4, 27n. 96, 212, 213		
		12:12–19	129n. 489, 176
		12:13	6n. 19, 9, 9n. 29, 9n. 31, 10, 13n. 45, 14t. 2, 15t. 2, 16t. 2, 19n. 68, 23t. 3, 24t. 4, 36n. 115, 127, 133, 157, 158, 158n. 591, 159, 160, 161, 161t. 32, 165n. 623, 166, 166t. 35, 167, 174, 178, 178n. 688, 180, 184, 185, 188, 189, 191, 192n. 748, 195, 196, 212, 213
10:37	106n. 415		
10:37–38	99n. 375, 100n. 379, 106n. 415, 208n. 788		
10:39	191n. 744		
10:40	64n. 243		
10:41	47n. 179		
10:41–42	65, 100n. 378		
11:1–44	130n. 497		
11:8	191n. 744		
11:9–10	41n. 140, 121n. 472		
11:16	191n. 744	12:13b-d	166t. 35
11:18	173n. 653	12:13c	160
11:20	15t. 2, 17n. 53, 151n. 574	12:13–15	196
11:27	39n. 134, 165n. 624, 175n. 662	12:14	159n. 594, 176, 181, 192, 193, 194
11:31	15t. 2, 17n. 53, 151n. 572	12:14–15	158, 177, 181
		12:14–16	167n. 630

Ancient Sources Index

12:15	2n. 3, 2n. 4, 5n. 18, 9n. 29, 13n. 47, 16t. 2, 19n. 67, 19n. 68, 20n. 71, 22n. 80, 23t. 3, 24t. 4, 127, 133, 158, 158n. 591, 159, 160n. 599, 161, 165, 165n. 623, 166, 167, 167t. 36, 168, 169, 170n. 645, 170t. 37, 173n. 656, 174, 174t. 38, 175, 175n. 664, 176, 178n. 688, 178t. 39, 179, 180, 180t. 41, 181, 184, 185, 187, 191, 193, 194, 212, 213		70, 70t. 11, 71, 72, 88, 92, 94, 97, 98, 104, 105, 105n. 404, 105n. 411, 106, 106n. 411, 107, 107n. 418, 108, 109n. 427, 110, 113, 114, 124, 141n. 538, 160n. 598, 212, 213
12:15a	168, 169	12:38–39	69n. 263
12:15b	169, 173	12:38–40	105n. 404, 110
12:15–16	10	12:39	108, 109, 110, 114, 122
12:16	127, 128, 132, 133, 133n. 503, 144, 157n. 587, 159n. 594, 193	12:39–40	10, 122
12:17	106n. 411, 127	12:40	5n. 18, 9n. 28, 10, 13n. 47, 16t. 2, 19n. 69, 20n. 71, 22n. 80, 23t. 3, 24t. 4, 25n. 86, 31, 32, 67, 68, 69n. 263, 72, 72t. 12, 73, 75n. 279, 77n. 285, 78, 79t. 14, 82, 83t. 16, 85t. 18, 86, 89, 95, 95t. 19, 96, 96t. 20, 97, 98, 105n. 404, 108, 110, 113, 114, 116, 117, 119, 120, 121, 122, 122n. 477, 124, 141n. 538, 161, 167, 169, 205, 208, 209n. 792, 212, 213
12:18	99n. 373, 109n. 426		
12:18–22	127		
12:19	175n. 663, 188n. 730		
12:20–26	175n. 663, 210n. 796		
12:23–36	193		
12:27	90n. 344, 109n. 420		
12:31	90, 90n. 342, 121n. 470, 155n. 586, 198n. 771		
		12:40a	74, 75, 77, 79t. 14, 81, 93, 117
12:32	175n. 663	12:40ab	73, 77, 82, 83, 88, 89, 91, 91n. 348, 94, 95, 95n. 362, 114, 115
12:34	16t. 2, 19n. 67, 212, 213		
12:35–36	41n. 140, 67n. 252		
12:35-36a	90n. 343, 121n. 471	12:40abd	75
12:37	67n. 253, 76, 98, 104, 105n. 404, 106, 107, 108, 110, 114, 118, 118n. 463	12:40a-d	83
		12:40a-e	77
		12:40b	75, 81t. 15, 82, 83
		12:40c	74, 75
		12:40cd	75, 82, 83, 94
12:37–38	114	12:40c-e	84
12:37–40	67n. 254, 69	12:40d	74, 75, 76, 84, 84t. 17, 96
12:37–41	31n. 99, 68, 69, 90n. 340, 98, 100, 119, 121, 157		
		12:40e	73, 74, 75, 76, 87, 91, 111, 115
12:38	2n. 4, 5n. 18, 6n. 19, 9n. 28, 9n. 31, 10, 13n. 45, 15t. 2, 16t. 2, 19n. 69, 22n. 80, 23t. 3, 24t. 4, 27n. 96, 31, 32, 67, 68, 69n. 263,	12:41	6n. 18, 32n. 100, 68, 68n. 255, 87, 87n. 323, 108, 110, 112, 112n. 437, 113n. 440, 124, 212, 213

12:41–42	88n. 327	14:28	174n. 658
12:42	87, 110, 111	14:29	76n. 280
12:42–43	67n. 253	14:30	90, 121n. 473
12:44	14t. 2, 36n. 114	14–17	100, 132, 143, 208, 209
12:44–45	104n. 402	15	153
12:44–46	90n. 343, 121n. 471	15:13–15	207n. 785
12:46	41n. 140, 175n. 662	15:16a-c	116n. 455
12:46–47	78n. 288	15:19	109n. 420, 116n. 455
12:47	90n. 335, 92n. 351	15:21	104n. 402
12:49	104n. 402	15:24	106n. 415
13	120n. 466	15:25	5n. 18, 7n. 22, 13n. 48, 16t. 2, 17, 18, 18n. 59, 18n. 60, 18n. 61, 19n. 67, 23t. 3, 24t. 4, 36n. 118, 69n. 263, 71n. 270, 115n. 448, 135, 136, 136t. 28, 138n. 527, 138t. 29, 139, 140, 141n. 538, 142, 160n. 599, 212, 213
13:1	207n. 783		
13:1–20:31	12, 157, 198–9, 206		
13:2	120n. 466, 120n. 467		
13:6	174n. 658		
13:10	83n. 307		
13:11	109n. 420		
13:18	5n. 18, 6n. 19, 13n. 46, 16t. 2, 19, 19n. 65, 19n. 70, 20n. 71, 23t. 3, 24t. 4, 27, 69n. 263, 141n. 538, 212, 213		
		16:5	104n. 402
13:18ab	116n. 455	16:7	174n. 658
13:20	104n. 402	16:11	90
13:27	120n. 467, 121n. 474	16:15	109n. 420
13:29	207n. 783	16:25–28	144n. 548
13:30	121n. 474	16:28	175n. 662
13–19	56	16:29–33	56n. 212, 209n. 795
14	146, 151, 152, 153	17:1	90n. 337
14:1	76n. 280	17:2	78n. 288, 89n. 333
14:1–2	9, 151, 151n. 571, 152, 153, 154, 154n. 584	17:4–5	116n. 453
		17:6	71n. 270, 89n. 332, 89n. 333
14:2	15t. 2, 17n. 53		
14:2–3	48	17:9	89n. 333
14:10	106n. 415, 154	17:11	154n. 581
14:10–11	99n. 375, 100n. 380, 104n. 403, 106n. 415, 208n. 788	17:12	6n. 19, 69n. 263, 212, 213
		17:20	105n. 411
14:15–18	152	17:20–21	154n. 582
14:17	151	17:25	176n. 667
14:18	174n. 658	18:8–9	6n. 19
14:20	154n. 580	18:9	89n. 333
14:23	152, 153, 154, 154n. 583, 174n. 658	18:14	82n. 303
		18:15–16	18n. 62
14:24	104n. 402	18:20–21	78n. 288
14:25–26	78n. 288, 132, 133, 204n. 774, 210n. 798	18:28	207n. 783
		18:33	191n. 743
14:27	76n. 280	18:33–38	8n. 27, 143n. 544

18:36	204n. 776	20:9	6n. 18, 128n. 486, 212, 213
18:37	90n. 335, 105n. 405, 165n. 624, 175n. 662, 175n. 663	20:14–16	87n. 320
		20:19–23	103n. 396
18:38–40	207n. 783	20:20	83n. 307
18:39	191n. 743	20:21	104n. 402
18:40	14t. 2, 36n. 115	20:24–29	207n. 786
19	8	20:25	207n. 787
19:1–22	8n. 27, 143n. 544	20:26–29	103n. 396
19:3	191n. 743	20:29	100n. 380
19:6	14t. 2, 36n. 115	20:29–31	208n. 789
19:11	109n. 420	20:30–31	99n. 374
19:12	14t. 2, 36n. 115	21:1	71n. 270
19:13	18n. 62	21:1–4	102n. 390
19:14	207n. 783	21:1–14	101n. 382, 103n. 396
19:14–15	191n. 743	21:6	102n. 390
19:15	14t. 2, 36n. 115	21:8	102n. 390
19:19	191n. 743	21:11	102n. 390
19:21	191n. 743	21:14	71n. 270, 101, 103, 103t. 21
19:23–24	9n. 30, 18n. 62		
19:24	2n. 4, 5n. 18, 6n. 19, 9n. 31, 13n. 45, 17t. 2, 18n. 60, 19n. 69, 22n. 80, 23t. 3, 24t. 4, 27n. 96, 69n. 263, 141n. 538, 212, 213	21:24	105n. 411, 106n. 412
		Acts of the Apostles 147	
		5:3	81n. 296
		6:12–14	148t. 31
		10:36–37	62n. 231
19:28	6n. 19, 23t. 3, 24t. 4, 69n. 263, 115n. 448, 135n. 513, 135t. 27, 138n. 527, 212, 213	13:10	41n. 141
		13:24	62n. 231
		13:24–25	42n. 149
		13:25	63n. 237
19:28–29	135, 135n. 513, 138t. 29, 139, 143	19	63
		19:3–4	65
19:28–30	9n. 30	28:24–28	97n. 368
19:29	135, 138n. 527, 207n. 783	28:25–27	68n. 256
		28:27b	97n. 368
19:30	83n. 307		
19:31	207n. 783	Romans	
19:35	106n. 412	10:16	68n. 256, 71n. 266, 72
19:36	9n. 30, 17t. 2, 19n. 69, 22n. 80, 23t. 3, 24t. 4, 160n. 599, 207n. 783, 212, 213	11:7	80n. 296, 81t. 15
		11:25	80n. 296, 82t. 15
		15:3	26, 136, 138t. 29, 142n. 540
19:36–37	6n. 18, 69n. 263		
19:37	2n. 3, 3, 9n. 30, 13n. 46, 17t. 2, 19n. 70, 20n. 71, 22n. 80, 23t. 3, 24t. 4, 25, 27, 27n. 91, 212, 213	2 Corinthians	
		3:12–14	94n. 356, 121n. 469
		3:14	80n. 296, 82t. 15
		4:3–4	91n. 348, 94n. 357, 120, 121n. 469, 121n. 475
19:42	207n. 783		

Ephesians
    4:17–18   82t. 15
    4:18   80n. 296

Hebrews
    10:27   15t. 2
    11:26   138t. 29, 142n. 540

James
    5:3   15t. 2

1 John 122
    1:2   71n. 270
    2:11   119, 120, 121, 121n. 475
    2:19   71n. 270
    2:28   71n. 270
    3:2   71n. 270
    3:5   71n. 270
    3:8   71n. 270
    4:9   71n. 270

2 John
    10   151n. 574

Targumim
Fragmentary Targum
    Genesis 49:10   165, 165n. 621, 184

Targum to Esther
    Esther 3:8   164, 164n. 615

Targum Isaiah
    Isaiah 6:1   32n. 100
    Isaiah 6:5   32n. 100
    Isaiah 6:10   86

Targum Kethuvim
    Psalm 8:3   163, 163n. 611

Targum Onqelos
    Genesis 49:10   165, 165n. 622, 184

Targum Pseudo-Jonathan
    Genesis 49:10   165, 165n. 621, 184

Early Christian literature
Gospel of the Ebionites
    Fragment 7   147n. 556

Gospel of Thomas, 147
    §71   148, 148n. 557, 148t. 31

Shepherd of Hermas
    Mandate 4.2.30:1   81n. 296, 82t. 15
    Mandate 12.4.47:4   81n. 296, 82t. 15

Theophilus
    Ad Autolycum 2.35 81n. 296

Tertullian
    Scorpiace 12   192n. 749

Origen
    Commentarii in evangelium Joannis
        6:24   38n. 129
    Fragmenta in evangelium Joannis 92   91n. 348

Epiphanius
    Panarion 30.16.4–5   147n. 556

Cyril of Alexandria
    Commentariorum in Joannem continuatio (PG 74:96–97)   91n. 348

MODERN AUTHORS INDEX

Abbott, E. A. 83n. 305
Abegg, M. G., Jr. 21n. 77
Achtemeier, P. J. 5n. 17, 7
Albl, M. C. 26n. 87
Alexander, P. S. 33n. 105, 54nn. 204–205, 57n. 216
Allegro, J. M. 34n. 105
Anderson, P. N. 143n. 544
Annese, A. 148n. 557
Ashton, J. 205

Baillet, M. 25n. 86, 117–18, 117n. 457
Barrett, C. K. 1n. 1, 8n. 27, 15n. 50, 26n. 88, 38n. 130, 39n. 131, 67n. 253, 77n. 285, 109n. 421, 128n. 486, 128n. 488, 129n. 489, 136n. 516, 137, 137nn. 519–520, 143, 154, 159n. 596, 159nn. 594, 596, 169n. 639
Barthélemy, D. 35n. 113, 93n. 353
Bauckham, R. 208n. 790
Bauer, W. 179n. 691
Bauer-Arndt-Gingrich-Danker (BAGD) 146n. 553
Becker, J. 91n. 348, 119n. 465
Bernard, J. H. 64n. 247, 109n. 421, 128n. 487, 137n. 522, 158n. 589, 159n. 594, 177n. 684
Beutler, J. 135n. 513
Blank, J. 116, 116n. 452
Blenkinsopp, J. 165, 165n. 625, 184
Böhl, E. 7n. 23
Boismard, M.-É. 8n. 26, 76n. 281, 99–104, 101n. 382, 102nn. 389–390, 103n. 394, 166n. 628, 195
Boyer, C. 147n. 556, 148n. 558, 148nn. 558–559
Braun, F.-M. 5n. 18, 9n. 31, 137n. 517, 158n. 590, 158nn. 590–591, 208n. 790, 212n. 800
Brooke, G. J. 58n. 217
Brown-Driver-Briggs (BDB) 144n. 550

Brown, R. E. 8n. 26, 27n. 94, 80n. 295, 111n. 438, 112n. 438, 118n. 461, 128n. 487, 129n. 489, 133n. 503, 158n. 589, 159n. 596, 166n. 628, 192nn. 747–749
Brownlee, W. H. 25n. 82
Bruce, F. F. 88n. 330
Bryan, S. M. 139–41, 139nn. 528, 530–531, 140nn. 532–535, 144
Bullinger, E. W. 10n. 33, 11n. 35
Bultmann, R. 8n. 26, 97n. 366, 106n. 414, 128n. 486, 130n. 490, 133n. 503, 137nn. 517, 521, 138n. 527, 158n. 589, 159n. 594, 206n. 780
Burge, G. M. 133n. 504
Burkitt, F. C. 164, 186
Burney, C. F. 34n. 106, 41n. 137, 78, 78n. 288, 137n. 517
Burrows, M. 23t. 3, 24t. 4, 25n. 82
Bynum, W. R. 3, 5, 25, 25nn. 83–84

Charles, R. H. 192n. 749
Charlesworth, J. H. 46n. 176, 58n. 217
Chazon, E. G. 117n. 457
Cheyne, T. K. 162–3, 163n. 611, 186
Clark-Soles, J. 1n. 1, 2n. 3, 3n. 7, 4, 6n. 19, 10n. 32, 21n. 75, 128n. 485
Clarke, E. G. 165n. 621
Coloe, M. L. 152–3
Colwell, E. 39n. 134
Culpepper, R. A. 146n. 553
Curtis, A. 191n. 743

Daise, M. A. 22n. 78, 129n. 489, 132n. 499, 133n. 504, 141n. 537, 147n. 555, 152n. 576, 153n. 577, 164n. 617
de Lagarde, P. 163n. 611
de Mérode, Marie 176n. 676
de Waard, J. 81n. 297, 93
Dimant, D. 58n. 217, 64, 117n. 457
Dodd, C. H. 8n. 26, 67

Ehrman, B. D. 147n. 556, 148n. 557
Elliger, K. 22n. 80
Evans, C. A. 69n. 263, 77, 77n. 285, 79n. 293, 90, 91, 114n. 444, 118n. 461

Farmer, W. R. 192n. 749
Feuillet, A. 192n. 748
Flint, P. W. 34n. 105, 70nn. 264–265, 72n. 272
Floyd, M. H. 168n. 631, 189nn. 731, 733
Fortna, R. T. 98n. 371, 103n. 395
Franke, A. H. 2n. 3, 9n. 31, 19–20, 19nn. 67, 69, 20n. 71, 27n. 91, 37n. 124, 52n. 197, 76n. 283, 77, 77n. 286, 81n. 300, 158n. 590, 162n. 609, 179n. 691, 211
Freed, E. D. 1n. 2, 2n. 5, 5n. 18, 11n. 37, 18n. 62, 20, 20nn. 73–74, 34n. 107, 35n. 113, 38n. 129, 39nn. 131,134, 135, 41, 41n. 141, 44–7, 47n. 178, 50, 53, 55, 65, 73n. 273, 78, 78nn. 288–289, 79n. 293, 81, 81n. 299, 88n. 330, 134n. 506, 137n. 521, 142n. 539, 158n. 590, 158nn. 590–591, 162n. 608, 163n. 613, 164n. 619, 170n. 643, 174n. 657, 175nn. 666, 176, 176n. 670, 177n. 684, 181
Fuller, R. E. 25n. 83

Goodacre, M. 148n. 557
Goodwin, C. 7n. 24, 27n. 95, 71n. 266
Gundry, R. H. 152n. 575

Haenchen, E. 32n. 102, 113
Hanhart, R. 25n. 84
Harris, J. R. 26n. 87
Heekerens, H.-P. 101n. 385, 103n. 395
Hengel, M. 25n. 84, 132, 132n. 500, 159n. 594, 213n. 801
Hollenbach, B. 88–9, 88n. 330, 89n. 331, 92n. 350, 111
Holmes, M. W. 82n. 301
Hoskyns, E. C. 97n. 365, 105n. 410, 128n. 486, 159n. 596, 187n. 726, 192n. 747, 193n. 752
Howard, W. F. 129n. 489
Humann, R. J. 20n. 71, 27n. 91, 39n. 131, 137n. 517, 158n. 590, 170n. 643

Jauhiainen, M. 6n. 19

Käsemann, E. 206n. 780
Keener, C. S. 38n. 126, 133n. 505
Klein, M. L. 165n. 621
Köstenberger, A. J. 206n. 780
Kubiś, A. 2n. 3, 3n. 8, 4–5, 4n. 15, 5n. 18, 5nn. 16–18, 6n. 19, 25, 25nn. 83–84, 168n. 631, 169nn. 637–638, 170n. 644, 173, 173n. 654, 175, 175nn. 660, 665, 176nn. 668, 675, 177n. 685, 178n. 687, 179n. 691, 180, 189, 195–6, 195n. 759, 212n. 800
Kühschelm, R. 79n. 293
Kysar, R. 118n. 461

Lamouille, A. 8n. 26, 76n. 281, 166n. 628, 195
Lappenga, B. J. 139–40, 139nn. 528, 530, 140nn. 532–533, 144
Levenson, J. D. 173n. 654
Lieu, J. M. 88, 88n. 330, 111, 119n. 465
Lightfoot, R. H. 128n. 487, 187n. 727
Lim, T. H. 7n. 22
Lindars, B. 67, 76n. 284, 129n. 489, 163n. 612
Lohse, E. 163n. 610
Loisy, A. F. 159n. 596

Marcus & Wikgren (LCL) 146n. 553, 149n. 563
Martone, C. 93n. 353
May, H. G. 191n. 743
Mayoral, J. A. 10n. 34
McCaffrey, J. 152n. 575
Menken, M. J. J. 1n. 2, 2n. 4, 3, 5, 5n. 18, 6n. 19, 8n. 26, 9nn. 31–32, 11n. 38, 14, 14n. 49, 15n. 50, 16nn. 51–52, 17–19, 17nn. 56–57, 18nn. 59, 62, 20, 21nn. 75–76, 22, 22n. 80, 23t. 3, 25n. 82, 26, 26nn. 90–91, 27n. 91, 34–6, 35n. 112–113, 36n. 116, 119, 38nn. 128–129, 39n. 131, 41–5, 41n. 141, 42nn. 143, 144, 148, 149, 43nn. 154, 155, 156, 44nn. 159, 167, 45n. 169, 46, 47–50, 47n. 180, 48nn. 183–184, 56, 56n. 208, 62, 62n. 230, 70n. 265, 71, 71nn. 266, 277, 270, 74n. 276, 75n. 279, 76nn. 280–281, 78nn. 288, 290, 292, 79n. 293, 80n. 296, 81n. 298, 82n. 304, 83–6, 83nn. 305, 308, 84nn. 309–311,

85n. 312, 86n. 316, 87n. 322, 90n. 336, 93, 95, 95n. 363, 98n. 370, 107n. 417, 115n. 451, 119nn. 464–465, 120n. 466, 135, 135n. 510, 137, 137n. 519, 138, 138nn. 523–524, 527, 141, 141n. 538, 158n. 590, 162n. 607, 168n. 634, 173, 173n. 656, 174nn. 657, 659, 175–7, 175nn. 660, 665, 176nn. 675–676, 177n. 682, 178n. 687, 179, 180–1, 180nn. 693, 695, 194, 196
Metso, S. 58n. 217
Metzger, B. M. 32n. 100, 74n. 278, 188n. 730
Migne, J.-P. (PG) 91n. 348
Miura, N. 174n. 659
Morgan, R. 10n. 32
Morris, L. 128n. 487, 159n. 594, 185n. 719
Moulton, H.K. 134n. 508
Moulton, J. H. 39n. 134
Myers, A. D. 2n. 4, 4n. 15, 105

Neirynck, F. 179, 180n. 693
Noack, B. 1n. 1, 27, 27nn. 93, 95, 96

Obermann, A. 1n. 2, 2n. 4, 3, 4, 4n. 12, 4nn. 12, 15, 5n. 18, 6n. 20, 21, 21nn. 75–76, 22, 22n. 80, 24n. 81, 24t. 4, 25n. 82, 32n. 102, 35nn. 108, 113, 38n. 130, 39n. 135, 53, 106n. 413, 128n. 485, 132n. 500, 134n. 506, 160n. 597, 163n. 612, 177, 177n. 683, 181n. 696, 184n. 716, 186, 186n. 724
O'Rourke, J. J. 77n. 285, 78n. 288, 86n. 316

Painter, J. 76, 77n. 286, 87nn. 323–324, 88nn. 327, 329, 90–2, 90nn. 339, 340, 344, 91n. 348, 92n. 350, 98n. 370, 107n. 418, 109n. 427, 110, 114, 116, 118n. 461, 119, 120, 121n. 471
Peters, H. 10n. 33, 69nn. 258, 259, 261
Pleše, Z. 147n. 556, 148n. 557
Plett, H.F. 69n. 258
Pope, M. H. 163nn. 610, 612
Preuschen, E. 38n. 129, 91n. 348

Quinn, A. 10n. 33, 69nn. 258, 260, 262

Rahlfs, A. 137n. 519
Rainbow, P. A. 108n. 419, 206, 207n. 785

Rathbun, L. 10n. 33, 69nn. 258, 260, 262
Reifferscheid, A. 192n. 749
Reim, G. 2n. 3, 3n. 10, 5n. 18, 31n. 98, 37n. 125, 38n. 127, 50n. 193, 76n. 284, 78, 78nn. 288–289, 122n. 477, 129n. 489, 137n. 521, 161, 161n. 602, 171n. 648, 173, 178n. 686, 179n. 691, 187n. 725, 189–90, 190nn. 740, 742, 197
Rensberger, D. 25n. 91
Richter, G. 7n. 23, 27n. 92
Rietz, H. W. L. 46n. 176
Ruckstuhl, E. 83n. 305
Rudolph, W. 22n. 80
Rytel-Adrianik, P. 4n. 15

Sahlin, H. 176n. 676
Schnackenburg, R. 8n. 26, 15n. 50, 27n. 91, 77n. 286, 82n. 304, 87nn. 320, 326, 88n. 328, 89, 90nn. 336, 339, 111, 112nn. 436, 439, 116, 133n. 502, 133n. 505, 138n. 527, 143n. 544, 154n. 584, 160n. 600
Schuchard, B. G. 1n. 2, 2n. 4, 3, 5, 5n. 18, 7, 8n. 26, 8n. 27, 9n. 31, 11n. 39, 20n. 72, 26n. 91, 27n. 91, 34–5, 35nn. 108, 110, 113, 36nn. 108, 110, 113, 38n. 128, 39n. 136, 41, 41n. 138, 44–6, 44n. 167, 45nn. 169, 173, 174, 47, 47n. 181, 50, 53, 55n. 207, 56, 65, 73n. 273, 76n. 283, 78n. 288, 80n. 294, 81, 81nn. 296, 298–300, 82n. 304, 83, 83nn. 305–306, 84n. 311, 85–6, 85n. 312, 86nn. 313, 317, 87nn. 321, 326, 92, 94–5, 98n. 371, 105n. 410, 105nn. 404, 410, 115nn. 448, 451, 118, 118n. 461, 119n. 465, 123–4, 137n. 517, 140n. 535, 158n. 591, 163n. 613, 166nn. 627–628, 168n. 634, 170n. 644, 173n. 656, 174nn. 657–658, 176n. 675, 177, 177n. 683, 178n. 687, 180, 188n. 728, 191n. 743
Schuller, E. 93n. 354
Schweizer, E. 83n. 305
Sheridan, R. 1n. 2, 2n. 4, 4–5, 4n. 15, 5n. 17, 6, 9n. 31, 21n. 75, 158n. 590
Silva, M. 48n. 182
Skehan, P. W. 72n. 272
Smith, D. Moody 69n. 263
Smyth, H. W. 107n. 416
Sperber, A. 32n. 100, 164n. 615, 165n. 622

Spitta, F. 101n. 385, 103n. 395
Stegemann, H. 93n. 354
Stemberger, G. 38n. 129, 76n. 281
Stendahl, K. 2n. 5, 38n. 127
Stinespring, W. F. 168n. 631
Strachan, R. H. 170n. 643
Strack, H. L. 38n. 129, 76n. 281
Strugnell, J. 34n. 105
Sukenik, E. L. 23t. 3, 24t. 4, 25n. 82

Tomson, P. J. 191n. 743
Torrey, C. C. 162n. 608, 163n. 613
Tov, E. 21nn. 76–77, 22n. 79
Trevor, J. C. 25n. 82
Trites, A. A. 133n. 504

Ulrich, E. 21n. 77, 34n. 105, 70n. 264, 72n. 272

van Belle, G. 84n. 309
VanderKam, J. 70n. 265

Vermes, G. 33n. 105, 54nn. 204–205, 57n. 216
von Wahlde, U. C. 71, 137n. 521, 159n. 593, 187n. 725

Wagner, J. Ross 71n. 267
Wellhausen, J. 101n. 384
Werner, E. 162n. 608, 163nn. 610–611
Westcott, B. F. 128n. 487, 187n. 726
Wiles, M. F. 91n. 348
Williams, C. H. 9n. 32, 11n. 40, 39nn. 132–133, 41, 43–5, 43n. 157, 44nn. 164, 166, 46, 47–50, 48n. 185
Wissowa, G. 192n. 749
Wright, R. B. 103n. 397

Yadin, Y. 23t. 3, 24t. 4, 25n. 82
Young, F. W. 87n. 324

Ziegler, J. 37n. 123

www.ingramcontent.com/pod-product-compliance
Lightning Source LLC
Chambersburg PA
CBHW070028010526
44117CB00011B/1751